Inside the Whirlwind

african christian studies series (africs)

This series will make available significant works in the field of African Christian studies, taking into account the many forms of Christianity across the whole continent of Africa. African Christian studies is defined here as any scholarship that relates to themes and issues on the history, nature, identity, character, and place of African Christianity in world Christianity. It also refers to topics that address the continuing search for abundant life for Africans through multiple appeals to African religions and African Christianity in a challenging social context. The books in this series are expected to make significant contributions in historicizing trends in African Christian studies, while shifting the contemporary discourse in these areas from narrow theological concerns to a broader inter-disciplinary engagement with African religio-cultural traditions and Africa's challenging social context.

The series will cater to scholarly and educational texts in the areas of religious studies, theology, mission studies, biblical studies, philosophy, social justice, and other diverse issues current in African Christianity. We define these studies broadly and specifically as primarily focused on new voices, fresh perspectives, new approaches, and historical and cultural analyses that are emerging because of the significant place of African Christianity and African religio-cultural traditions in world Christianity. The series intends to continually fill a gap in African scholarship, especially in the areas of social analysis in African Christian studies, African philosophies, new biblical and narrative hermeneutical approaches to African theologies, and the challenges facing African women in today's Africa and within African Christianity. Other diverse themes in African Traditional Religions; African ecology; African ecclesiology; inter-cultural, inter-ethnic, and inter-religious dialogue; ecumenism; creative inculturation; African theologies of development, reconciliation, globalization, and poverty reduction will also be covered in this series.

SERIES EDITORS
Dr. Stan Chu Ilo (DePaul University, Chicago, USA)
Dr. Esther Acolatse (Duke University, Durham, USA)
Dr. Mwenda Ntarangwi (Calvin College, Grand Rapids, USA)

"*Inside the Whirlwind* is a wonderful exploration of what a genuine encounter with African Christianity really looks like. This is contextual theology at its best."

—TIMOTHY TENNENT, President, Professor of World Christianity,
Asbury Theological Seminary

"Jason Carter's *Inside the Whirlwind: The Book of Job through African Eyes* is a major intervention in contemporary scholarship on the reading, reception, and uses of the Christian Scriptures in an African context. Through skillfully focusing on the reading practices of Christian communities in the Central African nation of Equatorial Guinea, Carter shows how the Book of Job is creatively mobilized by these readers to address a range of pressing local concerns, including the HIV/AIDS pandemic. He persuasively shows how readers find new grammars of affliction and suffering in the biblical text, using its narratives to offer redemptive interpretations of misfortune. Carter's book will be enthusiastically received by readers within Biblical Studies, Theology, and African Studies."

—JOEL CABRITA, Lecturer in World Christianities, University of Cambridge

"In this volume Rev. Dr. Jason Carter provides insights into African religiosity in Equatorial Guinea, Central Africa, focusing particularly on historic missionary Christianity and new Pentecostal and Charismatic expressions. The Book of Job in the Bible is often used as rationalization of the contradiction Africans experience between extreme affluence and extreme destitution. This volume adds penetrating theological insights to the accumulating scholarship on African Christianity in this Third Millennium."

—JESSE N.K. MUGAMBI, Professor of Philosophy and Religious Studies,
University of Nairobi

"Too much writing on African theology is at home in the university lecture hall but remote from the lives of ordinary Christians in their villages and townships. Jason Carter's study of popular interpretations of the book of Job among the Fang of Equatorial Guinea is a decided exception. Based on careful participant observation and a deep knowledge of Fang cosmology, Carter's book raises profound and unsettling questions for all rose-tinted interpretations of modern African Christianity. He calls on theology in Africa—and by implication in the North as well—to consider afresh whether it is in danger of losing its central focus on the sovereignty of God."

—BRIAN STANLEY, Professor of World Christianity, Director for the Centre
for the Study of World Christianity, University of Edinburgh

"For many of us living in the affluent West, the book of Job focuses on exceptional suffering, in the context of a mystical cosmic battle, in a world far from our experience. We read it theoretically or when we encounter unexpected loss or suffering, but few of us would look at the book through the eyes of normative living in the context of ongoing spiritual warfare. But for our brothers and sisters in many African contexts, Job's hardships appear as daily realities in the midst of a spiritual clash between God and the Devil. In *Inside the Whirlwind*, Jason Carter introduces us to people living in these daily realities and shows us how they read the book of Job as a foundation for hope. *Inside the Whirlwind* opens our eyes to understand suffering, spiritual warfare, and the book of Job as we never have before."

—PAUL BORTHWICK, Development Associates International; Author of *Western Christians in Global Mission: What's the Role of the North American Church?*

"Through this carefully researched and well written book, a great lacuna is being filled in the study of African Christianity. Much has been heard from Christians in Anglophone, Francophone, and Lusophone Africa, but rarely do we hear from the lone country that makes up Hispanic Africa—Equatorial Guinea. Reading Job in the context of the sufferings of the ordinary Christians of Equatorial Guinea, Carter provides significant theological insights and pastoral resources for addressing the problem of suffering in an African context."

—DAVID T. NGONG, Assistant Professor of Religion and Theology, Stillman College, Tuscaloosa, Alabama; Author of *Theology as Construction of Piety: An African Perspective*

"*Inside the Whirlwind* addresses an issue of enormous significance to contemporary Christianity, namely how the rapidly growing churches of the global South interpret scripture. Jason Carter here focuses on the Book of Job, a work of enormous relevance to societies deeply acquainted with suffering. He has written a thoughtful, rewarding, and provocative book, from which Northern-world Christians can learn much."

—PHILIP JENKINS, Distinguished Professor of History, Institute for Studies of Religion, Baylor University

"Carter's *Inside the Whirlwind* is a *tour de force*. It is a rich ethnographic and critical contextual reading of Job in Equatorial Guinea when the message of Job resonates fully as Africans and faith communities battle HIV/AIDS. Job's story comforts and challenges stigmatization. This is an extremely valuable resource for contextual studies."

—ELIAS KIFON BONGMBA, Harry and Hazel Chavanne Chair in Christian Theology, Professor of Religion, Rice University

Inside the Whirlwind

The Book of Job through African Eyes

Jason A. Carter

FOREWORD BY
Andrew F. Walls

PICKWICK *Publications* · Eugene, Oregon

INSIDE THE WHIRLWIND
The Book of Job through African Eyes

African Christian Studies Series

Copyright © 2017 Jason A. Carter. All rights reserved. Except for brief quotations in critical publications or reviews, no part of this book may be reproduced in any manner without prior written permission from the publisher. Write: Permissions, Wipf and Stock Publishers, 199 W. 8th Ave., Suite 3, Eugene, OR 97401.

Pickwick Publications
An Imprint of Wipf and Stock Publishers
199 W. 8th Ave., Suite 3
Eugene, OR 97401

www.wipfandstock.com

PAPERBACK ISBN: 978-1-4982-3069-8
HARDCOVER ISBN: 978-1-4982-3071-1
EBOOK ISBN: 978-1-4982-3070-4

Cataloguing-in-Publication data:

Names: Carter, Jason A. | Foreword by Walls, Andrew F.

Title: Inside the whirlwind : the book of Job through African eyes / Jason A. Carter.

Description: Eugene, OR: Pickwick Publications, 2017 | Series: African Christian Studies Series | Includes bibliographical references and index.

Identifiers: ISBN 978-1-4982-3069-8 (paperback) | ISBN 978-1-4982-3071-1 (hardcover) | ISBN 978-1-4982-3070-4 (ebook)

Subjects: LSCH: Christianity—Africa | Bible, Job—Criticism, interpretation, etc. | Bible—Hermeneutics | Suffering—Religious aspects—Christianity

Classification: BR1360 C18 2017 (print) | BR1360 (ebook)

Manufactured in the U.S.A.   12/08/16

Unless otherwise indicated, all Scripture quotations are from the New Revised Standard Version Bible, copyright 1989, Division of Christian Education of the National Council of the Churches of Christ in the United States of America. Used by permission. All rights reserved. Scripture quotations marked (ESV) are from the ESV® Bible (The Holy Bible, English Standard Version®), copyright © 2001 by Crossway, a publishing ministry of Good News Publishers. Used by permission. All rights reserved.

The map of the Fang Homeland entitled "Fang Territory" is used by permission © SIL International. Permission required for further distribution. The map entitled "Map of Equatorial Guinea" is used by permission © Graphic Maps. Permission required for further distribution.

*Dedicated to the students and professors at
Instituto Bíblico "Casa de la Palabra" (IBCP)
My life has been immeasurably enriched by your friendships.*

Contents

List of Maps, Tables, and Illustrations | ix
Key Fang and Spanish Terms | xi
Foreword by Andrew F. Walls | xiii
Acknowledgements | xv

Introduction | 1

Part 1: The Hermeneutics-Culture-Praxis Triad

1. Readings of the Book of Job as a Window on African Christianity | 13
2. The Fang of Equatorial Guinea: Their History, Beliefs, and Practices | 36
3. An Untold Story of African Christianity: Presbyterian and Pentecostal Expressions of the Christian Faith in Equatorial Guinea | 75

Part 2: Contextual Readings of the Book of Job: Themes, Theologies, and Trajectories

4. Theodicy and the Nature of Evil: Job between God and the Devil | 117
5. The Sting of Retribution and the Promise of Lament: Reading the Book of Job from the Experience of Leprosy and HIV/AIDS | 165

6. Hope in Suffering: Prayer, Eschatology, and
   Job's Final Liberation | 203

   Conclusion: African Christianity between Indigenization
   and Diabolization | 237

   *Appendix 1: The "Pentecostal Deliverance Liturgy" of Apostle Agustín
   Edu Esono: "Power against Incurable Sicknesses" | 255*

   *Appendix 2: Reading the Book of Job at Six Distinct Locations in
   Equatorial Guinea | 262*

   Bibliography | 267

   Index | 289

List of Maps, Tables, and Illustrations

Introduction

Table 1: Primary Textual and Thematic Blocks Prioritized in Readings of the Book of Job | 6

Table 2: Scope of the Study | 7

Chapter 1

Figure 1.1: The Hermeneutics-Culture-Praxis Triad | 17

Figure 1.2: Typical Relationship between Ideas and Stories in Western Preaching | 28

Figure 1.3: The Symbiotic Relationship between Oral Narration and the Communication of Ideas | 29

Chapter 2

Figure 2.1: Map of Equatorial Guinea | 38

Figure 2.2: Fang Territory | 47

Figure 2.3: Principal Ritual Cults of the Fang Identified in *Dulu Bon be Afri Kara* | 50

Figure 2.4: The Initiation Process of Fang Witchcraft | 62

Figure 2.5: Fang Disease Etiologies: The Category and Severity of Fang Sicknesses | 67

Chapter 3

Figure 3.1: Regional Map of Central Africa including Equatorial Guinea's island of Corisco | 78

Figure 3.2: Pentecostal Prayers of Deliverance as a Means of Breaking the Cycle of Fang Witchcraft | 97

Figure 3.3: The Center Holds: Motifs of the Prosperity Gospel at the Assembly of the Holy Spirit's Prophetic Seminar | 108

Chapter 4

Figure 4.1: The Pillars of Theodicy in the Western Theological Tradition | 123

Figure 4.2: The Pillars of a Contextualized Theodicy amongst the Fang | 124

Figure 4.3: Traditional Fang Cosmological Map of the Universe | 128

Figure 4.4: The Christianization of the Fang Cosmological Map according to Missionary Christianity | 130

Figure 4.5: The Christianization of the Fang Cosmological Map according to Fang Pentecostals | 136

Chapter 5

Figure 5.1: Components of Antonio's Initial Reaction to the Book of Job | 174

Key Fang and Spanish Terms

1. Key Fang Terms

abók misémm   "dance of/against 'sin'"; a ritual dance part of the Ndong Mba cult

akwann Fang   "Fang sicknesses"; sicknesses which are thought to originate in the nocturnal world of *mbwo* and thus treated by the Fang *ngangan*

akwann mbwo   "witchcraft sicknesses"; sicknesses which are thought to originate in the nocturnal world of *mbwo* and thus are treated by the Fang *ngangan*

akwann misémm   "sicknesses of sin"; sicknesses traditionally attributed to social agency

akwann ntangan   "sicknesses of the white man"; sicknesses which are thought to occur naturally through physical contagion and thus are treated in the hospital by the white man's doctors

Alar Ayong   *alar* ("unite"); *ayong* ("clan"); a clan re-grouping movement begun by the Ntumu Fang subgroup in the late 1940s which continued through the late 1950s as an indigenous response and protest against European colonialism

Biéri   the "cranium" of an ancestor; the Fang ancestral cult

biyem   "witches"; "the ones who know" about the nocturnal realm of *mbwo*; plural of *nnem* (see also *nnem*)

ekí	prohibitions/taboos
evus	the originating source of *mbwo* which is believed to live corporally in the human
Eyima Biéri	the Biéri figure; the small wooden figure which guarded the craniums for the Biéri ritual cult
mbwo	the nocturnal witchcraft of the Fang wherein a person's *evus* is thought to leave the body at night in order to engage in anthropography
miemie	innocent person; a category of persons thought to be uninvolved in *mbwo* (witchcraft)
mwan biang	"child of medicine"; the small wooden figure which guarded the craniums for the Biéri ritual cult
ngangan	Fang traditional healer (translated into Spanish as *curandero*)
ngbel	the nocturnal world of *mbwo* where the *evus* travels in order to participate in anthropography
Nguí	the traditional anti-witchcraft cult amongst the Fang
nnem	"witch"; a person whose *evus* travels in the nocturnal world of *ngbel*
nsem	an offense against the community; conventionally translated as "sin"
nsuk biéri	the bark box reliquary which kept the cranium or pieces of cranium of an ancestor
nzam	leprosy
Nzama	relatively marginal figure traditionally who was raised to divine status during the process of Christian inculturation; today translated "God"
okwann / akwann	sickness / sicknesses

2. Key Spanish Terms

curandero	Fang traditional healer; the Spanish translation of *ngangan*
curandería	the place where the *ngangan* (traditional healer) performs the healing

Foreword

SUB-SAHARAN AFRICA IS NOW one of the world's principal theatres for the Christian faith. It is the home of a large and growing proportion of the world's Christians and is beginning to hold the place in Christian discourse worldwide that was at one time occupied by Europe. But studies of African Christianity as it affects and is expressed in the lives of ordinary people are still not common; which is one good reason for welcoming this remarkable book.

It examines the understanding of the Bible and its application to daily life among a substantial number of African Christians; and it is particularly gratifying to find such a study based in Equatorial Guinea, for studies of Christianity there are particularly rare: a small country, with an unusual colonial background, (neither British, French, Belgian, nor Portuguese, but Spanish. The country also has, interestingly, the highest literary rate on the continent). Dr. Carter introduces us to a variety of church and institutional settings, some Reformed, some Pentecostal, some Catholic, some related to the historic churches of the West, some of indigenous origin, and he examines how Christians there understand and apply one substantial book of the Bible, the book of Job.

The Bible is at the heart of African Christian experience; to discover how people understand and respond to Scripture is central to any true comprehension of its nature. Nor is it surprising that the part of Scripture chosen for special attention should be from the Old Testament.

Western Christianity has often found the Old Testament a strange book, with some good stories, some wonderful passages of lyric beauty but with long passages of alien and intractable material. The consequence has been a tendency to anthologize the Old Testament, concentrating on the favored passages and ignoring those parts that seem alien. The Old Testament has been compared to a disreputable elderly relative staying in one's home, who must stay there because he is family, but whom one dreads might burst into the living room and frighten the visitors. The reason for this lies in the adjustment that Western Christianity made to the European Enlightenment, which involved acknowledging a frontier between the empirical and spiritual worlds. Christians had obviously to allow for crossing places on that frontier, but as they adjusted to the Enlightenment worldview, their theology strictly limited the number of crossing places and the frequency of the crossings. As a result, Western Christians came to live in a smaller universe than their predecessors; Western theology is designed for a small-scale universe.

But large numbers of African Christians live in a larger universe, where the frontier between the empirical and spiritual worlds is open and repeatedly crossed in both directions. And for African Christians, the Old Testament is not a strange book. Its family patterns, the relationships described, many of the institutions and customs are all familiar or recognizable. So is the age-long struggle between the worship of the God of Israel and the Ba'alim, the territorial spirits claiming to be the owners of the land. Familiar too is the vivid immediacy of the crossings of the frontier with the spiritual world. Perhaps, within the worldwide Christian Church, it may be one of the special tasks of African Christianity to reclaim the Old Testament and restore it to its place in Christian discourse. Perhaps Africa may provide illuminating commentaries on the Scriptures that Christians inherited from Israel that were the Bible of Jesus and the apostles.

At any rate, as Dr. Carter shows, the Fang Christians of Equatorial Guinea have devoured those Scriptures and identified with the issues they raise. Suffering is a central theme in Job, treated at length, realistically and unsparingly, and set within a lively consciousness of the Living God, and ending, not with easy solutions, but with hope and assurance.

In a telling aside, Dr. Carter remarks that in the society that he writes about, practically everybody has a story about suffering. Some of his studies reflect the experiences of leprosy sufferers and victims of HIV/AIDS (the latter, in particular, an issue of huge significance for Africa, and one giving rise to diverse theologies).

This book will illuminate and challenge. It may also show the way to further illumination and even greater challenges.

Andrew F. Walls
University of Edinburgh, Liverpool Hope University
and Akrofi-Christaller Institute, Ghana.

Acknowledgments

AS THE FANG REFRAIN states, *onuú ovóó wăá vea fwás á mbií:* "A single finger does not extract the larva from the hole." The refrain implies that communal cooperation is the only sure path in the pursuit of a goal. In the writing of this book, many fingers lent their help in extracting the *fwás* from the hole.

My life has been immeasurably enriched through my time spent amongst the Fang. The journey began in 1998–99 when I spent one of the most rewarding relational years of my life eating, working, and studying with several future leaders of the Protestant community in Equatorial Guinea. The many nights sharing, laughing, dreaming, and singing around a candle or kerosene lamp after supper have not been forgotten, and, in many ways, this book stands as a rather distant testimony to the impact those times had on my life.

Many people helped make this project possible. Most importantly, I want to thank the three churches that graciously agreed to host the Bible studies and sermons series on the book of Job. Within the Reformed Presbyterian Church, Manuel Nzôh Asumu, Alberto Mañe Ebo Asong, and Manuel Owono Akara Oke were all a wealth of information on Presbyterian church history, Fang culture, and Presbyterian ethos. I am also thankful for "Mama Lily" (one of the foremost Presbyterian matriarchs) who went out of her way to host a trip for me to the old missionary station in the village of Bolondo. Within the church Joy of My Salvation, Damián Ángel Asumu and Basilio Oyono proved extremely kind to the project. Both pastors were instrumental for gaining an appreciation for the dynamics of Pentecostal deliverance ministries as practiced by the church, and welcomed me not only to observe the deliverance prayer time but also encouraged me to sit alongside the counselees as they expressed their presenting problems. In the Assembly of the Holy Spirit, Augustín Edu Esono, along with his wife

Maria Dolores Nchama, were very gracious and hospitable hosts. Liborio Nvo Ndong was also extremely helpful in arranging the sermon series at the church. Yet these few names only begin to scratch the surface. I am indebted to so many others within all three church communities: pastors who preached, lay people who diligently prepared Bible studies, and other church members who simply spent time answering my various questions.

At the local seminary, *Instituto Bíblico "Casa de la Palabra"* (IBCP), professors Modesto Engonga Ondo and Esteban Ndong graciously agreed to co-teach the class on the book of Job despite their busy schedules as local pastors. It was also an absolute privilege to be so warmly received by the communities at the leprosarium of Micomeseng and the Good Samaritan HIV/AIDS support group. The Fang sense of hospitality shone bright even against the backdrop of the darkest of personal stories.

In addition to the hospitality of the three churches, my field research was enriched through extended stays with the families of Agapito Mang and his wife Maria Carmen (in Bata), Deogracias Bee and his wife Juanita (in Nsork), and Clemente Alogo and his wife Nely (in Kogo). All were surrogate families for me during my field research while also providing invaluable inroads into Fang culture. I am also grateful that one former graduate of IBCP seminary, Martin Mbeng Nze, who is known at the Spanish Cultural Center for his deep knowledge of Fang indigenous practices, took a particularly keen interest in the project by spending hours discussing Fang traditional rituals with me. Samuel Ndong and Allen Pierce, two members of the *Asociación Cristiana de Traducciones Bíblicas*, were both exceeding helpful at various stages of the research. My own missionary colleagues, Roly and Cristina Grenier and Jazmin Abuabara, were characteristically welcoming, and their friendships and hospitality in facilitating numerous logistical and practical details were most helpful.

The material in this book formed the basis of my PhD dissertation which was presented to The University of Edinburgh in February of 2014. Not enough kind words can be said about my primary supervisor, Brian Stanley, Director for the Centre for the Study of World Christianity. Of the many accolades Professor Stanley has accumulated over the years, one stands out as particularly unique to me. *African Christianity: An African Story*, a collection of essays written predominantly by Africans and edited by the late Ogbu Kalu, was dedicated to Andrew F .Walls and Brian Stanley stating, "many have bemoaned the collapse of Christian scholarship in Africa, you both have done something about it."[1] The tribute speaks to a remarkable respect for Professor Stanley's scholarship in the academy and

---

1. Kalu, *African Christianity: An African Story*, ix.

to the integrity of his Christian character to which I can only add my own small "Amen!" to this widely held consensus.

I am thankful for my parents, Steve and Sandra Carter, who gifted me with a sense of hard work and a love of knowledge. The plethora of educational opportunities which I have been granted is largely a testimony to their loving involvement in my life. And, finally, undoubtedly the most endearing support came from my wife Lisa who held down the fort with our rambunctious young boys while daddy was away doing field research "in Africa." I'll always be incredibly grateful for her love and support.

Jason A. Carter
Bata, Equatorial Guinea

Introduction

FOR THE LAST TWO centuries, the book of Job has undergone academic scrutiny from those centers of the global church most distant from the daily realities of suffering. Treatises of Job cooked in western ovens often wax eloquently about suffering or theodicy or retribution, but the grassroots interpreters whom we shall observe in this study soaked reflections on Job in the cold waters of harrowing personal experience. From my own experiences in Central Africa, engaging in a conversation about suffering is like offering a cup of tea or coffee to a friend. The mutual sharing of heartfelt stories and personal anecdotes often warmly ensues because nearly everybody has a story to tell about suffering. My personal interest in this study began with a vague sixth sense that grassroots African Christians would encounter the book of Job as uniquely empowering within their context. After reading the book of Job with over 200 participants at six different venues, I now believe that my original intuition was certainly correct: ordinary readers interpreted the book of Job as offering *profound* existential insights and *rich* theological perspectives. These popular African readings of Job frequently proved to be innovative and creative but also occasionally took quite surprising and unexpected directions. In this book, I compare these grassroots explorations of Job to a *window* which affords an inspection or a *prism* that captures the multi-colored themes, theologies, and trajectories currently pulsating within contemporary African Christianity.

In spite of the rise of Christianity in Africa, studies offering a descriptive analysis of how grassroots Christians interpret and appropriate the themes and theologies of a particular biblical book are remarkably atypical. This book seeks to close the gap between the growing Christianization of much of sub-Saharan Africa and the relative marginalization of ordinary

African voices in the areas of biblical hermeneutics and contextual theology. As Stephen B. Bevans has argued, "There is no such thing as 'theology'; there is only *contextual* theology" since all theology is inherently rooted in specific cultural contexts.[1] This study endeavors to capture and reflect upon the contextual theologies emerging from Christian communities in the small Central African nation of Equatorial Guinea with wider implications for African Christianity more broadly. As contextually-based studies provide the fuel and fodder for wider theological innovation and dialogue, the thematic and theological reflections on suffering, evil, and hope emerging from grassroots faith communities in Equatorial Guinea undoubtedly have the ability to resonate more widely, especially across the African continent.

Since grassroots readings of the Bible in Africa are often molded by "the harsh realities of daily living" and "the sheer struggle to survive,"[2] engaging in an exploration of popular readings of the book of Job—the quintessential biblical book on suffering—represents an exceptionally intriguing test case for African hermeneutics in particular and for African Christianity in general. Guided by the conviction that the Christian faith in Africa is taught and caught, sung and danced, lived and shared most noticeably through the lenses of scriptural interpretation, local culture and ecclesial practice—an interconnected triad that we term the *hermeneutics-culture-praxis triad*—themes and theologies occupying African Christianity will be explored with the book of Job serving as a catalyst into these discussions.[3]

Overview and Outline

Throughout this study, we argue that the *hermeneutics-culture-praxis triad* is pivotal to understanding the biblical hermeneutics and the dominant themes and theologies adopted by grassroots Christians in Africa. Providing the overall structure of the book, each "pole" or "source" of the hermeneutics-culture-praxis triad is explored at length in part one (chapters 1–3). With respect to hermeneutics, chapter 1 gives a general overview of the hermeneutics-culture-praxis triad by highlighting its wide-ranging and significant relationship to African Christianity as well as revealing why the book of Job provides a particularly suitable window into an exploration of

---

1. Bevans, *Models of Contextual Theology*, 1, italics in the original.

2. Riches, "Interpreting the Bible in African Contexts," 183.

3. Our own triad is clearly distinguished from most major interpreters of African hermeneutics by recognizing the role ecclesial practice exerts upon biblical interpretation. As Gerald West recognizes, "most characterizations of African biblical hermeneutics tend to portray a bi-polar approach"; West, "Biblical Hermeneutics in Africa," 21.

issues affecting contemporary African Christianity.[4] Chapter 2 offers a brief ethnography of the Fang peoples of Equatorial Guinea and their history, beliefs, and practices which inform local readings of the book of Job. Chapter 3 explores the ecclesial praxis of three major Protestant denominations of Equatorial Guinea: the Reformed Presbyterian Church of Equatorial Guinea and two Pentecostal churches—Joy of My Salvation and Assembly of the Holy Spirit.

On the basis of these locally-rich descriptions and contextually-anchored realities, part two (chapters 4–6) begins an exploration of central themes, theologies, and trajectories within African Christianity arising from the insights of "ordinary readers" in Equatorial Guinea in response to the book of Job.[5] In part two, we do not leave behind the *hermeneutics-culture-praxis triad* as is typically the case for strictly commentary-style interpretations of biblical texts. Instead we will be engaging in "interpretations and appropriations" of Job which seek to engage with the underlying implications of the hermeneutical circle of text and context. That is, not only will we explore grassroots exegetical readings of the *text* of Job ("interpretations") but the various cultural and ecclesial *contexts* of the biblical interpreters themselves will be exposed and placed in intimate dialogue with the text ("appropriations").[6] By exploring fully this hermeneutical circle of text-with-context, meaningful lines of dialogue within African Christianity will open up from the vista of the book of Job. To continue with the metaphor, we believe that the book of Job offers some particularly revealing panoramas which illuminate the themes, theologies, and trajectories currently occupying African Christian communities in the twenty-first century. These panoramas are made possible because at the popular levels of African Christianity people do not only "read" texts but the texts "read" people in their own context as Christians engage in a lively back-and-forth

---

4. As a methodological note, when referring to "Africa" or "African Christianity" this book is referring to sub-Saharan Africa unless otherwise indicated.

5. Following Gerald O. West, we define "ordinary readers" as typically untrained, poor, marginalized, and/or illiterate biblical interpreters who generally "read" the scriptures pre-critically. In general, an ordinary reader is a "typical" Christian at the popular level of African Christianity. See West, *The Academy of the Poor*, 10–11; West, "(Ac)claiming the (Extra)ordinary African 'Reader' of the Bible," 29–47. See also Kiriaku Kinyua, *Introducing Ordinary African Readers' Hermeneutics*; Akper, "The Role of the 'Ordinary Reader' in Gerald O. West's Hermeneutics," 1–13.

6. Throughout this study, our own use of the term "appropriation" signifies a response to the text from the whole person as situated in his or her context; Goldingay, *Models for Interpretation of Scripture*, 251; West, "Biblical Hermeneutics in Africa," 22–23.

dialogue with what is termed the hermeneutical circle and place their own lives within the framework of the biblical narrative.

In chapter 4, we explore the nature of evil and theodicy as confronted culturally, existentially, and theologically by Fang Christians. We contend that rooting theodicy in an African context requires a radical re-framing to reflect the contours of local African cultures. We advance the argument that *Christian theodicy acutely shapes the theological vision of grassroots Christians, leaving an indelible imprint upon the fabric of African Christianity*. Theodicy provides a critical lens through which local Christians interpret scripture, re-conceptualize the cosmology, and construct images of God and the Devil which decisively impact the nature of the Christian faith. In chapter 5, we analyze the roles of lament and retributive blame in the stigmatized suffering of leprosy patients and people living with HIV/AIDS by listening to their own engagement with Job's lament (Job 3:1–26) and the retributive blame levied on Job by his friends Eliphaz, Bildad, and Zophar. This chapter considers the challenge posed by the paradigm "Job the Innocent Sufferer" to theologies of blame which continue to characterize Christian rhetoric during the HIV/AIDS crisis. In contrast to the idiom of blame, we explore Job's lament as an authentic and liberating theological language capable of empowering churches to embody compassionate solidarity with those infected and affected by HIV/AIDS. In chapter 6, we turn to the eschatological orientation of grassroots Christians as they examine Job's experience of suffering and his final liberation. We suggest that the "theology of hope" which sustains Fang Christians in the midst of suffering is a *Deus* (rather than *Christus*) *Victor* paradigm expressed in the Christian practice of prayer. In the concluding chapter, we look to comment generally on the use of Christian scriptures in African Christian communities as well as offer some brief evaluative reflections on the dialectical relationship that exists between indigenization and diabolization within African Christianity.

Methodology

Academic articles and popular meditations by several leading African theologians and biblical scholars, including Gerald O. West,[7] E. Bolaji Idowu,[8]

---

7. West and Zengele, "Reading Job 'Positively' in the Context of HIV/AIDS in South Africa," 112–24; West, "The Poetry of Job as a Resource for the Articulation of Embodied Lament in the Context of HIV and AIDS in South Africa," 195–214; West, "Hearing Job's Wife," 107–31.

8. Idowu, *Job*.

Sam Tinyiko Maluleke,[9] and Madipoane J. Masenya,[10] seem to indicate that the identity and plight of Job connects viscerally with the sufferings of African Christians and that an in-depth study of the book of Job in Africa would be a welcome addition within the academy and the church.[11] In the context of the HIV/AIDS pandemic, African biblical scholars have occasionally excavated Job for spiritual nuggets in the construction of theologies able to speak powerfully within the doldrums of this unique modern health crisis.[12] These studies, however, do little to remedy Paul Gifford's lament that "there is obviously a serious dearth of research on (or lack of interest in?) how the Bible is actually received or understood or used on the ground,"[13] a complaint that our own project explicitly seeks to re-dress.[14]

In the present study, voices not commonly heard in African hermeneutics will foreground the discussion. Ordinary pastors, committed lay people, HIV-positive Christians, leprosy patients as well as local seminary professors and students will be observed engaging with the thematically rich and existentially challenging book of Job. Utilizing my own relational network with churches and individuals garnered from several years as a missionary-professor at a Protestant seminary, I approached three significant churches in the Protestant tradition in Equatorial Guinea to assess their willingness to make the book of Job a subject of hermeneutical reflection through sermons and Bible studies in their respective churches. I freely expressed my

9. Maluleke, "A Letter to Job—From Africa," 5.

10. Masenya, "Between Unjust Suffering and the 'Silent' God," 186–99; Masenya, "All from the Same Source?" 46–60; Masenya, "Her Appropriation of Job's Lament?" 283–97.

11. On the intersection between Africa and the book of Job, one-volume biblical commentaries written by African biblical scholars may be mentioned: Habtu, "Job," 571–604; Masenya and Sadler, "Job," 237–43; Ntreh, "Job," 141–50. For a Congolese reading of Job, see Mukenge, "Une Lecture Populaire de La Figure de Job Au Congo," 2–6. For a PhD dissertation, see Obeta, "Eschatological Concepts in Job."

12. See Tshikendwa Matadi, *Suffering, Belief, Hope*. In addition to West and Masenya's articles previously cited, see also Nadar, "Re-reading Job," 343–57; Nadar, "'Barak God and Die!,'" 60–79; Wittenberg, "Counselling Aids Patients," 61–68; Van Dyk, "The Tale of Two Tragedies," 7–13; Nelson, "Justice and Biblical Interpretation," 431–52, esp. 441–48; Nelson, *Power and Responsibility*, 166–200; Lwendo, "The Significance of the Doctrine of Retribution." As part of a HIV/AIDS curriculum developed by the World Council of Churches for African theological institutions, see Nadar, "Studying the Book of Job Part 1," 103–18; Nadar, "Studying the Book of Job Part 2," 119–36. For the use of Job in developing HIV-sensitive liturgy, see Mosupole, "Stigma and Discrimination," 125–27.

13. Gifford, Review of *The Bible in Africa*, 399.

14. To our knowledge, of all the biblical scholars who intersect the book of Job with an African context, only West and Zengele explicitly foreground grassroots responses to the text of Job; see West and Zengele, "Reading Job 'Positively,'" esp. 118–21.

own preference for the book of Job as the locus of this study, indicating to these church leaders that the West has interpreted the book of Job from the position of their own privileged socio-economic condition and within the milieu of their own cultures. My study, I told them, not only would seek to capture the theological and biblical perspectives of local Christian communities but also highlight popular, rather than academic, reflections of the book of Job from communities well-acquainted with suffering.

This proposal to study the book of Job was readily accepted by high-level leaders in all three church traditions. Yet the project was still confronted with a crucial methodological question from the outset: exactly how should the churches study the book of Job? Insofar as Job's considerable length (forty-two chapters) mitigated against a chapter-by-chapter exposition, should any texts in Job be prioritized as especially worth of consideration? Local pastors deemed Elihu's lengthy speech (Job 32:1—37:24) and the so-called Wisdom Poem of Job (Job 28:1-28) as two thematic blocks which least attracted their homiletical interest, and thus voiced their preference for six textual blocks to facilitate a manageable time-frame for conducting the sermon series and Bible studies within their churches.

Table 1:
Primary Textual and Thematic Blocks Prioritized
in Readings of the Book of Job

	Thematic Unit of Job	Text of Job
Part 1	The Prologue	Job 1:1—2:13
Part 2	Job's Lament	Job 3:1-26
Part 3	The Dialogue: The Friends	Speeches by Eliphaz, Bildad, and/or Zophar
Part 4	The Dialogue: Job Responds	A Response of Job from the Dialogue Sections
Part 5	The Whirlwind Speeches	Job 38:1—42:6
Part 6	The Epilogue: Job's Restoration	Job 42:7-17

For five months spanning October 2011 to June 2012, I observed, listened to, and recorded nineteen sermons, twenty-three Bible studies, and eighteen hours of seminary classroom discussions centering on the book of Job. In addition, I conducted eight interviews with leprosy patients and people living with HIV/AIDS in order to personalize their stories and gain greater access to their perspectives on suffering and retributive blame given that their communities did not engage homiletically with Job.[15]

Table 2:
Scope of the Study

Site of the Study	Sermons	Bible Studies	Semi-Structured Interviews
Reformed Presbyterian Church of Equatorial Guinea	6	8	—
Joy of My Salvation	7	6	—
Assembly of the Holy Spirit	6	—	—
Leprosarium	—	6	4
"The Good Samaritan" (NGO) with HIV-positive Christians	—	3	4
Total	*19 Sermons*	*23 Bible Studies*	*8 Interviews*

With a view towards prioritizing local agency and creativity, indigenous Christians led all the Bible studies and local preachers had complete autonomy to narrow their exegetical and homiletical focus to particular verses (or sections) of interest within the various thematic blocks.

As an ordained Presbyterian pastor and interdenominational missionary, I intentionally chose not to lead the Bible studies and was not engaged in commending any specific homiletical strategies, based on my own understanding of Job, to local pastors and leaders. In other words, I am not primarily attempting to "do" contextual theology in this study, but rather I am interested in observing contextual theology being "done" and "performed" by grassroots Christians as they engage with the book of Job in typical ecclesial practices: sermons and small group Bible studies. Therefore, while I had initially suggested the book of Job as the locus of hermeneutical reflection, I was also inviting these ordinary readers to dynamically engage with the text on their own terms.

---

15. For further methodological information, see appendix 2: "Reading the Book of Job at Six Distinct Locations in Equatorial Guinea."

Major Sites of the Study of Job

In this book, the reader will hear from a myriad of grassroots Christians in a diverse range of venues. The study is situated in six distinct interpretive communities which appropriated the book of Job: three Protestant churches (one Presbyterian, two Pentecostal), a grassroots seminary, a colonial built leprosarium, and a HIV/AIDS support group of the non-governmental organization (NGO) "The Good Samaritan." Since chapter 3 depicts a rich "ecclesial ethnography" of the three churches and their dominant ecclesial practices, only a brief word is needed here to explain the inclusion of these particular churches in the study.[16] In other words, why were these churches chosen for the study and not others? Simply put, the churches selected to read the book of Job represent the most influential churches from each of the three ecumenical Protestant networks of Equatorial Guinea.[17] Churches representing historic missionary Protestant Christianity are aligned together in a local networked called the *Council of Evangelical Churches of Equatorial Guinea* which maintains a connection with the World Council of Churches (WCC). In this ecumenical network, the Reformed Presbyterian Church of Equatorial Guinea is unquestionably the largest and most influential.[18] The second ecumenical consortium of churches amongst Protestants is known as the *Federation of Evangelical and Pentecostal Churches of Equatorial Guinea* which includes a broad spectrum of Pentecostal churches as well as the newer evangelical missionary churches. *Joy of My Salvation* is the church which represents arguably the fastest-growing indigenous church in this network and one of the largest expressions of Pentecostalism in the country.[19] The third Protestant ecumenical organization in the country, the

---

16. This "ecclesial ethnography" is based upon participant observation of Sunday morning worship services, Bible study groups, prayer meetings, deliverance ministries, evangelistic campaigns, prophetic seminars, women's groups, and young adult groups. In addition, semi-structured interviews with pastors, elders, deacons, catechists, and lay people as well as with variously named denominational figures (general secretary, church historian, superintendent, apostle) within the three churches were conducted with an eye towards providing a rich description of the diverse landscape of Guinean Protestant Christianity. For the term "ecclesial ethnography," see Healy, *Church, World, and the Christian Life*, 182–85, cf. 24, 169.

17. In Spanish, the three ecumenical networks are called (1) *Consejo de Iglesias Evangélicas de Guinea Ecuatorial* (CIEGE), (2) *Federación de Iglesias Evangélicas y Pentecostales de Guinea Ecuatorial* (FIEPGE), and (3) *Asociación de Iglesias Evangélicas y Pentecostales de Guinea Ecuatorial* (AIEPGE).

18. In Spanish, the church is known as *Iglesia Reformada Presbiteriana de Guinea Ecuatorial* (IRPGE). The two other churches involved in this ecumenical partnership are the *Iglesia Metodista de Guinea Ecuatorial* and *Iglesia Cruzada de Guinea Ecuatorial*.

19. In Spanish, the church is called *Gozo de la Salvación* whose nearest English

Association of Evangelical and Pentecostal Churches of Equatorial Guinea, is presided over by Apostle Agustín Edu Esono who leads the church *Assembly of the Holy Spirit*.[20] Assembly of the Holy Spirit can be distinguished from some of its local Pentecostal brethren by the conspicuous presence of expatriate prosperity gospel preachers. The influence of the prosperity gospel was at the heart of the division which precipitated the creation of two separate ecumenical networks dominated by Pentecostals even within the small confines of Equatorial Guinea. Considering the rapid growth of Pentecostals in Equatorial Guinea over the last fifteen years, the inclusion of two Pentecostal churches in the study seems appropriate for portraying the diversity of Guinean Pentecostalism, especially in the absence, to our knowledge, of any African Indigenous Church (AIC) originating in the country.

With respect to participants in non-ecclesial venues, the leprosarium built under Spanish colonialism in the village of Micomeseng provided Catholic participation in the study as all of the leprosy patients self-identified as Roman Catholic. Reading the book of Job at the leprosarium sought to add interpretive depth to cultural issues surrounding stigmatization and retributive blame while also providing a comparative perspective with HIV/AIDS. During its support group meeting for people living with HIV/AIDS, the non-governmental organization (NGO) "The Good Samaritan" read the book of Job during their weekly Bible study session before discussing other practical aspects of living with the disease (i.e., nutrition, medication). The final venue to participate in the study was a grassroots theological institution where two Fang professors—Esteban Ndong and Modesto Engonga Ondo—taught the book of Job to eight theological students during their third-year ministry practicum in the local churches.

As a final methodological note, as a fluent Spanish-speaker, I conducted all research, except at the leprosarium, in Spanish.[21] Since Equatorial Guinea boasts the highest literacy rate (93 percent) in all of Africa, local Christians who customarily preach in Spanish (with simultaneous translation into Fang) were able to main normal church praxis with respect to language for the sermons and Bible studies.[22] Throughout the book, the names

---

translation would be rendered "Joy of the Salvation." However, we have chosen to utilize the local English name "Joy of My Salvation" adopted by an Anglophone (mostly Nigerian) congregation which utilizes *Gozo's* church building in the city of Bata.

20. In Spanish, the church is called *Asamblea del Espíritu Santo*.

21. At the leprosarium, the six Bible studies and two female interviews were conducted in Fang. These recorded transcripts were later translated from audio recordings into Spanish by a small team of Fang speakers.

22. "Literacy Rate, Adult Total," *Index Mundi*. The sermons, Bible studies, and

of the leprosy patients, people living with HIV/AIDS, and participants in the Bible studies are anonymous while the names of the preachers (and professors at the seminary) are used with permission.

---

interviews in Spanish have been translated by the author into English throughout the book. In addition, Spanish and French secondary sources have been translated into English by the author.

Part 1

The Hermeneutics-Culture-Praxis Triad

1

Readings of the Book of Job as a Window on African Christianity

Introduction

> What lies ahead is a critical theological construction which will relate more fully the widespread African confidence in the Christian faith to the actual and ongoing Christian responses to the life-experiences of Africans. Here, academic discourse will need to connect with the less academic but fundamental reality of the "implicit" and predominantly *oral* theologies found at the grassroots of many, if not all, African Christian communities...[1]
>
> —Kwame Bediako (1945–2008), Ghanaian Theologian

KWAME BEDIAKO'S CONVICTION REGARDING the need for scholars to engage with lived expressions of the faith in African Christian communities defines the central scope and trajectory of this book. Scholars of African Christianity often recognize that "much more work needs to be done on how ordinary Africans interpret the Bible" not merely out of a "nostalgic or romantic yearning for a lost naivete" but because the Bible lies at the heart and center of African Christianity.[2] Philip Jenkins argues that Christian communities in the global south "are still in the initial phases of a love affair with the scripture" and evokes the axiom of Martin Luther ("The Bible is

---

1. Bediako, "Understanding African Theology in the 20th Century," 17, italics in the original.
2. West, "Mapping African Biblical Interpretation," 43.

alive—it has hands and grabs hold of me, it has feet and runs after me"),[3] which may be taken as quite a significant and astute insight as to the Bible's "aliveness" and "power" in African Christianity. Yet regrettably, studies of popular or grassroots interpretations of specific biblical books within African Christianity are remarkably atypical.[4]

Despite the centrality of the Bible within African Christianity and the growing scholarly interest in "African" approaches to the scriptures which have resulted in several major publications in recent years including the *Africa Bible Commentary*,[5] Gerald O. West and Musa W. Dube's substantial edited volume *The Bible in Africa*,[6] and Jenkins' *The New Faces of Christianity: Believing the Bible in the Global South*,[7] the tendency still remains for scholarly voices to dominate the conversation. Grassroots interpretations of the Bible which have sustained the vibrant expansion of the Christian faith all across sub-Saharan Africa remain largely unexplored academic territory. As Paul Gifford notes, the nascent resurgence of interest in African practices of biblical interpretation has largely been performed by "Western-trained academics" for the consumption of western audiences as "[t]here has been relatively little study of the way the Bible is actually used in churches, especially at the very grassroots."[8] In similar fashion, John S. Mbiti has acknowledged that three chief theological forms comprise contemporary African Christianity including *written theology* (academic expressions), *oral theology* (sermons, prayers, Bible study, songs), and *symbolic theology* (art, sculpture, drama) but laments that popular oral expressions of the Christian faith which are "produced in the fields, by the masses, through song, sermon, teaching, prayer, conversation" are "often heard only by small groups, and generally lost to libraries and seminaries."[9] Thus, the need to situate the hermeneutical process holistically within its most natural environment—in dialogue with cultural dynamics and ecclesial practices at the popular level—remains of utmost importance for not only recognizing the shaping influence that the Bible continues to play within African Christianity but also for understanding African Christianity itself, in all its complexities and nuances. By pitching our tent at the corner of local grassroots realities and

---

3. Jenkins, *The New Faces of Christianity*, 18.

4. Though see David T. Adamo's exploration of the Psalms amongst Nigerian Aladuran churches; Adamo, *Reading and Interpreting the Bible in African Indigenous Churches*.

5. Adeyemo, *Africa Bible Commentary*.

6. West and Dube, *The Bible in Africa*.

7. Jenkins, *The New Faces of Christianity*.

8. Gifford, "The Bible in Africa," 203.

9. Mbiti, "The Biblical Basis for Present Trends in African Theology," 84.

biblical interpretation, we can begin to appreciate not only the role that the Bible continues to exercise within African Christianity but also make great strides in understanding African Christianity "from below," as a loosely-connected series of movements, institutions, theologies, and histories which self-identifies itself intimately with biblical texts.

A central argument of this study is that experiences of the Christian faith as well as the dominant beliefs, values, and theologies adopted by local believers are uniquely informed by the dynamism of the *hermeneutics-culture-praxis triad*.[10] Based upon the presupposition that everyone reads the Bible in a certain way (hermeneutics), from a particular vantage point (culture), and with a certain group of people who distinctively engage in being the church (praxis), comprehending the dynamics of the *hermeneutics-culture-praxis triad* is essential to unveiling the contours of contemporary African Christianity. So, it is to this important triad that we now turn.

The Hermeneutics-Culture-Praxis Triad in African Christianity

Hermeneutics: What is African Hermeneutics? Reading the Bible in Africa

Despite the fact that the demographic changes of the global church have almost become yesterday's news amongst students of world Christianity, the facts bear repeating: the typical Christian in the twenty-first century is no longer an Anglo-Saxon of European descent living in the western metropolises of New York City, London, or Berlin but may be described more accurately as a Brazilian mother living in a *favela* of São Paulo or a young Nigerian man attempting to survive on the informal economy of Lagos.[11] These profound changes in the demographics of the global church are not without their consequences, particularly as Christians in the global south—like St. Augustine so many centuries ago—*tolle lege* ("take up and read") their Bibles in contexts very different than their northern counterparts.

---

10. It is also evident that the dialogical interaction between hermeneutics, culture, and praxis forms the constitutive basis of Christian self-identity in Africa. If there is a "pole" which is often excluded by academic theologians, it is typically the crucial element of ecclesial praxis and its significant impact upon both Christian identity and theology. For instance, Bediako's *Theology and Identity* leaves largely unexplored this crucial pole of ecclesial praxis which critically impinges upon the self-identity of African Christians; Bediako, *Theology and Identity*. For a similar critique of Bediako, see Katongole, "'A Different World Right Here,'" 206–34, esp. 209–18.

11. This is the main contour of the argument in Jenkins, *The Next Christendom*, 1–2.

Today nearly one out of every four Christians on the planet lives in Africa, which is estimated to contain some 495 million Christians.[12] This dramatic southward migration of the world Christian movement[13] has prompted Andrew Walls to insist that "anyone who wishes to undertake serious study of Christianity these days needs to know something about Africa."[14] Questions such as "how do Africans at the popular level read and interpret their Bibles?" or "what does biblical interpretation look like outside the western cultural hegemony of the Enlightenment?" or simply "what is African hermeneutics?" are remarkably important if we are to understand not only the *demographic* and *statistical* changes of world Christianity but also the very contours and practices shaping one of the major new hubs and centers of Christianity in the twenty-first century—the vibrant faith of millions of Christians in Africa.

This flourishing and spirited faith on the African continent is embedded within and nourished by three significant "poles" or "sources" which we have already introduced as the *hermeneutics-culture-praxis triad*. Biblical interpretation in Africa is likewise closely conjoined to this "tri-polar" orientation,[15] reflecting not only the central place the Bible occupies within African Christian communities but also illustrating the relative influence the Bible has exerted upon the whole of the African continent since the beginnings of European colonialism[16] wherein "reader" and "Christian" have often represented synonymous terms.[17] Generally-speaking, popular biblical interpretation in Africa is characterized by a constant dialectic between the "three poles" of hermeneutics, local culture, and ecclesial praxis wherein ordinary readers pay *close attention to the text* (hermeneutics), *close attention to the context* (culture), and *close attention to the community* (ecclesial praxis) (see figure 1.1). The robust and constant dialogical interaction be-

---

12. The statistic reflects the entire continent of Africa (not only sub-Saharan African); Johnson and Ross, *Atlas of Global Christianity*, 9, cf. 110; *Global Christianity: A Report on the Size and Distribution of the World's Christian Population*, 9, 53–56.

13. For a helpful overview of this seismic shift, see Tennent, *Theology in the Context of World Christianity*, 8–11.

14. Walls, "Eusebius Tries Again," 106.

15. Arguably, this triad may reflect the orientation of *popular* biblical interpretation in the majority of contexts in the global church, from South East Asia to Latin America to North Atlantic contexts. For coining the phrase "tri-polar," see Draper, "Old Scores and New Notes," 148–68 as cited by West, "Biblical Hermeneutics in Africa," 21.

16. "Along with gunboats, opium, slaves and treaties, the Christian Bible became a defining symbol of European expansion," Sugirtharajah, *The Bible and the Third World*, 1.

17. In Uganda, the policy of the Church Missionary Society (CMS) required every adult to learn to read before being baptized and every candidate for confirmation to own a copy of the New Testament; Ibid., 69.

tween these three mutually interpreting poles captures the spirit and posture of African biblical interpretation as well as its underlying uniqueness.

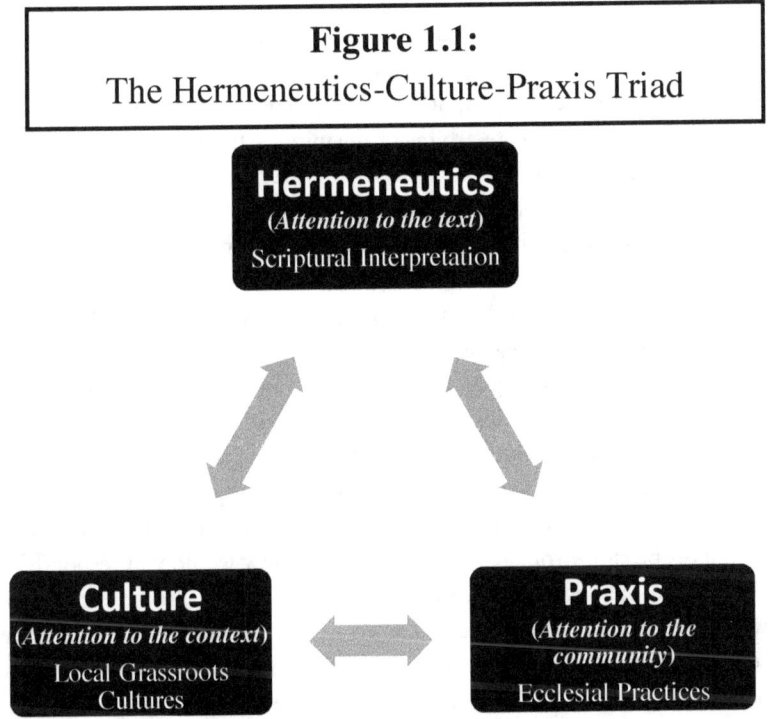

Figure 1.1:
The Hermeneutics-Culture-Praxis Triad

In placing African biblical interpretation on the map of modern approaches to the Bible, Nigerian biblical scholar Justin Ukpong argues that three prominent approaches to the scriptures may be identified in the modern era: (1) the "historical-critical approach" which focuses primarily upon the original text in its historical context wherein the author's original meaning as communicated to the original audience is thought to be determinative for unlocking the meaning of any particular text, (2) the "literary approach" which attempts to tease out literary nuances and latent structures within the text which may exert an organizing and decisive influence on the meaning of the text, and (3) the reader-centered "contextual approach" which is the method most broadly representative of African hermeneutics in general.[18] Although all three approaches are utilized in Africa, most readers of the Bible in Africa are not primarily concerned with getting "behind" the text

18. Ukpong, "Developments in Biblical Interpretation in Africa," 25.

(the historical-critical method) nor with positioning themselves "upon" the text (literary readings) but rather with approaching and engaging Christian scriptures from "within" the text. Ukpong observes that African Christians "are interested neither in the literary analysis of biblical texts nor in the history behind the text. They are interested in the theological message in the text and how that message might be useful to their lives."[19] For African hermeneutics, neither history, nor genre, nor complicated etymologies figure as the chief or ultimate arbiter of meaning. African hermeneutics is a highly personal and existential experience of reading the Bible by placing oneself "within" the biblical text. As I observed first-hand at almost every single Bible study group I attended, neither the particular denomination (Presbyterian or Pentecostal), nor the genre of the text (prose or poetry), nor the specific location (church, seminary, leprosarium, or HIV/AIDS support group) changed to any degree the most fundamental question for ordinary readers of the Bible in Equatorial Guinea. From my own experience, the most foundational, recurring, all-pervasive, and important question in African hermeneutics is: "Put yourself in the story—what would you do? How would you react? How would you respond?" Literally countless times during the course of my research, I heard articulated this main emphasis: "Take Job out of the story. You are there in his place. How would you respond?"

As Ukpong argues, African biblical interpretation largely eschews the two-tiered approach[20] between "meaning" and "application" that characterizes the historical-critical and literary approaches to scripture.[21] Whereas historical-critical or literary approaches to the scriptures engage first in "what the text meant" in order to discover "what the text means,"[22] thereby preserving (theoretically) interpretative objectivity while at the same time paying respectful homage to Lessing's "ugly ditch of history" as an epistemological gap separating the (historical) text from the (contemporary) reader,[23] African biblical interpretation generally suppresses such two-stage processes. By contrast, the ordinary reader in Africa dynamically *enters the*

---

19. Ukpong, "Popular Readings of the Bible in Africa," 588.

20. For example, John Barton writes: "The heart of the matter is this. Assimilating any text, the Bible included, is a two-stage operation. The first stage is a perception of the text's meaning; the second, an evaluation of that meaning in relation to what one already believes to be the case," Barton, *The Nature of Biblical Criticism*, 159, cf. 171, 176–77.

21. Ukpong, "Developments in Biblical Interpretation in Africa," 24–25.

22. For a helpful overview of major voices in vernacular biblical interpretation in the global south, see Nelson, *Power and Responsibility in Biblical Interpretation*, 87–119. We are indebted to Nelson here, 105, fn. 103.

23. Lessing, "On the Proof of the Spirit and of Power," 51–56, esp. 55.

text in "one process" whereby any epistemological distance from the text is foreshortened in order for the reader to explore applicational meaning from a positional relationship extremely close to the text itself.[24] Whereas western interpreters can arguably remain more easily unaffected by the interpretative process since *meaning* can be largely divorced from *application*, biblical interpretation in Africa evokes within the reader immediate "reactions, responses and commitments" within his or her context.[25] Musimbi Kanyoro argues that "we [in Africa] appropriate the words of the scriptures and assume that we are the intended audience" by alluding to a story when she read the Apostle Paul's concluding benediction to the Corinthian church ("My love be with all of you in Christ Jesus") in a northern Kenyan village:

> The community, which had been listening silently, responded in unison, "Thank you Paul." They were thanking Paul for sending them greetings, not the reader for reading the text to them.[26]

Such profound existential reactions to biblical texts are undoubtedly one reason which accounts for the power and vibrancy often associated with African Christianity.[27]

Culture: The Pursuit of the Abundant Life in Africa

At a broad conceptual level, biblical interpretation in Africa proceeds from the distinct concerns, questions, and pre-understandings which African Christians bring to the biblical text.[28] Often referred to as the "comparative method"[29] or the "inculturation hermeneutic"[30] and associated with the

---

24. Ukpong explains: "[T]here are not two processes, consisting of recovery of the meaning of a text through historical analysis and then applying it to the present context, but one process of a reader who is critically aware of his/her context interacting with the text analysed in its context.... This involves entering into the text with a critical awareness about the contemporary context and allowing it to evoke in the reader appropriate reactions, responses and commitments about the context," Ukpong, "Developments in Biblical Interpretation in Africa," 24–25.

25. Ibid., 25.

26. Kanyoro, "Reading the Bible from an African Perspective," 18. The verses were 1 Cor 16:21–24.

27. For example, Jenkins' second chapter in *The New Faces of Christianity* is entitled "Power in the Book"; see Jenkins, *The New Faces of Christianity*, 18–41.

28. Gornik, *Word Made Global*, 164.

29. Gifford, "The Bible in Africa," 204. For a critical evaluation of the comparative method, see Anum, "Comparative Readings of the Bible in Africa," 457–73.

30. Ukpong, "Rereading the Bible with African Eyes," 3–14, esp. 4–5.

"hermeneutical circle" of text and context[31] wherein the reader places herself at the center of the interpretive process,[32] the main emphasis involves placing the "texts and motifs" of the Bible alongside "supposed African parallels, letting the two illuminate one another."[33] Culturally, ordinary readers of the Bible often feel quite "at home" within the biblical text. Whether based upon shared social concerns, comparable ethical norms, or analogous ways of organizing the cosmological universe, the striking parallels between ancient Israel and modern-day Africa often resonate with ordinary readers:

> Many biblical stories sound familiar to Africans: people going out to fish for that day's breakfast, beggars and prostitutes on the streets, women carrying the family's load, exclusion of women and children in counts and censuses, light from oil lamps, neighbors going to ask for bread to feed an unexpected guest in the middle of the night, free "all-you-can-eat" weddings for all relatives and friends, demon-possessed men, women, and children. The list goes on and on[:] . . . lineage, age-groupings, the value of royalty, birthrights and inheritance laws, the value of the elderly, emotional attachment to ancestral lands. These affinities make the Bible sound true and relevant to the reader.[34]

In this sense, the second "pole" or "source" of culture provides one of *the* determinative lenses through which ordinary readers in Africa appropriate biblical texts. This experiential encounter between the text and the context contains the possibility for a two-way transaction which significantly illuminates both the reader's context (reader-in-context) and the biblical text itself (text-in-context): not only are the lives, beliefs, and practices of African Christians shaped by biblical texts but also the biblical texts themselves are negotiated by the ordinary reader in such a way that the Bible "may enhance rather than frustrate" the pursuit of life in his or her context.[35]

As the Tanzanian Catholic theologian Laurenti Magesa has recognized, the pursuit of the abundant life lies at the center of most African cosmologies.[36] As one of the foundational aspirations of African religiosity, a

---

31. Tim Meadowcroft argues that the metaphor of the hermeneutical circle originated with Friedrich Schleiermacher; Meadowcroft, "Relevance as a Mediating Category in the Reading of Biblical Texts," 611–27, esp. 614–16.

32. Ukpong maintains that the African "inculturation hermeneutic" seeks to make the reader-in-context the "subject" of biblical interpretation; Ukpong, "Rereading the Bible with African Eyes," 5.

33. Holter, *Old Testament Research for Africa*, 88.

34. Mwombeki, "Reading the Bible in Contemporary Africa," 123.

35. Maluleke, "Black and African Theologies in the New World Order," 13.

36. Magesa, *African Religion*.

diverse range of beliefs and practices are conceptually tied together through this focal impulse to acquire "life, life in its fullness."[37] From the importance of children (i.e., to safe-guard the continuation of life) to the legitimacy of a given ethical decision (i.e., does it promote life?) to the continuing presence of the ancestors in the community (i.e., they help procure life), the pursuit of the abundant life functions as a central category in the self-understanding within African cosmologies and provides one of *the* key filters through which people understand their world, communicate truths, and—we are arguing—process sacred texts like the Bible. That is, African cultural aspirations to the abundant life significantly shape the *position* and *posture* from which African Christians appropriate biblical texts.[38] The pursuit of the abundant life not only functions as the *raison d'être* for many of the traditional rites and rituals throughout Africa[39] but also provides reasons why certain biblical motifs are prominently highlighted. Healing narratives featuring the infertility of Hannah or the leprosy of Naaman or the Gospel stories portraying Jesus defeating demonic spirits powerfully resonate with African Christians in their pursuit of the abundant life, implicitly indicating that the realities generally affecting the African continent—the oppression of poverty, the scourge of war, and the affliction of sickness—are never far from the minds of ordinary readers in their appropriation of biblical texts.

In Africa, the often-cited use of the Bible as "bola" or "fetish" during the colonial era demonstrates that the Bible has a long history in Africa of being wrestled away from European interpreters and placed unmistakably within the framework of African cosmologies.[40] The fact that colonized Africans encountered the Bible in tandem with the technology and wealth of the white man often led Africans to appropriate the Bible, with the aid of indigenous worldviews, as another sacred object in their pursuit of the abundant life. Recounting an early incident in Southern Africa, the Scottish missionary Robert Moffat observed, "My books puzzled them; they asked if they were my 'Bola,' prognosticating dice."[41] Today African Christians do

---

37. Ibid., 77, see also 71.

38. After analyzing a 1,446 person survey of "favorite texts" of the Bible in Nigeria and Ghana, Eric Anum notices the elevation of the theme "the importance of life" in virtually all of the favorite texts; Anum, "The Reconstruction of Forms of African Theology," 157.

39. "African anthropology emphasizes vitality of life and abundant life as the chief goals for daily living. These are the ends of every religious ritual: to preserve, enhance, and protect life," Kalu, *African Pentecostalism*, 261.

40. See West, "The Bible as Bola," 23–37; LeMarquand, "The Bible as Specimen, Talisman, and Dragoman in Africa," 189–99; Draper, "The Bible as Poison Onion, Icon and Oracle," 39–56.

41. Moffat, *Missionary Labours and Scenes in Southern Africa*, 384.

not literally confuse the Bible with "bola" or "fetish," but West's insightful plea to follow "traces of the Bible as *bola* into the present" suggests that the pursuit of the abundant life still represents a dominant cultural motif in the appropriation of biblical texts.[42] In an illuminating study of the "reading" practices of Nigerian Aladura ("Praying") Churches, David T. Adamo highlights the appropriation of the Psalms alongside the use of traditional herbs, potent words, fasting, water, and other traditional remedies in order to procure healing, protection, and success in life. In this manner, the Bible is used therapeutically: Psalms 1, 2, and 3 are prescribed for stomach pain, Psalm 51 for infertility, and Psalm 16 for defective hearing, to name just a few examples.[43] This medicinal use of the Bible by the Aladura is illustrated by Adamo:

> For cough take honey, palm oil, mix them together, read Psalm 24, 84, 91 three times. Each time call the holy names *Jah-Kurajah Jah Kulah* three times at every reading of the Psalm. The mixture should be taken regularly. Pray and wait for the power of God.[44]

These various thematic mutations of the "Bible as bola" in the colonial and postcolonial periods serve to underscore our chief point with respect to African hermeneutics: ordinary readers hardly approach the Bible as a *tabula rasa* but with certain pre-understandings informed by local cultures.[45] In arguing that the pole of culture impacts African hermeneutics, however, we have also identified even more particularly *the pursuit of the abundant life* as a key feature within that pole of culture which critically impinges upon popular biblical interpretation.

Praxis: The Worshiping Community and Biblical Interpretation

The third "pole" or "source" of African hermeneutics is the ecclesial practices of local church communities. The communal orientation of ontology

---

42. West, "The Bible as Bola," 35.

43. Adamo, *Reading and Interpreting the Bible in African Indigenous Churches*, 55, 56, 58. See also Adamo, "The Use of the Psalms in African Indigenous Churches in Nigeria," 336–49.

44. Ibid., 59. See also Ademiluka, "The Use of Therapeutic Psalms in Inculturating Christianity in Africa," 221–27.

45. Today, the most prominent expression of the "Bible as bola" is arguably the preaching of the so-called prosperity gospel typically associated with the rise of the new Pentecostal and Charismatic churches. See Gifford, *Ghana's New Christianity*; Anim, "Who Wants to Be a Millionaire?"

in Africa, articulated by Mbiti as "I am because we are and since we are, therefore I am,"[46] clearly reverberates into the realm of epistemology with significant implications for hermeneutical reflection.[47] In Africa, biblical interpretation is not primarily a private individualistic reading exercise but rather a community event shaped by a confession of faith nurtured by the praxis and orality of a local church. First and foremost, ordinary readers of the Bible in Africa are disciples of Jesus Christ incorporated into a community of faith. Traditional beliefs and practices of African cultures play a centrally-defining role in biblical interpretation, but church communities often dynamically engage their own cultures on a spectrum ranging from facile acceptance to modified assimilation to outright rejection. Thus, popular readings of the Bible are not only rooted in particular cultural contexts but also are significantly shaped by the way in which ecclesial communities engage, re-engage, or dis-engage the various beliefs and practices of their cultural backgrounds.

As Stephen Fowl and L. Gregory Jones recognized in *Reading in Communion*, since Christian discipleship is not an individualistic pursuit but occurs as Christians are "incorporated into particular communities of disciples set on the journey of becoming friends of God," an ethos of reading-in-community permeates the life of discipleship.[48] In Africa, the unmistakable *sensus communis* ("sense of the community"), highlighted by John S. Pobee of Ghana as a distinguishing feature of African life, has undoubtedly infused many African churches with a particularly vivacious *sensus ecclesiae* ("sense of the church") at the local church level.[49] Carlos Mesters' observation regarding the intersection of the community and hermeneutics amongst Brazilian Catholics applies equally well in an African context:

> The community is the resonance chamber; the text is a violin string. When the people pluck the string (the biblical text), it resonates in the community and out comes the music. And that music sets the people dancing and singing. The community of faith is like a big pot in which the Bible and community are cooked just right until they become one tasty dish.[50]

---

46. Mbiti, *African Religions and Philosophy*, 127.

47. This dynamic is reflective of what Michael Horton succinctly notes: "Epistemology follows ontology"; Horton, *The Christian Faith*, 47.

48. Fowl and Jones, *Reading in Communion*, 70.

49. Pobee, *Toward an African Theology*, 49; Asamoah-Gyadu, "'The Evil You Have Done Can Ruin the Whole Clan,'" 52; Mesters, "The Use of the Bible in Christian Communities of the Common People," 14.

50. Mesters, "The Use of the Bible in Christian Communities of the Common People," 14–15.

The confessional, faith-centered approach to biblical texts—and the ecclesial practices nurturing and sustaining the Christian faith—play a defining role in shaping African biblical interpretation. For example, in a study of Malawian exegesis amongst African Indigenous Churches (AICs),[51] prayer represented one of the most frequently mentioned exegetical resources available to pastors in preparing sermons.[52] In fact, prayer was identified almost twice as much as the use of biblical commentaries in helping solve exegetical complexities, demonstrating the critical role ecclesial praxis often exerts in influencing grassroots interpreters.[53] All-night prayer vigils, days of fasting, periodic revivals, exorcism of demonic spirits, and the shared navigation of issues relating to sickness and death all represent potential ecclesial practices which inform interpretation of biblical texts at the popular level.[54]

As Itumeleng Mosala recognizes, ordinary readers of the Bible in Africa "have an oral knowledge of the Bible. Most of their information about the Bible comes from socialisation in the churches themselves as they listen to prayers and sermons."[55] This importance cannot be overstated. A colleague of mine from Germany once remarked, quite scathingly, that in Equatorial Guinea the churches have a virtual monopoly on church members' time. Based on his experience in Germany, setting foot inside a church more than once or twice per week was excessive. Yet in Equatorial Guinea, it is not uncommon to find Protestant Christians attending church four or five times per week. The local church is where the basic orality of the Bible depicting the story (text) as told by the storyteller (preacher) to the audience (church members) is enacted not merely on a weekly basis but typically several times during the week.[56] Considering that Africa has been described as "the oral

---

51. Though scholars also use the terms African Independent Churches or African Initiated Churches or African Instituted Churches, this book will use the term African Indigenous Churches to highlight that the movement constituted a radical embrace of indigenous African cultures which had often been denigrated by historic missionary Christianity.

52. Mijoga, "Hermeneutics in African Instituted Churches in Malawi," 365.

53. Ibid., 365–67.

54. In contrast to western scholars like John Barton who champion the need for a "nonconfessional approach" to biblical hermeneutics requiring "one to put one's own beliefs on hold," a confessional commitment nurtured by ecclesial practices plays a critical role in grassroots African hermeneutics; Barton, *The Nature of Biblical Criticism*, 173.

55. Mosala, "Race, Class, and Gender as Hermeneutical Factors," 55.

56. For hermeneutics as "performance," see Lash, *Theology on the Way to Emmaus*, 37–46; Young, *Art of Performance*.

continent par excellence"[57] where the power and prevalence of the spoken word has often been "extended into various configurations of modernity," a more nuanced understanding between orality and textuality is required.[58] The role literacy played in the rise and development of historic mainline Christianity in Africa was undoubtedly crucial: even as late as 1980 Mbiti could note the stark disparity between the literacy rates of Christians with those of other groups.[59] Nevertheless, understanding that African hermeneutics is embedded in sermons and Bible studies—the central ecclesial practices which nurture this "ecclesial orality" or "oral socialization" of the Bible at the grassroots—is critical for exploring the way in which ordinary readers express the Christian faith and relate the Bible to everyday life.[60]

In areas of high unemployment, the church often becomes a *de facto* part-time job and an alternative social network while also functioning as a community-center mediating conflicts and handling sicknesses. Within such a milieu, understanding the worshipping community, where the Bible is primarily heard, read, and appropriated becomes extremely important for rooting understandings of African biblical interpretation within its most natural environment—local churches.

Why Choose the Book of Job?

In light of the hermeneutics-culture-praxis triad which provides substantive lines of inquiry for biblical interpretation in particular and African Christianity more broadly, a case study of one specific biblical book at the popular level seems highly promising for furthering our understanding of contemporary African Christianity. Yet the question remains: why choose the book of Job? Given the overall mood of afro-pessimism which dominates the mainstream (western) media, wherein Africa is branded "the hopeless continent,"[61] the "Third World of the Third World,"[62] or colorfully portrayed with disturbing apocalyptic rhetoric (e.g., "The Coming Anarchy"[63]), the choice of Job seems risky, especially by a white westerner. The image of Job

57. Gunner, "Africa and Orality," 67.
58. Ibid., 69. See also Finnegan, *The Oral and Beyond*.
59. Mbiti, "The Bible in African Culture," 29.
60. Not coincidentally, we have prioritized these ecclesial practices as methodologically central in our own project.
61. "Hopeless Africa," *The Economist*, 17, cf. cover.
62. Morrow, "Africa: The Scramble for Survival," 40: "Africa has become the basket case of the planet, the 'Third World of the Third World,' a vast continent in free fall."
63. Kaplan, "The Coming Anarchy."

sitting memorably on a trash heap scrapping himself with broken pottery—utterly destitute yet defiantly clinging to his faith—is seared powerfully upon the consciousness of many Christians. Is not this project, by its very nature, implicitly portraying African Christians in the same light? Not at all. We must be careful not to let the epic and dramatic nature of the Joban prologue flatten out the full-orbed identity of this quintessential sufferer of the Hebrew Bible. Job was not only a hopeless victim but a courageous victor, not simply a paradigm of despair but a model of resolute faith and steadfast prayer. Job was not merely a disease-ridden shadow of a man but theologically courageous—even defiantly alive—in the midst of accusations, stigmatization, and shame. The book of Job suggests itself for study, not primarily because popular caricatures of Job converge with the equally under-nuanced rhetoric about the African continent in general, but because the book offers a unique angle from which to explore critical and pressing issues facing believers at the grassroots of African Christianity. In fact, the selection of Job rests primarily upon three main pillars which make the book of Job exceedingly relevant and uniquely suited for an exploration of contemporary African Christianity.[64]

African Christians and Hebrew Narratives

First of all, the book of Job suggests itself as a prime candidate for a case study in African Christianity because of the deep affinity and fondness African Christians have shown for Judaic expressions of the Christian faith. As Andrew Walls has observed, "You do not have to interpret Old Testament Christianity to Africans; they live in an Old Testament world."[65] Judaic features of church life are common throughout Africa,[66] especially

---

64. These three pillars broadly correspond to chapters four, five, and six respectively in part two of the study.

65. As cited by Quinn, "The Desert People," para. 6.

66. Mention can be made of the Ethiopian Orthodox Church which arguably represents the most Judaized form of Christianity in Africa. Besides its stature as one of the longest continuous expressions of the Christian faith in Africa, the Ethiopian Orthodox Church is also unique in the profusion of Hebraic elements which characterize church life. Church buildings reflect the tri-partite division of the Hebrew temple. Mosaic food laws are kept. Circumcision of males on the eight day is practiced. The traditional Jewish Sabbath, alongside Sunday, is observed. Ritual processions and prayers are made before replicas of the Ark of the Covenant (and the original Ark of the Covenant, according to Ethiopian tradition, is thought to reside in the town of Aksum). See Pawlikowski, "The Judaic Spirit of the Ethiopian Orthodox Church," 178–99, esp. 186–94; Shenk, "The Ethiopian Orthodox Church," 259–78.

amongst the African Indigenous Churches.[67] This profound identification of African Christians with the Old Testament led the late Kwesi A. Dickson, a prominent Methodist Ghanaian theologian, to call attention to the phenomenon with the memorable phrase the "African predilection for the Old Testament."[68] Dickson observed that the Old Testament provided a "'kindred' atmosphere" for many African Christians and a genuine "source of reference in matters of faith and practice."[69] This "African predilection for the Old Testament" is rooted in the parallels between ancient Israel and modern-day Africa which include, but are hardly limited to, the presence of sacrifices, the value of ritualistic observances, the importance of genealogies, the notion of covenants or pacts, the proverbial nature of wisdom, and (as we shall see) a causal universe.[70]

Besides the various cultural parallels to ancient Israel, the "African predilection for the Old Testament" also rests, in our view, upon a "narrative ethos" or "narrative way" which permeates the manner in which African Christians live within and conceive of the moral universe. A myriad of "family resemblances" is certainly found between ancient Judaism and modern African Christianity, yet arguably more important to *biblical interpretation*

---

67. For example, amongst the Akurinu AICs of Kenya, many Old Testament rules and rituals are kept including the following: "keeping uncut hair and beard (Numbers 6:5–7, 1 Samuel 1:11–13), restriction from wearing red clothes (Deuteronomy 27:26), removal of shoes in Church (Exodus 3:4–7), ritual uncleanness after child delivery (Leviticus 12:1–8), rejection of modern medicine (Jeremiah 46:11–12, Hosea 5:13–14), wearing of white robes and turbans (Leviticus 8:9–14, Exodus 29:6–7), raising of hands during prayer (1 Kings 8:22–23, 1 Timothy 2:8–9)"; Ndung'u, "The Role of the Bible in the Rise of African Instituted Churches," 241.

68. Dickson, *Theology in Africa*, 145; Dickson, "The Old Testament and African Theology," 32. See also Dickson, "'Hebrewisms of West Africa,'" 23–34.

69. Dickson, "The Old Testament and African Theology," 31–41, quoting 36. See also Dickson, "Continuity and Discontinuity Between the Old Testament and African Life and Thought," 95–108.

70. Ironically, this disposition towards Old Testament expressions of the Christian faith in Africa does not necessarily mean that the Old Testament is the "favorite Testament" or even that more "preaching texts" come from the Old Testament. Harold Turner's major study in the mid-1960s of 8,000 sermons in the Church of the Lord (Aladura) found that New Testament texts were slightly preferred (57 percent) over Old Testament texts (43 percent); Turner, *Profile Through Preaching*, 21. More recent surveys conducted in Nigeria between 1992 to 1994 also found that contemporary Christians preferred the New Testament (83.8 percent) to the Old Testament (16.2 percent) since ordinary readers of the Bible reportedly believed the New Testament to be "'more powerful than the OT' for the power of Jesus expressed in the miracles pervades it"; Riches, "Interpreting the Bible in African Contexts," 183. In another study, statistics of 1,446 respondents in Ghana and Nigeria also indicated that the New Testament (77.2 percent) is read more than the Old Testament (22.8 percent); Anum, "The Reconstruction of Forms of African Theology," 155.

in Africa is the narrative oral substructure implicit in the way ordinary readers think about the world, process sacred texts, and communicate essential truths. In the West, both in deductive and inductive preaching, narrative stories typically serve to clarify central points or memorably illustrate fundamental ideas (see figure 1.2).[71]

Figure 1.2: Typical Relationship between Ideas and Stories in Western Preaching

Main Point

Narrative Illustration

In the West, narrative stories serve primarily to illustrate, clarify, or memorably impact the main point.

The narration is subservient or subordinated to the main idea.

Amongst ordinary readers of the Bible in Africa, however, a more symbiotic relationship exists between the communication (and appropriation) of main ideas and the narrative substructures which inherently embody those ideas. In Africa, to communicate an idea, at least traditionally, one tells a story (see figure 1.3).[72]

---

71. For example, see one of the best-selling books on preaching in the western tradition: Robinson, *Biblical Preaching*.

72. See Okpewho, *African Oral Literature*. For oral literature in Equatorial Guinea, see Creus, *Curso de Literatura Oral Africana*.

> **Figure 1.3**: The Symbiotic Relationship between Oral Narration and the Communication of Ideas

> *In Africa, the communication of ideas takes place within a narrative epistemology significantly affected by orality.*
>
> *The narration and the idea are intertwined.*

Therefore, African story-telling is not only "the most widely used method in the expression and transmission of traditional wisdom,"[73] but also the transmission of the Christian faith in general and the Bible in particular is fundamentally impacted, perhaps even principally shaped, by this "narrative ethos" or "narrative way" of communicating sacred truths. In other words, narrative story-telling is deeply woven into the fabric of African epistemology. In shaping the substructures of orality and narrative, African epistemology is intimately fused with narrative stories which provide the "nuts and bolts" through which Africans typically understand the world, interpret events, and (as we have been arguing) process sacred texts like the Bible. Narrative story-telling provides a key paradigm of epistemological continuity between traditional African wisdom (stories) and the manner in which the Christian faith (*the* Story) is interpreted in the context of communities of faith which are still predominantly oral.

In this sense, an epistemology grounded in orality and story-telling within African cultures often encourages an Old Testament perspective on the *entire* Bible precisely because the vast majority of biblical narratives

---

73. Chima, "Story and African Theology," 61.

occur in the Old Testament.[74] For instance, African preaching on themes as diverse as personal holiness or the power of God might be introduced by a New Testament reading but many (or all) of the substantive illustrations which communicate and embody the idea will often hang on Old Testament narratives and stories which become not merely illustrative but rather constitutive of the way ideas are communicated by grassroots Christians. Biblical narratives, most of which are rooted in the compelling dramas (exodus and exile), the memorable personalities (patriarchs and kings), and the prophetic pronouncements (blessings and curses) of the Old Testament, often exert a tremendous shaping influence upon preaching, small group Bible studies, and extemporaneous forms of prayer—the very essence of popular forms of African Christianity.

It is within this light that the selection of the book of Job, with its narrative drama featuring the paradigmatic biblical sufferer caught between divine and demonic intentions, affords a particularly intriguing case study for probing the religious imagination of contemporary African Christians. What indigenous cultural, theological, and ecclesial resources do ordinary Christians employ as their narrative imagination is awakened to the figure and plight of Job? Considering African Christians' well-documented preoccupation with the believer's complex relationship to God *and* the Devil, the Joban narrative arguably occupies a unique position within the entire biblical canon for exploring precisely these critical issues.[75]

Suffering and Sickness: The Conversational Partners of African Christianity

The selection of the book of Job also holds promise for a contextual study within African Christianity because the realities of suffering and sickness—perhaps the most fundamental and vital dialogical partners of ordinary Christians—are uniquely explored from this Old Testament narrative. In stark contrast to the afro-pessimism and apocalyptic imagery that continues to plague the political, economic, and social sectors of African societies, one African institution above them all has displayed remarkable growth and vibrancy: the African church. Yet the church resides in an overall climate

---

74. See also Sundkler, *Bantu Prophets in South Africa*, 275–77; Turner, *Profile Through Preaching*, 22.

75. See especially Meyer, *Translating the Devil: Religion and Modernity*. With regard to the role of the Devil, Asamoah-Gyadu maintains that in charismatic ministries "every changed life is seen as the defeat of the power of the devil by the superior might of Jesus Christ"; Asamoah-Gyadu, *African Charismatics*, 143.

constituted by unparalleled suffering and pandemic sicknesses. The following statistics merit serious reflection:

1. In sub-Saharan Africa, 12.5 percent of children die before their fifth birthday, with more than half of those deaths attributed to diarrhea, malaria, and pneumonia.[76] Combined with the total fertility rate of 4.64 (children per woman),[77] a relatively small to medium-sized congregation wherein one-hundred women enter the door of the church means that fifty-eight children have died before the age of five in that congregation alone.

2. "Africans, on average, barely reach the age of 50 . . . Eastern Europe, the cultural block with the second lowest life expectancy in the world, has a life expectancy 20 years higher than in Africa."[78]

3. African countries account for more than two-thirds of the forty-eight countries on the United Nations list of Least Developed Countries (LDC).[79]

4. In sub-Saharan Africa, nearly one in every twenty adults (4.8 percent) lives with HIV.[80] By the end of 2014, nine sub-Saharan African countries still had HIV adult (15–49) prevalence rates above 10 percent, including Swaziland at 27.7 percent and Botswana at 25.2 percent.[81] In sub-Saharan Africa, an estimated 25.8 million people are HIV positive[82] (including 3.2 million children[83]), and an estimated 790,000 Africans had died from AIDS-related causes in 2014 alone.[84]

With regards to the African HIV/AIDS pandemic, all nine countries with a HIV adult (15–49) prevalence rate over 10 percent have overwhelmingly Christian populations which illustrates our point: African Christianity is embedded in contexts where multifaceted forms of suffering and sickness

---

76. "The Millennium Development Goal Report 2010," 2.

77. United Nations data on Africa from 2005–2010: "World Population Prospects," 11.

78. Daughtry, *The Changing World of Christianity*, 195.

79. "List of Least Developed Countries (as of 16 February 2016)," *United Nations*.

80. "UNAIDS: How AIDS Changed Everything, 2015," *UNAIDS*, 485.

81. "The World Factbook: Country Comparison, HIV/AIDS—Adult Prevalence Rate," *Central Intelligence Agency*. (Based on 2014 estimates.)

82. "HIV/AIDS Fact Sheet No. 360, Updated November 2015." *World Health Organization*, para. 3.

83. "Treatment of Children Living with HIV," *World Health Organization*, para. 1. Statistic based on 2013.

84. "Global Health Observatory (GHO) Data," *World Health Organization*, para. 3.

are daily realities. Simply put, these are the dialogical partners to which African Christianity is wed, at least for the foreseeable future.

Given the fact that for the last two hundred years, the book of Job has undergone academic scrutiny from the geographical centers of Christianity *most distant* from questions of unjust suffering, a contextual exploration of Joban themes amongst those mired in situations of suffering seems uniquely promising. As ordinary readers explore Job's lament, does Job provide a common voice to articulate their own sufferings? As leprosy patients and people living with HIV/AIDS engage the Joban text, how does Job challenge or reinforce the prevailing cultural assumptions with regard to sickness and stigmatization? With the book of Job providing an entry-point into the conversation, our engagement with the themes of suffering and sickness allows us to explore how Christians in Africa relate to arguably their most important dialogical partners, the realities of suffering and sickness ubiquitously present within their midst.

Worldview: Causality in African Cosmologies

Finally, the book of Job represents an intriguing case study for African Christianity because causality, with its resultant spirituality, not only undergirds the entire narrative of the book of Job but also resides at the heart of most African cosmologies. As early as 1885, missionary Noel Baudin captured in an elegant analogy the system of causality underpinning much of what was then termed the "fetishism" of Africa:

> Nothing moves in this universe of forces without influencing other forces by its movement. The world of forces is held like a spider's web of which no single thread can be caused to vibrate without shaking the whole network.[85]

Although the reduction of African traditional religion to "fetishism" is thoroughly antiquated, Baudin's image of a spider web of causality dynamically fusing the entire cosmology with a notion of cause and effect constitutes an enduring observation and insight. In African societies, where the sacred-secular divide is absent, an interconnectedness permeating all of life characterizes African indigenous thought. In this milieu, issues of causality are often quick to surface even in ordinary, everyday circumstances:

> If one trips on a stone while walking, for instance, one will realize and accept the fact that one has just tripped. Yet lingering at

---

85. As cited by Magesa, *African Religion*, 46; Baudin, *Fetichism and Fetich Worshipers*.

the back of one's mind will be the questions, Why me? And, why did I trip at this particular moment? Why wasn't the person I was walking with trip? Why did I take this particular side of the path where the stones are?[86]

Issues of causality are particularly prominent in issues of sickness and health. The *ultimate* causal reason is never far from the minds of many Africans, even if the *natural* cause is already known. This dynamic is well-depicted by missiologist David Burnett in his book *Unearthly Powers*:

> *Tribesman*: "This man is sick because someone worked sorcery against him."
>
> *Western Doctor*: "This man is sick from malaria because he was bitten by an infected mosquito."
>
> *Tribesman*: "Yes, he was bitten by a mosquito, but who sent the mosquito?"[87]

Akin to African contexts, the book of Job depicts a moral universe where the causal connections between sin and suffering are manifestly evident. "If Job suffers," reasons Job's friends, "then Job must have sinned." In this worldview, suffering and retributive blame become like two sides of the same causal coin: if an individual suffers, then retributive blame from the community quickly follows. In the scriptures, the doctrine of retribution is the notion that "God will punish the wicked and prosper the righteous"[88] whereby "linkages between deed and consequence became frozen into absolutist principle" in a legalistic application of the Torah.[89] And nowhere else in the Bible is the doctrine of retribution explored more thoroughly—and more memorably—than in the book of Job.

Thus, the unmistakable framework uniting causality in African contexts and retribution in Job provides a unique opportunity for exploring issues at the African grassroots. As David Clines recognizes, retribution is most commonly associated with the connection between sin and suffering, but it may also wear a decidedly "more acceptable face" wherein (religious) piety and (material) prosperity become closely linked.[90] In this light, how will ordinary readers react to Satan's pivotal question in the book of Job (i.e.,

86. Magesa, *African Religion*, 174.
87. Burnett, *Unearthly Powers*, 109.
88. Balentine, *Job*, 103.
89. Brueggemann, *Theology of the Old Testament*, 686, cf. 596–97. See also Brueggemann, *Old Testament Theology*, 182–84; Ticciati, *Job and the Disruption of Identity*, 59–65.
90. Clines, *Job 1–20*, xxxix.

"Does Job fear God for nothing?" Job 1:9) which poses a stark challenge to advocates of *interested* or *utilitarian* versions of religion? As ordinary readers engage with Job's experience *in the midst of* suffering and his final liberation *from* suffering, to what extent do causal paradigms impinge upon hermeneutical reflection and how does the spirituality of grassroots Christians shape their own responses to the suffering so prevalent in their midst?

Conclusion

In this study, we believe that the grassroots exploration of the book of Job provides a fascinating case study to view the themes, theologies, and trajectories currently shaping contemporary African Christianity. Issues of causality in African cosmologies, the presence of sickness and suffering on the African continent, and the shaping role Old Testament narratives play for African Christian communities all suggest that the book of Job is likely to provide a compelling case study for African hermeneutics and open a window to view some of the major contours of grassroots African Christianity from the perspectives of Equatorial Guinea.

A central argument of this book is that the Christian faith and the dominant themes and theologies adopted by ordinary Christians as they read biblical texts are informed by the constant dialogical intersection of biblical hermeneutics, local culture, and ecclesial practice: the *hermeneutics-culture-praxis triad*. This chapter has suggested that African *hermeneutics* is predominantly a reader-centered and existentially-grounded process with no epistemological distance between "meaning" and "application." By interpreting biblical texts from a positionality extremely close to the text itself, both the (biblical) text and the (reader's) context are mutually exegeted, helping to explain why a case study of African hermeneutics affords such a valuable window for viewing the themes and theologies of the readers themselves. With respect to *culture*, African biblical interpretation is often approached from the perspective of the concerns, questions, and pre-understandings that local readers bring to the interpretive process. We have argued that a dominant motif of most African cosmologies is the pursuit of the abundant life which represents one of the defining cultural centers from which grassroots Christians negotiate biblical texts. Finally, in terms of ecclesial *praxis*, we have observed how biblical interpretation in Africa is not primarily an individual exercise but takes place within a community of faith influenced by orality. This "oral socialization" of the Bible and the ecclesial practices of local faith communities also decisively impinge upon hermeneutical reflection.

In this book, the voices of ordinary Christians, albeit often marginalized by academic scholars, are intentionally engaged by prioritizing sermons and Bible studies from diverse communities in Equatorial Guinea. By listening to these voices "from below," we hope to capture some of the dominant thematic and theological trends currently characterizing African Christianity from the perspectives offered by Christians in Equatorial Guinea. To that end, the next chapter turns to the second "pole" in the *hermeneutics-culture-praxis triad* by focusing on the ethnography of the Fang people and their history, beliefs, and practices which most inform local readings of Job in Equatorial Guinea.

2

The Fang of Equatorial Guinea

Their History, Beliefs, and Practices

Introduction

IN THE HERMENEUTICS-CULTURE-PRAXIS TRIAD, the pole of *culture* will be explored in this chapter by highlighting those beliefs and practices of the Fang people of Equatorial Guinea which impinge most directly upon local readings of the book of Job. Because the ordinary reader of the Bible in Africa most notably utilizes the various paradigms and matrixes provided by his or her culture, the bulk of this chapter will focus on Fang conceptions of divinity, the nature of sin and evil, and causal views of sickness and healing. These cultural motifs will be shown in subsequent chapters to significantly impact the shape and contour of hermeneutical reflection and the dominant themes and theologies articulated by local Christians.

In addition, since Equatorial Guinea as a political entity largely drops off the map in studies of Africa, a brief history of the country will also help introduce the Fang people within their sociopolitical environment. In later chapters, we will come to see that ordinary readers deeply resonate with the sufferings of Job. This profound identification with Job's sufferings is undoubtedly facilitated by the socioeconomic and health concerns of ordinary Fang people, dynamics we draw explicit attention to in our brief history of Equatorial Guinea.

The Poverty of a Rich Nation: The Socio-Political History of Equatorial Guinea

Perhaps in no other modern economy has the "rags to riches" story been epitomized more drastically than in postcolonial Equatorial Guinea. Isolated linguistically as a Spanish enclave in Central Africa, Equatorial Guinea's tumultuous recent history may be captured by the various monikers commonly associated with the country since achieving independence in 1968. In the 1970s, Equatorial Guinea was referred to as the "*Dachau of Africa*" as a ruthless dictatorship rivaling Uganda's Idi Amin crippled the country, leaving economic destitution, a refugee exodus, and a history of brutal mass murder and torture in its wake.[1] In the 1980s, Equatorial Guinea could be described as the "*Haiti of Africa*," a forgotten country, about the size of Haiti, firmly situated as one of *the* poorest countries on the planet throughout the decade. Yet since the discovery of significant offshore oil reserves in 1995, Equatorial Guinea has now become known as the "*Kuwait of Africa*," quickly ascending to become the third largest oil producer in all of sub-Saharan Africa by 2003.[2] Based on economic indicators alone, the Equatorial Guinean populace should be enjoying one of the highest standards of living in the entire world. After a decade of the oil bonanza, Equatorial Guinea's GDP per capita (PPP) was estimated in 2005 at $50,240, the second highest in the world after Luxembourg.[3] Yet as the nation embarks upon a historic building boom related to enormous oil profits, the majority of the population continues to be plagued by rampant poverty, high unemployment, and tropical diseases.

While the discovery of off-shore oil reserves represents the latest watershed event in Equatorial Guinea's short tumultuous history, both Spanish colonialism and the Macías tyranny have also etched themselves unforgettably upon the soul of this small Central African nation. Though often confused with the Republic of Guinea (a former French colony) or Guinea-Bissau (a former Portuguese colony), Equatorial Guinea has the distinction of being the only country in Africa where Spanish is the official language.

---

1. Klinteberg, *Equatorial Guinea–Macías Country*, 55.

2. Frynas, "The Oil Boom in Equatorial Guinea," 536; Wood, "Business and Politics," 547.

3. McSherry, "The Political Economy of Oil in Equatorial Guinea," 23; Asongu, "A Curse or Blessing," 10.

Spanish Guinea: Spain's "Model" Economy and the Fang People

It was only at the dawn of the twentieth century that Spanish Guinea was established as a territory within its present-day borders (see figure 2.1).[4] The lingering conflicts between Spain and France from the 1884–85 Berlin Conference were decided conclusively by the Treaty of Paris in 1900 which demarcated Spanish territory as the islands of Fernando Po and Annabón along with a scant 26,000 square km of continental mainland (Rio Muni) and several tiny coastal-hugging islands (including, most notably, the island of Corisco).[5]

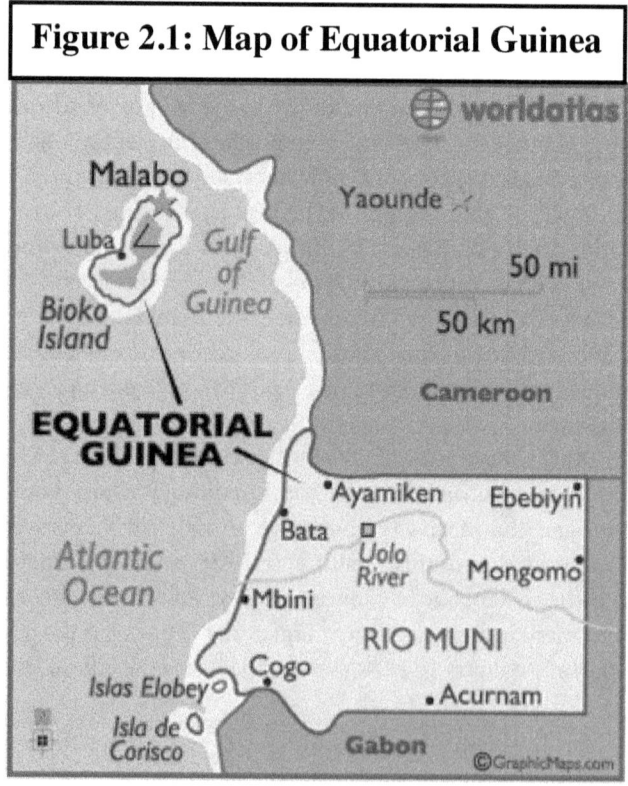

Figure 2.1: Map of Equatorial Guinea

---

4. Liniger-Goumaz, *Small Is Not Always Beautiful*, 20.

5. Ibid., 20; Fegley, *Equatorial Guinea: An African Tragedy*, 18–19. For the map, see "Equatorial Guinea," *World Atlas*. Used by permission, © Graphic Maps. Permission required for further distribution.

By the late nineteenth century, despite minimal Spanish involvement, the island of Fernando Po (later known as Bioko) "had become the watering hole of explorers, traders and missionaries" due to its strategic location in central Africa.[6] Yet with world demand and soaring prices for cacao in the last decade of the nineteenth century as an incentive—and with Fernando Po offering one of the finest places on earth for cultivating cacao—Spanish interest in her long neglected colony skyrocketed.[7] Due to the labor-intensive nature of cacao plantations and the limited indigenous population on the island of Fernando Po, the Spanish *casas fuertes* (cacao plantations) required a sizeable agricultural force to relocate to the island. For the Spaniards, repatriating the mainland Fang people onto Fernando Po represented one potential solution to kick-start the colonial economy. Yet partly because of the Fang's own defiance at being exploited for plantation labor and partly due to Spanish reluctance to "import Fang nationalism into Fernando Po for obvious political reasons," the Fang were never integrated fully into the socioeconomic structure of the colony.[8] While the native Bubis of Fernando Po were increasingly being drawn into cacao production and the Catholic school system, the dense forest of Rio Muni, occupied overwhelmingly by the Fang peoples, was left virtually unexplored by Europeans until the 1920s. Over time Spanish Guinea became a classic example of European diplomacy superficially linking two vastly different territories and peoples under the umbrella of one colonial state.

By the time winds of decolonization began sweeping across the African continent, Spanish Guinea appeared to the world as a model economy. By 1960, Spanish Guinea exports totaled $33,000,000,[9] making the colony's exports per capita of $135 the highest in Africa.[10] Energy consumption was the fourth highest for sub-Saharan Africa. The literacy rate was an astounding 89 percent.[11] Spanish Guinea boasted sixteen hospitals with 1,637 beds, a ratio of hospital beds per capita which even exceeded Spain's.[12] With cacao production reaching 35,000 tonnes per annum and the second cash crop of coffee producing 20,000 tonnes per annum by 1968, Spanish Guinea was apparently provided with a stable economic base to support its nationalistic

---

6. Liniger-Goumaz, *Small is Not Always Beautiful*, 13.

7. Ibid., 29; Fegley, *Equatorial Guinea: An African Tragedy*, 85–86.

8. Cronjé, *Equatorial Guinea—The Forgotten Dictatorship*, 11.

9. Sundiata, "The Roots of African Despotism," 12.

10. Fegley, *Equatorial Guinea: An African Tragedy*, 59. By comparison, South Africa's per capita exports were $87 and Ghana's were $48.

11. Ibid.

12. Ibid., 60.

aspirations.[13] Yet deep cleavages between the island of Fernando Po and the mainland of Rio Muni persisted. The population of Rio Muni, consisting mostly of Fang subsistence farmers, fishermen, and hunters (timber being Rio Muni's only major export) had an annual per capita income of only $40 compared to $250 for Fernando Po.[14] Moreover, since 94 percent of the labor force was imported from Nigeria by the 1960s[15] and Spain consistently purchased cacao and coffee from Spanish Guinea at prices artificially higher than the world market,[16] Spanish Guinea's economy on the eve of independence was externally tied to both Nigeria (for labor) and Spain (for favorable trade), a precarious situation for nationalistic postcolonial politics. Spain's "model" African colony, therefore, was largely an artificial construction which "created neither a unified national market, nor effective state institutions and left the masses egregiously impoverished."[17] The Fang majority, the very people who became most critical for guiding the new nation during the formation of national identity, represented the most impoverished and marginalized group to the sociopolitical and economic opportunities within the colony. These socioeconomic realities confronted by the Fang under Spanish colonialism would not bode well for the new nation.

The Macías Years (1968–79) and the Descent into Chaos

If the inability to understand the Fang socially and politically lies at the heart of Spain's mismanagement of her only Central African colony, then nowhere else is this failure epitomized more than in the career of Francisco Macías Nguema, perhaps the least-known tyrant of the twentieth century.[18] Thought to be malleable to Spanish business interests because of his limited intelligence, Macías enjoyed a meteoric rise to power while benefitting from Spanish nepotism and corruption to become the first elected president of the Republic of Equatorial Guinea on October 12, 1968. Yet the national euphoria of Equatorial Guinea's newly found independence would be sadly short-lived. As one commentator put it, "real independence did not last more than 145 days, from October 12, 1968 to March 5, 1969."[19]

13. Sundiata, "The Roots of African Despotism," 12.
14. Ibid., 13.
15. Ibid., 14.
16. Pélissier, "Spain Changes Course in Africa," 9.
17. McSherry, "The Political Economy of Oil in Equatorial Guinea," 24.
18. Such is the sentiment of Fegley, *Equatorial Guinea: An African Tragedy*, 49–50.
19. As cited by Decalo, *Psychoses of Power*, 47.

After a diplomatic incident with Spain escalated into chaos, Macías "executed a classic purge of the opposition" including the liquidation of significant political rivals and traditional chiefs after alleging that a *coup d'état* had been staged by senior level governmental officials.[20] The March 5, 1969 (alleged?) coup attempt signified a watershed moment for the new nation. By the end of the month, the vast majority (92 percent) of the Spanish expatriate community had fled the country.[21] When the Nigerian plantation workers similarly fled *en masse* in 1974–75 after a series of abuses, murders, and nonpayment of wages, the collapse of the model economy was all but complete. With an export economy depending on Nigeria for labor and Spain for management and expertise, cacao production plummeted from 38,000 tons in 1967 to 22,000 (1970) to 10,000 (1974) to 2340 in 1975.[22] As similar levels of economic paralysis were suffered in other sectors, basic household items and food stuffs became difficult to find. Inflation skyrocketed.[23] Roads and transportation deteriorated. Western medicine became unavailable. No milk was available for children,[24] and written permission was required to buy a bar of soap.[25] As Robert Klinteberg would later write, "After 1969 Equatorial Guinea slowly dropped out of the world."[26] Equatorial Guinea's descent into chaos had begun.

For eleven years, Macías ruthlessly reigned over Equatorial Guinea as if it were his personal fiefdom. After dissolving all opposing political parties, his own political party, *Partido Unico Nacional de Trabajadores* or PUNT (Sole National Workers' Party), which was linked to the paramilitary organization *Juventud en Marcha con Macías* (Youth on March with Macías), came to dominate national life.[27] Military exercises and parades with wooden model guns became mandatory.[28] Alleged *descontentos* (nonloyalists) were quickly, and often fraudulently, denounced to the regime. During the Macías years, the social cohesion of the Fang people was violently broken, producing a culture of mutual suspicion and distrust that continues to the present day.

20. McSherry, "The Political Economy of Oil in Equatorial Guinea," 24.
21. Decalo, *Psychoses of Power*, 48.
22. Fegley, *Equatorial Guinea: An African Tragedy*, 92. See also Decalo, *Psychoses of Power*, 56; Klinteberg, *Equatorial Guinea–Macias Country*, 26.
23. Klinteberg, *Equatorial Guinea–Macías Country*, 24.
24. Fegley, *Equatorial Guinea*, 106.
25. Klinteberg, *Equatorial Guinea–Macías Country*, 28.
26. Ibid., 23.
27. Fegley, *Equatorial Guinea: An African Tragedy*, 111–15.
28. Liniger-Goumaz, *Small Is Not Always Beautiful*, 55–56.

Two institutions composed the backbone of Spanish colonialism: the business interests of the *casas fuertes* (cacao plantations) and the Roman Catholic Church. After alienating through intimidation and incompetency the *casas fuertes* early in his regime, Macías subsequently turned his ire towards the Roman Catholic Church. Comprising fifty-eight priests, nineteen parishes, twenty-eight religious communities, sixteen mission stations, two cathedrals, four seminaries, 315 chapels, and wielding a virtual monopoly on education and medicine at independence, the large and unifying institution of the Roman Catholic Church, described as one of the "densest network of church organizations on the continent," aroused Macías' constant paranoia.[29] As the Macías reign of terror developed, priests began to disappear. Nuns were harassed and killed.[30] PUNT party declarations increasingly revered Macías using religious language: "*no hay más Dios que Macías*" ("there is no God other than Macías"), an overt Spanish wordplay comparing Macías to the Messiah.[31] The August 1973 PUNT Party Congress proclaimed Macías "the tireless and sole miracle (*único milagro*) of Equatorial Guinea."[32] Beginning with a series of decrees in November 1974, all religious activity was prohibited, including baptisms, Christian funerals, and monetary offerings. By May 1978, only months before the Macías downfall, Equatorial Guinea officially became Africa's only atheistic state.[33]

The concerted attack on organized Christian religion in Equatorial Guinea signified a decisive blow to both education and medicine. During the Macías tyranny, illiteracy increased as schools became instruments of PUNT rhetoric. Post-primary education, already underdeveloped by Spain's Franco during colonialism, fell on even harder times.[34] As doctors and nurses were harassed, liquidated, or replaced by PUNT loyalists, hospital facilities suffered from inattention and incompetency. Malaria, trypanosomiasis (sleeping sickness), and *pian* (yaws) went unchecked. Leprosy, which had been reduced to 3,000 recorded cases by 1955 and only 8 deaths by 1962, experienced a surge of cases during the Macías era.[35]

In spite of the economic, educational, and medical collapse Equatorial Guinea experienced under Macías, the most enduring legacy of the

29. Fegley, *Equatorial Guinea*, 76.
30. Liniger-Goumaz, *Small Is Not Always Beautiful*, 25.
31. Klinteberg, *Equatorial Guinea–Macías Country*, 51.
32. Liniger-Goumaz, *Small Is Not Always Beautiful*, 56.
33. Fegley, *Equatorial Guinea*, 99–100; Liniger-Goumaz, *Historical Dictionary of Equatorial Guinea*, xx.
34. Fegley, *Equatorial Guinea: An African Tragedy*, 78–80.
35. Fegley, *Equatorial Guinea*, 60, 80; Liniger-Goumaz, *Small Is Not Always Beautiful*, 28.

dictatorship was a reign of terror that René Pélissier labeled "Cambodia minus political philosophy."³⁶ Under Macías, systematic liquidation of opponents, mass executions, and barbaric methods of torture became regular features of the regime. The most infamous example occurred in a football stadium where the *Único Milagro* staged a mass public hanging in 1969 while the Mary Hopkins' song "Those Were the Days" played over the loudspeakers before a watching public, an event which scarred itself upon the country's collective conscience. Harassment and torture became especially rampant inside Malabo's prison *Playa Negra* (Black Beach) and Bata Prison as political prisoners, often numbering around 5,000, were victimized by ominous-sounding methods of torture with names such as *El Balanceo* (The Swing), *La Colgadura* (The Hanging), *Las Tablillas* (The Planks), and *Los Grilletes* (The Shackles).³⁷ With the Nigerian labor force ousted, Macías turned to forced coercion and a system of state slavery. In a last ditch effort to save the cacao plantations and the national economy, in 1977 Macías arrested 25,000 laborers and, along with their 15,000 dependents, transported these "national workers" to the island of Fernando Po as unpaid laborers. Working from 6 a.m. until 6 p.m. under threat of beatings, limited food rations, and no medical care or freedom, these national workers were often subjected to brutality and the occasional liquidation.³⁸ Spain's Francoism had bred its own tyrant in Equatorial Guinea.³⁹ With the Macías militia dominating national life, refugees poured out of Equatorial Guinea in record numbers. According to Klinteberg, "the refugees from Equatorial Guinea may represent the largest proportion of any nation ever to have gone into exile."⁴⁰ The Macías tyranny was responsible for approximately 50,000 deaths and for driving an astounding one-third of the estimated 300,000 population into exile, typically across the borders into Gabon and Cameroon.⁴¹

---

36. Pélissier, "Autopsy of a Miracle," 13.
37. Klinteberg, *Equatorial Guinea–Macías Country*, 37–38.
38. Ibid., 30–31; Fegley, *Equatorial Guinea: An African Tragedy*, 88–89.

39. In the 1920s, an internationally publicized indictment accused Spanish treatment of Liberian plantation workers on Fernando Po as practically indistinguishable from slavery; see Fegley, *Equatorial Guinea: An African Tragedy*, 27.

40. Klinteberg, *Equatorial Guinea–Macías Country*, 55.

41. Ibid; Randall Fegley, *Equatorial Guinea*, liii. Some scholars estimate that between 50,000 and 80,000 fatalities can be attributed to the Macías regime; Decalo, *Psychoses of Power*, 58.

The Social Impact of Oil:
The Questionable Blessings of Oil

The sword which eventually ended the Macías reign of terror came from within his own clan. Teodoro Obiang Nguema Mbasogo, head of the army and nephew of Macías, along with elites from the Esangui clan from the village of Mongomo, staged a successful *coup d'état* against Macías on August 3, 1979. Macías was officially indicted with "continued and repeated crimes of genocide, mass murder, embezzlement of public funds, damage to property, systematic violation of human rights and treason."[42] On September 29, 1979, eleven years to the day after being elected as the first president of Equatorial Guinea, Macías was executed along with six henchmen by a Moroccan firing squad.[43] With the fall of Macías, international aid and medicine began to pour into the bankrupt and devastated country. Padlocked churches reopened. Schools began anew. Markets began to replenish with basic foodstuffs and essential commodities. Yet the path of reconstruction in Equatorial Guinea would be slow and arduous. From 1981 to 1985, GNP fell from $180 million to $69 million, and per capita GNP likewise decreased from $470 to $172 as Obiang Nguema's new military government struggled to escape from the devastation caused by the Macías era.[44] As the local currency (*ekwele*) became increasingly worthless amidst hyperinflation, Obiang Nguema went on the offensive diplomatically. The decisive moment occurred on January 1, 1985 as Equatorial Guinea became the sixth member to be accepted into the French monetary zone BEAC (*Banque des etats de l'Afrique central*).[45] In adopting the new currency, however, the *ekwele* was devalued by 82 percent, prompting *The Economist* to note at the time that "Equatorial Guinea now counts itself among the poorest countries in Africa."[46] For those who had survived the bloody years of the Macías tyranny, the poverty which confronted the masses in the 1980s hardly seemed like an adequate recompense.

From the execution of Macías in 1979 through the mid-1990s, the abject poverty and misery which generally characterized life in Equatorial Guinea during the Macías years hovered over the small nation like a bad dream. For political elites, the nightmare would end almost miraculously

---

42. As cited by Fegley, *Equatorial Guinea: An African Tragedy*, 167.

43. Ibid., 168.

44. Liniger-Goumaz, *Small Is Not Always Beautiful*, 109.

45. Members of the BEAC utilizing the currency the Franc CFA include Equatorial Guinea, Gabon, Cameroon, The Republic of Congo, Central African Republic, and Chad.

46. "Quarterly Economic Review of Congo, Gabon, Equatorial Guinea," 23.

as offshore oil reserves were discovered in 1995. Within a few years, this cash-strapped and debt-burdened nation was transformed into an African oil giant, often dubbed "The Kuwait of Africa." Revolutionized by immense oil wealth, the country eventually became one of the world's fastest growing economies as real GDP growth peaked at an astonishing 71 percent in 1997.[47] By 2009 approximately US$10 billion per year of foreign direct investment was pouring into the country.[48] Yet as mansions are built amidst the ruins of poverty, no country in the world is characterized by such an extreme disparity between its economic and social indicators as is Equatorial Guinea. Despite the newfound oil wealth propelling the country to become the first high-income nation of sub-Saharan Africa, the estimated population of 700,000 has been characterized by one of the highest poverty rates (76.8 percent in 2006) in all of Africa.[49] Life expectancy stands at fifty-eight years.[50] The under-five mortality rate—a dozen years after the 1995 oil discovery—still represented the fourth highest in the world.[51] From 1997 to 2002, Equatorial Guinea spent a mere 1.23 percent of government expenditures on health compared to 5.95 percent in Nigeria and 12.1 percent in South Africa.[52] In spite of Marathon Oil's anti-malaria program, malaria and typhoid continue to plague the population, and the existing health infrastructure remains underdeveloped.

More than geopolitical history or regime changes, however, which often take place above the heads of most Africans, it is the cultural understandings and cosmological thought patterns that serve as the primary sources for Christian faith and hermeneutical reflection. Africa imbibes and appropriates the faith primarily through the paradigms of its own cultures. So, it is to the Fang people and their indigenous beliefs and practices that we now turn.

---

47. "Country Profile: Equatorial Guinea 2008," 20. By 2001, real GDP growth was still an impressive 67 percent.

48. "Country Profile: Equatorial Guinea 2009," 10.

49. Holmes, *Social Protection*, 1; "Equatorial Guinea," *The World Bank*.

50. "Health Profile: Equatorial Guinea," *World Health Rankings*. (From the World Health Organization, 2015.) For life expectancy, Equatorial Guinea ranks 171 in the world. The life expectancy of the global population is 71.4 years; see "Global Health Observatory (GHO) Data," *World Health Organization*.

51. In 2007, Equatorial Guinea had the fourth highest infant mortality rate in the world; see "The State of the World's Children 2009," 117.

52. Frynas, "The Oil Boom in Equatorial Guinea," 543.

Fang Indigenous Beliefs and Practices

With an estimated population of 3,500,000, the Fang represent one of the largest Central African people groups of the equatorial forest region.[53] Identified by various names historically, including Pahouin, Pangwe, or Pamue, today the Fang reside in significant numbers in the adjoining Central African nations of Equatorial Guinea, Cameroon, and Gabon while the northwest corner of the Republic of Congo (Brazzaville) also contains a small Fang population (see figure 2.2).[54]

---

53. According to 2010 population figures in *Operation World*, three countries register significant Fang populations: (1) Equatorial Guinea with 396,616 Fang inhabitants (or 57.2 percent of the total population of 693,385), (2) Cameroon with 2,554,669 Fang inhabitants (12.8 percent of the total population of 19,958,351, counting Ewondo 7.7 percent and Bulu Fang 5.1 percent), and (3) Gabon with 621,674 (41.41 percent of the total population 1,501,266). Thus, Fang peoples account for 3,572,959 inhabitants in the three adjoining countries; see Mandryk, *Operation World*, 320, 189, 350. This population estimate seems generally on the trajectory of the *Encyclopedia Britannica* which estimated Fang inhabitants at 3,320,000 during "the late 20th century"; see "Fang," *Encyclopedia Britannica*, para. 1.

54. For the map, see "Fang Homeland." Used by permission, © SIL International. Permission required for further distribution.

Figure 2.2: Fang Territory

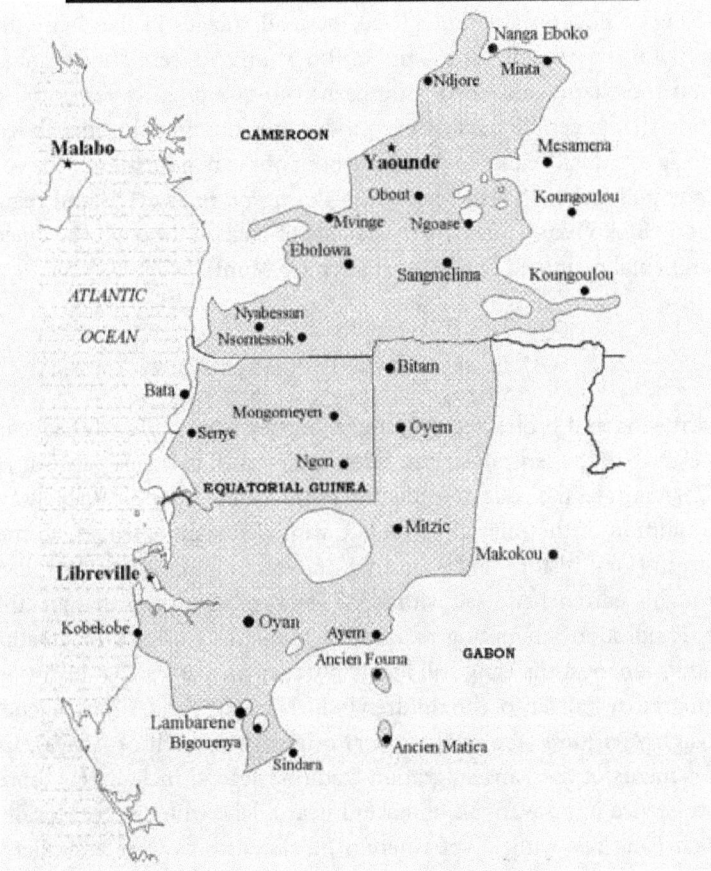

Although some nomenclature discrepancies exist amongst scholars in precisely how to designate the old Pahouin group which demonstrates considerable cultural uniformity across the various dialectical sub-groupings,[55] in

---

55. Some scholars, in choosing to highlight the subtle dialectical differences within the Pahouin group, posit a two-tiered nomenclature by dividing the cultural block into "Fang" and "Beti" (though sometimes "Fang Beti"). Other scholars utilize a three-tiered nomenclature: "Fang," "Bulu," and "Beti." Still other scholars, who tend to recognize cultural uniformity as the predominant characteristic of ethnicity, maintain that the nomenclature Fang, albeit originally referring to only a sub-group of the Pahouin, is nevertheless today the most widely utilized term to refer to the entire cultural block. Considering that it was European colonialism which generally insisted upon precise tribal boundaries, perpetuating artificially hard dialectical distinctions amongst the Fang seems at variance with the shared historical, migratory, and cultural affinities

Equatorial Guinea, the group is known as the Fang and is overwhelmingly the dominant indigenous people group in the country, accounting for 85.7 percent of the total population according to the 1994 census.[56] Traditionally, the Fang of Equatorial Guinea lived in small villages in the dense forest region of the continental mainland of Rio Muni and were divided into the Ntumu (northern) and Okak (southern) sub-groupings, a territorial distinction that generally persists even today. Beginning with independence, the Fang eventually came to dominate both of the major cities of the country: the political capital of Malabo on the *region insular* ("island region," formerly Bioko Island) and the coastal city of Bata on the *region continental* ("continental mainland region," formerly Rio Muni).

Afri Kara and the Fang Migration

A harrowing and protracted migratory journey from a previous savannah homeland[57] to the central African forest undertaken in stages between 1820 and 1890 forged the collective identity of the Fang in unmistakable ways.[58] The tradition of the migration, replete with rich symbolism which melds features of oral history and epic myth into a common heroic tale, has so thoroughly entrenched itself within the Fang consciousness that an ethnographic question attempting to unearth humanity's origins or creational accounts amongst the Fang will inevitably elicit an answer that begins with the migratory journey of the children (which are the Fang) of the legendary patriarch *Afri Kara* (the mythological original patriarch of Africa). Central elements of the Fang migration tradition-legend include: (1) a previous existence in a savannah homeland near a lake which serves locally to explain Fang ties with Egypt wherein Judaic customs were assimilated,[59] (2) an escape from mounted "red men"[60] who pursued the Fang in order

---

within the broader group. For a three-tiered classification, see Alexandre and Binet, *Le Groupe Dit Pahouin*, 4–6. For a scholar who classifies the older term Pahouin as Fang peoples, see Ndongo Mba-Nnegue, *Los Fan*, 15–19.

56. "The World Factbook," *Central Intelligence Agency*.

57. The previous homeland is typically identified by scholars as northwestern Cameroon and northeastern Nigeria although the Fang themselves find a connection with the Sudanic peoples of the Upper Nile region; Balandier, *The Sociology of Black Africa*, 88–89; Fernandez, *Bwiti*, 512.

58. Fegley, *Equatorial Guinea*, xvi. See also Chamberlin, "The Migration of the Fang," 429–56.

59. For the psychological impact of the Christianization of Fang legends, see Balandier, *Afrique Ambiguë*, 176–83.

60. The "red men" (*mvele me bot*) have been tentatively identified as the Fulani;

to sell them into the white man's slavery, (3) the treacherous crossing of the Sanaga river[61] with the timely and supernatural aid of either a giant snake, crocodile, or hippopotamus, and (4) the final penetration into the equatorial forest through the perforation of a giant *azap* tree which served as the last symbolic impediment before the successful domination of the autochthonous peoples and the ensuing acquisition of their new homeland.[62] These legendary stories of the Fang migration eventually resulted in an indigenously published work which circulated under the title *Dulu Bon be Afri Kara* (The Journey of the Children of Afri Kara)[63] written during the height of the *Alar Ayong* movement (*alar*: to unite; *ayong*: clan) in the 1940s and early 1950s which sought to reunite the Fang clans in response to the humiliation and domination of European colonialism.[64] The story of *Afri Kara* not only provided rich cultural descriptions of marriage, death, burial, the origins of evil (*evus*), the chicanery of witchcraft (*mbwo*), and the proud stories of military victories over the autochthonous peoples of the equatorial forest, but also served to explain in an accessible local idiom the wide diversity of dialects and clans scattered throughout the Fang territory by evoking Afri Kara as a single common ancestor.[65]

The "Big Three" Fang Rituals

As articulated in the story of *Afri Kara*, the collective identity of the Fang was fundamentally expressed by three rituals which today are considered the most important traditional rituals of the recent past: Ndong Mba, Biéri, and Nguí. Local informants conversant in the idiom of Fang traditional beliefs and practices explain the conceptual features of the three rituals in virtually an identical fashion as they are presented in the story of *Afri Kara*: (1) the ritual purification cult of Ndong Mba embodied the priestly function in village life which purified the *akwann misémm* (sicknesses of sin) in the village, (2) the ancestral cult of Biéri represented the kingly function in village life which was exercised in the acquisition of cultural goals, and (3)

Fernandez, "The Affirmation of Things Past," 444.

61. The Sanaga River is located in central Cameroon.

62. Fernandez, *Bwiti*, 64–69.

63. *Dulu Bon be Afri Kara* was written by Ondoua Engutu in 1948 and published by the American Presbyterian Press in Ebolowa, Cameroon in 1954; see Bibang Oyee, *La Migración Fang*; Fernandez, *Bwiti*, 64.

64. See Fernandez, "The Affirmation of Things Past."

65. The "children" of *Afri Kara* represent many of the major dialectical groupings within Fang territory; Fernandez, *Bwiti*, 67.

the anti-witchcraft cult of Nguí was compared to the justice system whereby a powerful judge rightfully exercised vengeance upon the witches thought to be disturbing the peace of the community (see figure 2.3).[66]

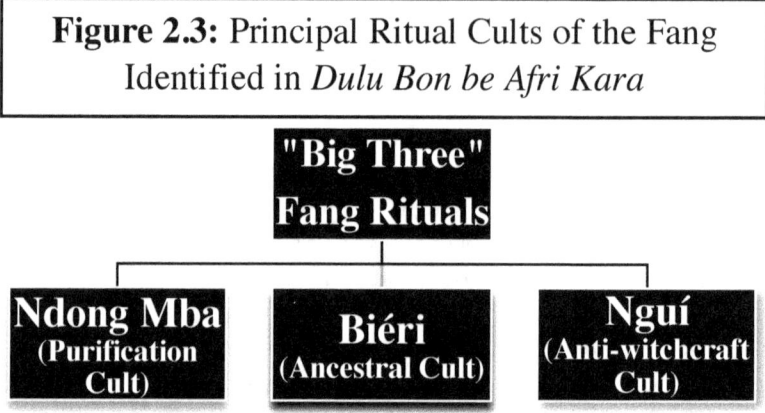

Figure 2.3: Principal Ritual Cults of the Fang Identified in *Dulu Bon be Afri Kara*

A detailed description of the three ritual cults is beyond our present scope, but conceptual features of these all-but-lapsed cults are significant for our purposes insofar as traditional practices (1) elucidate the interconnections between concepts of sin, sicknesses, and the ancestors, (2) illuminate how the Fang sought to acquire cultural goals in order to live an abundant life, and (3) clarify Fang representations and understandings of evil.[67]

The Purification Cult of Ndong Mba:
Placing nsem ("sin") in Fang Cultural Perspective

The principal conceptual feature of the purification cult of Ndong Mba consisted in purifying the village of *akwann misémm* which has been conventionally translated into Spanish as *enfermedades de pecado* ("sicknesses

---

66. Bibang Oyee, *La Migración Fang*, 61–65.

67. A local cultural magazine surmises that Biéri collapsed between 1940 and 1944 in Equatorial Guinea; Ondo Mangue, "El Culto a Los Ancestros de Los Fang," 35. Fernandez maintains that Ndong Mba and Biéri were mostly eradicated by colonial governments before the Second World War; Fernandez, *Bwiti*, 268. According to local informants, the Nguí cult was practiced in the outlining villages of Rio Muni into at least the 1960s.

of sin").⁶⁸ The primary *okwann misémm*⁶⁹ treated by Ndong Mba was *nnén-náng* (hemorrhoids) as this "sickness" was traditionally attributed to incest, arguably the most devious socio-familial offence imaginable to the Fang. As the Fang practiced double exogamy (and still do), meaning a person is forbidden to marry within either the patrilineal or matrilineal clans,⁷⁰ incest epitomized the great sexual transgression *par excellence*.⁷¹ Anthropologist James Fernandez, who worked amongst the Fang in Gabon from 1958 to 1960, described one central component of the cult:

> . . . instead of sitting down with the initiates, Ndong Mba led the men over to the kitchens where the women were all shut in. Beating against the walls they demanded the girls who had sinned with their brothers. The pregnant girl or a girl suspected of nsem [an offense against the community, translated conventionally as "sin"] was thrust forward. . . . Accusations were directed against the girl. Finally a purifying mixture of herbs and leaves was poured first over the boy and then over the girl. The girl was returned to the kitchen.⁷²

Central to the purification process was a confession of guilt by the accused followed by the entire village uttering a loud exclamatory "*oooooooooooh!*" which served both to shame the guilty participants and inculcate social restraint amongst the younger generation.⁷³ Alongside the public confession, the *abók misémm* ("*baile de pecados*," "dance of/against sins") symbolically served to purge the village of the offense and restore ancestral harmony. In the case of incest, the dance also helped ensure the future fertility of the guilty participants since miscarriages and sterility were often associated with incest.⁷⁴

68. Ndong Mba refers both to the name of the cult and the man wearing the traditional Fang mask leading the cult. Ndong and Mba are two of the most common names amongst the Fang.

69. Translated into Spanish in the singular as *enfermedad de pecado* ("sickness of sin").

70. Balandier, *The Sociology of Black Africa*, 121.

71. Fernandez, *Bwiti*, 245. Mvone-Ndong explains that incest was particularly vilified because it prevented the family group's expansion and created a surplus of people within the family system; see Mvone-Ndong, *Imaginaire de la Maladie au Gabon*, 151.

72. Fernandez, *Bwiti*, 250, brackets added to original.

73. Amongst the Yoruba of West Africa, those involved in incest are likewise "exposed to ridicule and are required to offer propitiatory sacrifice to assuage the anger of the ancestral spirits," Awolalu, "Sin and Its Removal in African Traditional Religion," 281.

74. Balandier, *The Sociology of Black Africa*, 149. According to Fernandez, the cult also worked to ensure a good harvest since it was typically celebrated in September (at

As an etiological category, *akwann misémm* represented a quite limited number of sicknesses, all of which were typically beyond the curative expertise of Fang traditional healers. In addition to hemorrhoids which were commonly associated with the social cause of incest, the "social etiologies" of *oñang* (glaucoma) and *mebara* (yaws)[75] likewise illustrate the way in which the Fang conceive of *nsem* ("sin") as primarily an offense committed against the social fabric of the community. In Fang practice, since a brother traditionally paid the dowry from the money the family obtained when his sister was wed, the children of such a matrimony were understood to owe a great deal of respect and gratitude particularly to the maternal aunt and uncle.[76] If children failed to respect these (especial maternal) aunts and uncles but instead engaged in mocking or making fun of these relatives, *oñang* (glaucoma) was understood to be the price these naughty children paid for their *nsem* ("sin"). Similarly, *mebara* (yaws) was thought to be the punishment bestowed upon those who chose to disrespect one's elders in a more general sense.[77] While the etiological connections of *akwánn misémm* provided a certain explanatory function for mysterious external "sicknesses" for Fang communities, the social function was also integral to the ritual insofar as adults could warn disrespectful children of the dire consequences of not respecting the community's elders. Indeed, the value of Ndong Mba in providing a certain amount of social cohesion for village life is illustrated by the fact that Ndong Mba was often celebrated in tandem with the boys' initiatory ritual of Soo.[78]

For the Fang, the ritualistic communal orientation of *nsem,* the word conventionally translated by the Fang as "sin," is helpfully placed in its proper cultural perspective by Ndong Mba. Not to be lost in the extremely

---

the end of the long dry season and before the planting of crops); Fernandez, *Bwiti*, 250.

75. Yaws is known by various names: pian, frambesia, tropical syphilis, paraangi, paru.

76. Balandier, *The Sociology of Black Africa*, 119–20.

77. Today, many Fang label *nzam* (leprosy) as an *akwann misémm* ("sickness of sin") with the social etiology of the disease having its roots in witchcraft. Historically, leprosy seemed to present such an etiological conundrum for the Fang that the disease, while frequently labeled an *akwann misémm*, does not appear to have been one of the chief sicknesses "treated" by the ritual Ndong Mba. While leprosy was frequently attributed to witchcraft, it also represented one of the possible judgments rendered against suspected witches by the anti-witchcraft cult of Nguí. Tessman indicated that the Fang of the early twentieth century believed that their traditional healers could cure the disease at the initial stages of its development; Tessman, *Los Pamues (Los Fang)*, 495.

78. In fact, Soo Ndong Mba was the name given to the cult when the two rituals were celebrated together; this may have been the case amongst the Fang of Rio Muni since the social etiologies of *oñang* and *mebara* are rather suggestive of an adolescent ritual; Fernandez, *Bwiti*, 245–53; Tessman, *Los Pamues (Los Fang)*, 375–94.

interesting connections between social causations and physical sicknesses is the central and decisive role of the *community* as the singular arbiter of "sin." For the Fang, the nature of *nsem* was conceived primarily as an anti-social act which harmed the well-being of the community. Recognizing the traditional communal orientation of the term "sin" amongst most African peoples, John S. Mbiti called attention to the semantic links that often exist between (1) physical sicknesses, (2) ritual impurities, and (3) behavioral "sins" in Africa by recourse to his own native Kenyan language of Kikamba. According to Mbiti, the term utilized by Protestants for sin is *nai*, a word that "actually means fever, malaria, flu."[79] In contrast, the Catholics translated "sin" as *thavu*, a word with ritualistic connotations which "refers to the state of being ritually unclean, as for example when a woman has menstruation."[80] Similarly for the Fang, the meaning of *nsem* slides easily into ritualistic overtones with physical sicknesses being the primary evidence that anti-social acts of *nsem* have been committed.

Anthropologists working amongst the Fang have defined *nsem* by appealing to precisely these ritual categories and communal prohibitions. L. Martrou defined *nsem* as "ritual impurities or moral blemishes."[81] Fernandez defined *nsem* as "sin, ritual sin in the sense of transgression of a taboo; act against cosmic nature such as incest within the clan."[82] For one Guinean author, the idea that behaviors against communal prohibitions or taboos may lead to tragedy or death is encapsulated by the Fang expression "*so, nsem; eky, bidjim*" ("the deer is sin and breaking the prohibition leads to misfortune").[83] In other words, the semantic range of *nsem* is suggestive of behaviors which are anti-communal against both the living and the "living-dead" (i.e., the ancestors).[84] The *communal* and *ritualistic* notions of *nsem* are not conceptualized by the Fang as two different aspects of "sin" but rather mutually intertwined. Through ritual performance, any disruption to the communal orientation of the group (which included the living and the ancestors) was called *nsem* and was dealt with *ritualistically*, which is to say *communally* across the boundaries of death. For this reason, Ndong Mba sought to remedy the problematic aspects of "sin" communally through the purification rituals.

79. Mbiti, "God, Sin, and Salvation in African Religion," 65.
80. Ibid.
81. Martrou, "Les 'Eki' des Mfang," 745–61 as cited by Balandier, *The Sociology of Black Africa*, 131.
82. Fernandez, *Bwiti*, 584.
83. Ocha'a Mve Bengobesama, *Tradiciones del Pueblo Fang*, 164.
84. Mbiti, *African Religions and Philosophy*, 83–91.

The Ancestral Cult of Biéri:
God and the Ancestors in the Procurement of Cultural Goals

The primary ancestral ritual for the Fang was the Biéri cult which used the craniums (*biéri*) of the clan's deceased ancestors whereby honor and veneration from the living were exchanged for the protective goodwill and benevolence of the ancestors.[85] Traditionally, the craniums were maintained in a bark box reliquary (*nsuk biéri*) guarded scrupulously by an initiated member of the cult chosen by the *nde bot* (literally, "house of people," the smallest patrilocal group of the village).[86] Placed upon the reliquary was a small wooden figure known as *mwan biang* (child of medicine) or *eyima Biéri* (the Biéri figure)[87] which served to ward off women, children, and the un-initiated from tampering with the craniums since blindness,[88] sickness,[89] or death[90] might all be attributed to an unsolicited peek at the craniums. Included within the praxis of the Biéri cult was the initiation of male members who, while fasting and abstaining from sexual intercourse,[91] ate *malan*, the bark of the *alan* bush[92] which produced temporary unconsciousness because of its hallucinogenic side-effects. Interpreting the narcotic state as symbolic of death, the initiate was believed to receive visitations and visions from the world of the ancestors.

While the Biéri cult solidified social cohesion amongst the initiated and promoted relationships across generational lines, the cult's *raison d'être* was the acquisition of communal goals deemed essential for the procurement of life, success, and prosperity. Large herds, success in hunting, productive crops, fertile wives, ability to pay the bride-price, healthy deliveries of babies, and communal prosperity could all be sought through the Biéri cult. In turn, respect and honor, in the form of libation, the bestowal of ancestral names upon one's progeny, and the proper celebration of the *ádzémé awú* (literally "celebrate death," *defunción* in Spanish) after the burial of the

---

85. For a description of Biéri, see Tessman, *Los Pamues (Los Fang)*, 442–53; Fernandez, *Bwiti*, 253–67; Laburthe-Tolra, *Initiations et Sociétés Secrètes au Cameroun*, 337–49; Balandier, *The Sociology of Black Africa*, 145–46; Alexandre and Binet, *Le Groupe Dit Pahouin*, 110–11; Ondo Mangue, "El Culto a Los Ancestros de Los Fang," 32–35.

86. Fernandez, *Bwiti*, 256.

87. Ibid.

88. Blindness was particularly remembered by local informants.

89. Tessman, *Los Pamues (Los Fang)*, 445.

90. Fernandez, *Bwiti*, 258.

91. Ibid., 259.

92. Ibid; Balandier, *The Sociology of Black Africa*, 145.

deceased, was given to the ancestors.[93] For the Fang, an ancestor was held to be an exceptional individual characterized as "simple, friendly, peaceful and loved" by their relatives and was also considered *miemie* (an innocent person), a term related to one's innocence of any activity associated with *mwbo* (witchcraft).[94] Yet the ancestors could also be impetuous, jealous, or resentful of the living, and often their actions were deemed malevolent and far from wholly beneficial to the living.[95] Due to this temperamental nature of the ancestors, a certain amount of ritual manipulation and coercion often accompanied Biéri rituals in order to induce the ancestors to "behave" in ways that promoted the well-being of the community. Interestingly, this coercion of the ancestors and its implied manipulative or utilitarian posture toward the spiritual realm (i.e., veneration of the ancestors *in exchange for* protection and benevolence for the living) stands in sharp opposition to the pivotal question in the book of Job which initiates the entire narrative of suffering: "Does Job fear God for nothing?" (Job 1:9). To what degree the dis-interestedness of Job's piety challenges or contests this basic orientation of Fang indigenous religiosity will be a theme which occupies us in later chapters.

For now, it will be sufficient to observe that traditional Fang religiosity displays a certain semblance to the advice of Eliphaz, Bildad, and Zophar—Job's three friends—who all encourage Job to confess his sin in order to leverage God to restore his health and wealth. Fundamental differences obviously exist between the Biéri cult and the Near Eastern counsel Job received, but the conceptual framework is analogous enough to engage briefly in a comparative analysis. First, *the conceptual framework driving both Biéri and Job's friends is predominantly the human-centered acquisition of benefits or blessings.* For Biéri this has already been noted. Even amidst a quite sociologically-driven portrayal of Biéri, Fernandez described a concluding prayer offered before *mwan biang* (the wooden figure) as displaying "that contractural coerciveness of early Old Testament prophecy."[96] The prayer, translated by Fernandez from Fang, is rendered thus:

> Fathers and grandfathers I tell you now. You left me the village. But that village is dark—no game, no children, no brides brought here. I am tired of counting the ways you have not given [from your side of the agreement—zia, to calculate, used primarily in respect to marriage payments]. But now I bring you (an offering

---

93. The *ádzémé awú* is typically celebrated one year after the death of the deceased.
94. Ondo Mangue, "El Culto a Los Ancestros de Los Fang," 32.
95. Fernandez, *Bwiti*, 253–54.
96. Ibid., 264.

of) sheep and cooked food. I tell you to give me much blessing so that the village will go well. You must tell me what I must do that the village will go well.[97]

In this prayer, the earthiness and materiality of Biéri comes explicitly to the foreground, as does language bordering on an attempt to chastise or manipulate the ancestral realm in the acquisition of material gain. This posture to the Fang ancestors stands in an analogous relationship to the theology of Job's three friends Eliphaz, Bildad, and Zophar. For instance, Zophar's "if-then" insistence that Job confess his sin is couched almost formulaically or mechanistically as having the power to enact Job's restoration:

If iniquity is in your hand, put it far away,

And let not injustice dwell in your tents.

Surely then you will lift up your face without blemish;

You will be secure and will not fear. (Job 11:14–15 ESV)[98]

The centrality of Zophar's lavish promises for Job ("your life will be brighter than the noonday," vs. 17; "you will feel secure," vs. 18; "none will make you afraid"; vs. 19) also suggests that the procurement of "blessings" for Job resides as the principal focal point of such counsel with God playing the role of a mechanistic arbiter or restorer of Job's entitlements. Related to the preceding point is the second: *the relational aspect of dealing with God is far from primary.* In Biéri, the role which *Nzama* (the term utilized today to refer to the Supreme Being) played in the actual proceedings of the ritual was marginal to non-existent. Even the theoretical idea, hinted at only vaguely by anthropologist Günter Tessman,[99] that the ancestors were intermediaries between humans and *Nzama* is suggestive of an imposition of the Christian worldview upon Fang ideas rather than being a true description of Biéri's conceptual dynamics. Even as the Biéri ancestral cult was increasingly "Christianized" in the Fang imagination—by arguing or speculating that *Nzama* stood behind the ancestral prayers—the role of *Nzama* in the Biéri rituals remained marginal and distant for the actual devotees of the ritual by any objective standard.[100] With respect to God, the posture of Job's friends indicates many of the same perspectives. For Job's friends, faith

97. Ibid., brackets and parenthesis in the original.
98. Bildad issues a similar "if-then" statement; see Job 8:4–6 ESV.
99. Tessman, *Los Pamues (Los Fang)*, 442.
100. In fact, Fernandez could provide a rich description of Biéri without any implication that the ancestors were originally conceived as intermediaries for a Supreme Being; see Fernandez, *Bwiti*, 253–67.

in God, as Samuel Terrien argued, had become "a mere projection of their idea of justice"—what they were primarily asking for was an admission of wrongs.[101] The incessant accusations of Eliphaz, Bildad, and Zophar calling for Job to repent of his hidden sins are hardly calls for contrition and tears due to a breach in Job's primary relationship with God. Relating dynamically to God was not a significant feature of religious experience either for Job's friends or for Biéri ritual participants.

In fact, the traditionally weak conceptual space for God within the Fang cosmology is poignantly illustrated by the difficulty presented to the earliest Christian missionaries in selecting a Fang equivalent term for the Creator God or Supreme Being. According to many of the earliest interpreters of the Fang, *Nzama* was originally the created son of the supreme god *Mebege*. Tessman's *magnum opus* of Fang anthropology, in one prominent account, even places *Nzambe*[102] in the fourth "generation" of the divine genealogy and states unequivocally that "Nsambe (God) has created all living creatures, but has not created the world, [Nsambe] is not at the beginning of all things, but himself is the result of development."[103] One of the oldest creation myths of the Fang, captured by Victor Largeau in 1901, not only represents the most widely circulated creation myth amongst students of the Fang but also highlights *Mebege's* creation of *Nzama* during primordial beginnings:

> Mebege created man with clay. He made him first in the form of a "lizard" (*a nga sum nye ane nsvie*), and then he placed this lizard in a pool of water. For five days and then for seven more days and on the eighth he went to look at him and said, "Come out." He came out and he was man. Then he knelt and said, "Thank you." Mebege asked him, "Whence do you come?"
>
> He replied, "I know not. I was in the water. Suddenly I stand here." Mebege said, "Go." Mebege said, "It is I that created you." Then they went to the village of Mebege and the son asked:
>
> "Father, what is my name? What is yours? They shall call you Mebege who created all things; myself they shall call Nzame ye Mebege." In the creation Mebege created man in this way.[104]

---

101. Terrien, *Job: Poet of Existence*, 69.

102. *Nzama*, *Nzambe*, and *Nzame* reflect regional dialectical differences but all names refer to the same entity.

103. Tessman, *Los Pamues (Los Fang)*, 347.

104. Largeau, *Encyclopédie Pahouine*, 210–13 as translated into English by Fernandez, *Bwiti*, 54.

By various interpreters, *Nzame* is ambiguously considered the "*premier home*" created by *Mebege*,[105] the "*organisateur de la creation*,"[106] or as an "ancillary deity as ignorant about the facts of creation as man himself."[107] As a classic otiose deity, *Mebege's* relative lack of involvement in human affairs in comparison with *Nzama*, who, as the progenitor of the clans, became identified with Fang ancestral traditions, apparently led the early missionaries to elevate the status of *Nzama* to "God" when seeking an equivalent term for the Judeo-Christian tradition.[108] Pierre Alexandre and Jacques Binet explain: "One needs to underline that *Nzame (Zambe) is not the creator god* but rather the ancestral overseer; it is from him that all the genealogies stem."[109] As the name *Mebege* was rarely pronounced, Alexandre and Binet argue that the earliest Christian missionaries' mistaken elevation of *Nzama* to the Creator God made it difficult, if not impossible, to return to the use of *Mebege* to refer to the Creator God. Nevertheless, despite the relatively new status afforded to *Nzama* as the Supreme Being, the conceptual space occupied by *Nzama* within the Fang cosmology seems scarcely to have surpassed *Mebege's* otiosity. Tessman compared *Nsambe* to an absent and decrepit boss of a large company,[110] while Fernandez observed the "relatively weak category" occupied by God amongst the Fang.[111] In subsequent chapters, we will explore how this rather weak conceptual "space" for God in the Fang cosmology affects the contours of both ecclesial praxis and hermeneutical reflection with respect to Job.

The Anti-witchcraft Cult of Nguí: The Apotheosized Rise of the Evus

As frequent as the lamentation over corruption at the geopolitical level or the constant frustration about the lack of electricity at a developmental level or the numerous grievances of sickness and disease at a medical level, is

---

105. Alexandre and Binet, *Le Groupe Dit Pahouin*, 108. See also Ndongo Mba-Nnegue, *Los Fan*, 57.

106. Mallart Guimera, *Ni Dos Ni Ventre*, 30.

107. Fernandez, *Bwiti*, 54.

108. The historicity of Fang anthropology appears to be ambiguous with respect to which early Christian missionaries first decided to elevate *Nzama* to divine status.

109. Alexandre and Binet, *Le Groupe Dit Pahouin*, 109–10, italics in the original. Fernandez posits that *Nzama's* ancestral function essentially gave him "a status midway between divinity and humanity"; Fernandez, *Bwiti*, 54.

110. Tessman, *Los Pamues (Los Fang)*, 347.

111. Fernandez, *Bwiti*, 244.

the Fang lament over the apparent rise of witchcraft at the societal level. As Spanish colonialism, with the aid of the Roman Catholic Church, stamped out Fang ritual cults as "primitive" and "pagan," the Fang were left without any ritual and communal recourse to address that one societal evil which was most feared: witchcraft. As one elderly *ngangan* (traditional healer) indicated, "Now witchcraft is on the rise. Witches aren't scared of anything with the disappearance of the Nguí."[112]

As the Fang anti-witchcraft cult, Nguí referred to both the ritual cult and the masked man chiefly responsible for the cultic oversight.[113] At times of extreme distress for the village (i.e., death of multiple children, tragic loss of crops, women not giving birth) or after particularly heinous anti-communal crimes (i.e., adultery, robbery, or murder when the culprit was unknown[114]), the Nguí was called upon to perform its lone and severe function: execute punishment upon the witches. Local informants explain that Nguí initiates were often given a certain eye drop *biang* (medicine) which allowed them to "see" the witches responsible for the village's problems. The Nguí acted as both judge (in determining exactly who was guilty) and executioner (afflicting the guilty witches with death or disease), and the mere presence of the Nguí in the village was thought to install so much fear in the witches that they often transformed into plants or animals to escape detection. Death (usually) or leprosy[115] (occasionally) were the typical punishments which served to restore therapeutic wholeness to the village by providing retributive justice.[116] As a classic power-encounter at the traditional level, the Nguí was conceived as performing a communal and thus a benevolent type of *mbwo* (witchcraft) in contrast to the individualistic and egotistical *mbwo* which increasingly began to be utilized for self-advancement and the individualized procurement of cultural goals.

As the traditional rituals broke down under the pressures of colonialism, Christianization, and modernization, Fernandez argues that two principal successors vied for the religious vacuum left by the recession of the ancestors symbolically represented by the disappearance of the Biéri cult: *Nzama* and the *evus* (a corporal entity of witchcraft).[117] Considering the relatively restricted conceptual space allocated to *Nzama*, it is hardly surprising that the *evus*, with its machinations of witchcraft, "flowed into

112. Interview, Eugenio Esono Moyo, May 14, 2012.
113. Balandier, *The Sociology of Black Africa*, 146.
114. Tessman, *Los Pamues (Los Fang)*, 417–18.
115. Ibid., 417, 421.
116. Balandier, *The Sociology of Black Africa*, 147.
117. Fernandez, "Christian Acculturation and Fang Witchcraft," 249.

the vacuum and grew out of all proportion."[118] Today, the *evus* of witchcraft, rather than the ancestor realm, represents the chief "religious" vehicle in the acquisition of the Fang cultural goals of success, wealth, and health. The fact that individuals traditionally sought these cultural goals of large crops, dowry payments, fertile wives, and large families through the *evus* of witchcraft is not disputed.[119] But what Fernandez aptly recognizes is that during the time in which the communal ancestral cult of Biéri and the anti-witchcraft cult of Nguí functioned, the egotistical, individualistic, and aggressive pursuit of the "good life" as symbolically represented by the *evus* was largely suppressed. Yet today, through its embodiment of evil and by occupying the conceptual terrain once dominated by the ancestors,[120] the apparent rise of the *evus* within Fang society has been labeled by Fernandez as the "apotheosis of evil."[121]

The Evus and the Dynamics of Mbwo (Witchcraft)

For the Fang, the *evus* is the originating source of *mbwo* (witchcraft) represented as a monster or beast which resides corporally in the human person (typically the stomach).[122] The Fang often depict the *evus* as a crab, bat, spider, frog, or small ball[123] leading Guinean author Joaquín Mbana to argue that the *evus* is "*animalidad encarnada en lo humano*" ("an animal condition incarnated in the human") since the Fang typically distinguish between *osang* (the stomach of a human) and *evus* (the stomach of an animal).[124] The witchcraft of the *evus* is best understood conceptually as a carnivorous principle in which the savagery of the forest is corporally represented in the human person wherein the Fang attributes of hospitality, solidarity, and dialogue are rent asunder in favor of deceptive, selfish,

118. Ibid.

119. Mallart Guimera, *Ni Dos Ni Ventre*, 63–67.

120. In part, Fernandez interprets the Bwiti cult as a "resurrection of the ancestors from the oblivion to which Christian evangelization has consigned them"; Fernandez, "Christian Acculturation and Fang Witchcraft," 251.

121. Fernandez, *Bwiti*, 5, 227–28, 230, 239, 266, 283–84, 286, 303.

122. Throughout the book, we will utilize of the Fang word *mbwo* which is translated locally as "witchcraft" by the Spanish word *brujería* in describing the phenomenon of "noctural flights." *Sorcellerie* ("sorcery") is the term more attested in the French secondary literature related to *mbwo*, but no such distinction between witchcraft and sorcery is recognized amongst the Fang.

123. Mallart Guimera, *Ni Dos Ni Ventre*, 43–54.

124. Mbana, *Brujeria Fang en Guinea Ecuatorial*, 53.

anti-social behavior which eventually transforms the *mbot* (person) into a *ko-mbot* (non-person).[125]

In contrast to the virtually forgotten creational stories featuring *Nzama*, the mythic origins of the *evus* are widely preserved amongst the major Fang groupings (Ntumu and Okak) of Equatorial Guinea. Despite regional differences,[126] several conceptual features of the mythic origins of the *evus* may be identified: (1) the *evus* originally inhabited the forest, a Fang symbol of anti-social, carnivorous danger and evil compared to the socially organized tranquility and safety of the village;[127] (2) a woman agrees to transport the *evus* back to the village (most often) because of her ambition to eat the fresh animals provided by the *evus*. Thus, the woman becomes the primary human scapegoat for society's misfortunes; (3) the *evus*, demonstrating some deceit and trickery, refuses to be carried on the woman's back or transported in a basket; (4) the woman finally agrees to sit on the ground and spread her legs apart while the *evus* penetrates her vagina. Thus the *evus* takes up residence in the stomach by an overtly sexual act of aggression which implicitly links sex (especially by a woman) with evil and taboo; (5) finally, the *evus* asks to eat the woman's children thereby initiating the anthropography (the eating of human flesh and blood) which is the quintessential characteristic of Fang *mbwo* (witchcraft). Typically, the myths conclude with a melancholy air of resignation noting the dangerous presence of the *evus* amongst the descendants while laying the blame squarely on the woman: "Today, the *evu* reigns throughout the entire country. Previously, it was not like this. It was the woman who, by her greed, brought the *evu* to the village."[128]

In the Fang conception, *mbwo* (witchcraft) is rooted in the nocturnal flights by those who possess an anti-social *evus*. At night when the body is sleeping, the witch's *evus* travels (typically by airplane) to eat the flesh and blood of one's enemies, thereby increasing its power, vitality, and success in the nocturnal realm of *ngbel*.[129] Similar to the traditional Fang

---

125. Ibid., 51–53, 63.

126. Mallart Guimera has identified several different versions of the myth; see Mallart Guimera, *Ni Dos Ni Ventre*, 24–38. A few mythic strands in Cameroon appear to associate the cosmic withdrawal of *Nzama* from humanity through the deception of a woman by the *evus* in an analogous "African Fall" reminiscent of the Genesis 3 account. Yet in Equatorial Guinea, the mythic tales of the *evus* typically begin with the existence of the *evus* in the forest without any mention of *Nzama* (i.e., "*the evus originally lived in the forest . . .*"). Based on our own fieldwork, the Ntumu and Okak accounts seem to correspond most closely with the Evuzok versions five and six recorded by Mallart Guimera.

127. A typical symbolic dichotomy amongst the Fang, see Ibid., 31–32.

128. Ibid., 28.

129. *Ngbel* is the nocturnal world of witchcraft, as referred to in the story of *Afri*

rituals wherein initiation often played an important sociological function, the dynamics of Fang witchcraft also includes an initiatory process which serves as the necessary mechanism whereby the *evus* is "activated" and thus becomes capable of traveling nocturnally in *ngbel*. In this sense, Fang witchcraft is essentially a two-stage process (see figure 2.4).

Figure 2.4:
The Initiation Process of Fang Witchcraft

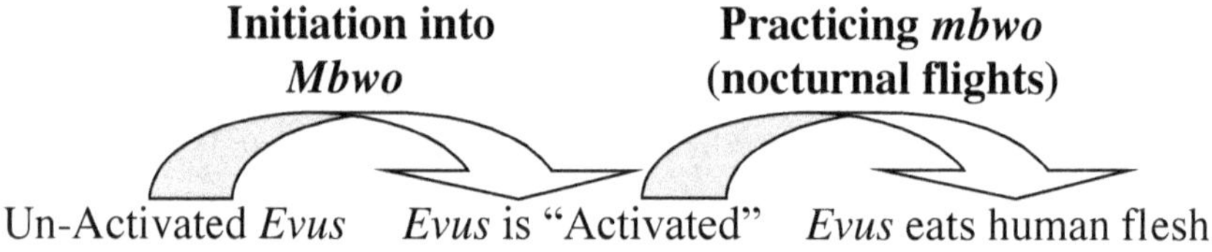

| Initiation into *Mbwo* | Practicing *mbwo* (nocturnal flights) |

Un-Activated *Evus*   *Evus* is "Activated"   *Evus* eats human flesh

While some ambiguity exists as to whether every person is born with the *evus* or simply with the latent capability to acquire it, it is only through the initiation ritual that the anthropographical potential of the *evus* is fully released to feed on human flesh and blood. Unlike the elaborate initiatory rituals of Biéri or Nguí, the initiation of *mbwo* centers upon the simple consumption of food[130] which traditionally entailed a *carne del bosque* ("bush meat") such as antelope, snake, or turtle. Today the initiatory meal is rather commonplace with the staple of *calabaza* (squash) or even candy or gum providing the master *nnem* (witch) with the initiatory "meal" necessary to seal the pact with a would-be apprentice.[131] The relative ease and pervasiveness with which initiation into witchcraft is thought to occur within the Fang society of today is encapsulated by a simple yet often-repeated Spanish refrain: "*Ya los niños inician otros niños*" ("children now initiate other children"). In a sense, "children initiating other children" is a demoralized lament expressing the imbalances of modern culture for many Fang who believe witchcraft has run amok without any of the traditional checks and balances such as Nguí to curtail such aggressive and individualistic behavior.

Conceptually, the *evus* explains quite a diverse range of societal symptoms such as the polarities between health and sickness and the discrepancies between prosperity and poverty. For the Fang, society is starkly divided

---

Kara; Bibang Oyee, *La Migración Fang*, 62.

130. Or occasionally, nowadays, drink.

131. This information was communicated to the author by multiple informants.

into three different classes of persons: innocent persons (*miemie*), "prepared persons" (*akomnge*, "preparation/initiation"), and witches (*biyem*, plural of *nnem*).[132] Generally lauded for their good nature by the community, the *miemie* are thought to live in peaceful relationships with family and neighbors and embody the Fang ideals of simplicity, hospitality, and community. Yet the ambiguous nature of the *miemie* is nevertheless highlighted in the fact that while non-witchcraft participation is one prerequisite for being venerated as an ancestor, a *miemie* is otherwise regarded, in Mallart Guimera's words, as a "*homme de rien*" ("a nobody, a man of nothing").[133] Since *miemie* are thought to be defenseless and easy targets for the *biyem* (witches) because of their lack of any knowledge of the nocturnal realm, their individual place in society is typically outside the halls of power and circles of wealth:

> Sociologically, the mmimye belong to this class of individuals whose human and material success never surpasses that of its neighbours.... He represents the young, the poor, the unmarried, the unlucky. In short, the man fails to create any prestige in the social group to which he belongs. However, there is some ambiguity: on the one hand he is considered lucky because it does not have evu; on the other hand, for the same reason he is considered very unlucky.[134]

While society is often portrayed dualistically between the extremes represented by the *miemie* (innocent ones) and *biyem* (witches), certain persons are thought to be "prepared" (i.e., *akomnge* for "preparation/initiation") during childhood/early adolescence for success or greatness.[135] Recalling the two-stage initiation for *mbwo* is critical for understanding this second stage: a prepared person's *evus* is "activated" but may not necessarily participate in nocturnal flights nor feed upon human flesh. The initiatory meal alone does not signify the person is yet a witch; only by *áke á mbwo* ("going to witchcraft"), as represented by nocturnal flights which activate the carnivorous hunger of the *evus*, is the person considered a witch. In traditional society, prepared persons typically occupied positions of power within the community such as traditional healers (*ngangan*), clan chiefs

---

132. Several anthropologists have recognized a three-fold distinction within Fang society, see Tessman, *Los Pamues (Los Fang)*, 457–58; Fernandez, *Bwiti*, 211–12; Mallart Guimera, *Ni Dos Ni Ventre*, 55–71.

133. Mallart Guimera, *Ni Dos Ni Ventre*, 42.

134. Ibid., 70.

135. Fernandez, *Bwiti*, 208–13. It should be noted that this second category of "prepared persons" is highly ambiguous. With the apparent rise of *mbwo*, this second class of "prepared persons" is often conceptually collapsed into the third category of *biyem* (witches).

(*nkúkúmá*), or the wealthy (*nkúkúm*), all who (theoretically) utilized their acquired knowledge, power, or wealth for the health and advancement of the community.[136] Therefore, a prepared person's "socialized *evus*," to use the terminology of anthropologist Mallart Guimera, was thought to bestow success on the individual which theoretically was re-invested into the community.[137]

Yet once the *evus* has tasted human flesh by participating in nocturnal flights, the entity becomes the embodiment of personalized evil and henceforth destructive by nature. As a third class of people, *biyem* (witches, plural of *nnem*) are ambitious, power-hungry, anti-social individuals who attempt to manipulate, but eventually succumb to, the power of the never-satiated appetite of the *evus* for human flesh. Today, an individual who garners immense wealth or success deemed out of proportion to the wider community is often labeled a witch: "If you're a great soccer player, you're a witch. If you're a successful businessman, you're a witch. If you're an important politician, you're a witch. If you're a famous medical doctor, you're a witch."[138] Locally, there is even widespread belief that nobody is ordained as priest in the Roman Catholic Church without participating in the eating of human flesh and blood (i.e., witchcraft anthropography).[139] Yet quite paradoxically, the stereotypical portrait of a witch as a lonely, impoverished, and destitute individual on the margins of society additionally holds true. The savage, carnivorous, forest-dwelling *evus* dwells in the human person quite precariously as suggested by the forest-village dichotomy inherent in the mythic origins of the *evus*. Therefore, the *nnem* (witch) who engages in nocturnal warfare utilizing his or her *evus* fails to recognize the basic ontology of the noctural anti-social *evus* as a radically evil entity which continually "obliges the possessor to kill humans and eat them."[140] When the *nnem* can no longer provide the human flesh that the *evus* so single-mindedly craves, the *evus* will eventually turn on its possessor resulting in death or destitution. As the traditional Fang refrain *evus ene guemosoc da ka* ("the *evus* is like a tail of a monkey that hangs itself")[141] makes abundantly clear, the constant nocturnal warfare of the *evus* leads eventually to the demise of the *nnem*.[142]

---

136. Mbana, *Brujeria Fang en Guinea Ecuatorial*, 41.

137. Mallart Guimera, *Ni Dos Ni Ventre*, 57, 62.

138. Interview, Modesto Engonga Ondo, Antonio Hill, and Leoncio Ndong, May 9, 2012.

139. Mbana, *Brujeria Fang en Guinea Ecuatorial*, 36.

140. Mbana, *Brujeria Fang en Guinea Ecuatorial*, 40. For the terminology of "social"/"anti-social" *evus*, see Mallart Guimera, *Ni Dos Ni Ventre*, 57–67.

141. Interview, Vicente Ndong Esono with Deogracias Bee, May 1, 2012.

142. In similar fashion, the Fang refrain *medjem mensua mayam nsua* meaning "the

A fundamental characteristic of Fang *mbwo* is the night-day dichotomy between "those who know" (*biyem*) and "those who are innocently exploited" (*miemie*) wherein true power, knowledge, and success in life are accessed through the nocturnal realm. As one informant put it, "the witch is not poor at night. He can be poor during the day but this is not important. The witch is powerful at night."[143] For the Fang, this central night-day dichotomy of *mbwo* closely parallels its own complicated relationship with the "White Man." In a sense, the harrowing journey and escape from the "Red Men" in the savannah who wanted to dominate the Fang ended rather unfortunately (and ironically) as the Fang were placed in the analogous role of *miemie* ("those who are innocently exploited") compared to the wealth and technology of the White Man during European colonialism.[144] By conceptualizing the nocturnal realm as a place of riches, power, and technology, the idiom of witchcraft served to relativize the Fang's own sense of inferiority and loss of self-confidence suffered "during the day" under European colonialism since the Fang could still point to powerful and successful feats of their own in the nocturnal realm. Arguably the most popular story currently circulating about *mbwo* in Equatorial Guinea illustrates precisely this White Man-Black Man distinction in highlighting the concept of nocturnal power:

> Once there was such a powerful witch that he was able to design, create, and manufacture a spectacular type of airplane that became famous the world over. People as far as America were shocked by the incredible technology and engineering of the airplane. It was far ahead of its time in both technology and design. The creator of this great airplane had traveled far and wide (even to America and Europe!) and was known to the Whites in that part of the world for his genius design of this new technology.
>
> One day, a group of white people (*ntangan*) came from America to find their friend, the designer of this magnificent airplane.[145] When they arrived in Akurenam [sometimes an unknown town in Cameroon], they were surprised to learn that this master inventor lived far out in the middle of the bush. Undeterred, the whites continued their trek using the small paths in the forest thinking very soon they would see the great mansion of their

---

water in the elephant [the water which springs from its own body] finally ends up cooking the elephant" was likewise applied to the dynamics of the *evus* by one informant; Interview, Martin Mbeng Nze, April 24, 2012.

143. Interview, Martin Mbeng Nze, May 5, 2012.

144. See Fernandez, *Bwiti*, 68–71.

145. The story is occasionally told as the visit of only one white friend.

famous friend. Yet as the whites asked more and more people where this famous mastermind of technology lived, they were continually told to trek even further into the bush. When the whites finally met their friend they were incredulous! The whites found this great inventor sitting in a kitchen all alone, dressed in worn-out clothes, and living in a small dilapidated house with a thatched roof.[146]

For the Fang, the story's humor lies precisely in its anticlimactic ending. The comic portrait of a great inventor and master of technology sitting idly in a kitchen underscores the great paradox of witchcraft: the witch can access a world of riches, success, and fame at night but ruin and destitution are equally its end result. Like this modern popular story, the mystical pursuit of riches and success was a thematic staple in Fang traditional stories and fables.[147] In the postcolonial era, these modern manifestations of "witchcraft riches" have also become quite entrenched in the urban legends amongst the Fang.[148] For instance, a widespread rumor developed in Bata and Malabo in the year 2000 that a boat of Chinese women would be dispersed amongst the males of Equatorial Guinea. Identifying this urban legend as a type of cargo cult, Spanish anthropologist Gustau Nerín argued that the women represented a highly desired "commodity" that mystically would appear from the other side of the world.[149] This cultural fascination of "white" western riches being acquired through mystical avenues is hardly repudiated within the local Christian community. The prevalence of the prosperity gospel in segments of Fang Pentecostalism, notwithstanding the transnational aspects of the prosperity movement, suggests a radical congruence with local beliefs and practices.

The Causal Universe: Sickness and Healing in Fang Cultural Perspective

The causal relationship between the nocturnal world of the *evus* and humanity's diurnal world represents a foundational concept for understanding the Fang cosmological universe. In the previous chapter, we alluded to Noel Baudin's elegant analogy referring to African causality as a "world of forces" which "is held like a spider's web of which no single thread can be caused to

---

146. The story is a concise summary recreated by the author.
147. For example, see Mbana, *Brujeria Fang en Guinea Ecuatorial*, 42–44.
148. See Ekomo et al., *Palabras que No Tienen Boca*.
149. Nerín, "El Barco de Las Chinas en Guinea Ecuatorial," 129–36.

vibrate without shaking the whole network."[150] For the Fang, nowhere is the spider web imagery more *apropos* than in the causal relationship between sickness and health.

In classifying disease etiologies, David Westerlund's typology of disease causation in African communities is instructive. Westerlund argues that three main categories of disease causation exist in Africa: *natural* (mainly physical), *religious* (supra-human, including the ancestors), and *social* (human).[151] Unlike some societies, the Fang recognize all three categories of sicknesses, but the severity of the illness is thought to be directly related to its etiological category. In the disease etiology of the Fang, natural (mainly physical) sicknesses are conceived as being the least troublesome whereas the nocturnal sicknesses caused by the *evus* are believed to be the most dangerous (see figure 2.5).

Figure 2.5: Fang Disease Etiologies: The Category and Severity of Fang Sicknesses

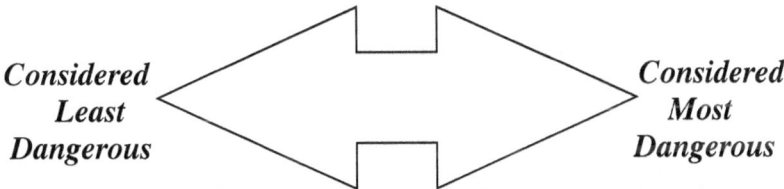

Category:	**Natural/Physical**	**Religious/Supra-human**	**Social/Human**
Origin:	(Contagion)	(Ancestors)	(Witchcraft)

For the Fang, sicknesses stemming from *natural* or *physical* causes exhibit relatively benign effects and are typically traced to ailments such as the common cold, cough, back pain, or diarrhea. Such sicknesses are referred to semantically as *akwánn ntangan* in Fang ("sicknesses of the white man") or *una enfermedad del hospital* in Spanish ("a hospital sickness"), and the

---

150. As cited by Magesa, *African Religion*, 46; Baudin, *Fetichism and Fetich Worshipers*.

151. Westerlund, "Pluralism and Change," 179. Semantically, the most problematic term is the "religious" or "suprahuman" category which includes the role of the ancestors. Westerlund assigns the ancestors to the "world of religion" since the ancestors as "spiritual beings" are conceptually distinct from "living humans" in their socio-religious cultic role.

symptoms are typically treated by visiting the doctors of the white man in a western hospital, although traditional herbalists or (more recently) Chinese pharmacies may also be consulted. Tessman indicated that with respect to these ordinary sicknesses, the Fang "generally does not think much about the origin of the sickness."[152]

The *religious* or *supra-human* category of disease causation is generally the least defined, albeit the broadest category amongst the Fang. As we have already seen, a limited number of sicknesses (*akwann misémm*, "sicknesses of sin") were attributed to breaching the community's social norms established by the ancestors. Fang ancestors also regulated clan life by affecting a broad and diverse range of behaviors known as *ekí* (prohibitions or taboos) which included sexual taboos (i.e., no sex during the day), gender-specific prohibitions (i.e., women cannot eat turtle), clan-specific prohibitions (i.e., the Okas clan cannot eat chicken), and life-stage prohibitions (i.e., pregnant women cannot eat snake because their babies will not learn to crawl well), to name a few.[153] Today prohibitions continue to impinge upon the daily life of many Fang, but the occurrence of actual sicknesses attributed to the ancestors due to breaking *ekí* seems to have undergone a major devaluation in recent years. With the apparent rise of witchcraft coinciding with the increasing prominence of western medicine, many Fang now tend to exclude the ancestors as a significant causal origin for sicknesses. Nowadays, local disease etiology is often conceived as a dualistic system whereby naturally-occurring sicknesses (*akwánn ntangan*) are best treated by western (i.e., "white") medicine in hospitals whereas sicknesses which involve the *evus* (*akwann Fang*, "Fang sicknesses") can only be treated by Fang traditional healers (*ngangan*).[154]

Utilizing Westerlund's schema, sicknesses amongst the Fang thought to be caused by the *social-human* agency of witchcraft are those sicknesses regarded by the Fang as unusual, severe, or most likely to lead to (especially premature) death. As an etiological category, *akwánn fang* ("Fang sicknesses") or *akwánn mbwo* ("witchcraft sicknesses") are those sicknesses attributed to the effects suffered by the *evus* during noctural flight. Just as local Guinean airlines have experienced numerous accidents and tragedies during the last decade, airplane travel by the *evus* in the nocturnal realm also represents a potentially dangerous journey.[155] To use local parlance, the airplane utilized

---

152. Tessman, *Los Pamues (Los Fang)*, 494.

153. The examples are all taken from the author's fieldwork.

154. See also "Ministerio de Sanidad y Bienestar Social de Guinea Ecuatorial," 30.

155. To reference only the crash with the highest number of fatalities, see "Sixty Killed in Equatorial Guinea Plane Crash," *The Sydney Morning Herald*.

by the *evus* may suffer an "accident" or even "crash." Or, a person's *evus* may be overpowered by stronger witches in the nocturnal realm. Whatever the case, while a person is sleeping calmly in his or her bed, the *evus* is thought to expose the witch to tremendous risks and dangers during its nocturnal flights, *with accidents suffered in the nocturnal realm having causal repercussions during the day in the form of sickness or death.*

As with any society, identifying the etiological source of the sickness is crucial for receiving the appropriate restorative remedy. *Evus*-related sicknesses (*akwánn fang*) originating in the nocturnal world cannot simply be treated by diurnal western medical science unaware of the realities and internal dynamics of the *evus*. In fact, the *evus* is often said to suffer *further* damage if treated in a western hospital, being particularly susceptible to puncture by a needle. As the nomenclature itself suggests, *akwann fang* are necessarily treated by the Fang themselves by visiting a traditional healer (*ngangan*). According to Mallart Guimera, the *ngangan*, possessing a socialized *evus*, can attempt to restore a patient's anti-social *evus* by rendering it "*inopérant*," conceptually reversing *mbwo*'s initiatory process.[156] In Equatorial Guinea, perhaps the most widely told *ngangan* healing technique involves both the *ngangan* and the sick patient vomiting their respective *evus* alone in the forest in order for the *ngangan* to compare his or her healthy *evus* with the damaged *evus* of the patient. In such a manner, the *ngangan* is therapeutically able to sew and stitch together the lesions of the injured *evus*.[157]

Since *evus*-related sicknesses are thought to be acquired in the nocturnal realm of witchcraft, vehement accusations of witchcraft are often directed at the sick and dying. Whereas some African societies highlight the innocence of the person thought to suffer from witchcraft or sorcery (i.e., "I saw someone approach your hut late last night, who do you think is trying to bewitch you?"[158]), the Fang's most typical reaction when faced with *okwánn mbwo* (witchcraft sickness) is to blame the sufferer (i.e., "You are sick. Do you want to die? You must confess your witchcraft before it's too late!").[159] Therefore, the sick person not only confronts the physical symptoms of the ailment itself but is often forced to cope with particularly acute familial or communal pressures to confess his or her deeds of witchcraft. At a conceptual level, witchcraft might theoretically serve to assuage, at least partially, day-time hostilities by elevating social hostilities and confronta-

156. Mallart Guimera, *Ni Dos Ni Ventre*, 208–10.
157. Ibid., 209.
158. For example, see Silla, *People Are Not the Same*, 60–62.
159. Mallart Guimera, *Ni Dos Ni Ventre*, 201: "La première démarche du grand guérisseur consiste à engager le dialogue avec le malade afin que celui-ci avoue ses actes de sorcellerie."

tions to the nocturnal realm. During witchcraft accusations, the pacific Zande people remained polite and avoided anger, as evidenced by Evans-Pritchard's classic study.[160] Yet for the Fang, who readily describe themselves as aggressive and warlike, these witchcraft accusations which are typically directed against the sufferer in the midst of familial tensions[161] often act like pouring gasoline on an already raging fire as tempers flare and underlying clan rivalries escalate.

In issues of sickness and health, the Fang cosmology is dominated by concerns to identify the moral etiology of the sickness. Simply put, moral blame typically follows—or is latently present in—the diagnoses of sicknesses related to *mbwo*. Physical etiology and moral etiology represent two sides of the same causal coin within the Fang cosmological universe. Blame must be assigned. This culture of blame and accusation surrounding issues of health and healing is particularly toxic to sick and suffering patients when the sickness has been attributed to *mbwo*. A story told to the author aptly illustrates the way in which *evus*-related explanations generally tend to scapegoat the sufferer.[162] In the village of Nkumekieñ, a mother was suffering from a prolonged and unusual birth lasting twenty-four hours. (With one of the highest infant mortality rates in the world, stories of the *evus* frequently surface with problematic pregnancies and births.[163]) As the baby finally exited the womb, the midwife and the rest of the older women attending the birth reportedly saw the mother's *evus* in the form of a grotesque frog trying to eat the baby's flesh. As the midwife protected the newborn by holding the baby high overhead, the *evus*—with the consent of the mother—was allowed to slip back into the mother's vagina. The implication of the mother's action was a confirmation to all present (and to those to whom the story was told!) that the mother was a *nnem* (witch) trying to eat her own baby. In the advent of the stillborn death of her baby, the mother would have suffered the inscrutable accusations of witchcraft. As this vignette reveals, *mbwo* amongst the Fang not only serves to "explain unfortunate events"[164]—in this case, a long and complicated birth—but also tends to breed a culture rife with blame and accusation.

Interestingly, a logical inconsistency of *mbwo* surfaces precisely at the moment of accusation. Theoretically, *biyem* (witches) are often thought to

---

160. Evans-Pritchard, *Witchcraft, Oracles and Magic Among the Azande*, 43, 46.

161. Since severe health concerns are, *ipso facto*, familial matters; Mallart Guimera, *Ni Dos Ni Ventre*, 214.

162. Interview, Modesto Engonga Ondo, Antonio Hill, Leoncio Ndong, May 9, 2012.

163. "Infant Mortality Rate," *U.S. Global Health Policy*.

164. Evans-Pritchard, *Witchcraft, Oracles and Magic Among the Azande*, 18–32.

prey on *miemie* (the innocent). But precisely at the moment of a prolonged or unusual sickness, any accumulated good-will or innocence accrued by the individual as a *miemie* is instantly forfeited as the family or community accuses the person of being a *nnem* (witch). As we shall see, some Fang Christians will recognize this same dynamic in the book of Job: the figure of Job is presented as thoroughly innocent (*miemie*), but he is accused in the same manner as a witch (*nnem*) in Fang culture. It is in this sense that Job defies Fang cultural categories. "Innocent sufferer" is as much a conceptual oddity and irregularity in Fang culture as it was for Job's friends in the Ancient Near East. Insofar as part of the purpose of the book of Job was to counteract the doctrine of retribution wherein deed and consequence became absolutized in a mechanistic cause and effect principle by positing a more dynamic and mysterious conceptual category of "innocent suffering" for ancient Israel, a reading of the book of Job theoretically offers many of the same possibilities for Fang Christians. In other words, within the Fang causal universe, the book and figure of Job offers a challenging new paradigm for thinking about suffering.

The Abundant Life and the Presence of Suffering

Within the causal cosmology of the Fang, suffering elicits genuinely human, albeit contextually framed, questions of existential angst: who is responsible and why is this happening? As Tessman observed over a century ago, "The Pamue does not know coincidence, since everything exists for a reason."[165] The endeavor to find the "cause behind the cause" represents a chief component driving the Fang worldview in issues of sickness and suffering. In the Fang causal universe, chance or mystery is excluded, but life is affirmed. For the Fang, the pursuit of the abundant life in the community is characterized by the centrality of the word *mvwaa*. Utilized in perfunctory greetings (*ye one mvwaa*/how are you?) and replies (*me ne mvwaa*/I am well), *mvwaa* also communicates a robust sense of "peace" and "well-being" in the deeper holistic sense. As Donald S. Arden has observed, the word for peace in many African languages "has deep overtones of the Hebrew *shalom*."[166] Suffering represents the opposite of *mvwaa*, but having *mvwaa* signifies that the person is presently enjoying health and at peace with the community. (Fernandez suggests that *mvwaa* is a conjunction which includes the word

---

165. Tessman, *Los Pamues (Los Fang)*, 339.
166. Arden, "Out of Africa Something New," 19.

avweñ, a term related to witchcraft meaning "cool."[167] If this is the case, possessing *mvwaa* would include the concept of living a life free from *mbwo*, a quintessential aspect of suffering in the Fang cosmological universe.) As our conceptual description of the "Big Three" Fang rituals demonstrated, an overarching theme of Fang religiosity is the celebration and affirmation of *life*: Biéri sought "cultural goals" (fertility, good crops, good health) with a view towards possessing or re-establishing *life*; the Nguí was summoned when the *life* of the community was threatened by witchcraft; Ndong Mba purified individuals, placated the ancestors, and re-oriented the community towards *life*. Therefore, because the *causal universe* and the *celebration of life* are both central tenets within the cosmology, the presence of suffering exists as an unwelcome intruder within these dual pillars which co-exist only amidst extreme tension but nevertheless serve to support the framework of the entire cosmology.

Laurenti Magesa, a Tanzanian Catholic theologian, has argued convincingly that the notion of the abundant life represents a foundational element of traditional African religiosity. For Magesa, African religiosity exists primarily to restore the status quo in bringing life back to its "normal" or "ideal" state characterized by abundance.[168] Affliction and suffering are contrary to the basic ontology of the universe which is conceived in fairly optimistic terms. Magesa explains: "The world ought to be harmonious, balanced, and good. Accordingly, misfortune, which means imbalance, and disharmony in the universe, *does not just happen*."[169] For the Fang, the assumption of the abundant life, together with the notion of causality, represent foundational elements of the cosmology which serve to mutually exclude suffering and affliction as naturally occurring or normative elements within the worldview. That is, the abundant life, rather than suffering, is the status quo. And when suffering *does* occur, the community has culturally conditioned mechanisms to causally eliminate evil by enacting the traditional rituals. Therefore, in spite of Mbiti's famous quip that "Africans are notoriously religious,"[170] it is humanity that resides at the center as the "most important element or aspect" of the moral universe.[171] Neither the otiose figure *Nzama* who was raised to divine status nor the dwindling presence of the ancestors occupies such a central place in the Fang religio-

---

167. Fernandez, *Bwiti*, 582. In Equatorial Guinea, the term is *avweñ* (rather than *avwe* which Fernandez observed in Gabon).

168. Magesa, *African Religion*, 35–114.

169. Ibid., 174–75, italics added.

170. Mbiti, *African Religions and Philosophy*, 1.

171. Magesa, *African Religion*, 72.

cultural universe as humanity.[172] Therefore, when the existential need to explain suffering naturally arises from the tensions inherent in the cosmology, humans are often assigned the moral blame for suffering utilizing the most dominant idiomatic discourse available, namely, that of witchcraft. In other words, humans, rather than *Nzama* or the ancestors, receive the predominant share of blame in the Fang moral universe. This immediacy to blame, incidentally, may account for a general tendency to project blame and suffering onto the nocturnal world of witchcraft and account for the same tendency to scapegoat the Devil in Fang Pentecostalism. It is not that the Fang essentially refuse to take responsibility for culpability but that their cosmology places them in an epistemological proximity and intimately-related relationship to blame that is existentially uncomfortable in a culture rife with both suffering and its accompanying accusations. Throughout our study of Job, these contextualized questions of moral etiology will surface repeatedly and poignantly.

Conclusion

In chapter 1, we argued that African Christianity engages in a constant dialogical interaction between biblical hermeneutics, local cultures, and ecclesial praxis. Contemporary African Christianity owes much of its unique dynamism to precisely this tri-polar orientation. In this chapter, we situated the Fang of Equatorial Guinea within those cultural paradigms and motifs which will become especially prominent as Fang Christians engage in hermeneutical reflection upon the book of Job. After a brief sociopolitical and economic history of Equatorial Guinea which accented the Fang people during the colonial and postcolonial periods, we presented several cultural *leitmotifs* including Fang understandings of sin and the ancestors, the relative marginality of *Nzama* (who was elevated to the Supreme Being in the Judeo-Christian tradition) within the cosmology, the causal relationship between sickness and health, the nature of witchcraft, and the centrality of the abundant life. In our anthropological foray into Fang culture, we have been primarily concerned to describe these features conceptually. Although Fang Christians do not explicitly link scriptural

---

172. Magesa's basic argument is that humanity occupies the central place in the ritual cults since "only human beings carry the responsibility of maintaining the bond between the two [visible/invisible] spheres of the universe," Ibid., 172. We argue that this human-prioritized centrality in Fang traditional beliefs and practices also accounts for humans receiving the predominant share of moral blame when suffering arises, as any medical doctor, missionary, or person with close friendships with the Fang may easily observe during times of crisis and suffering.

texts or ecclesial practices to traditional rituals such as Ndong Mba, Biéri, or Nguí, the underlying conceptual perspectives of Fang religiosity will be shown, in subsequent chapters, to significantly impact the appropriation of themes and theologies in their interpretation of the book of Job. Yet before launching straightaway into these contextual readings of the book of Job amongst Fang Christians, one last element of the hermeneutics-culture-praxis triad awaits: the pole of ecclesial praxis.

3

An Untold Story of African Christianity

Presbyterian and Pentecostal Expressions of the Christian Faith in Equatorial Guinea

Introduction: Telling an Untold Story

THE STORY OF CHRISTIANITY in Equatorial Guinea has, up until the present study, been told solely in terms of the historical prestige and dominance of the Roman Catholic Church[1] or narrated through the lenses of the triumphs and challenges of western Protestant missionaries and their societies[2] or focused exclusively upon the early history of Christianity during the Spanish

---

1. For the definitive history of the Roman Catholic Church in Equatorial Guinea, see Pujadas, *La Iglesia en la Guinea Ecuatorial: Fernando Poo*; Pujadas, *La Iglesia en la Guinea Ecuatorial: Rio Muni*. See also Ndong Mbá Nnegue; *Origen e Implantacion de la Iglesia Católica en Guinea Ecuatorial*. For the history of the Claretian mission, see Claretian Missionaries, *Cien Años de Evangelización en Guinea Ecuatorial*. For the memoirs of a Spanish Catholic who in 1904 became the first bishop of the Apostolic Prefecture of Fernando Po, see Coll, *Segunda Memoria de Las Misiones de Fernando Póo y Sus Dependencias*.

2. With respect to the Presbyterians, see Nassau, *My Ogowe*; Nassau, *The Gabon and Corisco Missions*; Nassau, *Corisco Days*; McNeill, *Compilation of the First Half-Century of Mission Work in Rio Muni 1850–1900*; Brown, *One Hundred Years*, esp. 213–18; Lowrie, *A Manual of the Foreign Missions of the Presbyterian Church in the United States of America*, esp. 76–78; Lowrie, *A Manual of Missions*. With respect to the Baptists, see Fuller, *Cameroons and Fernando Po*. With respect to the Methodists, see Boocock, *Our Fernandian Missions*; Roe, *Fernando Po Mission*. With respect to the Crusade Church (*Iglesia Cruzada*) founded by WEC International, see Grubb, *Penetrating Faith in Spanish Guinea*; Thorne, *God at Work in Spanish Guinea*.

colonial[3] or pre-Spanish periods.[4] In exploring the hermeneutics-culture-praxis triad, the pole of ecclesial praxis will be highlighted in this chapter as we update the story of arguably the most significant missionary-founded Protestant Church in the country as well as introducing, for the first time in a scholarly account, the emerging forms of Guinean Pentecostalism.[5] Two principal objectives form the basis of this chapter: (1) to introduce three Protestant traditions in Equatorial Guinea which form the basis of the readings of the book of Job in subsequent chapters and (2) to explore the ecclesial ethnography of these three churches by analyzing the discourse and praxis of each church on themes central to their interpretations of Job, namely, responses to sickness and suffering as well as understandings of healing, divine blessing, and the nature of evil.

---

3. More recent scholarship on Protestant Christianity in Equatorial Guinea focuses almost exclusively upon the Reformed Presbyterian Church during the late nineteenth century and early twentieth century period; see A'Bodjedi, "Las Iglesias Presbiterianas Ndòwĕ," 49–74; A'Bodjedi, "Los Pastores Presbiterianos Ndòwĕ," 73–100.

4. For the Portuguese influence of Roman Catholicism in the region from 1469 to 1778 with particular reference to the islands of Formosa (later Bioko) and Annobón before Spanish colonialism, see Ndong Mbá Nnegue, *Origen e Implantacion de La Iglesia Católica en Guinea Ecuatorial*, 10–21.

5. The image of hundreds and thousands of Africans walking *en masse* to church on Sunday mornings would be a seriously flawed stereotype of twenty-first century Christianity in Equatorial Guinea. Within the Roman Catholic Church, Christmas, Corpus Christi, Easter, first communions, and baptisms are festive (*"fiesta"*) events which draw heavy attendance in celebrating the mass. Yet on non-*fiesta* Sundays, it remains an open question whether more Catholics than Protestants actually find themselves in a church service in the cities of Bata and Malabo—despite the fact that studies of religious adherence estimate that 80 to 90 percent of the populace is Roman Catholic. In the rural villages, the Roman Catholic Church is undoubtedly more intertwined to the social fabric of village life, but religious life in the cities of Malabo and Bata tell a different story. In numerous neighborhoods in the cities of Malabo and Bata, the lone Catholic neighborhood church is surrounded by several (often six to eight) different Pentecostal churches, suggesting that the country is presently in the midst of experiencing a dramatic demographic shift, at least as far as church attendance is concerned. The *Atlas of Global Christianity, 1910–2010* estimates Equatorial Guinea is 90.6 percent Roman Catholic while *Operation World* places the estimate at 80.33 percent. See Johnson and Ross, *Atlas of Global Christianity*, 338; Mandryk, *Operation World*, 321.

A Historic Mission Church in Crisis: *Iglesia Reformada Presbiteriana de Guinea Ecuatorial* (Reformed Presbyterian Church of Equatorial Guinea)

The Corisco and Coastal Years: Early Presbyterian History

The story of Guinean Protestantism begins in earnest in the mid-nineteenth century as both the Baptist Missionary Society and the Primitive Methodist Missionary Society, both proceeding from Britain, arrived in Fernando Po in 1841.[6] Nearly a century later, C. T. Studd's[7] Worldwide Evangelization Crusade[8] began establishing the *Cruzada* churches amongst the Fang Okak in southern Rio Muni in 1933.[9] Yet the church which holds the distinction of being the largest expression of historic mainline Protestant Christianity in the country is the *Iglesia Reformada Presbiteriana de Guinea Ecuatorial* (Reformed Presbyterian Church of Equatorial Guinea). While the Baptists, Methodists, and Presbyterians all pre-date the arrival of the Spanish Catholic missions in 1856,[10] it was the Reformed Presbyterian Church, founded in 1850 on the tiny island of Corisco,[11] which made the most significant Protestant inroads amongst the autochthonous peoples (see figure 3.1). Through its early mission efforts amongst the Ndowean[12] peoples of the Rio Muni

---

6. Brown, *One Hundred Years*, 1:203. Though the Baptists can actually trace their (pre-missionary society) story to a small chapel in Port Clarence built by the Sierra Leonean Baptist minister Mr. Scott who arrived in 1827 with the expedition of the Royal Navy Captain Fitz-William Owen; Fegley, *Equatorial Guinea: An African Tragedy*, 24; Pujadas, *La Iglesia En La Guinea Ecuatorial: Fernando Poo*, 32; Stanley, *The History of the Baptist Missionary Society*, 106–10.

7. Grubb, *C. T. Studd, Cricketer and Pioneer*.

8. In 1982, Worldwide Evangelization Crusade changed its name to WEC International with the letters W-E-C standing for Worldwide Evangelization for Christ; *Coordinating Council Conference*, 23. For the recent history of WEC International, see Davies, *Whatever Happened to CT Studd's Mission?*

9. See Grubb, *Penetrating Faith in Spanish Guinea*.

10. Liniger-Goumaz, *Small Is Not Always Beautiful*, 23.

11. Brown, *One Hundred Years*, 203, 213. After numerous missionary deaths in Liberia, Corisco was selected based upon the relatively healthy experience in Gabon by the American Board of Commissioners for Foreign Mission (ABCFM); see Lowrie, *A Manual of the Foreign Missions*, 22, 76–78. For the ABCFM's arrival at the Gabon River in June of 1841, see Phillips, *Protestant America and the Pagan World*, 221–25. The mainline Presbyterian Church (U.S.A.) is currently the denomination which maintains a minimal ecumenical partnership with *Iglesia Reformada Presbiteriana de Guinea Ecuatorial*.

12. The Ndowe peoples, who are often referred to as *playeros* ("people of the beach") in Spanish, is the name given to the linguistically-related cluster of ethnicities on the continental region near the coast and the nearby islands.

coastline and by later establishing congregations amongst the Fang majority, the Reformed Presbyterian Church eventually came to elevate itself as the undisputed face of Guinean Protestantism as judged by its historic influence as well as its current scope and size.[13]

Figure 3.1: Regional Map of Central Africa including Equatorial Guinea's island of Corisco

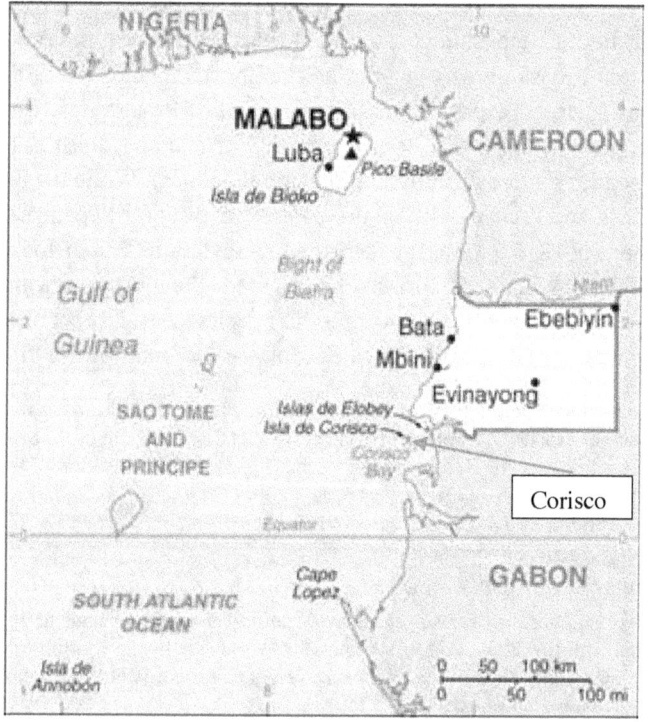

The tiny island of Corisco became the second West African mission chosen, after Liberia, by The Board of Foreign Missions of the Presbyterian Church in the United States of America. The island, measuring only five miles long by three miles wide, is located off the southwestern coast of the continental mainland region.

---

13. For the map of Equatorial Guinea, see "The World Factbook: Equatorial Guinea," *Central Intelligence Agency*.

The story of Presbyterianism in present-day Equatorial Guinea can be traced to 1850 as the Benga chief Imùnga ja Nyèmbanyango (circa 1795–circa 1865) from Corisco engineered a rather fortuitous partnership for the small island. Upon hearing the American missionaries Rev. and Mrs. James L. Mackay and Rev. and Mrs. George L. Simpson express interest in establishing a Presbyterian Church in the region,[14] Imùnga reportedly told the missionaries:

> Do not think about establishing your mission here on the mainland. These tribes are too savage and stupid. You will not be able to teach them anything. Come to Corisco: we are a civilized tribe and we will treat you well. Give us a school, like the one in Gabon, and you will have a good mission there. I, Imunga, will bring you to the island in my boat, and I will show you my people.[15]

As promised, the first Presbyterian school in the village of Evangesimba was founded in 1853 for Benga girls, one of whom managed to memorize entirely all four Gospels.[16] As seven new Presbyterian missionaries arrived in Corisco from 1851–55,[17] the mission occupied itself inaugurating the first Presbyterian congregation in Evangesimba on September 25, 1856,[18] translating portions of the scriptures into Benga,[19] and opening a total of three schools on the island.[20]

Buoyed by frequent missionary reinforcements to offset the perils of death and disease, Presbyterian missionaries often clashed with the surrounding peoples and their cultures. Denouncing the evils of polygamy, prohibiting Mokuku dances (an Ndowean secret society), and combating the lingering effects of the slave trade became the mission's most polemical and contentious issues. Though European powers, including Spain in 1817, had officially abolished the slave trade decades before Presbyterian missionaries arrived in 1850,[21] evidence points to the continuing presence

---

14. Lowrie, *A Manual of the Foreign Missions*, 252–54, 303–9.
15. See A'Bodjedi, "Las Iglesias Presbiterianas Ndòwě," 56.
16. Ibid., 57.
17. Mañe Ebo Asong, "Resumen Histórico," 5–6.
18. Ibid., 6.
19. Lowrie, *A Manual of the Foreign Missions*, 78.
20. Mañe Ebo Asong, "Misioneros Protestantes Presbiterianos Norteamericanos," 15. See also Lowrie, *A Manual of the Foreign Missions*, 78.
21. For the most comprehensive treatment of slavery in the Gulf of Guinea, see Sundiata, *From Slaving to Neoslavery*. See also A'Bodjedi, "Los Pastores Presbiterianos Ndòwě," 75.

of slaves on the island of Corisco and the clandestine selling of Benga girls to neighboring tribes.[22] Such realities evidently prompted the Presbyterian Church in Corisco to make a formal decision in 1868 declaring all slaves as free persons while ensuring the educational freedom for children of former slaves.[23] The Presbyterian Church in Bolondo, inaugurated on December 31, 1865 as the first Protestant church on Rio Muni, specified that one of the conditions for membership was not to be a slave-owner.[24] As the Presbyterian faith eventually spread northward on the Rio Muni coastline, early evangelistic efforts occasionally led to intense antagonism with indigenous religiosity. The aggressive evangelism by Mbàyi a Moliko, an indigenous Presbyterian Christian in charge of the local school near the church in Mbònda (organized in 1881[25]), seems to have resulted in one of the first known Christian martyrdoms of present-day Equatorial Guinea in the early twentieth century.[26]

Shortly after the founding of the first church on Corisco, the first two Presbyterian converts, Andekĕ ya Injĭnji and Ibìya J'Ikĕngĕ,[27] were baptized on October 1, 1856, subsequently becoming two of the first indigenous pastors ordained by American Presbyterians in central Africa on April 5, 1870.[28] Compared to the Roman Catholic Church, the speed with which Presbyterian missionaries moved to ordain indigenous leadership was unparalleled. As Randall Fegley observes, "A good indication of the level of Spanish paternalism is the fact that it was not until sixty years after Ikenge's ordination that a Bubi, Joaquin Maria Sialo, became

---

22. Pujadas suggests the presence of 200 slaves on Corisco as late as 1888; Pujadas, *La Iglesia En La Guinea Ecuatorial: Rio Muni*, 153.

23. Mañe Ebo Asong, "Misioneros Protestantes Presbiterianos Norteamericanos," 4–5, 12, 16.

24. A'Bodjedi, "Las Iglesias Presbiterianas Ndòwĕ," 58–59; Mañe Ebo Asong, "Misioneros Protestantes Presbiterianos Norteamericanos," 16.

25. A'Bodjedi, "Las Iglesias Presbiterianas Ndòwĕ," 62.

26. Here is the martyrdom account: "Hated by these [*ngònjĕ*, the traditional priests of *Mokuku*] because of his zeal and troublesome preaching about the imminent arrival of Jesus Christ and the urgency of repentance, those spiritual leaders took advantage of an accidental shooting, in the early twentieth century, to carry out their revenge.... After tying him firmly with the course rope *molângâ*, used to tie up witches and other criminals, the *One ngònjĕ* [note: the *One* is a small Ndowean tribe] carried Mbàyi out to sea in a canoe. There in the high seas they threw him overboard with his Bible, rejoicing in his drowning," Ibid., 63.

27. The European spellings often appear as Andrés Andeke and Ibia J. Tkenge (or Ibia Dy'Ikegue).

28. Rabat Makambo, "Estudio Preliminar," 6; Mañe Ebo Asong, "Misioneros Protestantes Presbiterianos Norteamericanos," 15.

the first Spanish Guinean African to become a Roman Catholic priest."[29] While Andekĕ "gave into polygamy,"[30] thereby fading quietly into the background of the annals of the Presbyterian Church, J'Ikĕngĕ's pastoral career was much more impressive. In many respects, J'Ikĕngĕ was a Benga man who embodied the amalgamation of Christianity, culture, and civilization so entrenched in the missionary ideology of the mid-nineteenth century. Educated theologically in a Presbyterian college in the United States,[31] J'Ikĕngĕ wrote a scathing 268-page diatribe *Costumbres Bengas y de los Pueblos Vecinos* depicting the vices of his own Benga tribe in comparison to the virtues of the Christian religion.[32] In addition to becoming one of the first indigenous intellects and authors of Central Africa, J'Ikĕngĕ was also a pioneering evangelist who shared in the establishment of several churches on the Ndowean coast and provided pastoral oversight for all the Corisco island churches when the last white missionary left in 1875 for the new mission center in the village of Bolonda in Rio Muni.[33] Yet apparently J'Ikĕngĕ's vision for the Benga people entailed more than a spiritual "pie in the sky" gospel. According to Ndowean author Enènge A'Bodjedi, J'Ikĕngĕ organized plans for a large-scale School of Agriculture and Industry based in Corisco which ambitiously sought to "replicate the Industrial Revolution" in Central Africa.[34] In spite of J'Ikĕngĕ's plea to his white counterparts that "African Christians, as an orphaned chick, should depend on their own beaks," his plans for the promotion of Benga commerce and civilization were judged by the Presbytery of New York in 1873 as too overtly secular to warrant support.[35] J'Ikĕngĕ's local prominence as a Presbyterian leader also landed him in the political crosshairs of the Roman Catholic Church. As the Claretians made a power play for land and influence on Corisco, the preeminent indigenous face of the Reformed Presbyterian Church was eventually exiled to Fernando Po in a kind of religious *coup d'état* which sought to undermine Presbyterianism on the island.[36] In many respects,

29. Fegley, *Equatorial Guinea: An African Tragedy*, 29.

30. Mañe Ebo Asong, "Misioneros Protestantes Presbiterianos Norteamericanos," 15.

31. Liniger-Goumaz, *Historical Dictionary of Equatorial Guinea*, 79.

32. See Dy'Ikengue, *Costumbres Bengas y de Los Pueblos Vecinos*. In English: *Benga Customs and Neighboring Peoples*.

33. Rabat Makambo, "Estudio Preliminar," 5–6. Most notably, J'Ikĕngĕ participated in the establishment of churches in the villages of Mbòde (1865), Mbonda (1874), and Batanga (1879).

34. A'Bodjedi, "Los Pastores Presbiterianos Ndòwĕ," 75.

35. Ibid.

36. Liniger-Goumaz, *Historical Dictionary of Equatorial Guinea*, 79.

the early history of the Presbyterian Church, portrayed most strikingly through the complexity of J'Ikĕngĕ's ministerial career, illustrates many of the themes which continue to characterize the church up until this present day: the complicated and often uneasy relationship between evangelization and social activities, the hunger for assimilation into western society while remaining within the milieu of traditional culture, and the identity of a religious minority community vying for respect against the larger and politically dominant Roman Catholic Church.

Mission Stagnation and Inland Expansion: The Importance of Indigenous Agency in the Presbyterian Evangelization of the Fang

A full decade before the Treaty of Paris (1900) which would inaugurate a major Catholic takeover and irrevocably alter the religious landscape of Spanish Guinea in unparalleled ways, the Reformed Presbyterian Church in 1890 counted approximately 1,090 members in nine *parroquias* (parishes)[37] from Corisco in the south to the coastal village of Batanga in the north.[38] The slow but steady expansion of the Presbyterian faith had, as of yet, occurred only amongst the coastal Ndowean tribes. The Fang interior of Rio Muni remained for the church, as for commerce and "civilization," virtually untouched. (In fact, Spanish colonial exploration of Rio Muni did not occur until 1926.[39]) One of the side-effects of the monopoly on trade and commerce possessed by the Ndowe *playeros*, a stranglehold which even prevented European merchants from journeying into the interior of Central Africa, was that the ministry of the Reformed Presbyterian Church stagnated for nearly six decades on the coast after its initial establishment on Corisco.[40] Further complicating the Protestant evangelization of the Fang were the Claretians who took advantage of pro-Catholic Spanish political policy by making life increasingly difficult for Presbyterian missionaries. In 1924, Presbyterian missionaries decided to withdraw from the Catholic

---

37. A *parroquia* (parish) in the Reformed Presbyterian Church represents a major church center/congregation which often includes several smaller chapels in the surrounding areas.

38. Rabat Makambo, "Estudio Preliminar," 16.

39. Fegley, *Equatorial Guinea: An African Tragedy*, 20.

40. Nassau, *My Ogowe*, 13; A'Bodjedi, "Las Iglesias Presbiterianas Ndòwĕ," 60. The *playeros* is a Spanish term meaning "beach peoples" which refers to the linguistically-related cluster of ethnicities known as the Ndowe peoples who reside on the continental mainland region near the coast and the nearby islands.

hegemony of Spanish Guinea to the less hostile territory of present-day Cameroon.[41]

In spite of the mission's eventual reestablishment in Spanish Guinea in 1932, the bulk of the Protestant evangelization of the Fang stemmed not from white missionaries but from indigenous Christian migrants as familial networks and various historical events spilled into Spanish Guinea from Cameroon to the north.[42] A case in point was the World War I defeat of the Germans in Cameroon in 1916–17 whereby "a very unique refugee situation occurred" as a sizeable number of German troops sought refuge in Spanish Guinea.[43] In the estimation of historian Randall Fegley, these defeated German troops represented "probably the only large group of Europeans to ever become refugees on the African continent."[44] Accompanying this defeated German force were some 60,000 Cameroonian soldiers and villagers, including numerous Presbyterian Christians who, by staying in Rio Muni after the war, spread the Christian faith to their Fang brethren.[45] From 1919 to 1930, no less than thirty-four Presbyterian *capillas* (chapels) were established amongst the Fang, even though the first recorded visit to the Fang interior by a Presbyterian missionary seems to have occurred as late as 1924 by a single female on a short visit from her mission station in Cameroon.[46] The local church historian, Alberto Mañe Ebo Asong, is surely correct in recognizing that the chapels surrounding the villages of Niefang, Micomeseng, Ebibeyín, Mongomo, Evinayong, and Bata were established in the 1920s as Fang Christians—displaced because of the War or having otherwise migrated to Spanish Guinea—celebrated "church services and evangelized their neighbors without any [outside] help."[47] By 1936, as a result of indigenous evangelization, a growing number of Fang Christians could also be counted amongst the estimated 3,000 Presbyterians in Spanish Guinea, with many of these Presbyterian congregations predating the arrival of Roman Catholicism in those areas.[48]

---

41. Brown, *One Hundred Years*, 215.

42. Most notably, Joseph and Lois McNeill helped re-establish the mission in 1932, see "McNeill Family Papers, 1918–1970," *Presbyterian Historical Society*.

43. Fegley, *Equatorial Guinea: An African Tragedy*, 19.

44. Ibid., 19–20.

45. Mañe Ebo Asong, "Resumen Histórico," 31.

46. Ibid., 37. The female missionary is remembered locally only by her African name "Mfum Esep."

47. Ibid., 35.

48. Brown, *One Hundred Years*, 215. See also Pujadas, *La Iglesia en la Guinea Ecuatorial: Rio Muni*, 56–57, 313.

Political Ascendancy and Spiritual Decline: The Rise of National Identity and the Decline of the Church

In describing the Reformed Presbyterian Church of the 1940s and 1950s, one can still hear stories told excitedly, if not nostalgically, by elderly Presbyterian Christians of the evangelization and catechism of tiny rural villages, the burning of *biéri* (the craniums of deceased ancestors) to demonstrate Christian repentance, and vivid tales featuring the power of prayer. One Presbyterian pastor, Mbula Ngubi, who died in 1932, reportedly brought a dead goat back to life through the power of prayer![49] Yet stories featuring the spiritual vitality of the church slowly start to become distant historical memories at the dawn of the 1960s. With the neighboring nations of Cameroon and Gabon gaining their independence in 1960, leaders of the Reformed Presbyterian Church, frustrated with the snail's pace of Spanish intractability, increasingly became one of the principal agitating organs for Guinean independence.

In Spanish Guinea, the leaders of the Reformed Presbyterian Church enjoyed close links to the most notable advocates of national independency. Missionary Joseph McNeill's close relationship with Enrique Nvo—the most celebrated national hero of Equatorial Guinean independence—helped facilitate Nvo's communication with the United Nations pleading for independence, as letters sent by whites circumvented colonial censorship.[50] Rev. Samuel Zoe Obiang, a Fang of Cameroonian origin who often agitated for independence by sharing nationalistic stories of Cameroon's independence, enjoyed close ties with Acacio Mañe who (alongside Nvo) was proclaimed a national hero and martyr of independence.[51] During the run-up to independence, Rev. Gustavo Emvelo (the first General Secretary of the Presbyterian Church) accompanied Bonifacio Ondo Edu (President of the Autonomous Government who later lost to Macías on the second ballot in the national elections) to the United States as Spanish colonialism drew to a close.[52] After independence, Emvelo would don his ambassador's hat under Macías as the Guinean representative to the United Nations. The second General Secretary of the Presbyterian Church, Rev. Pablo Mba Nchama, likewise walked the halls of political power as an advisor to Macías and was

---

49. Mañe Ebo Asong, "Resumen Histórico," 21–22. Evidently the story is well-remembered locally as Mañe Ebo Asong cites an eyewitness testimony.

50. For a brief biography of Enrique Nvo, see Liniger-Goumaz, *Historical Dictionary of Equatorial Guinea*, 123.

51. For a brief biography of Acacio Mañe, see Ibid., 97.

52. For the political career of Bonifacio Ondo Edu, see Fegley, *Equatorial Guinea*, 45, 47–48, 55–58.

nominated to the *Consejo de la República* (the congressional senate).[53] Even the mother of Obiang Nguema, the current President of Equatorial Guinea, raised her son for a time within the cradle of the Presbyterian faith.

The story of mainline churches providing African societies with the nucleus of a literate elite who eventually turned the tables on their European colonial masters is woven into the fabric of African Christian historiography. Across Africa, the connection between mainline missionary churches and nation building is unmistakable. Yet without downplaying the fruits of self-governance and the formation of national identity, increased political participation by the church and her ecclesial officers in the emerging nation-states of Africa often required much sacrifice of time and energy. However, very seldom is the question raised by scholars: what exactly was sacrificed?[54] Precisely at the time missionary-founded churches were moving towards a post-missionary situation due to calls for a moratorium on western missionaries or because of unfavorable political climates (as was the case in Equatorial Guinea),[55] ecclesiastical leaders were often busy tackling political posts in the newly formed independent governments. In Equatorial Guinea, local stories abound of General Secretaries and Presbyterian pastors holding the reins of ecclesiastical power while dedicating vast amounts of time and energy to nation-building. Such involvement may have been one of the first steps toward decreased viability for the Reformed Presbyterian Church. While prayer and politics may coalesce into a *kairos* moment as was the case in South Africa, in Spanish Guinea, the precarious balance between political activism and spiritual piety seems to have led to slippage in core ecclesial practices beginning in the 1960s.

In many respects, John V. Taylor's study of the Anglican Church in Buganda is highly descriptive of the ecclesiastical processes which have likewise affected the Reformed Presbyterian Church of Equatorial Guinea since the formation of national identity.[56] Taylor described a church process which he labeled *disengagement*, an idea which is closely linked to the church's pursuit of *institutionalization*. According to Taylor, disengagement (or institutionalization) comprised four central components: paternalism, clericalism, centralization, and specialization. To various degrees, all four patterns can be observed in the Reformed Presbyterian Church of Equato-

---

53. Liniger-Goumaz, *Small Is Not Always Beautiful*, 23.

54. Though see Hastings, *A History of African Christianity, 1950–1975*, 262–63.

55. American Presbyterian missionaries left in 1968 shortly before independence; see "Reformed Presbyterian Church of Equatorial Guinea," *World Council of Churches*, para. 3.

56. Taylor, *Processes of Growth in an African Church*, esp. 12–15. See also Taylor, *The Growth of the Church in Buganda*, esp. 85–108.

rial Guinea. Today one of the central institutional concerns for Presbyterians, namely, an unlivable and extremely inadequate pastoral stipend, is arguably the direct by-product of missionary *paternalism*. As Rev. Manuel Owono Akara laments, "The missionaries taught us very poorly about tithes and offerings."[57] Despite the fact that the Reformed Presbyterian Church comprises the most predominantly middle-class membership of any Protestant denomination in the country, pastors receive only 80,000 Central African francs (less than $150) every three months. With virtually all Presbyterian pastors dedicating themselves to full-time secular jobs,[58] pastoral leadership is often very minimal during the week, and mid-week programs are in a state of steep decline.[59] The last fifty years has also witnessed a general trend towards *clericalism* and *centralization* within the church. As ordained pastors increasingly centralized power in their own hands in the post-missionary era, indigenous leadership was often left with a declining ability to maintain pastoral oversight over extensive territories amidst astonishing patterns of church growth. In Nigeria, for example, the Tiv Nongo u Kristu church (from a Dutch Reformed Mission) in 1967 maintained only thirty-seven indigenous pastors to contend with 1,367 places of worship, 11,829 communicants, and an average worshipping Sunday attendance of 162,884.[60] Even within the small geographical confines of Equatorial Guinea, the Reformed Presbyterian Church faced comparable challenges, albeit on a much smaller scale. In 1968, when Equatorial Guinea gained independence, the Reformed Presbyterian Church consisted of fourteen parishes and fifty chapels in Rio Muni which received oversight from only five ministers; these ministers were aided, however, by fifty catechists and evangelists.[61] Yet as missionary oversight rescinded and pastoral clericalism ascended, the importance of local catechists and evangelists—the very instruments historically responsible for strengthening the vitality of the church at the grassroots—increasingly became marginalized within the Reformed Presbyterian Church structure. As catechists and evangelists eventually became overshadowed by ordained pastors, practices such as prayer and Bible study—precisely the hallmarks which characterize the rise of the new Pentecostal churches—suffered

---

57. Interview, Manuel Owono Akara, October 17, 2011.

58. By contrast, several local Pentecostal denominations, whose membership is considerably more poverty-stricken, ensure that their pastors work full-time.

59. Interview, Manuel Nzôh Asumu, General Secretary of the Reformed Presbyterian Church, October 24, 2011; Interview, Manuel Owono Akara, October 17, 2011.

60. Hastings, *A History of African Christianity, 1950–1975*, 270, 166–67.

61. Liniger-Goumaz, *Historical Dictionary of Equatorial Guinea*, 104.

debilitating losses of participation and waning enthusiasm.[62] With pastoral leadership huddled in the city of Bata forced to earn a living wage, the rural parishes of today suffer from infrequent pastoral visits.[63] In this situation, institutional church maintenance often takes precedence over evangelistic expansion.

The fourth component leading to the decreased vitality of the Anglican Church in Buganda within Taylor's study was a process whereby the *specialization* of missionaries—and their corresponding external projects—became increasingly central in the life of the church. In making way for indigenous leadership, Taylor argues, the withdrawal of western missionaries from church posts did not necessarily coincide with a decreasing level of missionary influence over the church since their withdrawal also tended to foster non-ecclesial projects which they often controlled from higher positions of leadership within the missionary hierarchy.[64] In Equatorial Guinea, this process was abetted through the harassment of institutionalized Christianity during the Macías regime which forced the indigenous Presbyterian leadership to forge a centralized ecumenical partnership with the Methodist and *Cruzada* churches in an effort to maintain a unified face for Protestant Christianity.[65] Post-Macías, this ecumenical partnership increasingly focused on the cultivation of international contacts through the World Council of Churches (WCC) in an effort to secure foreign funds for specialized, non-church-related activities.[66] During the 1980s, this ecumenical partnership received external aid from places like Holland, Norway, Germany, and Switzerland for projects as diverse as latrines, preventative medicine, and the cultivation of rice.[67] Working in tandem with these concerns for institu-

---

62. Interview, Alberto Mañe Ebo Asong, October 14, 2011.

63. Interview, Manuel Nzôh Asumu, General Secretary of the Reformed Presbyterian Church, October 24, 2011.

64. Taylor, *The Growth of the Church in Buganda*, 85–105.

65. Interview, Manuel Nzôh Asumu, General Secretary of the Reformed Presbyterian Church, October 24, 2011; Interview, Alberto Mañe Ebo Asong, October 14, 2011.

66. Interview, Alberto Mañe Ebo Asong, October 14, 2011; Interview, Manuel Nzôh Asumu, General Secretary of the Reformed Presbyterian Church, October 24, 2011. The name of the partnership has changed names several times throughout its existence. According to local Presbyterian Church historian Mañe Ebo Asong, the partnership was initially formed in 1973 and known as *Iglesia Reformada de Guinea Ecuatorial* (IRGE), followed by *IRGE-Union* in 1980, and finally as *Consejo de Iglesias Evangélicas de Guinea Ecuatorial* (CIEGE) in 1995.

67. In many respects, these were essentially Presbyterian projects due to their numerical strength relative to the Methodists and *Cruzada* churches. Interview, Alberto Mañe Ebo Asong, October 14, 2011; Interview, Manuel Nzôh Asumu, General Secretary of the Reformed Presbyterian Church, October 24, 2011.

tionalization already enumerated, Paul Gifford's argument that the western donor industry has often proven a diversion from the priorities of prayer, Bible study, and evangelism seems particularly descriptive of the Reformed Presbyterian Church. Gifford writes:

> An enormous amount of Christian involvement is not obviously about relating to the divine; it is most obviously about access to Western resources and the whole range of things this brings: education; employment; modernization and global opportunities . . . the point is that as Africa becomes increasingly marginalized, these aid flows and what they involve become increasingly significant for, even constitutive of, parts of mainline Christianity.[68]

For instance, a sister Presbyterian denomination, the Evangelical Presbyterian Church of Ghana, established a partnership in 2011 with the Alliance of Religions and Conservation (ARC), a secular group based in England, pledging to "integrate the theme of climate change into worship, liturgy, preaching and into the curricula of the Church's theological institutions"[69] while also agreeing to train "around 200 firefighter volunteers" and "plant 200,000 seedlings in degraded areas and plant 100,000 seedlings in community woodlots."[70] A key point made by Taylor[71] and resurrected more forcefully by Gifford[72] is that although the missionary apparatus withdrew to make way for autonomous African leadership, specialized (non-ecclesial) western projects such as building latrines or training fire fighters often provided an enormous obstacle to, if not a complete diversion from, the more traditional pastoral responsibilities of local African leaders. In the Reformed Presbyterian Church, while the spiritual decline begun in the 1960s has hardly been uniform and might be described by "institutional growth" as much as "spiritual decline," the cumulative effect of this decline spanning several decades has been severe.

---

68. Gifford, "African Christianity and the Eclipse of the Afterlife," 420.

69. "Evangelical Presbyterian Church of Ghana," *ARC: Alliance of Religions and Conservation*, 2.

70. Ibid., 3.

71. Taylor, *The Growth of the Church in Buganda*, 85–105.

72. Gifford, *African Christianity: Its Public Role*, 44–47, 308–25.

The Idiom of the Present Crisis: Between a Glorious Past and a Troubling Future

"The crisis of the church is a moral crisis."
—Rev. Manuel Awono Akara, Sunday October 2, 2011 from the pulpit of the largest Reformed Presbyterian Church in Bata

Since the 2010 National Synod, the most common word circulating today amongst the leadership and laity of the Reformed Presbyterian Church is the word "crisis." Allegations of the moral lapses of pastors, once well-kept church secrets, are increasingly talked about openly and honestly. Charges of adultery and alcoholism within the pastoral fraternity abound and continue to plague the testimony of the church both internally and locally amongst other Christian groups. Three pastors have recently died at *curanderías* (the traditional place of healing), events which are viewed by faithful members as capitulations to Fang traditional practices. The embezzlement of church funds, channeled through the WCC, by selected national church leaders in the past is also frankly acknowledged by many church members. At one sparsely attended meeting convened to dialogue about the self-diagnosed crisis, one elderly pastor evoked the provocative idea of Israel's *remnant* to describe faithful Presbyterians in the midst of the present decline.

Further complicating the moral crisis of the church is a lingering uncertainty of how to reach the next generation within a fast-changing society. Simply put, the church is ageing. On a typical Sunday, adults between the ages of 50–70 lead the prayers, collect the offering, and give the announcements. Ecclesial processes typically exclude the younger generation, which is largely confined to singing in the church choir. Though a few younger people have begun attending the newer Pentecostal churches, many have apparently become so disenfranchised with the church that they have stopped church attendance altogether. A succinct description of the crisis may be articulated like this: the Reformed Presbyterian Church is most *marginal* to precisely those questions and concerns that are most *central* to indigenous religiosity. Sickness, suffering, and the nature of evil, the quintessential concerns which invigorate Fang religiosity, are left largely unaddressed by the Presbyterian hierarchy, and no definitive guidance for coping with the existential fears and anxieties of witchcraft is given to ordinary Presbyterian members.

Perhaps the most surprising element in the long developing crisis within the Reformed Presbyterian Church has been the remarkable absence of revitalization as evidenced by the lack of significant prayer groups, holiness preachers, or pietistic-separatist prophets calling for a more radical discipleship. As a whole, the church has managed to preserve her unity even amidst the spiritual decline. The fact that the idiom of the present crisis is often attributed to the low salaries of an educated pastoral elite or voiced as disappointment that the church has been "orphaned" by western church sponsors suggests that the general contours of the present crisis may linger for some time. The African church historian, Adrian Hastings, reflecting in 1979 on the turmoil of decolonization in the years 1950–75, offered his own explanation for the rise of the new independent churches:

> No church can wholly escape a political dimension to its behaviour but for few churches are politics a primary concern. It is far more in terms of prayer that they understand themselves, hold the loyalty of their members and discover a future laced with hope. . . . It is impossible to understand very much about churches without taking very seriously indeed a sociology of prayer, and it could be argued that it was precisely because the mission-church leadership tended to get away from this central axis of ecclesial meaning, preoccupied with school management, scientific medicine, radio stations and printing presses that the independent churches were able time and again to steal their clothes and grow very effectively as just this and little else: churches of prayer.[73]

While revitalizing ecclesial practices such as Bible study and prayer were buried underneath a myriad of institutionalizing concerns within the Reformed Presbyterian Church, new Pentecostal churches burst onto the ecclesial landscape in Equatorial Guinea with a steady diet of prayer, aggressive evangelism (conducted by and for the young people), and dynamic healing and deliverance ministries seeking to address people's fears and anxieties of witchcraft.

Indigenous Guinean Pentecostalism I: *Gozo de la Salvación* (Joy of My Salvation)

Growth and Conflict: The conversion of Damián Ángel Asumu and Joy of My Salvation's Holiness Ethos

Compared to other African countries such as Nigeria, Ghana, or Kenya where indigenous Pentecostal churches were already blossoming into pioneers of ecclesial innovation in the 1980s and becoming the newest

---

73. Hastings, *A History of African Christianity, 1950–1975*, 265.

ecclesial powerhouses within African Christianity as growth accelerated in the 1990s,[74] the Pentecostal movement in Equatorial Guinea arrived relatively late upon the scene.[75] Yet since the beginning of the twenty-first century, Pentecostal churches in Equatorial Guinea have multiplied, divided, evangelized, planted new churches (and divided again) in a consistent and steady fashion. As Harvey Cox observed, "The most amazing thing about the runaway divisiveness in the young Pentecostal movement is that while the spats and squabbles continued, so did its spread. The more the Pentecostals fought, the more they multiplied. One of the most astonishing features of the movement is that it seems to thrive not only on opposition (which many religious movements have), but also on division. This is another reason for its growth."[76] This is particularly *apropos* with respect to the first generation of Guinean Pentecostals who have experienced intensified growth, alongside the pains of schism, during the past fifteen years.

Arguably the fastest growing indigenous Pentecostal church in the country is *Gozo de la Salvación* (hereafter Joy of My Salvation). The early history of Joy of My Salvation hinges on two significant events which continue to impinge upon the church's ethos up until the present day: the conversion of the church's charismatic founder and a decisive church-split based upon holiness principles. The story of Joy of My Salvation begins with the 1989 conversion of the church's founder, Damián Ángel Asumu, who

---

74. See Kalu, *African Pentecostalism*, 103–46; Anderson, *African Reformation*, 172–82. Scholars have referred to the rise of these pneumatologically-oriented churches with various terms. In our study, we will refer to these churches as "indigenous Pentecostal churches." By "indigenous," we mean to distinguish these Pentecostal churches from the more "classical" expressions of Pentecostalism, such as the Assemblies of God (*Asambleas de Dios de Guinea Ecuatorial*) which originated in the West but without any polemical intent implied about the indigenous nature of missionary-founded Pentecostalism. Pentecostal, rather than the adjectival term charismatic, is also the term of self-designation locally.

75. As late as 1996, a local study conducted by Pioneer Bible Translators (later *Asociación Cristiana de Traducciones Bíblicas*) indicated that only ten non-Catholic churches were found in the entire city of Bata. Despite the fact that five of those ten churches self-identified as Pentecostal, the Pentecostal movement accounted for a mere 900 total church members in 1996 on the entire continental mainland of Equatorial Guinea. Yet since the turn of the twenty-first century, Pentecostal growth has been remarkable. Today, it is not difficult to find six to eight Pentecostal churches surrounding the lone Catholic neighborhood church in numerous, if not most, neighborhoods in the cities of Malabo and Bata. This dynamic suggests that actual church attendance amongst Pentecostal believers in Malabo and Bata may rival, if not surpass, Catholic church attendance—despite studies of religious adherence which suggest Equatorial Guinea is overwhelmingly (80–90 percent) a Catholic country. See Pierce, et al., "Findings of Church Language Use," 3.

76. Cox, *Fire from Heaven*, 77.

made a decisive break from his Catholic upbringing when he "accepted Christ" in *Iglesia Paloma* (Dove Church). Twenty-five years later, Asumu is now one of the most respected, charismatic, and sought-after Pentecostal leaders in Equatorial Guinea. Yet the beginnings of Joy of My Salvation were initially mired in controversy. Due to rumors and accusations centering upon the sexual purity (accusations of adultery) and the moral integrity (consuming alcoholic beverages) of the *Paloma* leadership, Asumu made the decision to leave *Iglesia Paloma* in 1994 to establish his own prayer and Bible study group. Even though two decades have passed, the significance of Asumu's "founding action," made ostensibly to preserve the holiness and purity of the church, is seldom lost on the present-day leadership within Joy of My Salvation.[77] Holiness principles, defined by strict sexual and moral purity—no fornication, no drinking—are enforced by rigorous church discipline. The argument that "the centrality of the founding story" for African Indigenous Churches (AICs) often continues to influence the "spiritual and moral orientation" of the church applies equally well here.[78] In other words, the church was birthed out of a desire to experience Christianity based on a lifestyle of holiness, and on January 1, 1995, Joy of My Salvation celebrated its first church service as approximately twenty-five people met in a restored colonial cocoa warehouse in the city of Bata.

The ability of African Pentecostalism to thrive and network from humble beginnings is illustrated remarkably well by Joy of My Salvation. In 1995, Asumu was ordained as the sole pastor of Joy of My Salvation by a now unknown Congolese pastor who was (from an insider's perspective) providentially passing through Bata to attend Archbishop Benson Idahosa's All Nations for Christ Bible Institute in Nigeria.[79] Turning down a promising medical scholarship to Switzerland, Asumu embarked upon several campaign-style crusades which quickly led to the formation of new churches. The dual commitments to evangelism and deliverance ministry produced a steady pattern of church growth. By 1997, Joy of My Salvation officially joined the 400,000 member Wesleyan Church headquartered in Fishers, Indiana (USA) after a visiting evangelist helped Asumu make the first international contacts for the young church.[80] The appeal of the Wesleyan holiness emphasis, together with the nature of the cooperation

---

77. As one prominent pastor succinctly stated, "Those who wanted to preserve the holiness left." Interview, Basilio Oyono, October 12, 2011.

78. Adogame and Jafta, "Zionists, Aladura, and Roho," 278–79.

79. Cephas Omenyo has analyzed the spread and diffusion of African Pentecostalism via sociology's "diffusion of innovation theory"; see Omenyo, "William Seymour and African Pentecostal Historiography," esp. 253–56.

80. See "The Wesleyan Church."

(hands-off but potentially helpful), has produced a limited partnership for Joy of My Salvation whose most visible fruits have been the recent overseas trips to Latin America (Costa Rica, Columbia, Puerto Rico, Brazil) and Spanish-speaking areas of the United States (Texas, Arizona, Florida, California) for the church's charismatic leader. In fact, during a visit to Costa Rica in 2006, Asumu was "episcopized" as "Superintendent" by the Wesleyan hierarchy.

Holistic Ministry: Deliverance, Conversion, and Healing

While Joy of My Salvation's holiness ethos implies a certain relationship to culture, the prominent place deliverance ministry occupies within the life of the church communicates the dynamic far more clearly. Deliverance is based upon the belief that demonic powers which are brought about predominantly by witchcraft, ancestral curses, and participation in traditional or modern occult activities (though any sin potentially provides a doorway for the demonic) are often responsible for sickness and suffering in life and must be driven out "in the name of Jesus" by Spirit-filled prayers. These deliverance prayers are often accompanied by the "laying on of hands" by a spiritually anointed "Man of God" and the use of the "oil of anointing."[81] In Equatorial Guinea, Pentecostals primarily practice deliverance as a way of healing *evus*-related sicknesses (*akwann mbwo*), though some churches also emphasize deliverance prayers in order to achieve financial prosperity, advancement, and success in life. Birgit Meyer interprets the deliverance phenomenon in African Pentecostalism as a reaction to modernity whereby Africans are given an opportunity to experience traditional forms of possession but from a ritualized Christian perspective.[82] For Meyer, deliverance from demonic powers and the image of the Devil is primarily about providing modern Christians with the opportunity to sever "all previous ties with old and new spiritual entities, as well as from the social relations they imply."[83] Paul Gifford believes that the rise of deliverance ministries, at least in Ghana, can be explained as a side-effect of the unrealized expectations and promises created by the prosperity gospel, a kind of negative counterbalance to the positivity of the "name it, claim it" or "word of faith"

---

81. For the theology and practice of anointing with oil in African Pentecostalism, see Asamoah-Gyadu, *Contemporary Pentecostal Christianity*, 121–43.

82. Meyer, *Translating the Devil: Religion and Modernity*, 171–72.

83. Ibid., 171.

movement.[84] Whatever else they may be, deliverance ministries in Equatorial Guinea are a front door evangelistic tool to funnel people into Pentecostal churches. Deliverance ministries have played a critical role in spurring the lion's share of church growth for Guinean Pentecostalism in general and Joy of My Salvation in particular.[85]

For Pentecostals at Joy of My Salvation, a symbiotic relationship exists between deliverance and conversion. Theologically, the healing ministry of deliverance can be likened to an evangelistic seed which ideally germinates into conversion. In the words of Asumu, if only a demon is cast out during deliverance, "we haven't done a big thing."[86] That is, though the *seed* of deliverance ministries may not always yield the *fruit* of conversion, *demonic expulsion is almost always regarded as a necessary ingredient for conversion to take place in Fang Pentecostalism*. Demonic expulsion anticipates conversion proleptically as the fulfillment of "pneumatological soteriology."[87] In the construction of soteriology, Fang Pentecostals generally tend to rearrange the two-fold conversion process of classical Pentecostalism (being "born again" and speaking in tongues) into a two-stage process which distinguishes "demonic expulsion" from "Holy Spirit filling" by recognizing that demonic expulsion does not simultaneously, or automatically, imply pneumatological conversion.[88] (Incidentally, this is part of the reason why many Pentecostals often complain of people in the broader society utilizing or leveraging the church for health and well-being while neglecting the salvific purposes of God, despite rather ironically linking their ecclesiology to practices which promote precisely this tendency.) This two-stage conversion process of *demonic expulsion* and *Holy Spirit filling* is rooted in an extremely polemical stance towards both Fang indigenous culture and the Roman Catholic Church. Interestingly, two prominent Joy of My Salvation pastors independently articulated their belief that 90 to 95 percent of the people in Equatorial Guinea "have demons."[89] For Joy of My Salvation, being a Christian entails a radical departure from the initiations, curses,

---

84. Gifford, *African Christianity*, 105.

85. See also Anderson, "Deliverance and Exorcism in Majority World Pentecostalism," 101.

86. Interview, Damián Ángel Asumu, October 27, 2011.

87. Anderson, *African Reformation*, 233.

88. Compared with classic western Pentecostals, speaking in tongues or *glossolalia* is not a predominant practice for Guinean Pentecostals.

89. Interview, Basilio Oyono, October 12, 2011; Interview, Damian Ángel Asumu, October 27, 2011. Oyono gave percentages of people who "have demons" at 90 to 95 percent while Asumu placed the number at 95 percent. Both figures were unsolicited by the author.

fetishes, and alleged witchcraft—the demonic pacts—of Fang culture while simultaneously requiring a decisive breaking of one's ties with the Roman Catholic Church. In light of this severe demonization of virtually the entire Catholic populace, Ogbu Kalu's axiom that "Pentecostals allege that it is easier for a camel to go through the eye of a needle than for a Roman Catholic to be born again" perhaps may be viewed as reaching its zenith in Equatorial Guinea.[90]

On the morning of November 7, 2011, about thirty-five people arrived at Asumu's mid-week deliverance session. An important, and often overlooked, aspect of "prayer and deliverance" within African Pentecostalism is the holistic counseling provided, in the case of Joy of My Salvation, by theologically trained pastors. Asumu's availability for the surrounding community in providing an emotional and psychological outlet for the disadvantaged poor who could otherwise ill-afford western-style clinically-based counseling is undoubtedly part of the attraction. Conflict disputes, bereavement counseling, marriage therapy, parental guidance, and sage advice regarding the best ways to navigate the complexities of the modern medical landscape are all addressed during one-on-one counseling sessions before the prayers begin. After attending to the presenting issues, Asumu calls the group together to commence the prayer time with a short exhortation based on Psalm 23. Combining his disarming sense of humor with penetrating biblical vignettes, Asumu's stories often pack a punch. During the exhortation, Asumu contrasts the perils of Fang traditional practices with the liberating value of Christian prayers. A story is told of a man from the village of Ebebiyín who spent the entire night, under the direction of a traditional healer, in a cemetery buried up to his neck in dirt. Asumu recalls that the traditional healer eventually solicited payment from the poor man—building to the climactic moment—by requesting a human hand! To remedy such foolish devilry, the Superintendent reads Psalm 23: "You prepare a table before me in the presence of my enemies." The inference is abundantly clear: "my enemies" are Fang indigenous sources of spiritual power, their chief architect is the Devil, and bizarre forms of suffering inevitably result from participation in these devilish rituals. In contrast, prayers of deliverance made *voz en cuello* ("at the top of your lungs") offer true hope and relief: "You can leave from this place with your problem resolved."[91] After the short exhortation, worship songs such as "There is Great Power in the Name of Jesus" and "The Spirit of God is Here" accompany fervent

---

90. Kalu, *African Pentecostalism*, 66.

91. Damian Ángel Asumu, "Joy of My Salvation," Bisa Church of Bata, November 7, 2011.

group prayer led by the Superintendent. Applying the "oil of anointing" liberally, Asumu casts out demons "in the name of Jesus" through the "laying on of hands." During the prayers, one woman pounds her chest defiantly (the demon's way of indicating "this is my property"[92]), others violently convulse, nine women lie writhing on the floor, and three women physically vomit. In Fang Pentecostalism, physical "manifestations," often quite violent by nature, are typical reactions to the spiritual power of prayer. Multiple Joy of My Salvation pastors indicated that vomiting, urinating, defecating, or even women bleeding from the uterus may occur during deliverance prayers as demons try to exit through bodily orifices.[93] Thus, mops to clean up the messes are always kept close at hand. Before closing the prayer time, Asumu offers some final advice: "If you are coming for prayer in the church and have amulets in your house, these two things are incompatible. If you have something in your house which you are afraid of, let us know and we'll deal with it. Or, better yet, burn it."[94]

In Equatorial Guinea, Pentecostal churches are generally considered part of the medical landscape in dealing with sicknesses alongside Fang *curanderías*, western-style hospitals, and the recently arrived Chinese pharmacies. In other words, Pentecostal churches are one of the four major centers for coping with sickness in the country. For deliverance ministry practitioners like Asumu, distinguishing between witchcraft-related sicknesses (*akwann mbwo*, "witchcraft sicknesses" or *akwann Fang*, "Fang sicknesses") and naturally occurring sicknesses (*akwann ntangan*, "sicknesses of the white man") is critically important. While all who attend deliverance services at Joy of My Salvation receive prayers for divine intervention, special attention is typically given to those people believed to be suffering from *mbwo* (witchcraft). Demonic activity is thought to parade in the guise of witchcraft. Witchcraft and demonology, in the words of Anderson, "are now virtually interchangeable and synonymous terms in African Pentecostalism."[95] The leader of the largest Pentecostal denomination in Ghana, Opoku Onyinah, has coined the term "witchdemonology" to depict the way demonic influences and Akan witchcraft beliefs are dynamically synthesized in his own Church of Pentecost.[96] Much of the same dynamic is

92. Interview, Basilio Oyono, October 12, 2011.

93. See also Gifford, *African Christianity*, 98; Allan Anderson, "Exorcism and Conversion to African Pentecostalism," 129; Asamoah-Gyadu, *African Charismatics*, 187.

94. Damian Ángel Asumu, "Joy of My Salvation," Bisa Church of Bata, November 7, 2011.

95. Anderson, "Exorcism and Conversion to African Pentecostalism," 121.

96. Onyinah, "Akan Witchcraft and the Concept of Exorcism in the Church of

witnessed amongst Pentecostals in Equatorial Guinea. At Joy of My Salvation, the dramatic physical reactions to deliverance prayers (most typically vomiting) can be viewed as strictly corresponding to Fang witchcraft initiations which are commonly thought to occur through the simple consumption of food or drink (see figure 3.2).

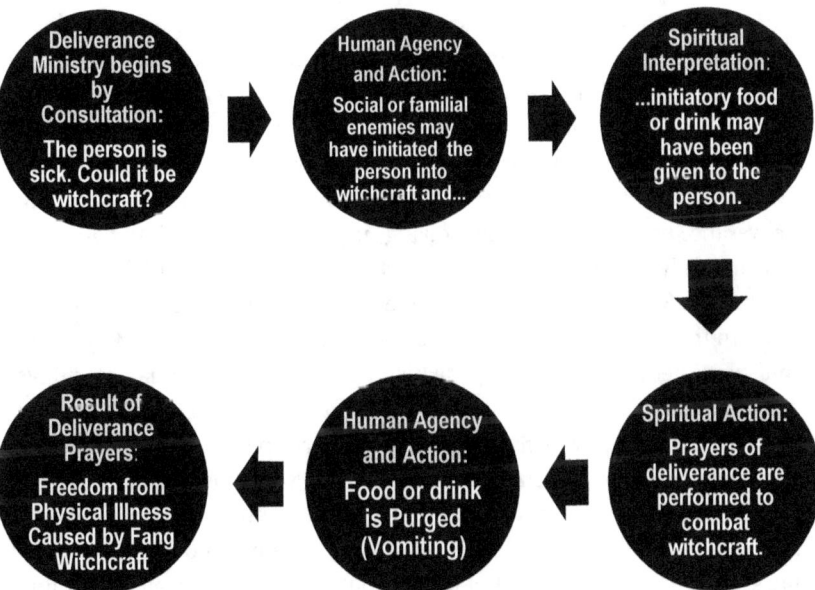

Figure 3.2: Pentecostal Prayers of Deliverance as a Means of Breaking the Cycle of Fang Witchcraft

When the demonic expulsion occurs, a physical purge frequently accompanies these deliverance prayers because the underlying cause of witchcraft—which was initiated through food or drink—has to be "driven out" before healing can occur. In other words, since demonic possession/oppression manifests itself *physically* in the form of sicknesses, spiritual deliverance is also experienced *physically* as prayers seek to reverse the effects of *mbwo*. Kalu's recognition that "Christianity in Africa has absorbed the *old goals* of primal religion while reordering the worldview and introducing *new*

Pentecost," 231–38; Onyinah, "Deliverance as a Way of Confronting Witchcraft in Modern Africa," 125.

symbols and sources" should not be construed as to overlook the fact that many of the *old* symbols and sources remain key elements in Pentecostal cosmologies in general and Fang deliverance ministries in particular.[97] For instance, two of the most indispensable elements required for successful treatment at Fang *curanderías*—confession (of the witchcraft) and fasting—are also believed to be imperative for healing in Fang deliverance ministries.[98] While new Christian symbols such as the Bible, Satan, and the Holy Spirit significantly expand the worldview of local Pentecostals, it is also the case that traditional conceptions of healing have been thoroughly integrated into deliverance practices through Christian inculturation.

At Joy of My Salvation, deliverance ministries are a preeminent ecclesial praxis which most poignantly illustrates the boundary between the Christian faith and Fang witchcraft that so intrigues and fascinates local Pentecostals. The degree to which pastoral ministry is founded upon the bedrock of deliverance ministry can scarcely be over-emphasized. Basilio Oyono, who represents a key voice in the denomination, hosts deliverance ministry services on Monday and Tuesday mornings in the church. From Wednesday to Friday, the church functions much like a prayer camp with deliverance participants fasting, praying, and sleeping in the church in order to come fully prepared for the special deliverance service on Friday night. Though the Sunday morning worship service still constitutes the high-water mark in the life of the church, the pastor's schedule largely revolves around mid-week deliverance ministries which begin early on Monday mornings and culminate late on Friday night. On October 21, 2011, after an hour of holistic counseling with approximately thirty people, Oyono initiated the prayer time by focusing on Felipe, a man who was suspected of being initiated into witchcraft by alcoholic drink. Within moments of being anointed with oil, Felipe was on the ground writhing and grunting like a pig as Oyono shouted: "Spirit of the pig, out, out, out! If you ate something or drank something [connected to Fang witchcraft initiation], come out by vomits! Vomit everything!"[99] The next case requiring Oyono's attention was a middle-aged woman who had danced in Bwiti rituals.[100] Indicating that demonic possession in the woman's spinal column sought to paralyze her,

---

97. Kalu, *African Pentecostalism*, 74, italics added.

98. The Spanish term *curandería* refers to the place where the traditional healer performs his or her healing. Many deliverance practitioners in Joy of My Salvation hold that, in the absence of confession, deliverance prayers will be ineffective since the person has given a legal or covenantal right to the demon to possess or oppress; see also Asamoah-Gyadu, *African Charismatics*, 182; Kalu, *African Pentecostalism*, 80–82.

99. Basilio Oyono, Joy of My Salvation, Ngolo Church in Bata, October 24, 2011.

100. For the most accomplished scholarly work on Bwiti, see Fernandez, *Bwiti*.

Oyono rebuked Satan directly: "You can't hide from God. Satan, now you are in the stomach. You've moved from the spine to the stomach, but you can't hide from God. Get out! In the name of Jesus!"[101] The next morning, the vast majority of the participants returned, and Oyono commenced the session on October 22, 2011 by reading Jeremiah 17:5–8 which he summarized: "Cursed is the one who trusts in *curanderos* [traditional healers], but blessed is the man who trusts in Jehovah."[102] The exhortation consisted of miraculous testimonies to engender hope ("I have personally seen people healed of cancer and AIDS!") and centered primarily on a scathing polemic against *curanderos*: traditional healers destroy families, traditional healers reduce people to servitude ("you are practically a slave"), and traditional healers leave people in financial ruin ("you are left with neither mattresses nor pots"—reflecting typical bartered commodities to pay for *curandero* services).[103] "God is not a thief," Oyono concludes, "The Devil, the *curandero* is the thief. Satan makes you suffer until your last day and then he puts you into hell."[104] As with much of African Pentecostalism, the Devil is understood to be embodied in traditional religious rituals as well as in more modernizing forms of witchcraft. Deliverance "in the name of Jesus" is believed to offer solutions to sicknesses and sufferings rooted in the local religio-cultural universe. At Joy of My Salvation, pastoral ministry entails constant attention to the Devil, engaging in frequent polemics against the *ngangan*, and operating with authoritative prayer against the demonic. These discourses and practices centering upon a robust interconnection between evil, suffering, and the Devil, as we shall see, significantly impinge upon the task of hermeneutical reflection on the book of Job.

Situating Joy of My Salvation within Guinean Protestant Christianity

Joy of My Salvation is unmistakably proud of its Pentecostal roots and practices. Nonetheless, the church belongs to the Federation of Evangelical and Pentecostal Churches of Equatorial Guinea[105] which encompasses several of the newer missionary-founded evangelical churches and the more "moder-

---

101. Basilio Oyono, Joy of My Salvation, Ngolo Church in Bata, October 24, 2011.

102. Basilio Oyono, Joy of My Salvation, Ngolo Church in Bata, October 25, 2011. *Curandero* is the Spanish term for the traditional healer (*ngangan* in the Fang language).

103. Ibid.

104. Ibid.

105. In Spanish: *Federación de Iglesias Evangélicas y Pentecostales de Guinea Ecuatorial*.

ate" wing (as the President of the *Federación* expressed it) of Guinean Pentecostalism.[106] By identifying with this local coalition of evangelicals and Pentecostals, the leadership of Joy of My Salvation primarily endeavors to distance itself from the preaching of the so-called prosperity gospel in local Pentecostal churches whose invited international conference speakers have caused quite a scandal and point of contention within the Pentecostal community.

Indigenous Guinean Pentecostalism II: *Asamblea del Espíritu Santo* (Assembly of the Holy Spirit)

The Apostolic Couple and the Birth of Indigenous Pentecostalism in Equatorial Guinea

A history of Protestant Christianity in Equatorial Guinea would not be complete without a description of *Iglesia Betania* (Bethany Church), the first Pentecostal church which burst significantly onto the Guinean ecclesial landscape. For the sake of clarity, the history of Assembly of the Holy Spirit, the third church of this study, was birthed out of a cantankerous division from *Betanía*. Assembly of the Holy Spirit's history thus properly begins with the early years of *Betanía*.

In similar fashion to the Presbyterian faith which seeped southward amongst the Fang from their northern Presbyterian counterparts in Cameroon, the Pentecostal gospel arrived in Equatorial Guinea as the result of indigenous African agency amidst the global forces of migration, this time coming northward from the Libreville region of Gabon. After experiencing a heavenly vision and deliverance from a series of afflictions in *Eglise Bethany* in Libreville, Maria Dolores Nchama, a charismatic nineteen-year old young woman, established *Betania* in 1988 in the village of Evinayong (central Rio Muni) as she returned to her country of birth.[107] According to Nchama, miraculous results quickly ensued, including sight for the blind, healing of the lame, deliverance from witchcraft, and numerous baptisms.

---

106. The nomenclature of "moderate Pentecostalism "and "extreme Pentecostalism" was articulated by the then-president of the *Federación de Iglesias Evangélicas y Pentecostales de Guinea Ecuatorial* in 2011; Interview, Modesto Endo Ongonga, November 20, 2011.

107. From personal accounts in Equatorial Guinea, *Eglise Bethany* seems to have begun as a prayer movement amongst Gabonese youth from *Eglise Evangelique du Gabon* (founded by North American Presbyterians but later partnering with the Paris Missionary Society) which may have also attracted youth from *Eglise de l'Alliance Chretienne due Gabon* (founded by the Christian Missionary Alliance).

After receiving a vision, Nchama began using holy water with deliverance prayers since "evil spirits couldn't withstand even a drop of holy water."[108] Within the rural Catholic confines of Equatorial Guinea, Nchama's healing ministry—including the baptism of former Catholics—became a lightning rod of controversy which eventually landed her a night in jail when she adamantly refused, before a Catholic priest, to terminate her new ministry. Undeterred, but sensing a new beginning for the ministry, Nchama moved to Bata where she eventually evangelized her future husband, Agustín Edu Esono. "After eleven years in the *curanderías*," Esono recalled, "the Lord healed me in a single day."[109] A few years after his healing and conversion, Esono was ordained a pastor of *Betania* by Gabonese leaders in 1993, graduated from a Pentecostal Bible School in 1999, and was later bestowed the title of Apostle by two Congolese visitors in 2003. Today, numerous Guinean Pentecostal churches trace their lineage to *Betanía* due to the church's fissiparous nature, and many Pentecostals identify Nchama as the "founding mother" of Guinean Pentecostalism. Coinciding with Esono's appointment to the apostleship, *Betanía* suffered an internal feud amongst upper level leadership which eventually saw Gabonese leaders from *Eglise Bethany* side against Esono-Nchama. In the division, Assembly of the Holy Spirit was born with Esono-Nchama firmly occupying the leadership helm of the new church while also retaining the original *Betanía* building, undoubtedly the most recognizable face, in terms of physical locale, of the nascent Pentecostal movement in the country. Today the Assembly of the Holy Spirit is one of the largest indigenous Pentecostal churches in Equatorial Guinea with numerous congregations within the continental mainland region of the country.

Francophone "Men of God": Between External African Agency and Indigenous Autonomy

One of the most obvious elements of Assembly of the Holy Spirit is the Cameroonian bishops, Ivorian Coast prophets, Gabonese apostles, and Congolese preachers from Francophone Africa who have become increasingly ubiquitous in the life of the church for the past several years. To some degree, this development within the church corresponds to the political life of the nation as visitors have flocked to Equatorial Guinea to celebrate some of Africa's most significant sporting and political events, including the 2012

---

108. Interview, Maria Dolores Nchama, May 18, 2012. The use of holy water represented a departure from the ecclesial practice of *Eglise Bethany*.

109. Interview, Agustín Edu Esono, May 18, 2012.

and 2015 African Cup of Nations (football) and the 2011 African Union Summit. Today it is quite common for these Francophone spiritual "Men of God" to dominate church pulpits for weeks at a time while also being exclusively featured for week-long "prophetic seminars." As these Francophone leaders occupy local pulpits and receive top billing at frequently held local conferences, the question naturally arises: to what degree has Fang or Guinean autonomy within the church been compromised or subverted to external influences?

In his landmark study *African Christianity: Its Public Role*, Paul Gifford sought to problematize the assumption that the indigenization or Africanization of the continent's churches—rhetoric which generally coincided with the period of decolonization of the 1950s and 1960s—still represents an accurate portrayal of African Christianity today in light of the modernizing forces of globalization. Gifford writes: "For all the talk within African church circles of localisation, inculturation, Africanisation or indigenisation, external links have become more important than ever."[110] For Gifford, the sociopolitical and economic collapse generally characterizing African nations in the 1980s and 1990s was instrumental in accelerating the growth of external ecclesial networks as life became increasingly unbearable and poverty-ridden for the majority of Africans.[111] In such a milieu, so the narrative goes, African churches have eagerly turned to western church "partnerships" for financial viability. Gifford argues that this dynamic tends to make the rhetoric of indigenization and autonomy increasingly meaningless as external influences often tend to drive the programmatic structures and ideologies of local African congregations.[112] While Gifford acknowledges that African agency and creativity have been at the center, rather than at the periphery, of the expansion of the Christian faith in Africa, he also argues that such African "creativity should not be so emphasised that it glosses over the West's cultural significance."[113] For Gifford, evidence indicating that "[s]o much of Africa's mushrooming Christianity is closely linked" with forms of Christianity from the United States suggests that African leaders, in lieu of championing indigenization, have instead decided to "opt in" to globalization and modernity through precisely these external ecclesial partnerships.[114] This argument merits serious reflection. In the city of Bata, a trip

---

110. Gifford, *African Christianity*, 308.

111. Ibid., 324, cf. 8–16.

112. Ibid., 308–25, cf. 44–47; Gifford, "African Christianity and the Eclipse of the Afterlife," 416–21.

113. Gifford, *African Christianity*, 322.

114. Ibid., 321.

to a local internet café can often yield new pastoral acquaintances as one encounters Pentecostal leaders surfing the internet for international partnerships with churches in Latin America and Spanish-speaking parts of the United States. Many Pentecostals speak quite openly about the advantages of having a "spiritual covering" which some even define—returning to the mission church rhetoric of previous centuries—as having a "mother church." International church travel,[115] hosting international visitors, establishing western partnerships, and securing a "mother church" all are signs which visibly increase local prestige and prominence.[116]

Yet despite Gifford's provocative analysis, the question in many respects remains ambiguous: does ecclesial extraversion necessarily imply a subversion of indigenization? David Maxwell suggests that Gifford inverts the Bayart thesis, part of which argues that African political extraversion often skillfully exploits—from a position of power—western global partners.[117] Gifford recognizes that the western donor industry—including the missionary enterprise—in a sense "needs" Africa, which implies a position of weakness for western donors because their objectives necessarily require African participation.[118] African Christians, like their political counterparts, often creatively and astutely negotiate the power dynamics involved in external ecclesial partnerships.[119] In Equatorial Guinea, the internet equivalent of "cold calls" issuing from local Pentecostal pastors who invite, via email, zealous Latino evangelists and preachers to conduct campaigns or explore partnerships has yielded numerous visits. Yet Fang Pentecostals are occasionally frustrated by Latino aspirations when extraversion implies relinquishing local autonomy, engaging in dubious mission strategies,[120] or simply being a puppet in planting the flags of Latino denominations. The aspiration for external contacts amongst Fang Pentecostals is nearly universal, yet external partnerships which supply finances with minimal local interference are the most coveted. The partnership secured by Asumu

115. Both Esono of Assembly of the Holy Spirit and Asumu of Joy of My Salvation have traveled extensively in the United States. See also Maxwell, "'Delivered from the Spirit of Poverty?'" 367.

116. Just as such partnerships may increase the local prominence of western churches and their leaders.

117. Maxwell, Review of *African Christianity*, 476. See Bayart, "Africa in the World," 217–67, esp. 218–19, 226–28; Bayart, *The State in Africa: The Politics of the Belly*, 25–26. See also Marshall-Fratani, "Mediating the Global and Local in Nigerian Pentecostalism," 84, 99, 101.

118. Gifford, *African Christianity*, 315.

119. See Englund, "Christian Independency and Global Membership," 83–111.

120. For example, one Mexican mission focused exclusively upon teaching Spirit-filled local Pentecostals how to do "praise and worship" Mariachi-style.

with the Wesleyan Church is the classic example. Without sacrificing local autonomy—indeed many church members at Joy of My Salvation know next to nothing about the Wesleyan Church—Asumu has secured multiple overseas trips, funds for a church roof in the village of Mongomo, and the assistance of a Peruvian missionary for one year.

Yet considering the true nature of the global Pentecostal network, discussions of ecclesial extraversion cannot be simplistically reduced to the dichotomy of pitting western (typically U.S.) externality against African indigenous agency or creativity. For microstates like Equatorial Guinea, such duality hardly begins to scratch the surface or match local realities on the ground. The constant stream of Ivorian prophets, Cameroonian apostles, Gabonese pastors, and Congolese bishops to Assembly of the Holy Spirit necessarily entails reframing the conversation to include yet another paradigmatic discourse: African agency negotiating the dynamics of *African extraversion*. In light of the Christianization of much of sub-Saharan Africa, the discourse of extraversion which highlights only the most prominent *western* expressions of global Christianity is bound to be a caricature. For Fang Pentecostals in particular, negotiating the power dynamics involved in cross-cultural partnerships *within the African continent* not only facilitates increased cultural understandings but also ostensibly preserves greater local autonomy than might otherwise be possible in a western-based partnership. Though Guinean Pentecostalism exists as a younger and less-developed enterprise than many of its African brethren, it nevertheless self-consciously negotiates from a position of economic strength with its African neighbors due to (in Pentecostal rhetoric) the "blessing" of the country's oil money.

The question of whether *African* externality implies a reduction of local agency or problematizes issues of indigenization is quite complex. Ivorian prophets or Gabonese apostles, albeit preaching in French, are all masters of communicating in idioms quite accessible to the Fang cultural universe. These Francophone spiritual "Big Men," with their unrelenting discourse on witchcraft, accompanied by frequent references to poverty, unemployment, sickness, infertility, singleness, and familial tensions move virtually seamlessly into the socioeconomic and religio-cultural realities confronting the Fang, while embracing, if not embodying, the church's transnational Pentecostal rhetoric. In many ways, these Francophone prophets and apostles resemble their Fang counterparts in the Assembly of the Holy Spirit with one significant exception: their messages are disproportionately tied to the preaching of the prosperity gospel when compared to the church's indigenous leadership. That is, local pastors and leaders of the Assembly of the Holy Spirit enthusiastically preached on deliverance from witchcraft but characteristically stopped short, in my experience, of proclaiming unequivocal messages of financial prosperity. Thus, while the prosperity gospel is broadcast with great regularity from indigenous pulpits, Francophone guests are the predominant mouthpieces of these prosperity messages. This arrangement suggests that these Francophone guests, although treated almost reverentially in church gatherings, are nevertheless "hired workers" who provide a particular service for the church's top-tiered leadership. A certain amount of mutual back-scratching is evident and is illustrated most poignantly in the double offerings which accompany these Francophone guests wherein one offering is taken for the Francophone "Man of God" while a second offering fills the coffers of the local church and its leaders.[121] Paradoxically, this intentional self-subversion of local autonomy through African extraversion is welcomed enthusiastically by the church's high-level leadership for the financial returns such an arrangement secures for local leaders and their churches. In other words, Fang indigenization is *intentionally* compromised as the prosperity messages of Francophone "Big Men" become increasingly popular and vital elements within the life of the church. Local leaders, headed by Apostle Esono, are thus able to stand a comfortable distance away from the actually preaching of prosperity messages, which have caused quite a point of contention within the local Pentecostal community, while nevertheless receiving many of the financial and social perks that these practices afford.

Prophetic Seminars: Celebrating the Message of Prosperity

In its local form, the prosperity gospel is the teaching that believers can access wealth, health, success, and advancement by defeating the powers of witchcraft, by prayers of faith which lay authoritative claim on divine blessings, and by the payment of tithes and offerings to the church and/or to the anointed "Man of God."[122] In the Assembly of the Holy Spirit, the

---

121. This arrangement is also mutually beneficial in other ways. These Francophone guests are not only showered with adulatory praise but also collect multiple offerings each week even as lodging and many meals are freely provided by the church for weeks (or months) at a time. On the other hand, Assembly of the Holy Spirit utilizes these Francophone guests to create its own niche in the local religious marketplace which attracts people (and their money) into the church; local pastors continue to receive weekly offerings (and *daily* offerings during the week-long prophetic seminars), but the work of preparing the daily or weekly messages has effectively been "outsourced" to these Francophone hired workers.

122. See Wright, et al., "Lausanne Theology Working Group Statement on the Prosperity Gospel," 99.

prosperity gospel is disseminated widely by these Francophone leaders in week-long "prophetic seminars" organized every few weeks by local church leaders. One such prophetic seminar commenced Sunday morning April 22, 2012 featuring the prophet Frederic Fouahouly (aka "Prophet Frederic") from Ivory Coast. As if whetting the appetite of the congregation for the week ahead, Prophet Frederic began by promising that "God has blessing upon blessing, prosperity upon prosperity, victory upon victory, success upon success for you."[123] A general prophecy quickly followed: "Today suffering in your life leaves you. Somebody [here] has been oppressed, in three days you will receive a call that will change your life, change your business, change your success."[124] The morning's scriptural text was 1 Chronicles 29:10–12 with special emphasis on verse 12: "Riches and honor come from you, and you rule over all." People were asked to turn to their neighbor and say "recognize God in your life" as Frederic depicted *God as the source* and the *Christian faith as the path* for attaining material blessings: "Who wants success? Who wants victory? Who wants to be married? That only happens here on the earth. Here there are cars, here there are marriages, up there is only prayer and adoration."[125] Alluding to his own testimony, Frederic often held himself up as a tangible representative of "collective aspiration."[126] Evoking the image of Joseph who went from "prison to the Prime Minister," Frederic indicated that he once wandered the streets eating in trash dumps as a "crazy person" on the streets of Ivory Coast: "For four years—four years—I didn't even touch a 25 [referring to the smallest coin in the Central African monetary system]."[127] Frederic continued: "My parents thought I had died. Now they've heard their son has become a great prophet. Now people want to see me, political ministers want to see me."[128] Without a doubt, Frederic's zero-to-hero testimony embodied the main point he wished to make: "God doesn't destroy, he builds. God doesn't make poor, he makes rich. God doesn't put down, he raises you up. If someone tells you, 'you can't make it', cast that witch out."[129] To conclude the morning's prophetic ministry, Frederic bestowed several succinct and often ambiguous prophecies on specific individuals:

123. Frederic Fouahouly, Assembly of the Holy Spirit, Central Church of Bata, April 22, 2012.
124. Ibid.
125. Ibid.
126. Maxwell, "'Delivered from the Spirit of Poverty?,'" 363.
127. Frederic Fouahouly, Assembly of the Holy Spirit, Central Church of Bata, April 22, 2012.
128. Ibid.
129. Ibid.

> To a middle-aged man: "You are a man that should be in Europe. But your father has blocked you."
>
> To pre-teen child: "You are hard-headed. You don't obey your parents, you are going to have a short life. Be careful."
>
> To a man in his 20s: "The girl you long for—the one you love—you will have problems maintaining this girl you want. But if you want, go after her."[130]

During the course of Frederic's message, dozens of people made their way to the front of the church to donate to the prophet's offering bucket placed prominently on the center of the stage.

By way of contrast, at Joy of My Salvation, spiritual blockages are generally named as cultural-religious phenomena such as Fang *mbwo*, *curanderías*, *ekong*,[131] Bwiti, or traditional fetishes. But during the prophetic seminars at Assembly of the Holy Spirit, the demons typically masquerade under the more modern socioeconomic guises of poverty, unemployment, bad grades, rejection of a VISA, or the privation of modern goods (epitomized by possession of a car and international travel). For example, the demonic blockages that were "broken" by Frederic in the spiritual realm were touted as instrumental for prosperity and success during the first night of the prophetic seminar:

> To a man on the front row: "You are a zero. You have a small house. Even the roof is not finished, and it drips water. Everything your hands touch doesn't prosper. But today I end the blockage."
>
> To a woman in her 40s or 50s: "You've deposited an application with a company, you'll receive the call. And you'll receive a good salary."
>
> To a teenage girl: "Sometimes you study hard for an exam, but at the moment of your exam, everything you studied seems to vanish. This is from your father's ties in witchcraft. But you are going to break out of this! You will have success in school and then marry a great man of God."[132]

---

130. Ibid.

131. *Ekong* is one of the most popular and newer forms of witchcraft in Equatorial Guinea. Instead of eating his or her victim, a witch steals the victim's body from the grave so that the post-mortem victim can work as a kind of zombie to enrich the witch. See Geschiere, "Witchcraft and New Forms of Wealth," 43–76, esp. 47, 57–60.

132. Frederic Fouahouly, Assembly of the Holy Spirit, Central Church of Bata, April 23, 2012.

The rest of the prophetic seminar often followed a similar script. To a young man: "I see a VISA to Spain for you. It's on the desk at the Embassy in Spain."[133] One congregant even suffered from a "'spirit of forgetfulness'. You lose things. I proclaim this spirit broken today."[134]

Distinct but subtle emphases have led to a wide variety of labeling the prosperity gospel phenomenon including "health and wealth," "word of faith," "positive thinking," "name it-claim it," and "birthright theology." Prophet Frederic moved with ease amongst the various motifs but the overarching thematic and theological framework was inescapably tied to financial prosperity, physical healing, and success/advancement in life, the central tenets of the prosperity gospel (see figure 3.3).

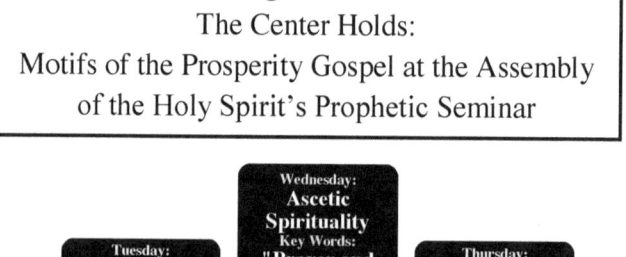

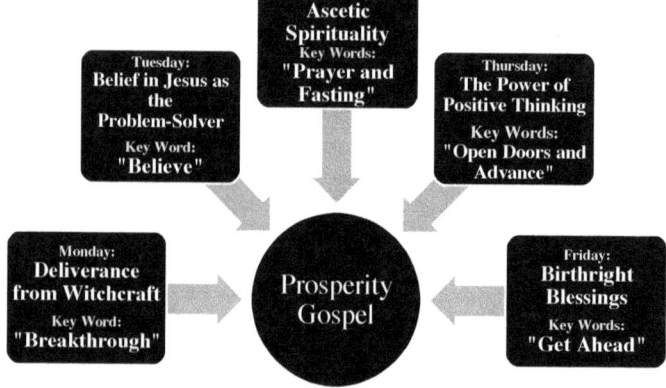

The circuitous biblical and thematic routes taken to arrive at prosperity messages were wildly divergent, perhaps none more surprising than Wednesday's treatment on April 25, 2012 of prayer and fasting.[135] For

---

133. Frederic Fouahouly, Assembly of the Holy Spirit, Central Church of Bata, April 26, 2012.

134. Ibid.

135. For the paradox of Pentecostal discourses centering upon both the message of prosperity and the seductiveness of wealth, see Meyer, "Pentecostalism and Neo-Liberal Capitalism," 22–23.

Frederic, prayer and fasting, primarily, are neither spiritual practices rooted in personal holiness nor ascetic forms of spirituality fostering detachment from this-worldly desires, but practices suitable for leveraging God to bestow material prosperity. Miraculous results from the Ivorian prophet's own life were all credited to the power of "prayer and fasting" including the healing of a paralytic girl, heavenly visitations from three persons in white robes, and increased visibility and success in ministry (i.e., "When you get to Gagnoa, a town twice the size of Bata, you can ask, 'Where is the great prophet Frederic?' and any person will take you by the hand and lead you to my house").[136] "Prayer and fasting," Frederic proclaimed, "are the only solutions you have as a Christian."[137] With Frederic, stories of extreme spiritual asceticism[138] were championed in the same breath as banal worldly trivialities. The Ivorian Prophet shared about one woman who cried out to God in prayer after her recently-paid-for pedicure was damaged on a rock: "As soon as it happened, the woman cried out in the name of Jesus for God to restore her pedicure. And, since the woman loves pedicure, and God loves what the woman loves, God healed the pedicure and restored the broken nail in that same moment."[139] By connecting prayer and fasting to unrelenting discourses of financial prosperity, the internal essence of these spiritual practices was subverted, if not completely reversed, in their relationship to God: it is not that believers, through prayer and fasting, are taught to love what God loves, but God is portrayed as baptizing the desires of believers without any accompanying transformation of the human appetite for prosperity or self-aggrandizement. After five consecutive nights, the prophetic seminar culminated with the message "Today is your day not to stay behind but get ahead"—memorably illustrated by Frederic ceremoniously emptying the entire contents of an offering bucket over the head of a young woman. For Frederic, "today" was the woman's time to "get ahead" and be "in front" and the dozens small coins and numerous bills which rained down over her life were symbolic signs of the nature of divine blessing.[140]

136. Frederic Fouahouly, Assembly of the Holy Spirit, Central Church of Bata, April 25, 2012.

137. Ibid.

138. Frederic frequently belittled local fasting practices as "lower level" compared to his own fasts where neither food nor drink (including water) was consumed. On day seven of one such fast, the Prophet indicated that "my mouth began bleeding and all my teeth became loose. Obviously it was the devil trying to distract me. But I didn't care if I lost all my teeth. God is able to grow new ones!" Ibid.

139. Ibid.

140. Frederic Fouahouly, Assembly of the Holy Spirit, Central Church of Bata, April 26, 2012.

Deliverance Liturgy

In contrast to countries such as Nigeria (Aladura), Ghana (*sunsum sorè*), or South Africa (Zionists), no local African Indigenous Church (AIC) can be identified as a precursor to the Pentecostal movement in Equatorial Guinea. In the historiography of African Christianity, scholars have often observed that AICs and Pentecostals are "cut from the same cloth" by drawing special attention to their shared pneumatological orientation, kindred historical origins, and corresponding mining of indigenous worldviews to inform ecclesial practices such as prayer.[141] Nevertheless, African Pentecostals *themselves* frequently engage in a radical demonization of AICs[142] and arguably save their most severe chastisement for AIC healing rituals which incorporate the use of holy water, ritual candles, indigenous herbs, and practices such as bathing in a river. These healing rituals, as judged by Pentecostals, are frequently considered to be "demonic doorways" because of their entanglement with traditional techniques.[143] As Rijk van Dijk has argued, African Pentecostal churches

> critiqued the missionary churches for denying what was so obviously a part of everyday African life: occult forces. . . . It was also on this account that these Pentecostal churches have remained dismissive of the healing churches' syncretic practices. As the traditional practices for healing, protection or exorcism may in themselves be contaminated by demonic influences, it followed that these churches could not be trusted either. . . . Herbs, candles, water, fire, or other substances that are commonly used in both traditional healing practices and in healing churches tend not to be found among these Pentecostal churches . . . .[144]

The majority of Fang Pentecostals, judging by their demonization of the *Iglesia del Cristianismo Celeste* ("Celestial Church of Christ") which locally was founded by Beninois, would forthrightly concur with van Dijk. Local Pentecostals, by and large, practice healing and deliverance with authoritative prayers accompanied by the "oil of anointing" (in accordance with James 5:14–16) but without the use of indigenous herbs, ritual candles, or holy water.

---

141. See Kalu, *African Pentecostalism*, 65–83, esp. 68–75; Anderson, "African Independent Churches and Pentecostalism," 22–42; Meyer, "Christianity in Africa," 447–54.

142. Kalu, "Estranged Bedfellows?" 121–42; Kalu, *African Pentecostalism*, 75–82.

143. Asamoah-Gyadu, *African Charismatics*, 181–85.

144. Van Dijk, "Witchcraft and Scepticism by Proxy," 101.

Yet this proclivity to denigrate the healing rituals of AICs does not signify that Fang Pentecostals are without their own creativity in developing rich liturgies for healing and deliverance. Apostle Esono is one such deliverance practitioner who frequently augments the more customary practices of prayer and anointing oil within Fang Pentecostalism by introducing the repeating of mantras, the swallowing of one's own saliva, the deep "breathing in" of the Holy Spirit, the evocation of the "fire of God" to burn away sickness, and the commanding of scientific bodily systems (e.g., endrocrine, digestive, circulatory) to be free from sicknesses. Esono's creative use of what may be described as a "Pentecostal Deliverance Liturgy" entitled *Power against Incurable Sicknesses* is a participatory-style, mantra-based prayer time focusing on utilizing spiritual resources against sicknesses of demonic origin (see Appendix 1). The morning deliverance service on May 22, 2012 led by Esono included several elements from this "deliverance liturgy" which entailed the communal repetition of the following mantras:

"Every evil food that I ate at the table of the devil, I vomit."

"Every seed of evil in my life, I reject."

"I drink the blood of Jesus" (accompanied by the participants swallowing their own saliva).

"Fire of the Holy Spirit, burn from my head to the bottom of my feet."[145]

As participants clenched their fists, punched the air, stomped their feet, and shouted the mantra prayers, a rhythmic virtually trance-like cadence was produced amongst the group. Each phrase was repeated approximately 200–300 times during the course of several ten to fifteen minute segments. In a sense, participants were physically enacting the unity of the body-spirit connection so characteristic of the Fang worldview. As the participants shouted "I drink the blood of Jesus" and proceeded to swallow their own saliva after each repetition, the Apostle explained this physically-charged symbolic act to the participants: "The blood of Jesus has power. The blood is now defeating the demons. The blood is now defeating the witches."[146] For the last liturgical response, Esono encouraged the participants to simply breathe in deeply the Holy Spirit. Soon sounds of vigorous breathing filled the sanctuary as the Apostle began crying out to God on behalf of the people: "Fire, fire, fire, burn, burn, burn, AIDS, cancer, diabetes in the name

---

145. See "Power Against Incurable Sicknesses," appendix one.
146. Agustín Edu Esono, Assembly of the Holy Spirit, May 22, 2012.

of Jesus."[147] As this creative "deliverance liturgy" suggests, while Fang Pentecostals frequently demonize traditional healing techniques, their churches are nonetheless the vanguards of instituting new Christianized healing practices in concert with elements of the local worldview.

Conclusion

In terms of Protestantism in Equatorial Guinea, this chapter has sought to balance ecclesial histories with a description of the fundamental core practices of three influential local denominations. The largest historic mission-founded church in the country, the Reformed Presbyterian Church, boasts a rich history dating back to 1850 on the island of Corisco and counts significant contributions to the formation of national identity among her many historic accomplishments. The ordination of one of the first indigenous Presbyterian pastors in the region, the translation of parts of the Bible into the Benga language, and the founding of the first Protestant congregations amongst the Benga, Ndowe, and Fang peoples in present-day Equatorial Guinea represent some of the more notable achievements. Yet preoccupations with political processes and a myriad of institutionalizing concerns, coinciding generally with the period of decolonization, eventually placed the church on a trajectory wherein critical ecclesial practices such as prayer, Bible study, and evangelism became increasingly marginalized within the life of the church. Today a severe self-diagnosed crisis confronts the church. Yet, no aspect of the crisis is more existentially central to the lives of ordinary Presbyterians than questions of Fang religiosity which include concerns about sickness, suffering, and witchcraft which are not adequately addressed by Presbyterian leaders.

In contrast to the missionary-founded Reformed Presbyterian Church which has generally failed to provide culturally satisfying ecclesial practices capable of contesting (witchcraft) evil and its concomitant sicknesses, indigenous Pentecostal churches in Equatorial Guinea have energetically embraced combating *mbwo* and *evus*-related sicknesses through deliverance and healing ministries. Behind Damián Ángel Asumu's charismatic leadership, Joy of My Salvation has burgeoned into one of the fastest growing Pentecostal churches in the country with a strict holiness ethic and deliverance ministries designed to promote pneumatological conversions. The Assembly of the Holy Spirit also places deliverance ministries at the forefront of ecclesial praxis but prominently features messages of financial prosperity from Francophone preachers alongside such healing-related activities.

147. Ibid.

Finally, a common theme running through the history of Protestant Christianity in Equatorial Guinea for both Presbyterians and indigenous Pentecostals is that migration from surrounding African nations has often played a decisive role in the spread of the Christian faith amongst the Fang.

With the exploration of the hermeneutic-culture-praxis triad now complete, we now turn in the second part of the book to themes, theologies, and trajectories of Protestant Christianity in Equatorial Guinea as viewed through the window of the book of Job. In the realm of biblical interpretation, we proceed from the general contours of African hermeneutics (as outlined in chapter 1) to a specific case study of Job. With respect to Fang culture, we move from a treatment of traditional Fang conceptions of divinity, witchcraft evil, and sickness (chapter 2) to a descriptive analysis of themes and theologies central to Fang Christians vis-à-vis their cosmologies and worldviews. And in terms of church praxis, the ecclesial histories and practices of these three influential churches in Equatorial Guinea (discussed in the present chapter) shed light in the chapters that follow on Joban interpretations and the way in which certain themes and theologies are more or less prominently accentuated within the perspectives provided by their particular church tradition.

Part 2

Contextual Readings of the Book of Job

Themes, Theologies, and Trajectories

4

Theodicy and the Nature of Evil

Job between God and the Devil

"I would like us to see that three figures are found in the book of Job . . . the figure of God, the figure of Job, and the figure of Satan. We have to observe that of these three figures, *Job is found in the middle*. I would say that on the right side is God; and on the left side is the Devil; and Job is in between."

—Rev. Alberto Mañe Ebo Asong, Reformed Presbyterian Church of Equatorial Guinea, Sermon on Job 4

"In other words, the life of Job is being thrown about *between God and the Devil*. The Devil asking for the life of Job—and all that he had—and God allowing it."

—Pastor Basilio Oyono, Joy of My Salvation, Sermon on Job 3

Introduction

UNBEKNOWNST TO HIM, JOB is in quite the predicament. In the opening scene in the book of Job, God and Satan are engaged in a rather casual conversation about Satan's recent travels. Satan indicates that he has been "going to and fro on the earth" (1:7) when suddenly God begins to brag about his servant Job: "Have you considered my servant Job? There is no one like him on earth, a blameless and upright man, who fears God and turns away from evil" (1:8). Satan takes exception. Satan accuses God of bribing Job with prosperity, riches, and success in life in exchange for Job's faithful service.

Who would not choose to serve God in return for such lavish abundance and extravagant blessings? Satan's challenge does not fall on deaf ears, as God takes this devilish wager by exposing Job's business empire to ruin and his family to catastrophic loss. Eventually, even Job's health withers away.

As Job's life is engulfed in a cycle of chaos and suffering of epic proportions, the narrator of Job does not fail to mention the secondary causes of Job's calamity. The Sabeans, the fire of God, the Chaldeans, and a mighty wind all have a role to play in Job's sufferings (1:13–19). Yet the way in which the narrative drama unfolds, life begins to unravel for Job after this heavenly conversation between God and Satan. The conversation is the lynch pin of the story. The dialogues between God and Satan (1:6–12; 2:1–6) represent both the spark *and* the gasoline which ignites a raging fire of tremendous suffering, terrible sickness, and horrendous evil around Job which threatens to choke off his faith in God. Job is caught in the middle.

Perhaps no better analogy exists in the Bible to describe the Christian existence faced by millions of Christians in Africa than the portrait of Job caught between God and the Devil. According to ordinary readers, Job lives precariously "in the middle" between God and the Devil,[1] and his sufferings stem from "being thrown about between God and the Devil."[2] Consistent with their own interpretations of Job as a man living dangerously "in the middle" between God and the Devil, Fang Christians also experience themselves as living in the midst of a dynamic cosmic conflict between *Nzama* (God) and the *deble* (Devil). Yet whereas the cosmic conflict for Job occurred above his head in the heavenly realm, ordinary African Christians are consciously aware of the conflict between spiritual powers as a daily reality that explains the incidence of sickness and suffering in their lives.

This chapter seeks to unravel the Gordian knot of theodicy in an African context where many people, including most Christians, wrestle with the existential dilemma of living in a cosmos enchanted with mystical forces, nocturnal witchcraft, and demonic oppression while nevertheless believing in God as the Supreme Being and Creator. In Africa, the existential angst, spiritual *gravitas*, and intellectual tensions embodied by the nature of theodicy are lived out by all—whether Christian or not—on an everyday basis. The classic western formulation of theodicy, defined by the tensions inherent in God's omnipotence, God's benevolence, and the presence of evil, has been honed in the west for the last three centuries. *Yet theodicy in an African context requires a radical re-framing to reflect the contours of local African*

---

1. Alberto Mañe Ebo Asong, Reformed Presbyterian Church, Sermon, Job 4:1–11, October 23, 2011.

2. Basilio Oyono, Joy of My Salvation, Sermon, Job 3:1–4, October 16, 2011.

cultures. In this chapter, therefore, we constructively set forth a specific proposal for a theodicy grounded upon dominant cultural motifs amongst the cultures of sub-Saharan Africa. The framework of this contextual African theodicy is then developed locally by examining the changing cosmologies of Fang Christians in Equatorial Guinea and by demonstrating how theodicy issues become the critical lens through which local Christians construct images of God and the Devil and interpret Christian scriptures like the book of Job which decisively impact the nature of the Christian faith.

Thus, after our exploration of each pole of the *hermeneutics-culture-praxis triad* in part one of the study (chapters 1–3), we now turn to view the dominant themes and theologies occupying Fang Christians through their contextual readings of the book of Job (chapters 4–6). In this chapter, the Joban prologue (Job 1:1—2:12) with its archetypal portrait of Job's sufferings and its arresting conversation between God and Satan will be the primary text explored by ordinary believers through sermons and Bible studies. Through engaging with the text of Job, these ordinary readers provide a critical lens to observe the prevailing questions, concerns, and pre-understandings that grassroots Christians bring to the biblical text.

Characteristic Concerns of Theodicy in the Western Theological Tradition

Historically, theodicy is a relatively late addition to the theological vocabulary of the West. The term, apparently coined only in 1710 by the German philosopher Gottfried Leibniz based on an amalgamation of *theos* ("god") and *dike* ("justice"), nevertheless has a long, storied past.[3] Epicurus (341–270 BC), a Greek philosopher, is commonly credited with formulating theodicy's basic contours,[4] suggesting that the *underlying concerns* of theodicy evade simple identification with a single cultural or religious worldview.[5] As John Hick indicates, the term theodicy connotes "a kind of technical shorthand" of "the defense of the justice and righteousness of God in face of the fact of evil,"[6] a threefold problem which, at least for the western philosophical tradition, received arguably its most succinct formulation by David Hume:

---

3. Leibniz, *Theodicy*.
4. Hick, *Evil and the God of Love*, 5, fn. 1; Surin, "Theodicy?" 225.
5. For a multicultural and multi-religious exploration of the nature of evil, see Parkin, *The Anthropology of Evil*.
6. Hick, *Evil and the God of Love*, 6.

> Is he willing to prevent evil, but not able? then he is impotent.
> Is he able, but not willing? then he is malevolent. Is he both able and willing? whence then is evil?[7]

The foundations of theodicy in the western tradition, therefore, are historically assumed to rest upon the tensions inherent in (1) God's omnipotence, (2) God's benevolence, and (3) the presence of evil.

In the West, particularly since the horrors of Auschwitz, the problem of evil has been embedded as a non-negotiable empirical reality in western discourse. Susan Neiman argues that the problem of evil has even acted as an "organizing principle for understanding the history of philosophy" for the last two centuries.[8] Given the non-negotiable fact of evil, *western theodicies often proceed by investigating the tenuous relationship between the two divine attributes* in the face of evil.[9] In other words, in the West, the conversation of theodicy is pulled centripetally *towards the divine center* in a re-examination of God's omnipotence or God's benevolence.

In the western philosophical tradition, as the term *theo*-dicy itself implies, an epistemological prioritization has emerged which tends to cement the divine attributes (*theos*) as indispensable to any discussion of theodicy. As Kenneth Surin argues, most western theodicies are inescapably tied to the philosophical theism of the seventeenth and eighteenth centuries which, in typical Enlightenment fashion, posits an abstract causal being existing in a cosmos divested of all other supernatural agents.[10] Theodicy's conversation then rationalistically tends to unravel the conundrum of divine omnipotence, divine benevolence, and the presence of evil by engaging in metaphysical debates rooted in what Michael Foucault referred to as the "archaeology of knowledge."[11] In other words, western theodicy concerns

---

7. Hume, *Dialogues Concerning Natural Religion*, Part X, 134.

8. Neiman, *Evil in Modern Thought*, 7, see also 1–5, 238–58.

9. Recent theodicies bear this imprint. The protest theodicy of John Roth, for instance, displays a robust view of God's omnipotence but questions the essential goodness of God. In conceiving of God as "everlastingly guilty" for history's victims, protest theodicy construes God's benevolence as a repugnant concept given the horrendous evils in the world; faith, at its core, constitutes an honest protest against the God who omnipotently sanctions evil, a kind of clinging to God *against* God in the face of despair; see Roth, "A Theodicy of Protest," 14. On the other hand, the process theodicies of John Cobb and David Griffin posit a God of absolute goodness but place radical restrictions on God's power, effectively limiting God's power to historical processes; see Cobb and Griffin, *Process Theology*. Only a cursory glance at western theodicies underscores the basic point: western theodicies hinge on probing God's omnipotence and benevolence—the underlying assumptions of monotheistic religion—in the face of evil.

10. Surin, *Theology and the Problem of Evil*, 2–7, esp. 4, cf. 39–46.

11. Foucault, *The Archaeology of Knowledge* referred to in Surin, *Theology and the*

may be viewed as being contextually rooted within the broader contours of Enlightenment cosmologies and the history of western thought.

Yet what if the foundational assumptions underpinning western theodicies cannot be presupposed outside the cultural hegemony of the North Atlantic? What occurs if the problem of evil and suffering is explored from a radically different basis than philosophical monotheism? In Africa, locally calibrated theodicies do not simply collapse into a dialogue of mindless chatter in the absence of the foundational assumptions of western monotheism. This dynamic suggests that the entire conversation of theodicy in Africa warrants a radical re-framing to be sufficiently embedded in the local thought patterns and the accompanying worldviews of African cultures.

Theodicy in an African Context

The Tone and Tenor of an African Theodicy: Theodicy as Moral Etiology

In Africa, theodicy is not first and foremost a theoretical exercise. The conversation of theodicy amongst African Christians proceeds in an entirely different tone and tenor. The endless labyrinth of discussions centering upon exonerating God in the face of evil in the western tradition is noticeably absent amongst the Fang and many other African peoples. As Kwame Bediako observes: "For theodicy here, in light of the African experience, does not consist in asking 'Where was God, and what was God doing in our experience of suffering?'"[12] Indeed, in my field work I found ordinary Christians genuinely ambivalent about—even uninterested in—probing or assessing the image of God in the book of Job. Whenever I tried to raise poignant questions *of God* such as "Doesn't the image of God in the book of Job concern you?" or "Do you want to serve a God like that? God seems to be working in concert with the Devil!" or "If we serve the same God as Job, does this not create profound and disturbing questions of faith for you?" my questions were always handled matter-of-factly and never provoked a visceral response which matched the intensity or urgency with which I asked the question. I found that such questions, rooted in traditional understandings of western theodicy, were hospitably ignored.

Yet traditionally, the Fang were hardly immune to concerns about evil and suffering. Historically, Fang religiosity was galvanized and rituals were performed precisely when evil was perceived as threatening the well-being

---

Problem of Evil, 39.

12. Bediako, "Toward a New Theodicy," 50.

of the community. At its core, Fang religiosity is rooted in theodicy. Fang traditional beliefs and practices were primarily concerned to eliminate evil and suffering at the communal level. Yet rather than theodicy scrutinizing the divine nature as in the western tradition, the concerns of the Fang centered primarily upon asking the questions: "who is chiefly responsible for evil in the causal universe?" and "what can be done pragmatically about it?" In African cosmologies preoccupied with discovering the causal origins of sickness and suffering, determining the "cause behind the cause"—or what we term the *"moral etiology"* of evil and suffering—may be identified as a dominant and paradigmatic motif. *Theodicy rooted in an African context is primarily concerned in identifying the moral etiology of evil and suffering.* For only by establishing the moral etiology of the sickness or suffering can evil be eliminated and the cosmos restored back to its benevolent (default) status, an ideal experienced across Africa as the celebration of the abundant life. This preoccupation with identifying the "cause behind the cause"—or the moral etiology of evil—is not only deeply rooted in indigenous religiosity and thoroughly implanted within the psyche of the Fang but also represents a radical contrast with the God-centered theodicies of the West.

Thus, the radical reconfiguration that Christian theodicy necessarily undergoes in Africa is significant.[13] For the Fang, questions of moral etiology, embedded in the traditional rituals, provided the framework for dealing with evil despite *Nzama's* otiose nature. Thus, we interpret the tone and tenor of theodicy amongst Fang Christians, whereby suffering and evil do not appear to cause local Christians to question *Nzama's* character, not as evidence that these Christians are uninterested in theodicy or even necessarily as a sign of a robust piety or a profound faith in the face of suffering (though these Christian virtues are often demonstrated) but primarily as evidence that Christian religiosity shares a more basic continuity with traditional religiosity which generally tended to marginalize *Nzama* to the periphery of religious consciousness. In other words, Fang Christian theodicy develops along the same trajectory of traditional religiosity whose *raison d'ètat* was grounded in pragmatically dealing with evil rather than engaging with a supreme deity.

---

13. In African contexts, even the retention of the term theodicy itself, given its etymological roots, may be viewed as problematic for some. Yet the term's continued usefulness, based upon its ability to capture succinctly the issues raised for a monotheist by the problem of evil, suggests its permanence as a theological category even as the substance of the term itself is significantly altered in non-western contexts.

The Parameters of Theodicy in an African Context

If the tone and tenor of Christian theodicy amongst the Fang are decidedly different than in the West, so too are the conceptual parameters with which theodicy is constructed. The monotheistic orientation of theodicy in the western theological tradition, built upon the conundrum of God's omnipotence, God's benevolence, and the presence of evil, is radically alien to the Fang. As previously indicated, the Fang cosmology is predicated upon two interconnected principles which, in the face of suffering and evil, co-exist only amidst extreme tension: the causal universe and the celebration of the abundant life.[14] As suffering and evil encounter these interconnected principles of the Fang cosmology, Christian theodicy is transposed from a *concentration upon the deity* in the western tradition, which often morphs into dense metaphysical discourse, to a decidedly more anthropocentric and pragmatic conversation in Africa which *concentrates upon the nature of evil* (see figures 4.1 and 4.2).

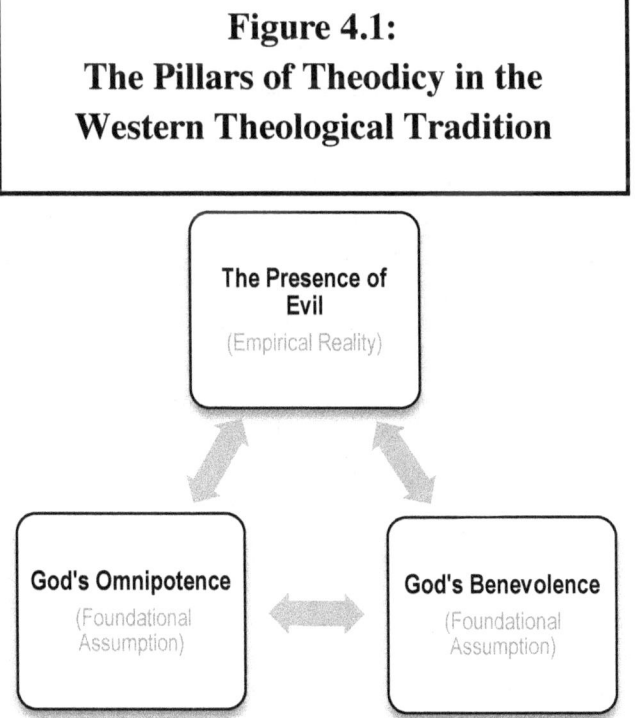

Figure 4.1: The Pillars of Theodicy in the Western Theological Tradition

---

14. See chapter 2, section "The Abundant Life and the Presence of Suffering."

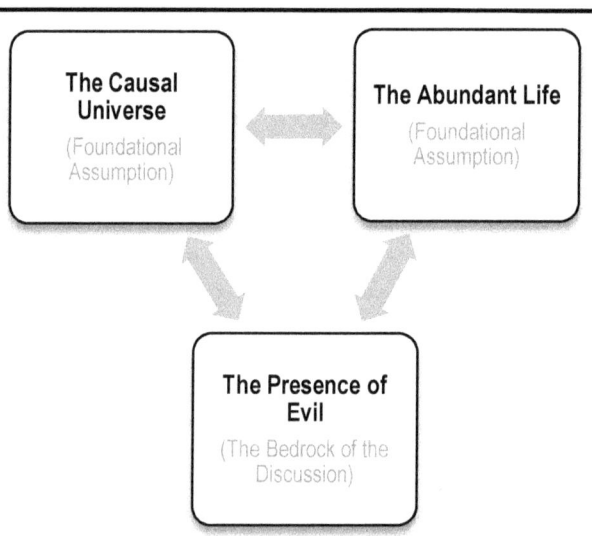

Figure 4.2:
The Pillars of a Contextualized Theodicy amongst the Fang

In Africa, rather than the conversation focusing on divine attributes often embedded in metaphysical categories, the bedrock of Christian theodicy shifts towards a more pragmatic and experiential discourse focusing on the nature of evil. Whereas the Judeo-Christian tradition may be distinguished as a God-centered religious tradition, the "center" of Fang traditional religiosity is orientated around an anthropocentric quest for the abundant life with its attendant and causal desire to eliminate evil. Thus, notwithstanding that many African worldviews appear to have conceived of a Supreme Being who played (or who came to be given) at least some role in the creation of living things, belief in such a Being was typically neither the dominant motif nor the organizing center around which traditional beliefs and practices tended to be structured. Andrew Walls makes the point as follows:

> *The elements of religious life are not the same as the structure of religious life.* Most obviously, the tradition of a people may include a Being who, when that people came into contact with a God-centered religious tradition, will be invested with all the characteristics of the Supreme Being; or the tradition may in

some other way recognize the ultimate unity of the transcendent world, a single principle underlying life. And yet such a recognition may impinge very little on the life of most members of the community, though ritual acts and words may be of regular occurrence.[15]

That is, despite the *presence* of an indigenous figure or deity whose character becomes invested with Christian attributes of the Supreme Being,[16] the *structure* of indigenous religiosity often served to leave this figure as an outside observer in the celebration of rituals or rites, the central *loci* of indigneous religiosity. For the Fang, the relationship with transcendence has always been rooted in traditional rituals of power, not in a god-centered ontology. Thus, we should note at the outset that amongst grassroots interpreters of Job the hermeneutical disinterestedness in exploring the image of God corresponds more nearly to a basic continuity not with the God-centeredness of Judeo-Christian monotheism but with the distant otiose figure *Nzama* from the Fang's pre-Christian past.

Therefore, *theodicy as moral etiology* amongst the Fang completely flips on its head the entire conversation of theodicy as typically conducted in the West. In the western Judeo-Christian tradition, the foundational assumptions of God's benevolence and God's omnipotence generally provide the parameters of theodicy's entire conversation. Yet amongst the Fang, the parameter of the presence of evil tends to be dominant, capturing most of the conceptual weight and existential concern of ordinary people. To place in perspective the radical transformation Christian theodicy undergoes in

15. Walls, *The Missionary Movement in Christian History*, 122, italics in the original.

16. James L. Cox is one of several scholars who suggest that the simple equation of Africa's indigenous figures and deities with the God of the Judeo-Christian tradition is not without its problematic assumptions. Rather than rehearsing this admittedly important albeit complex discussion of secondary literature here, we have sought to explicitly underscore the divergent "organizing centers" of African religiosity and the Christian tradition, especially considering that re-creating traditional beliefs and practices before the incursion of Christianity represents an almost impossible task for much of Africa. With respect to the Fang, the concerns of scholars like Cox are poignantly illustrated since *Nzama's* elevation to the category of Supreme Being seems to indicate a "categorical evangelization" or "cultural imposition" of western Christianity upon Fang indigenous thought. See Cox, *The Invention of God in Indigenous Societies*; Cox, "The Invention of the Christian God in Africa," 315–28; Cox, *From Primitive to Indigenous*, 16–22. For Okot p'Bitek's critique that the first generation of African Christian scholars (e.g., John S. Mbiti, E. Bọlaji Idowu, J. B. Danquah) were "intellectual smugglers" who sought to introduce "Greek metaphysical conceptions into African religious thought," see P' Bitek, *African Religions in Western Scholarship*, quoting 88. See also Shaw, "The Invention of 'African Traditional Religion,'" 339–53; Mudimbe, *The Invention of Africa*, esp. 58–83.

Africa, it is important to remember that "one of the deepest and most enduring desires of all African societies" is "the anxiety to eliminate evil."[17] By conceptualizing evil in relatively broad and nebulous terms—J. Kwabena Asamoah-Gyadu defines evil as "anything that destroys life"[18] while Richard Gray observes that "evil was experienced as that which destroyed life, health, strength, fertility and prosperity"[19]—*the propensity for evil to be viewed as nearly ubiquitous within African societies is almost inescapable*, especially considering the prevalence of suffering on the continent due to socioeconomic and political realities. In addition, whereas infertility or prolonged sicknesses typically tend to fall outside the semantic domain of "evil" for western societies, in African communities, where (western) scientific causation and pure chance are often excluded, the vocabulary of evil often mushrooms to voluminous proportions as anything inimical to the abundant life.

The nature of evil, being antithetical to the abundant life, also emerges as a prodigious category because its discourse is inextricably bound to witchcraft. Amongst the Fang, we may recall that anthropologist James Fernandez, by identifying the *evus* of witchcraft as the "apotheosis of evil," effectively argued for the divinization or deification of evil amongst the Fang.[20] In other words, not only is the nature of evil, rather than the attributes of the deity, the central preoccupation for Fang Christian theodicy, but also the nature of evil tends to encroach upon those areas which, for the western theological tradition, are typically reserved for God alone. Indeed, it may be argued that the nature of evil amongst the Fang functions psychologically in analogous fashion to the doctrine of divine providence amongst western Reformed Christians.[21] For John Calvin, the providence of God was an existentially comforting and calming doctrine, serving to ease the anxiety of believers in the face of suffering:

> Yet when that light of divine providence has once shone upon a godly man, he is then relieved and set free not only from the extreme anxiety and fear that were pressing him before, but from every care. . . . His solace, I say, is to know that his Heavenly Father so holds all things in his power, so rules by his authority

---

17. Gray, *Black Christians and White Missionaries*, 5.
18. Asamoah-Gyadu, "Conquering Satan, Demons, Principalities, and Powers," 87.
19. Gray, *Black Christians and White Missionaries*, 5.
20. Fernandez, *Bwiti*, 5, 227–28, 230, 239, 266, 283–84, 286, 303.
21. See Gray, *Black Christians and White Missionaries*, 101.

and will, so governs by his wisdom, that nothing can befall except he determine it.[22]

Yet amongst the Fang, the nature of evil and its elimination tend to play this role. That is, only by keeping the moral etiology of evil "close at hand" through constantly engaging in dialogue so as to discover its ultimate causal origins in order to eliminate evil ritually, can evil be divested of its accompanying fears and terrors.[23] Psychologically, one gets the distinct impression that for the Fang an evil which is "out of sight, out of mind" becomes an existential burden almost too heavy to bear. Evil, as the Fang would have it, deserves its idiomatic discourse "during the day" when the anxieties of nocturnal witchcraft can be discussed—and when its burden can be shared and communally alleviated—in order to assuage the conscience of its malevolent possibilities.

Cosmological Maps: Traditional, Presbyterian, and Pentecostal Cosmological Maps of the Universe amongst the Fang

Worldviews or cosmologies can be helpfully conceptualized as "mental maps of the universe" which, consciously or unconsciously, serve to aid people in their navigation of the moral universe.[24] Features of these "cosmological maps" include elements of cosmogony (how the world began), ontology (what the world consists of), and socialized patterns of experiencing life (how the world works and what is our own place in it).[25] As Walls has succinctly stated, "African Christianity is shaped by Africa's past."[26] As the Christian faith was placed upon locally available cosmological maps of the universe, Christianity in Africa has often retained the goals of indigenous beliefs and practices even while Christianizing—and thus re-shaping— traditional worldviews by introducing new symbols and re-configuring the prominence of old elements within traditional cosmologies.[27]

For the Fang, theodicy and reflection on the nature of evil played a pivotal role in the re-drawing of the traditional cosmological map during the process of engagement with Christianity. As the Christian faith wrestled with local forms of evil, Fang cosmologies adapted under the weight of the Christian message even as the basic shape and contours of the map

22. Calvin, *Institutes of the Christian Religion*, 1.17.11, 224.
23. See Harries, "Good-by-Default and Evil in Africa," 151–64, esp. 152–53.
24. Walls, "Worldviews and Christian Conversion," 155.
25. Kyriakakis, "Traditional African Religion, Cosmology and Christianity," 132–154, esp. 135.
26. Walls, "African Christianity in the History of Religions," 187.
27. Ibid., 189; see also Walls, "Worldviews and Christian Conversion."

remained largely unaltered. Relying on ethnographic fieldwork and anthropological literature, the traditional cosmological map of the Fang before the process of Christianization can be rendered with the following depiction (see figure 4.3).[28]

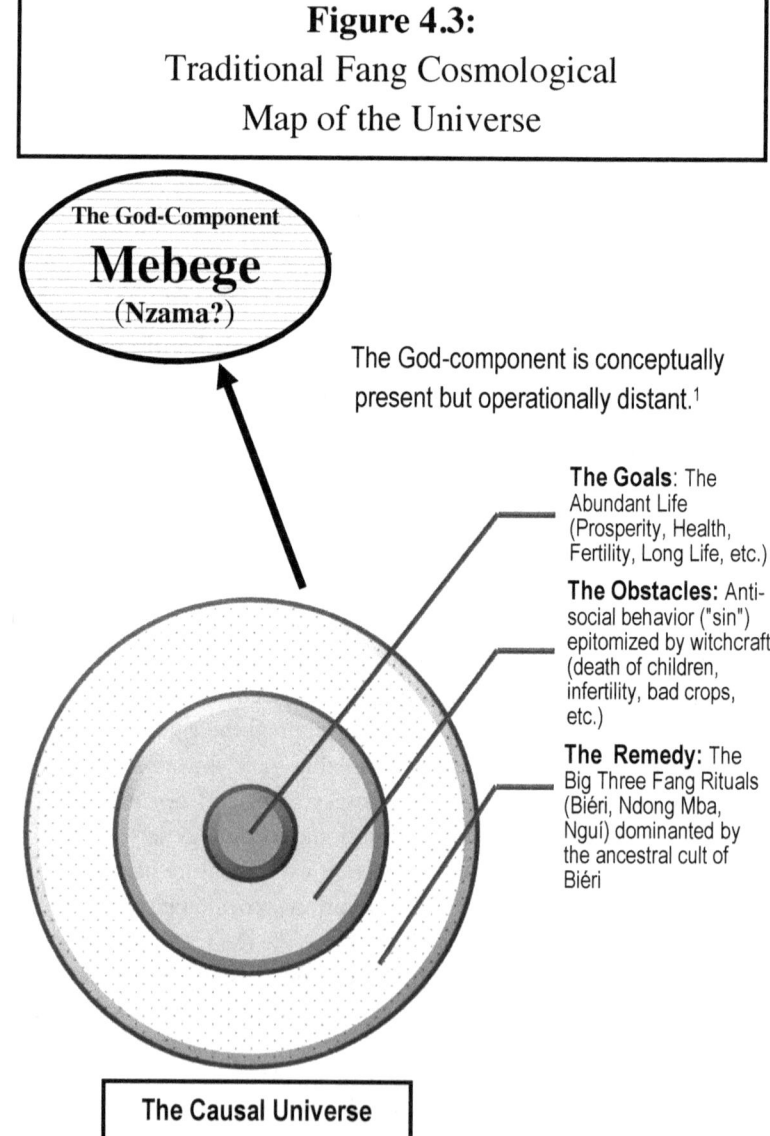

28. Walls, "Worldviews and Christian Conversion," 156.

Admittedly, recovering the shape of the traditional Fang cosmology before the incursion of Christianity represents an almost impossible task, but the most notable features of the cosmology were indisputably the ritual cults. The ancestral cult of Biéri played the most central role in securing the Fang cultural goals of prosperity, health, and success whereas the anti-witchcraft cult of Nguí and (to a lesser extent) the purification cult of Ndong Mba served to eliminate obstacles in the achievement of the abundant life. The fact that the early missionaries elevated *Nzama*, rather than *Mebege*, to the status of the Supreme Being suggests that *Mebege* played a historically marginal role within the cosmological structure. Yet even as *Nzama* was "divinized" through missionary misunderstanding, the God-component continued to be a relatively weak and marginal concept, only tangentially related to the day-to-day causal activity of the cosmos.

Yet during the mid-twentieth century, the principal ancestral cult of Biéri, the anti-witchcraft cult of Nguí, and the purification cult of Ndong Mba all buckled under the pressures of Christianity and colonialism. As the ritual cults were demonized by missionary rhetoric and driven underground by colonial governments, *the ancestral component underwent a major devaluation within the Fang cosmology* as Christianity began to transform the traditional cosmological map. Colonial governments, by identifying the communally-oriented rituals as themselves indigenous embodiments of evil forces, failed to grasp that the real epitome of evil for the Fang was the nefarious individualism of witchcraft.[29] In stamping out these ritual cults, including the anti-witchcraft cult of Nguí, the Fang were left without any locally satisfying recourse to address the problem of witchcraft. To compensate for the void represented by the recession of the ancestors, various forms of missionary Christianity have attempted to enlarge the God-component by bringing *Nzama* more centrally into the operational purview of the Fang cosmological map (see figure 4.4).

---

29. Rowlands and Warnier, "Sorcery, Power and the Modern State in Cameroon," 127–28; Fernandez, "Christian Acculturation and Fang Witchcraft," 249.

130   PART 2: CONTEXTUAL READINGS OF THE BOOK OF JOB

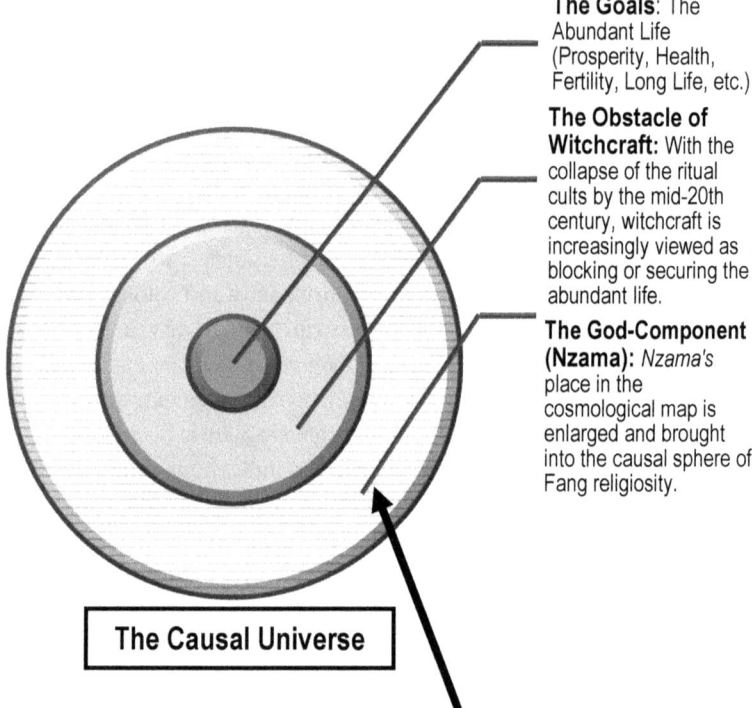

Figure 4.4:
The Christianization of the Fang Cosmological Map according to Missionary Christianity

The Goals: The Abundant Life (Prosperity, Health, Fertility, Long Life, etc.)

The Obstacle of Witchcraft: With the collapse of the ritual cults by the mid-20th century, witchcraft is increasingly viewed as blocking or securing the abundant life.

The God-Component (Nzama): *Nzama's* place in the cosmological map is enlarged and brought into the causal sphere of Fang religiosity.

The Causal Universe

The God-component is conceptually enlarged and brought into the causal and operational sphere of the Fang cosmology.

Yet even as missionary Christianity conceptually sought to bring *Nzama* more centrally into the Fang cosmological map, the elements of causality and the pursuit of the abundant life—the two most foundational elements of the cosmology—remained largely unaltered. Though *Nzama*, rather than the ancestors, was now theoretically depicted as the final arbiter of the causal universe, *Nzama* always existed rather uncomfortably for Christians within this causal and operational universe which he had never played a significant role. Indeed, it might be argued, it was always a role which *Nzama* was rather ill-equipped to play particularly since he had never been involved in the traditional rituals.

In Spanish Guinea, the Fang became increasingly exposed to Christianity following the 1926 Spanish exploration of Rio Muni.[30] The most prominent expression of the cosmological changes produced by Christianity was undoubtedly the influence of a widespread folk Catholicism that developed as the result of Spanish colonialism. In Spanish Guinea, educational opportunities were largely tied to one's baptismal membership in the Roman Catholic Church, a situation which hindered Protestant development and encouraged widespread Catholic baptisms. Although the diffusion of Christianity amongst the Fang in Rio Muni occurred relatively late for Central Africa, by the time of national independence (1968), the majority of the Fang populace were baptized Catholics, a situation somewhat analagous to the Catholicism which developed during the Spanish conquest of the Americas.[31] As Laurenti Magesa has recognized, the inculturation debate within Roman Catholicism is no longer strictly between missionary Christianity and African traditional religion but principally between *official* inculturation and *popular* inculturation.[32] At the level of official inculturation, several features of the Catholic faith theoretically provided a relatively dynamic canopy for Fang religiosity as its own traditional rituals collapsed under colonialism and Christianity. The ritualized celebration of the mass, the canon of saints, baptismal liturgies, the organized celebration of Catholic feast days, and first communions officially sought to fuse together ritualized religious observance and social cohesion for Fang rural villages.[33] In particular, Roman Catholic baptismal liturgies centering upon elaborate prayers, the symbolic blessings of salt and water, the invocation of holy words, and the exorcism of the Devil to protect the child from sicknesses and evil were theoretically well-suited to provide a viable Christian substitution for Fang religious needs centering upon protection against evil forces within the cosmology.[34] At the popular level of inculturation, however, many Fang Catholics have not regarded these Catholic rituals as existentially capable of providing a full substitution for dealing with the proliferation of witchcraft.[35] For the majority of Fang Catholics, neither the ritualized observa-

---

30. Fegley, *Equatorial Guinea: An African Tragedy*, 20, 77; Pujadas, *La Iglesia En La Guinea Ecuatorial: Rio Muni*, 313.

31. Pujadas, *La Iglesia En La Guinea Ecuatorial: Rio Muni*, 19.

32. Magesa, "The Present and Future of Inculturation in Eastern Africa," 70. See also Wijsen, "Popular Christianity in East Africa," 39.

33. Pujadas, *La Iglesia En La Guinea Ecuatorial: Rio Muni*, 50–51.

34. See Duffy, *The Stripping of the Altars*, 280–81.

35. As David Maxwell has argued with respect to Catholicism in northeast

tion of the mass nor the baptismal liturgy has fundamentally replaced the *raison d'être* of the traditional rituals in a culturally satisfying way. In this "South Americanization" of Catholicism amongst the Fang of Equatorial Guinea,[36] the development of a substantial Christian vernacular, including the enlargement of the God-component (*Nzama*), does not appear to have fundamentally altered recourse for dealing with witchcraft through the indigenous channels embodied by the *ngangan*. Within this milieu of folk Catholicism, many Fang Catholics seem to have adopted dual identities without a major existential tension or conflict between the two centers of their religious identities; rather, these two religious spheres—Fang religiosity and the Catholic ritualized faith—appear to exist side-by-side with minimal dissonance.

For the Reformed Presbyterian Church, the re-conceptualization of the Fang map of the universe has resulted in several existential difficulties for local believers, chief amongst them being this conundrum: while *Nzama* was now credited as being the Creator God and Supreme Being and hence responsible for the entire causal universe, witchcraft (*mbwo*) nonetheless continued to flourish. With the Fang traditional rituals no longer functioning to protect people from the evils of *mbwo* (witchcraft), the Presbyterian rhetoric of God's power and protection in Christ theoretically served to assuage the conscience of believers in a causal universe now seen as increasingly malevolent.[37] Yet traditionally, ritual rather than rhetoric was the gateway to securing healing and restoration. As Walls puts it, "previously there was a pathway marked on the map that linked the place of danger to the source of protection. With the deletion of the old source of protection, that path has now disappeared from the map, and *there is no clear pathway from the (still clearly marked) concrete danger of witchcraft to the theological*

Zimbabwe, the pre-Vatican II posture towards indigenous cultures which sought to supplant indigenous rituals with ritualized observance of the mass increasingly gave way to the incorporation of indigenous religiosity into Catholic practice in the post-Vatican II era. For the folk Catholicism of Equatorial Guinea, the true impact of Vatican II (1962–65) is difficult to gauge, but it may have provided further impetus for a rather wide acceptance of indigenous practices amongst Fang Catholics; Maxwell, "The Spirit and the Scapular," 299.

36. For the term "South Americanization," see Bucher, *Spirits and Power*, 14.

37. Tessman, who lived amongst the Fang in Cameroon from 1907 to 1909, indicated that those possessing the *evus* were a minority; yet by the time Fernandez spent time amongst the Fang in Gabon (1958–60), his informants indicated that over half of the Fang people possessed the *evus*. Today, many Fang believe that everyone is born with the *evus*, providing evidence for the assertion that, for the local populace, witchcraft has been on the rise in the twentieth century since the elimination of the anti-witchcraft cult of Nguí. See Fernandez, "Christian Acculturation and Fang Witchcraft," 249.

statement about the love and power of Christ."[38] And herein lay the distinctive difficulty for Protestants: despite not providing a ritual substitution to assure its members of God's protective benevolence during times of sickness, many Presbyterians nevertheless continued to portray the decision to seek spiritual protection within the church or to visit the *ngangan* as the benchmark for Christian faithfulness. An elderly Presbyterian catechist expressed it this way:

> Because in many occasions, what has happened? In order to get the cure, you go there [to the *ngangan*]. *You abandon the faith.* On the other hand, there are those that endure. How many people are missing among us now? "No, it's that I wanted, I looked for my health." But the God that we believe in here [in the Presbyterian Church]: He can't heal?[39]

Thus, Fang Presbyterians are often faced with an existential dilemma of sizeable proportions during times of crisis: *Nzama* or *ngangan*? This existential crisis, often referred to as a kind of religious schizophrenia, not only pits Fang religiosity in sharp opposition to Christian identity, but also can be described as the difference between the pragmatic ritual action of the Fang and the "wait and see" trust of the Christian. Yet this Christian posture is often deemed as nonsensical in the eyes of the Fang extended family since such non-action is frequently viewed as a sign of utter resignation and as a complete failure to act in the face of the crisis. Considering that three Presbyterian pastors have recently died at *curanderías* (traditional places of healing), the Christian pathway from *mbwo* (witchcraft) to *Nzama* (God) has not been clearly demarcated even amongst the Presbyterian leadership.

As Birgit Meyer has argued with respect to the Evangelical Presbyterian Church amongst the Ewe peoples of Ghana, dealing with witchcraft amongst historic missionary Christianity often produces great ambiguities at the level of the local church.[40] Manuel Awono, pastor of the largest Reformed Presbyterian Church in the city of Bata, indicates that part of the role of the local pastor consists of shepherding members to help them carefully discern between "good" and "bad" *curanderías*. Pastor Manuel would not hesitate to send a church member to a *curandería* wherein the person is only encouraged to drink some herbs, mixed with water, from the bark of a tree or have broken bones reset in the traditional fashion.[41] For Pastor

---

38. Walls, "Worldviews and Christian Conversion," 158, italics added.
39. Reformed Presbyterian Church, Bible Study, Job 11:1–20, October 24, 2012.
40. Meyer, "'If You Are a Devil, You Are a Witch,'" 98–132.
41. Interview, Manuel Awono, November 9, 2011.

Manuel, all healing is God's healing, a stance which reflects the Presbyterian redrawn cosmological map wherein healing is linked to the Creator God.[42] God created the herbs and gave knowledge of medicine before the white man placed those medicines into fancy packages. Yet other Presbyterian church members, as already demonstrated by the catechist's remarks, view visiting a *curandería* as one of the chief signs of "abandoning the faith" since it entails a *de facto* admission of God's impotence in the face of sickness and suffering (i.e., "the God that we believe in here [in the Presbyterian Church]: He can't heal?").[43] The resulting tension prevalent in the same local church produces complex ambiguities, or two divergent ways of conceptualizing the Fang cosmological universe which, to utilize Meyer's language, essentially refer to two distinct processes of Africanization: an Africanization "from above" and an Africanization "from below."[44] For some Presbyterian leaders and members, living with the paradox that God is the Creator in a universe filled with evil is part and parcel of affirming *Nzama's* role within a biblical framework: evil exists yet God rules. Yet other Presbyterian members are rather reticent and dissatisfied in placing God, rather than the Devil, as the chief causal being in a world filled with *mbwo*, particularly since *Nzama* seems no more willing or able to combat (witchcraft) evil ritually than he was in the traditional cosmology. As such, the redrawn cosmological map of missionary Christianity (figure 4.4 above) reflects an Africanization "from above." Yet in the absence of significant Christian rituals in the Presbyterian Church to combat *mbwo*, this Africanization "from above"—with all its existential ambiguities—can be viewed as being the main model informing the ministries of the church.

By contrast, the ambiguities and tensions of theodicy faced by Presbyterians are to some extent resolved by Fang Pentecostals as they radically re-draw the Fang cosmological map. As a whole, Fang Pentecostals are generally less predisposed to consider God as the figure primarily responsible for the entire causal universe, especially with regard to witchcraft. If Presbyterian leadership, by calling their members to live with the tension between God's sovereignty and the reality of evil, can be viewed as encouraging

---

42. Manuel Nzôh Asumu, General Secretary of the Presbyterian Church, also indicated that "one cannot totally reject" the *curanderías* since Christians must "measure the good and the bad" in all things. Alberto Mañe Ebo Asong, Director of Christian Education and local church historian, reiterated the stance of Presbyterian leadership by stating "if the *curandería* inclines toward death, it's bad; if it helps, it's good." Interview, Manuel Nzôh Asumu, October 31, 2011; Interview, Alberto Mañe Ebo Asong, October 14, 2011.

43. Reformed Presbyterian Church, Bible Study, Job 11:1–20, October 24, 2012.

44. Meyer, "'If You Are a Devil, You Are a Witch,'" 122–23.

Christian witness precisely in this paradox, then Pentecostal leaders can be understood as loosening this tension by warning that where evil exists, there the Devil must rule. If Presbyterians sing the old hymn "This is My Father's World," Pentecostals are more apt to bellow out a newer chorus:

> We conquer Satan
>
> We conquer demons
>
> We conquer principalities
>
> We conquer powers
>
> Shout Hallelujah.[45]

As the depiction of the Fang Pentecostal map illustrates (see figure 4.5), the dominant Christian element on the cosmological map has conceptually changed from God (in figure 4.4) to Satan (in figure 4.5), reflecting the theological emphasis that the Devil, rather than God, is ultimately responsible for (witchcraft) evil in the causal universe.

An observation by Walls relating to African Pentecostals and AICs applies equally well here with respect to Fang Presbyterians and Fang Pentecostals: "They use the same maps of the universe even if they colour them differently."[46] By deeming the Devil as the chief causal architect of *mbwo*, Pentecostals have placed the Christian notion of the Devil, rather than God, at the center of the cosmological universe.

---

45. As cited by Asamoah-Gyadu, "Conquering Satan, Demons, Principalities, and Powers," 86.

46. Walls, "African Christianity in the History of Religions," 193.

Figure 4.5:
The Christianization of the Fang Cosmological Map according to Fang Pentecostals

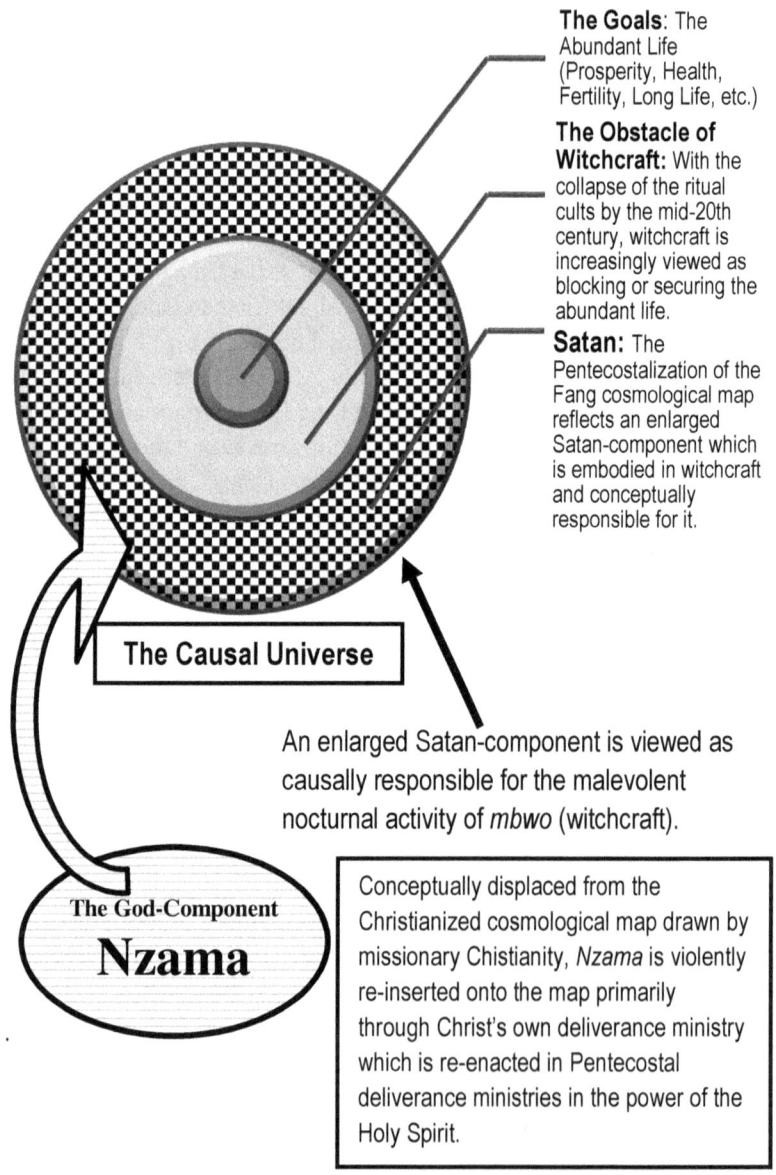

In Africa, although several Bible translations have claimed to have found indigenous equivalents for Satan including Èsù for the Yoruba Bible (Nigeria), *Legba* for the Ewe Bible (Benin), and *Rwuba* for Kirundi Bible (Burundi), these translations can be viewed as highly debatable since the local divinities concerned do not seem originally to have been innately evil like the New Testament figure of Satan.[47] In the case of the Fang, the enlargement of the God-figure (*Nzama*) has corresponded with a foreign importation of the Christian concept of an intrinsically evil being. The Fang adopted a borrowed word (*deble*), probably derived from West African pidgin English, to refer to the Devil while the character of Satan in the book of Job is simply rendered orally in Fang as *Sátan*.[48] The absence of any indigenous content of these "zero-meaning" terms, as David Bosch described them, paved the way for the religious imagination of the Fang to regard the *deble* as *Nzama*'s dark counterpart and the originating source and power of *mbwo*.[49] In the Fang conception, this invested the *deble* with traits of the deity, albeit in a negative fashion.[50] Yet the *deble* was not only conceptualized, in dualistic opposition to *Nzama*, as an intrinsically evil "deity" but also was thoroughly "humanized" by being closely linked to anti-social human malevolence as epitomized by *mbwo* (witchcraft).

This foreign importation of the *deble* onto the cosmological map of the universe has been radically accentuated by Fang Pentecostals. In the worldview of Fang Pentecostals, the "incarnation" of the *deble*—a spiritual being linked to all that is evil in the world—can hardly be described as otiose, distant, or remote but represents an immanent expression of evil conceived in highly familiar terms. In this Pentecostalization of the cosmos,[51] not only have witches and demons become virtually synonymous concepts but also the *deble* has been inserted as a nearly ubiquitous presence within the causal universe who has been hitched to the prodigious category of witchcraft in the societal psyche.[52] To utilize language from the Nicene Creed, the *deble* comes fairly close to being *homooúsios* (of the "same substance") to the

---

47. Gbádégesin, "Changing Roles of Èsù," 33–53; Bosch, "The Problem of Evil in Africa," 40.

48. Allen Pierce, email message to author, March 11, 2013. Pidgin English is spoken on the *region insular* (formerly Bioko island). Pierce served as a missionary for approximately twenty years working on the translation of the Fang New Testament.

49. Bosch, "The Problem of Evil in Africa," 40.

50. Fernandez, *Bwiti*, 227–28.

51. See Kalu, "Preserving a Worldview," 110–37; Kifleyesus, "Cosmologies in Collision," 75–92.

52. Onyinah, "Akan Witchcraft and the Concept of Exorcism in the Church of Pentecost," 231–32.

divine realm and *homooúsios* to the human realm: divinized like *Nzama* (God) and humanized through *mbwo* (witchcraft). At the same time, although this radical re-drawing of the cosmos has effectively substituted the *deble* for *Nzama* as the ultimate causal agent in the universe, quite paradoxically, Pentecostals have nonetheless brought *Nzama* more "into" or "within" the causal and operational worldview of the Fang through Pentecostalizing the old routes and traditional rituals to deal with witchcraft. In other words, by re-inserting *Nzama* violently into the causal universe primarily through deliverance ministries, *Nzama* has been given a "ritual space" in which to operate, a space in the causal universe which *Nzama* had never occupied before—either within the Fang traditional cosmos or within missionary Christianity. In traditional terminology, Pentecostal deliverance ministries function like a Pentecostalized version of Nguí, the now defunct witchcraft eradication cult which nonetheless has been conceptually raised to life through Pentecostal practice.[53]

Job between God and the Devil

The Figure of Job and Reader-Centered Hermeneutics

Considering the centrality of how issues of moral etiology affected the cosmology during the process of Christian inculturation, it is hardly surprising that these issues come prominently to the foreground as ordinary readers appropriate the scriptures, particularly with respect to the book of Job. For Christians in Equatorial Guinea, the chief character of the book of Job is the quintessential sufferer of Job himself. Simply put, the figure of Job deeply resonates with ordinary readers. Reflecting a hermeneutical framework which predisposes readers to accentuate highly personal experiences, the *context* of ordinary readers and the *text* of Job were often placed in a dynamic existential dialogue. In fact, in searching for Job, interpreters often went in search of themselves:

---

53. Daneel, "Coping with Wizardry in Zimbabwe in African Initiated Churches (AICs)," 52. In a study of the Masowe weChishanu church in Zimbabwe which does not read the Bible, Matthew Engelke suggests that performative ritual speech both creates experiences of the divine and constitutes religious authority. In this sense, as Fang Pentecostal pastors occupy the role of the *ngangan* in the modern religious marketplace, Pentecostals can be viewed as not only re-creating (in Pentecostal fashion) the traditional rituals to ward off evil but also the ritual performative speech which mediates access to the spiritual realm and constitutes religious authority; see Engelke, "Text and Performance in an African Church," 77.

Assembly of the Holy Spirit: It is not the history of the "Job in the past," it is the history of the life of each one of us today. *It is the life of me and you.* Amen?⁵⁴

Reformed Presbyterian Church: We do not limit ourselves simply by saying: "Ah, this man suffered much, poor guy, now it's over." No. *We proceed as if reading our own lives right alongside Job.*⁵⁵

Joy of My Salvation: You, being Job, what would you do?⁵⁶

The quest for "Job as an example" was one of *the* central leitmotifs in Fang interpretations of the Joban text. The Presbyterian Bible studies, for instance, spent hours arguing about the substance of Job's sin in order to determine exactly *how* and *how far* contemporary Christians should replicate Job's response as a template in the midst of suffering. Jesus of Nazareth, whilst unique among biblical figures for Fang Protestants, hardly owns squatter's rights in being elevated from narrative stories and commended to believers as an example to follow. Ordinary readers of Job tended to dynamically read their own lives "side by side" with the figure of Job. And while such hermeneutical postures presumably contain the seeds of personal transformation, reader-centered hermeneutics may also be critiqued for opening the door to the possibility that the identity of the reader dominates or overshadows the concerns of the biblical text.

In the search to identify the "Job" worthy to emulate, echoes of William Lane Craig's critique (paraphrasing George Tyrell) that each historical Jesus interpreter "looked down the long well of history and saw his own face reflected at the bottom," may faintly be heard in characterizing the reader-centered approach to the scriptures.⁵⁷ *In Equatorial Guinea, the grassroots studies of Job produced several instances where "Job" began to reflect the idiosyncratic identities and priorities reflected in each church tradition.* For instance, Prophet Frederic, preaching in the Assembly of the Holy Spirit, began by describing with dramatic flair the vast riches and wealth of Job:

> The Bible says that Job had a multitude of servants. The Bible says that this man was the most esteemed of all the men of the East. Hallelujah! Job occupied first place! He was rich! Hallelujah. [Proceeds to list all of Job's animals a *second* time.] He was a rich man. A man *very* rich! He had *many* servants. His servants

54. Marcellino Abeso Nsu, Assembly of the Holy Spirit, Sermon, June 6, 2012.
55. Reformed Presbyterian Church, Bible Study, Job 11:1–20, October 24, 2012.
56. Joy of My Salvation, Bible Study, Job 3, November 9, 2011.
57. Craig, *Reasonable Faith*, 218. Craig is paraphrasing Tyrrell, *Christianity at the Cross-Roads*, 44.

shared in his possessions. And *they* were very rich. The servants! . . . Job was a blessed man.[58]

For Prophet Frederic, *Job the Prosperous* was the perfect prototype for his celebration of the message of prosperity.[59] For Joy of My Salvation, Job represented the consummate spiritual and godly man who "prayed to God in all moments" and "sought a total purification" from sin, reflecting the holiness principles upon which the church was founded.[60] In Joy of My Salvation, Job's *spiritual* qualities as "blameless and upright" and as "one who feared God and turned away from evil" (Job 1:1b) most centrally distinguished Job as a "man of God" or a "servant of God"—favorite Pentecostal descriptions of the ideal Christian type. In the Presbyterian Church, the first response to the question "who was Job?" indicated that "Job was a good person" who was also identified as a responsible and hard-working family man:

Leader: The first response is that Job was "a good person" . . . What more can we say about him, in order to understand Job?

Juan: Yes, there is another thing: Job took care of his family. He cared deeply about his family.[61]

Later, the leader marveled at "the ability of the person of Job to be able to control so many servants. . . . We can say that Job was a responsible man. Quite responsible."[62] Whilst the picture of Job amongst Presbyterians cannot be collapsed into a simple caricature of Job as a good and responsible family man, the fact that more middle-aged employed adults attend the Reformed Presbyterian Church than any other single Protestant denomination in the country underscores the general point: reader-centered hermeneutics often tends to reflect the identity of the interpreters themselves, a projection of their idealized self. Whereas Craig argued that the quest for the historical Jesus resulted in identifying "Strauss's Hegelian Jesus, Renan's sentimental Jesus, Bauer's non-existent Jesus, Ritschl's liberal Jesus and so forth,"[63] in the reader-centered search for the figure of Job, different portraits of Job emerged: *Job the Prosperous*, *Job the Spiritual Man*, and *Job the Responsible*

---

58. Frederic Fouahouly, Assembly of the Holy Spirit, Sermon, Job 1:1–5 and various passages, June 15, 2012.

59. See chapter 3, section "Prophetic Seminars: Celebrating the Message of Prosperity."

60. Basilio Oyono, Joy of My Salvation, October 9, 2011.

61. Reformed Presbyterian Church, Bible Study, Job 1–2, October 17, 2011.

62. Ibid.

63. Craig, *Reasonable Faith*, 218.

Family Man, each reflecting the respective latent characteristics of the three strands of Fang Protestantism.

The Image of Job "between God and the Devil"

Amongst the portraits of Job explored by Fang readers, undoubtedly the most common was the image of Job situated perilously between God and the Devil. In other words, more than the characteristics which *divide* Fang Protestants in their interpretations of the figure of Job are the *commonalities* rooted in the worldview which helped formulate key questions that ordinary readers brought to the Joban text. For Fang Protestants, Job resided in the midst of a precarious cosmological situation analogous to traditional Fang fishermen whose boats are often violently subjected to the waves and roar of the sea:

> I would like us to see that three figures are found in the book of Job . . . the figure of God, the figure of Job, and the figure of Satan. We have to observe that of these three figures, *Job is found in the middle*. I would say that on the right side is God; and on the left side is the Devil; and Job is in between.[64]

> In other words, *the life of Job is being thrown about between God and the Devil*. The Devil asking for the life of Job—and all that he had—and God allowing it.[65]

To continue the metaphor, Job was caught in the eye of a cosmic storm in "being thrown about between God and the Devil," a situation not unlike Fang Protestants who live in the midst of a complex cosmic conflict between *Nzama* (God) and the *deble* (Devil). For Fang interpreters, one of the most frequently occurring questions which surfaced throughout the study of Job was the question of responsibility or culpability. In the Fang worldview, blame must always be assigned; blame is a practical consequence and outworking of its preoccupation with finding the moral etiology of evil and suffering. In light of the Bible's unequivocal initial portrayal of Job as "blameless and upright" (Job 1:1b) and the unfolding narrative drama wherein Job's suffering (Job 1:13–19) occurs on the heels of the God-Satan dialogue (Job 1:6–12), Fang appropriations of the Joban prologue primarily centered upon unraveling this Gordian knot relating to the problem of evil:

---

64. Alberto Mañe Ebo Asong, Reformed Presbyterian Church, Sermon, Job 4:1–11, October 23, 2011.

65. Basilio Oyono, Joy of My Salvation, Sermon, Job 3:1–4, October 16, 2011.

who was chiefly responsible for Job's suffering? Yet in answering the question for Job, ordinary readers were also engaged in answering it for themselves.

Presbyterians, the Causal Conundrum, and the Image of God

As the Fang cosmological map underwent schematic changes during the encounter with Christianity, easily the most dissatisfied group were ordinary Presbyterians who felt a deep loss as ritual practice was subordinated to the Reformed emphasis on intellectual belief. Simply put, intellectual retreat to *Nzama* as the Supreme Being is not a natural Fang response when confronted with the evil of witchcraft. During hermeneutical reflection upon Job, Presbyterian pastors and lay people maintained neither an existential immediacy to the Devil nor engaged in a rich narrative description of Satan's work. Nevertheless, the ambiguities of conceiving of *Nzama* as central and prominent within the causal universe were not without their difficulties, particularly since God's eternal opponent, the Devil, "prowls around like a roaring lion" virtually begging to be blamed for evil and suffering (1 Pet 5:8 ESV). These ambiguities of moral etiology, reflected in their Christianized cosmology, were often contemplated by ordinary Presbyterians. During a Bible study on the Joban prologue (Job 1–2), Presbyterian lay people disputed the causal origins of Job's sufferings in a heated and cantankerous discussion:

> *Lucas:* Who is the responsible one?
>
> *María Carmen:* Satan.
>
> *Lucas:* I believe that Satan could do all those things because God ordered him to do so.
>
> [*Several women vehemently disagree amongst themselves.*]
>
> *Lucas:* Who is the one responsible for all of these things? Of all that was done? And give arguments. Let's see.
>
> *Tomás:* I believe that he that has the power . . . is the responsible one. When God permits a certain thing, it's in order to fulfill a purpose. He's not responsible like the one that can crush you but God permitted evil for a purpose. God has an indirect responsibility. God is indirectly responsible.
>
> *Isabella:* The one with the blame is Satan. Permit is one thing. It's another thing [to say]: "I'm going to kill my child." . . . Satan is the one with the blame.

María Carmen: Satan is the one to blame because he has a purpose. The work of Satan is to move us away from God.... When Job loses everything that he has, Satan wants Job to say the same thing that we are saying here now: "God is the one responsible." And in this way, Satan gets to separate us from the protection and love of God that we have. Satan—those are his works.

Tomás: I'm going to insist upon what exactly is responsibility. God has the power to say to Satan: "Stop." And nothing will happen. But since he permits it, God is now responsible. But he's responsible with a purpose.... What is the purpose of God? That we believers learn from Job. God is not responsible in a way which makes him guilty. No. I don't talk about blame. No. I talk about responsibility.

Isabella: I still say that the Devil is the responsible one. And that he's the one to blame.[66]

As this back-and-forth argument developed, an interesting division amongst the group became apparent: men advocated God as the primary causal actor while women vehemently laid the blame at the doorstep of Satan.[67] Yet ordinary Presbyterians, both men and women, are faced with the same dilemma: whether conceptualizing God or Satan as the chief causal being in the universe, all are urged by their ministers to *believe* that God is more powerful than the *ngangan* during times of suffering and sickness:

Preacher: "Naked I came from my mother's womb, and naked shall I return there; the Lord gave, and the Lord has taken away; blessed be the name of the Lord." This is the response that we should give in difficult situations. But brothers and sisters, in many occasions we do not arrive at expressing those words.... I believe that if we were like Job—in a situation like that—we would have finished up in the *curanderías*. We would have went around asking: "*Who* did this to me?" ... And Job could have attributed that situation to some family members, such as we do on many occasions, but he didn't behave in this manner. There

---

66. Reformed Presbyterian Church, Bible Study, Job 1–2, October 17, 2011.

67. In a patriarchal society, men are predisposed to conceptualizing responsibility and power in family dynamics "behind the scenes" (e.g., men have the "last word"), perhaps influencing their belief that God would be primarily responsible for Job's sufferings. On the other hand, women's immediacy to witchcraft is regularly magnified since women are the primary care-givers to children who frequently experience sicknesses regarded as originating in the nocturnal realm of witchcraft, perhaps making women more predisposed to regarding the Devil as the entity most responsible for Job's sufferings.

> are families that do not get along because the brother, the sister attributed [misfortune] to something that cursed their child which is the cause of the misfortune that they have in their life.
>
> But brothers and sisters, this should not be our behavior in the difficult situations of our lives. The spiritual maturity of Job helped him to recognize God and bless God. Therefore, spiritual maturity should help us to endure the bad and bless God in the good in acting with faithfulness before our God. In moments of pain, we raise our voice to God and we should ask for strength. In moments of happiness we should also raise our voice to God to bless his name. . . . Job gives us a good example of the reactions of a person of faith when one goes through tragic moments in their life. The example [of Job] serves us although our own customs demand the contrary. *Sometimes in difficult situations, we feel alone because it seems that God doesn't intervene in order to change the circumstances*, the [circumstances] that surround us. And in those moments, we are in the habit of cursing the name of our God. Brothers and sisters, in moments like this, we can lift our voice to God to express to him our love and faithfulness as Job did.[68]

Behind this heartfelt homiletical appeal for believers to trust God (like Job) in the face of adversity lie the ambiguities of a causal universe. Whereas Meyer makes the Devil the watershed figure between an Africanization "from above" and an Africanization "from below" amidst the Evangelical Presbyterian Church in Ghana, she does not thoroughly address the larger issue rooted in the religio-cultural worldview—the notion of causality. In contrast, the ambiguity sensed by Presbyterians in Equatorial Guinea is related less to the centrality now given to the Devil and more to the dissatisfaction some Presbyterians have felt in integrating *Nzama* into the causal universe. Even amongst Presbyterian Bible study participants who tended to lay the blame for Job's suffering at the doorstep of the Devil, the role of the Devil in the Joban story was never amplified nor was a rich characterization of his personality considered. Amongst Presbyterians, the description of Satan's involvement in Job's story was matter-of-fact and marginal to the overall trajectory of the Joban narrative. For these Presbyterians, the dynamic local idiom of *mbwo* (witchcraft) can survive without retreating to "Christian discourse" about Satan.[69] For many Presbyterians, the problem

---

68. Manuel Owono Akara Oke, Reformed Presbyterian Church, Sermon, Job 1, October. 9, 2011.

69. See also Merz, "'I Am a Witch in the Holy Spirit,'" 202. Merz argues that diabolization often "does not accredit witchcraft its own discourse in its own right."

lies more with a sense of frustration that while *Nzama's* conceptual space is now theoretically writ large upon the cosmological universe (due to *Nzama's* position of being elevated to the Creator God and Supreme Being), *Nzama's* integration within the day-to-day causal universe has never been rendered wholly satisfactory personally or existentially. In this situation, Presbyterians hear frequent pastoral pleas to retreat to God in the midst of suffering. But the pastors themselves are often keenly aware that many feel God's abandonment precisely during these times of crisis. To reiterate the sentiment of Pastor Manuel: "Sometimes in difficult situations, we feel alone because it seems that *God doesn't intervene* in order to change the circumstance. . . . And in those moments, we are in the habit of cursing the name of our God."[70] In other words, the feeling of abandonment by God is explicitly linked to God's refusal or (more likely) his inherent inability to affect the causal universe from within the cosmological imagination of missionary-founded Christianity. This feeling of "God-abandonment" was a frequent sentiment arising from Presbyterian pulpits and Bible studies:

> But when we find ourselves in a difficult situation, for many of us, it is easy to blaspheme the name of our God.[71]

> Many of us, when we receive the good that God has blessed us with, we do not thank him. We even forget him. "Everything is good. I have everything. I have a car. I have money. I have powers." God—a little bit a part. Everything's fine. But when suffering comes, when problems arrive, when you find yourself in a difficult situation, many of us now begin to accuse God.[72]

This frustration with *Nzama*—and blaming him for suffering or evil—is directly tied to their Christianization of the cosmos wherein God's role is defined as preeminent over the entire causal universe. But blame being directed towards *Nzama* can also be understood as being rooted in a basic continuity with indigenous religiosity whose orientation often accounts for suffering by blaming the nocturnal realm of *mbwo* (witchcraft) or the ancestors' fickle temperament. Traditionally for the Fang, no entity in the cosmos was conceived as so intrinsically "good" as to be exempt from being a causative agent in suffering. As the Fang proverb suggests, "good and bad walk together" (*abe ye mbeng ba wulu nsama*).[73] A moral

---

70. Manuel Owono Akara Oke, Reformed Presbyterian Church, Sermon, Job 1, October 9, 2011.

71. Ibid.

72. Reformed Presbyterian Church, Bible Study, Job 3, October 18, 2011.

73. Fernandez, *Bwiti*, 215, 227.

universe where good and evil exist in a Manichean duality is foreign to the Fang, if not to most African societies traditionally.[74] On the other hand, the traditional entity of the *evus*, though often malevolently connected with an individualized and anti-social pursuit of cultural goals, was also traditionally held to invest traditional healers (*ngangan*), clan chiefs (*nkúkúmá*), and the wealthy (*nkúkúm*) with socialized privileges for the greater good of the community.[75] As Mbiti writes, "Mystical power is neither good nor evil in itself; but when used maliciously by some individuals it is experienced as evil."[76] For the Fang, evil is not an abstract concept but manifested primarily through concrete evil actions.[77] In this light, when the moral etiology of evil and suffering cannot be linked to a malicious *human* action because the causal source of the suffering remains a mystery, God often serves as a convenient scapegoat for suffering owing to his prominent position in the Presbyterian cosmos.

As local Presbyterians engaged with Joban texts, plain-spoken responses like "God wants to know to what extreme we love him" (Claudia) or "God wants to see how far Job's faith reaches" (Tomás) or "God gives us these tests; He gave them to Job, He also gives them to us" (Lucía) all rested upon a critical assumption that the Christian faith will always be tested.[78] As one elderly Presbyterian woman succinctly put it, "In our culture, friendship is not deemed friendship until a child dies."[79] In other words, only when retributive blame and witchcraft accusations are *not* directed at family members and friends during a crisis is that friendship counted as genuine. In very practical terms, the preoccupation with establishing the moral etiology of evil means that friendships are often tested in the crucible of suffering, and this ordinary reader analogously applied this same logic to God: only when accusations are *not* directed at God in the midst of suffering is that relationship considered genuine. Although Fang Presbyterians more typically focused on the anthropocentric "level of faith" or "level of love" Job was called upon to display during the crisis, an image of God nevertheless emerged through the back-door of faith: the image of God as a testing God. *Nzama* is a God who undeniably tests his children. The *Nzama* or *ngangan* litmus test of Christian faithfulness inculcated by the early missionaries

---

74. Bosch, "The Problem of Evil in Africa," 39–41.

75. Mbana, *Brujeria Fang en Guinea Ecuatorial*, 41.

76. Mbiti, *African Religions and Philosophy*, 205.

77. See also Gregor, "Evil and Salvation in African Religion and Christianity," 4.

78. Reformed Presbyterian Church, Bible Study, Job 9:27–35; 13:13–19; 16:18–22; 19:23–27, October 25, 2011.

79. Ibid.

has arguably been woven so deeply into the fabric of Presbyterianism as to become stamped or projected upon the very image of God. This image of a *testing God* offers a particularly helpful image to Presbyterians who are confronted by *disappointing aspirations of the abundant life* and a *Christianized causal universe which does not function or cooperate according to local patterns of religiosity*. Since *Nzama* exists as the ultimate causal being in the cosmos—albeit with an almost inherent *in*ability to helpfully impinge upon causal problems arising within the worldview (i.e., witchcraft)—being faithful to *Nzama* during the crises of life is viewed by Presbyterians as one of the most genuine and authentic signs of faith. Aided by their Christianized cosmos, that idea that *Nzama* gives these tests to Job (and to believers) is virtually taken-for-granted within this ecclesial worldview. In the virtual absence of a charismatic Devil figure, the construction of the image of God as a testing God arguably represents such a pivotal and integral theology for undergirding Christian faith in the midst of suffering that the internal dynamics of the Reformed Presbyterian Church virtually demand it.[80]

Pentecostals, Fang Witchcraft, and a Rich Narrative Description of the Devil

Whilst Fang Pentecostalism was not directly birthed out of indigenous dissatisfaction with missionary-founded churches in Equatorial Guinea, the Pentecostal movement nevertheless seems to have an intuitive sense of the inadequacies bequeathed from missionary Christianity, centering principally upon the subordination of rituals to belief and the conceptual problem of locating *Nzama* as the chief causal being in a universe filled with *mbwo* (witchcraft). By integrating the figure of the Devil more centrally into ecclesial praxis and through offering a rich narrative description of his character and deeds, Fang Pentecostalism offers a tangible way to navigate the causal universe and ritually combat *mbwo* without visiting the *ngangan* while simultaneously carving out a more culturally-satisfying cosmological space for *Nzama*.

Informed by their organization of the causal universe, it would hardly be an overstatement to say that the Devil has captured the interpretive

---

80. This tension of conceiving of the cosmos as fused with suffering from divine (God) or nearly divine (Satan) actors while nonetheless retaining the traditional view of the cosmos as generally benevolent, may help explain the paradox often found in many African believers who teeter between resignation (e.g., "it is the will of God") and the frenzied, sometimes fanatical, search for a solution in the midst of suffering. For the tendency towards resignation amongst Gambian Muslims, see Sanneh, *Summoned from the Margin*, 3–22.

imagination of Fang Pentecostals like no other biblical figure. For Fang Pentecostals, the figure of Satan in the book of Job was depicted with a narrative artistry which rendered the Devil as playfully feisty, relentlessly brutal, and singularly responsible for *mbwo* (witchcraft). Rather than bracketing off the conversations between God and Satan in the Joban prologue (Job 1:6–12; 2:1–6) as a unique literary dialogue quite exceptional within the Old Testament canon, the idea of Satan "going to and fro" throughout the earth (displaying *de facto* ubiquity) and audaciously entering into the heavenly court was viewed as prototypical activity for Satan amongst local Pentecostals:

> *Preacher*: The Devil seeks his life every day. Amen?
>
> *Congregation*: Amen.
>
> *Preacher*: The Devil seeks [Job's] life every day. Every time. Every moment. If the Devil could get where God is every day, he could ask for *your* life also everyday. In order to do something in *your* life every day. In order that every day that you wake up, you'll have a new problem—a new problem with the Devil.[81]

In the Assembly of the Holy Spirit, one preacher portrayed the Devil through a veritable montage of narrative images: as a brutal criminal, like a witch who visits believers "in your bed at night" (a blatant allusion to the *evus* of witchcraft), and as a landed aristocrat surveying his estate:

> *Preacher*: And I wonder: what job is Satan doing? It says that he goes around throughout the whole earth as if he was the owner of the whole earth. It's like someone who has done a great work! For example, you have planted a great plantation and someone sees you going around in your great plantation and asks you: "What are you doing?" And you say: "I'm going around to look at my work." That's how Satan was responding. "That I've just finished going around the whole earth!" [God to Satan:] "But why have you gone around the whole earth? What are you looking for on the earth?" To do all this work, *Satan doesn't sleep*! He always goes around the earth. You don't know how many times he arrives at *your bed at night* because he comes to look for you. You don't know how many times he goes around *your village*. Going around all the earth!
>
> Satan considers this first test [referring to Job 1:13–19] like a game. Because already he had taken everything from Job. . . . Listen to how criminal all of this is! For us, Satan is a criminal who hopes to destroy all of our lives. Now I'm amazed at

81. Basilio Oyono, Joy of My Salvation, Sermon, Job 1–2, October 9, 2011.

the people who say: "I'm going to go with Satan!" Satan is so criminal that he could take a needle and poke you in the eye. Hallelujah! He's a criminal for the children of God because he is working to win your lives.[82]

As was the case for Presbyterians, the search to determine the moral etiology of Job's sufferings was foundational for local Pentecostals. Yet for Pentecostals, it was principally the figure of Satan, depicted in all his "Christian glory" as the embodiment of Fang witchcraft, whom Pentecostals deemed most responsible for Job's suffering:

> *Marta*: When something happens to you, suffering or whatever thing that can occur in your life, do we tend to think that this comes from God?
>
> *Elena*: I would say no. The majority of the time we think that it is the Devil that pursues us. And everything that comes to us as suffering, we cannot think that this could come from God if it's evil. We think that all the good things come from God because God is good, God is marvelous. But if something bad reaches you—a sickness so rare—you cannot think that God can permit it, but "it's the Devil that torments me. The Devil is pursuing me. How many things is he bringing to me now?" But I do not believe that in these moments of suffering—I say of pain, of true pain—you cannot say to me that this comes from God! . . . We say. "what is here now is from the Devil—he seeks me, he wants to take me away, he wants to frustrate me." *We attribute everything to the Devil.* That is what I think.[83]

Pentecostals presented a rich narrative description of Satan as a figure who, despite being traditionally absent from the Fang cosmology, nevertheless behaves according to locally-satisfying patterns of causality with regards to the nature of (witchcraft) evil.

For Fang Pentecostals, the moral etiology of Job's evil and the rightful blame for his sufferings was clearly laid at the feet of a charismatic Devil figure. Fang Pentecostals even tended to read "against the text" by contrasting Job's *limited* knowledge to the *certain* knowledge of Pentecostals with respect to the causal origins of their sufferings. As one preacher put it, "Job was not a person that could understand what we want to understand this morning."[84] For this preacher, Pentecostal ideology clearly superseded the

---

82. Liborio Nvo Ndong, Assembly of the Holy Spirit, Sermon, Job 2, May 11, 2012.
83. Joy of My Salvation, Bible Study, Job 1–2, November 16, 2011.
84. Basilio Oyono, Joy of My Salvation, Sermon, Job 1–2, October 9, 2011.

vague knowledge that Job possessed insofar as suffering should be *rightly* attributed not to God but rather to the chicanery and malevolence of the Devil. As Pastor Liborio from Assembly of the Holy Spirit articulated, "Job began with God. Here we find the difference between our life and the life of Job. We suffer nowadays first because we haven't begun with God. We've begun with tradition, we've begun with witchcraft, we've begun with traditional pacts."[85] Therefore, even if interpretive clues in the text of Job provided Pentecostal preachers with sufficient ammunition to suggest that God was responsible for Job's sufferings, their own Pentecostalized cosmos—which conceives of the Devil as causally responsible for evil—provided the decisive paradigm in attributing the moral etiology of Job's sufferings as rooted primarily in the activity of the Devil.

By way of summary, we may observe that the causal universe not only provided the interpretative *agenda* for the Joban prologue by prioritizing questions of moral etiology (i.e., "who is ultimately responsible for Job's sufferings?") but also shaped the interpretative *response* to this central question so that it reflected the way in which local Christians organized the cosmological universe. In this respect, local readings of the Joban prologue primarily were rooted in, if not driven by, what we may term *theocosmology*—a cosmologically-oriented theology—which provided the dominant lens through which both Fang Presbyterians and Pentecostals negotiated the biblical text. Thus, as local Christians renegotiated their own cosmological maps of the universe in response to Christianity, the (biblical) text can be viewed as dynamically altering the (cultural) context. Yet this process is hardly a one-way street. These Christianized cosmologies, calibrated differently by various church traditions, have served in turn as templates which guide ordinary readers in their appropriation of the biblical text.

The Irony of Indigenization: A Theologized God vs. A Narrated Devil

Yet the question lingers: what accounts for this fascination with the Devil amongst Fang Pentecostals? As Meyer has insightfully recognized, "Nowhere in the Scriptures is it [the Devil] presented coherently. The Devil is the most obscure figure in the Christian doctrine, only vaguely described in the Bible. He therefore supplies room for speculation about his existence and actions in the world."[86] Meyer emphasizes that the Devil is "good to think with" for Ewe Christians in Ghana because the image of the Devil

---

85. Liborio Nvo Ndong, Assembly of the Holy Spirit, Sermon, Job 1, May 9, 2012.
86. Meyer, "'If You Are a Devil, You Are a Witch,'" 106.

provides a strict boundary-marker between Christianity and Ewe religion while nevertheless keeping traditional explanatory concerns close to Ewe Christians.[87] For Fang Pentecostals, we might additionally argue, the ubiquity of the Devil can also be squared with the narrative ethos or narrative way in which the Fang typically tend to explain the moral universe. The image of the Devil, though unparalleled in the traditional cosmology, connects powerfully, viscerally, and seamlessly to indigenous narrative discourse about the ubiquity of evil. In fact, amongst Fang Pentecostals, the narrative conceptualization of the Devil grew to such proportions as to lay *de facto* claim to attributes traditionally reserved for God alone:

> *Preacher*: Satan knows our weak points. Hallelujah! He knows our weak points. This does not mean that he knows your thoughts. The only one that knows our thoughts is God. Satan does not know your thoughts. Hallelujah. *But in the way that you move, this one [Satan] knows that "this one is thinking such a thing."* Hallelujah. Satan is not omniscient. God is omniscient. But Satan, if he does this to you: "Whoa" [The preacher makes a loud shout, personifying Satan shouting at the believer to scare him or her], you begin to tremble. *He [Satan] begins to read everything that you say. Hallelujah! Everything that you say, he begins to read your thoughts with only this one gesture.*[88]

Although acknowledging a theological category which technically reserves omniscience for God alone, this narrative description of Satan, in practical terms, essentially serves to bestow omniscience on God's dark counterpart.

The Fang penchant for story-telling becomes the epistemological basis for the dynamic and near ubiquitous appropriation of the figure of the Devil amongst local Pentecostals. As Evans-Pritchard recognized for the Azande, nearly everyone is an authority or expert on witchcraft.[89] In Equatorial Guinea, the situation is no different: stories of witchcraft not only proliferate and race through communities at astounding speeds but also represent one of the chief talking points within the entire society.[90] Though the actual terms may have changed with the arrival of Christianity (from *evus* to *deble*), the basic "lexicon of evil" with its evocative, personified, and explicatory portrayal of evil remains virtually the same. In other words, just as

---

87. Meyer, *Translating the Devil: Religion and Modernity*, 111; Meyer, "'If You Are a Devil, You Are a Witch,'" 113–14.

88. Liborio Nvo Ndong, Assembly of the Holy Spirit, Sermon, Job 1, May 9, 2012.

89. Evans-Pritchard, *Witchcraft, Oracles and Magic Among the Azande*, 1: "Every Zande is an authority on witchcraft."

90. See Ekomo et al., *Palabras que No Tienen Boca*.

witchcraft is one of the most robust and pervasive talking points within the entire society, the church's near ubiquitous discourse and praxis revolving around the Devil represents a basic point of continuity with the larger societal narrative. Thus, when Fang Pentecostals (1) conceptualized the Devil as one who absorbs the widespread nighttime activity of Fang *mbwo* as well as modern representations of witchcraft currently *en vogue* in Fang territory (e.g., *ekong*,[91] *Mami Wata*[92]) and (2) heralded the church as *the* Christian alternative to Fang *curanderías*, it hardly came as a surprise that the Devil often took on characteristics approaching divinity: nearly omniscient, enormous powerful, and seemingly ubiquitous.

As ordinary Pentecostal readers interacted with the Joban text, they portrayed the Devil's role in the book of Job with a vividness and immediacy that surpassed the role given to God by any strand of Fang Protestantism. Whereas the Devil naturally seemed to capture the narrative imagination of these Fang Pentecostals, *Nzama* was often allocated to less robust theoretical categories and described with terms such as "omnipotence," "omnipresence," and "omniscience." That is, whereas the Devil was portrayed using a traditional style of narrative story-telling, thereby coming alive to these Pentecostal believers, the figure of God, in both Presbyterian and Pentecostal churches, was often referred to utilizing rather remote theoretical constructs or ideas derived from the western-Hellenistic theological tradition.[93] Ironically, despite utilizing indigenous terminology for God (*Nzama*) whilst having to import a borrowed word, probably derived from West African pidgin English,[94] to refer to the Devil (*deble*), it was the conceptualization of the Devil, rather than the figure of God, who was typically portrayed in more robust terms in the appropriation of the book of Job. At the grassroots, God (*Nzama*) was theorized and theologized while the Devil (*deble*) was

---

91. *Ekong* is one of the most popular and newer forms of witchcraft in Equatorial Guinea. Instead of eating his or her victim, a witch steals the victim's body from the grave so that the post-mortem victim can work as a kind of zombie to enrich the witch. See Geschiere, "Witchcraft and New Forms of Wealth," 43–76, esp. 47, 57–60.

92. *Mami Wata* is a water spirit, typically described like a female mermaid with European features, who entices men with promises of wealth and money in exchange for sex. See Frank, "Permitted and Prohibited Wealth," 331–46.

93. The point is that God's character and attributes during the Joban studies were presented with neither the vividness nor the immediacy which characterized portrayals of the Devil by Fang Pentecostals. For example, one Presbyterian argued that Satan was ultimately "held accountable" by God for Job's sufferings by stating: "A little explanation. Because God is omniscient. God is who created everything." In general, Hellenistic categories seemed to hinder a robust depiction of God's agency; Reformed Presbyterian Church, Bible Study, Job 1–2, October 17, 2011.

94. Allen Pierce, email correspondence with author, March 11, 2013.

powerfully narrated, helping to account for the relative nearness and immanence of the Devil for Fang Pentecostals compared to the relative remoteness of God and the hermeneutical indifference afforded to him.

Live Options in Contextualized Theodicy

In exploring Job's sufferings, ordinary readers have been shown to sympathize deeply with the figure of Job, recognizing in Job their own analogous situation as living hazardously "in the middle" between God and the Devil. Like Fang fishermen who diagnose the perils of their trade in order to ensure their own safety, these ordinary readers can analogously be viewed as existentially wrestling with the burdens of theodicy. In order to live peacefully within the cosmos, grassroots Christians sought to negotiate the cosmological foundations of theodicy which co-exist only amidst extreme tension in the face of evil: the celebration of the abundant life and the causal universe. To that end, two dominant theodicies may be identified from appropriations of the book of Job, both chiefly espoused by Pentecostals who tend, more than Presbyterians, to foreground theodicy concerns *pragmatically* in ecclesial praxis and *discursively* through constant reflection upon the nature of evil and suffering. The final section of this chapter, therefore, turns to an examination of two of the most prominent theodicies advocated by Pentecostals in their appropriation of the book of Job.

Theodicy as Pentecostalization and Pentecostalization as Theodicy: Radically Embracing the Causal Universe

In many respects, the rise of Pentecostal Christianity in Africa can be viewed against the backdrop of missionary Christianity's inability to adequately integrate the God-component into the causal worldview of indigenous African peoples. Another way of expressing this state of affairs within missionary Christianity is by focusing on the nature of evil, a dynamic portrayed eloquently by David Bosch:

> the missionaries proclaimed a Christ who released people from guilt which had been induced and who forgave sins of which the church, but not their consciences, found them guilty. On the other hand the area of real sin and evil in society, as Africans experienced it, was left untouched by the church. Thus the true relevance of the Christian message of sin and redemption was

subverted. Redemption was made superficial for it did not penetrate to the heart of the problem of evil.[95]

By placing theodicy and the nature of evil at the forefront of the theological agenda of the church, Pentecostalism has aligned itself more centrally with the preoccupations which traditionally galvanized African ritual practices. Anticipated to some extent by the African Indigenous Churches (AICs)[96] and eventually spilling over to affect Catholic[97] and mainline Protestant churches,[98] part of the attraction of Pentecostalism in Africa resides in its basic affirmation and willingness to engage with the causal universe, including its most prominent discourse of witchcraft.

Yet the allure of the Pentecostal affirmation of causality, with its concomitant attention to witchcraft, begs the question whether Fang Pentecostalism, by embracing the reality and rhetoric of witchcraft, represents a contextualization of, or a capitulation to, the Fang causal universe. Does the frequent Christian rhetoric about *mbwo* (witchcraft), accompanied by the pervasive ecclesial praxis of deliverance ministry, represent an endorsement of indigenous paradigms of evil by paradoxically bolstering or reinforcing belief in *mbwo*?[99] Or, do Pentecostal practices offer liberation by meeting the felt "existential needs and fears of people in a ritually understandable and therefore psychologically and religiously satisfying manner"?[100] These questions are not easily or unequivocally answered, even by Pentecostal insiders themselves. The Assembly of the Holy Spirit's Apostle Esono compared deliverance ministry to having regular *chequeos* (check-ups) at the doctor's office or to the practice of regularly taking the car to the mechanic.[101] Yet Pastor Liborio, also from the Assembly of the Holy Spirit, wondered "how many times can one person be delivered from evil spirits" while openly expressing frustration that some women come habitually "every three

---

95. Bosch, "The Problem of Evil in Africa," 52.

96. As Kalu observes, "The early Pentecostals emerged in the garb of Zionists;" Kalu, "Preserving a Worldview," 124. See also Anderson, "African Independent Churches and Pentecostalism;" Asamoah-Gyadu, *African Charismatics*, 36–63.

97. Konings, "Religious Revival in the Roman Catholic Church and the Autochthony-Allochthony Conflict in Cameroon," 31–56; Lado, "African Catholicism in the Face of Pentecostalism," 22–30.

98. Omenyo, "From the Fringes to the Centre," 39–60.

99. See Shorter, *Jesus and the Witchdoctor*, 197ff; Bosch, "The Problem of Evil in Africa," 55–60; Behrend, "The Rise of Occult Powers, AIDS and the Roman Catholic Church in Western Uganda," 44, 53–55.

100. Daneel, "Exorcism as Combating Wizardry," 311. See also Anderson, "Exorcism and Conversion to African Pentecostalism," 130.

101. Interview, Agustín Edu Esono, Assembly of the Holy Spirit, May 22, 2012.

months" for these deliverance *chequeos*.[102] In Equatorial Guinea, evidence suggests that while combating witchcraft through deliverance ministries *does* provide psychological relief and may *occasionally* lead to conversion, the consolation may only be temporary or for a short duration for many. Just as the Fang visited the *ngangan* for every new case of *okwann mbwo* (witchcraft sickness) so too many people sitting in Pentecostal pews continue to visit the Christian *ngangan*—the "Big Man" Pentecostal pastor—with every new fear, suffering, or sickness related to demonic oppression epitomized by witchcraft. As a movement which displays an uncanny ability for self-criticism, the notion that the Devil often takes "center stage" within the life of the church is not lost upon Pentecostal leaders:

> "The Lord gave and the Lord has taken away; blessed be the name of the Lord." Can somebody [here] say it? I don't believe so. Who can swallow this bitter drink? When they are looking at you as a son of God and now you are suffering, how do we interpret suffering? Witchcraft! Satan! Hallelujah! That's how we interpret suffering. "I suffer because witches are behind me!" *And you give the witches a superior rung.* "I suffer because Satan never wants to leave me in peace." *Satan says:* "Ahhhh, you already have placed me on a higher rung [preacher moves his hand above his head]. I'm already there!" Hallelujah.[103]

By adopting the goals of Fang indigenous religiosity, including the ritual elimination of evil, Pentecostals have essentially embraced a Spirit-filled *curandería-ecclesiology* for their model of the church, which positions the church in the local religious marketplace as *the* Christian alternative to the *ngangan* in combating *mbwo*. But just as *mbwo* keeps the *ngangan* "in the business" of eradicating evil, the Devil also provides Pentecostals with a central and sinister combatant which fuels the cosmic conflict so prevalent within their churches. We would argue, in fact, that the Devil provides such a key sociological function for African Pentecostalism that the whole edifice might well collapse without this demonic image.[104]

As Meyer has observed, "there is no reason to assume that conversion to Christianity would result in a decline of demonology."[105] By tying their ecclesial orientation explicitly to a radical demonology, Pentecostal leaders themselves can often be viewed, quite paradoxically, as being gravely

---

102. Interview, Liborio Nvo Ndong, Assembly of the Holy Spirit, May 16, 2012.

103. Liborio Nvo Ndong, Assembly of the Holy Spirit, Sermon, Job 1, May 9, 2012.

104. Bosch argues for a similar sociological function for witchcraft in African societies; Bosch, "The Problem of Evil in Africa," 43–44.

105. Meyer, "'Delivered from the Powers of Darkness,'" 237.

concerned that *not even the church* provides a place of sanctity from the chancery of witchcraft:

> One has to think: what I'm going through now, where does it come from? Many of us, we have a common enemy that is the Devil. But in our context, what bothers us so much are the problems that have entered in the church on us. Many of us, we have come to the church to escape witchcraft because witchcraft is one of the things that destroys our society. Sometimes when one of us is suffering, the first thing that one thinks of is witchcraft. "Witches are pursuing me. Witches won't let me sleep. Witches pursue [me] even in the church." And this is true. *Witches pursue you even in the church.* Because they have asked for your life. They have chosen [your life] in order to destroy it because they wanted to destroy Job's life. Witches. That's why, many times, these witches enter even in the churches to do their witchcraft in the church. I have heard many testimonies of brothers and sisters who share testimonies that they were sent here by Satan. And they came into the church to make you their people. Witches enter even in the church wanting to destroy lives.[106]

As Abraham Akrong indicates, "although [Pentecostal churches] have exposed the reality of the devil, people are still afraid of the devil."[107] As Pentecostals themselves recognize, witchcraft is messy and its chaotic effects of blame, fear, and accusations often enter the church. (In fact, divisive church splits and pastors being accused of witchcraft are virtually synonymous events in the local Pentecostal community.) Fang Pentecostals have radically embraced the causal universe with its affirmation of *mbwo* (witchcraft), and in so doing, have made the Devil their indispensable "sparring partner" which energizes and informs nearly everything they do. The Devil looms large over the entire Pentecostal landscape: from their hermeneutics, to their sermonic discourses, to their most dominant ecclesial practices. Church attendance at a local Pentecostal church invariably succeeds in placing people within range of—and in a greater proximity to—the rhetoric and practices that focus upon the Devil and his evil machinations. Simply put, the Devil has completely captured center stage in the biblical interpretation and in the theology of local Pentecostals.

Yet the pervasive embrace of causality by Fang Pentecostals likewise has radical implications for their doctrine of God. Whereas the Devil is perceived as the primary causal *problem*, God is touted as the primary

---

106. Liborio Nvo Ndong, Assembly of the Holy Spirit, Sermon, Job 1, May 9, 2012.
107. Akrong, "Towards a Theology of Evil Spirits and Witches," 22.

causal *solution*. Through Spirit-empowered deliverance ministries which declare power "in the name of Jesus," Pentecostals have effectively integrated *Nzama* "into" or "within" a causal cosmology despite the relative marginality of the God-component traditionally. Yet even for Pentecostal insiders, the question whether this theological innovation makes God more accessible for sufferers or narrowly restricts God to solely running the gauntlets of traditional religious causality remains an open question. That is, has God been freed to work within the causal universe of witchcraft or trapped within its confines?

By embracing the *curandería-ecclesiology* paradigm within their churches, Fang Pentecostals are often acutely aware of the dilemmas posed by heralding *Nzama* as a God of solutions. Amongst seminary students and professors, spirited conversations centering upon divine healings are a frequent topic of conversation:

> *Professor*: I preach "Jesus as the best *ngangan*" [traditional healer].
>
> *Alejandro*: Jesus is the best doctor.
>
> *Frederico (Baptist student)*: Yes, they also sing about this. I have heard it one time from a choir: "Jesus is *ngangan*, oooooooh." I don't know how they go about singing that!
>
> *David*: But it's a reality that [Jesus] is *ngangan*, is it not? He heals everything.
>
> *Alejandro*: Jesus heals!
>
> *David*: Jesus heals![108]

Yet such Pentecostal enthusiasm is often tempered by a reticence based upon suspicions that people might be "using" God and the church as a religious "means to an end" without understanding the nature of faith or the character of God:

> *Professor*: That's why, really, when we evangelize the Fang—I am talking about the culture—when we evangelize the Fang, until somebody reaches one year in the church, don't count on it that you have a member.
>
> *Ildefonso*: More!
>
> *Santiago*: One year and a half.

---

108. *Instituto Bíblico "Casa de la Palabra"* (IBCP Seminary), Class on Job, June 8, 2012.

Professor: The person is there with a purpose, bringing to God a prayer and truthfully if time goes on [without God answering the prayer or providing the solution], he's going to blaspheme and leave the church.

David: Because they [in the church] have made a prayer for her and she has stayed there for good health.

Professor: It is a cultural weakness.

David: That's why the Christian churches are full, especially the churches that do deliverance. They are full for that reason, not because the person has faith in Christ.

Daniel: Yes, it's true.[109]

As a movement embodying theodicy concerns, Pentecostal Christianity in Africa has effectively restored the "pathway" from the "concrete danger of witchcraft" to God's love and power in Christ.[110] But the theological danger Fang Pentecostals intuitively seem to recognize is whether God has been *restricted* to those pathways as simply the mechanistic arbiter of the Fang causal universe. In its most pronounced form, God essentially becomes dependent upon causality, meaningless without reference to witchcraft, and defined primarily in relation to the Devil. The rich narrative description of the Devil embraced by local Pentecostals has essentially become the controlling metaphor shaping the very contours of their doctrine of God. One wonders whether the doctrine of God for African Pentecostals has become so wedded to theodicy concerns that other biblical loci (i.e., creation, redemption) which traditionally have shaped the doctrine of God have been effectively muted. One cannot dismiss out of hand the question of whether the doctrine of God, for African Pentecostals, has essentially been reduced to "God the Exorcist" or restricted to "God the Healer." In this theological trajectory, the most pressing question of theodicy for local Pentecostals becomes: if God is defined by the terms set by causality and conceived primarily as the Divine Solution to devilish problems, then is there any worship of God when *Nzama* fails to solve life's problems?

Ironically, despite Fang Pentecostalism's radical embrace of causality, some Pentecostals can be viewed as being deeply suspicious of the latent tendencies the *curandería-ecclesiology* model of the church seems almost

---

109. *Instituto Bíblico "Casa de la Palabra"* (IBCP Seminary), Class on Job, June 1, 2012.

110. Walls, "Worldviews and Christian Conversion," 158.

predisposed to encourage: a propensity to place the abundant life, rather than God, at the center of the religious universe:

> *Catalina*: It's how the people in the world have God. When they have problems, they call the church.... The church goes to pray for him and when he is healed, he returns to his things. Now he has God there as ...
>
> *Marta*: [interrupting] Manipulating God.
>
> *Catalina*: One that is only there [in the church] so that God helps you.
>
> *Lucia*: People are only there to receive from God. But they aren't interested in what God does, what God needs, what God asks of us.[111]

Interestingly, this underlying suspicion that people might be "manipulating God" closely corresponds to the reticence early European missionaries to Africa often expressed about the genuineness of religious conversion and church attendance amongst "the natives."[112] Just as white missionaries in the nineteenth century openly lamented that "the natives" were often interested only in the technology and wealth of the white man (while nevertheless continuing to display a conspicuous consumption of European goods), some Fang Pentecostals of today lament that people are only interested in "manipulating God" in order to secure health and healing (while nevertheless continuing to champion an ecclesial paradigm which unmistakably proclaims a "God of solutions").[113] In positioning the church in the wider society as the Christian alternative to traditional *curanderías*, an openly expressed concern amongst local Pentecostals is that the external pragmatic benefits offered by Pentecostalism may actually serve to overshadow God insofar as *Nzama* is regarded as a functional or mechanistic solution provider to problems occurring within the causal universe.

---

111. Joy of My Salvation, Bible Study, Job 4–5, May 16, 2012.

112. See Peel, *Religious Encounter and the Making of the Yoruba*, 215–47.

113. For another example of this dynamic with respect to the Fang Pentecostals involved in this study, see chapter 6, section "Human Prayer, Divine Sovereignty, and the *Deus Victor*," para. 7 of the section.

The Normalization of Suffering as Theodicy: Destabilizing the Abundant Life

The second dominant theodicy demonstrated in the appropriation of Job by Fang Pentecostals was the attempt to *normalize suffering*. For the Fang, the default ontology of the cosmos is characterized by prosperity, good health, fertility, and long life, the quintessential elements of the abundant life. As the abundant life is affirmed, suffering is excluded. When suffering *does* occur, ritual manipulation of the causal universe is seen as part and parcel in restoring the general benevolence of the cosmos. Simply put, suffering is "not the way it's supposed to be." The causal universe *should* restore life back to its ideal state. Therefore, ordinary readers of Job who attempted to "normalize suffering" by utilizing Job as their model can be viewed as swimming decidedly upstream against the prevailing cultural current.

As we have seen, Pentecostalism's primary theodicy resides in a radical embrace of causality with a view towards the elimination of evil. Evil is viewed as intrinsically incompatible with the foundational assumptions of the abundant life and the causal universe. Evil is a reality which, to utilize a favorite idiom of Fang Pentecostals, requires aggressive *combate* (combat, battle) rather than idle acceptance. Yet Pentecostals intuitively seem to recognize that questions of the nature and origin of evil represent complexities far too dense and variegated to comprise only a single response. Thus, a secondary theodicy embraced by some Pentecostals, namely, the "normalization of suffering," tends to act as a kind of "safety valve" in the event that their primary theodicy proves ultimately inadequate in providing the kind of ideal solution envisioned. Before engaging in a diabolization of Job's sufferings, Pastor Liborio of the Assembly of the Holy Spirit, reflected early on in both of his sermons on the Joban prologue about the naturalness or normalcy of suffering:

> Sermon on Job 2: In the moment that you are born, you are born accompanied by death.... We cannot forget this when we are rejoicing. That one day, there will be suffering. Suffering comes at any moment. The kings of the earth suffer. Presidents suffer. Women suffer. Men suffer. The poor suffer. Thus, suffering is next to joy. If there is joy, there is also suffering. Hallelujah. Therefore, we cannot deny this reality. And we are talking about this reality because every day is like a blow that we suffer on the head.[114]

---

114. Liborio Nvo Ndong, Assembly of the Holy Spirit, Sermon, Job 2, May 11, 2012.

> *Sermon on Job 1*: Brothers and sisters, what we are going to study this afternoon is that first: suffering exists for good people and for bad people. For those that are in the church and for those that aren't in the church. Suffering on an initial level is natural. Hallelujah. If you have been born, one day you are going to suffer.[115]

In a denomination known to frequently host prosperity gospel preachers, Pastor Liborio nonetheless spends considerable pedagogical energy with an eye towards destabilizing the assumptions of the abundant life.

Yet the message of the normalcy of suffering is not a message easily heard within Pentecostal churches. Particularly since ecclesial praxis seems to work in precisely the opposite direction in its aggressive pursuit of the abundant life. Ordinary readers of Job, reflecting on this dynamic, admitted that "escaping from Satan" can be easily misconstrued as "escaping from suffering" in the context of Pentecostal rhetoric in church services which emphasize the key words of victory, deliverance, power, healing, triumph, and breakthrough:

> When you come to the church, what is in your mind is that: "Now I have escaped from Satan. Now I am in the hands of God. And there God is going to protect me. *Now I'm not going to have more suffering.* I'm not going to be hungry. . . . I am in the hands of God." Many times what allows us to remain in the church is when you have come sick [and] God heals you. You see a miracle. This allows you to remain in the church. *Then, being in the church, when things happen to you—when things go bad—what you think is to return to the world.* Or, what you think is "I don't believe God has power, eh?" Everything that happens to me, they have told me: "'Jesus heals', 'Jesus delivers', 'Jesus has power', 'Jesus has such and such'. And now, what is happening to me?" And sometimes you think that even *now* Satan is in you, he is dominating your life, even *now* he has power in your life. It's what you think. But I know that once we accept Christ as Lord and Savior, God takes control of our lives. *But when we are still in the world of suffering, we are not exempt* [from suffering]. All those things we are going to receive even being Christians, *but many times we don't think like that.*[116]

As this middle-age woman in Joy of My Salvation church indicates, as Pentecostals engage in divine healing and deliverance from the demonic,

---

115. Liborio Nvo Ndong, Assembly of the Holy Spirit, Sermon, Job 1, May 9, 2012.
116. Joy of My Salvation, Bible Study, Job 1–2, November 16, 2011.

the frequency of testimonies highlighting "Jesus heals," "Jesus delivers," and "Jesus has power" not only provides hope but also engenders despair. By testifying to the God of solutions, Pentecostal rhetoric can empower and disempower. Just as "escaping from Satan" may be construed as an indomitable victory (i.e., "now I'm not going to have more suffering"), prolonged frustration with the causal universe, on the other hand, may be interpreted in precisely the opposite direction (i.e., "sometimes you think that even now Satan is in you . . . dominating your life").[117]

For Pentecostals, *theodicy as the normalization of suffering* may be understood in much the same way as this middle-aged woman portrayed it: as the necessary corrective to their primary theodicy of radically affirming the causal universe. Yet whereas the primary theodicy is rooted in ecclesial praxis and pragmatically directed towards the elimination of witchcraft evil (e.g., deliverance ministries, divine healings, testimonies), this secondary theodicy—an attempt to normalize suffering—is built mostly upon rhetoric alone which may make its assimilation minimal, if not marginal, to the basic contours of the Pentecostal faith.

Conclusion

In this chapter, we have contended that the underlying concerns of theodicy are contextually framed by Fang Protestants as a moral etiology of evil and suffering. In contrast to theodicy in the western theological tradition which is constituted by the triad of God's omnipotence, God's benevolence, and the presence of evil, the basic parameters of a theodicy of moral etiology in an African context consists of the foundational cosmological assumptions which we have identified as *causality* and the *pursuit of the abundant life* which co-exist only amidst extreme tension in the face of evil and suffering. Reflecting these foundational premises, Fang Christian theodicy is constructed upon a more pragmatic and anthropocentric conversation centering upon the presence and elimination of evil than the God-centered nature of theodicies of the western tradition. We have argued that this contextualized theodicy, identified as a moral etiology of evil and suffering, decisively impacts the nature of the Christian faith in Africa by providing a critical lens through which grassroots Christians organize the cosmological universe, interpret Christian scriptures like the book of Job, and construct images of God and the Devil.

As the Reformed Presbyterian Church sought to insert *Nzama* (now identified with the Christian God) in a central place within the Fang

117. Ibid.

cosmological map of the universe, the ambiguity of *Nzama*'s relationship to a causal universe where *mbwo* (witchcraft) continued to flourish resulted in deep-seated existential difficulties for many Presbyterians. The resulting religious schizophrenia for some Presbyterians, manifesting itself precisely in the moment of *okwann mbwo* (witchcraft sickness), not only pits Christian identity in sharp opposition to Fang religiosity but also poses an existential dilemma for Presbyterians insofar as Reformed orthodoxy has always subordinated traditional *ritual action* to combat evil to sound Christian *belief* in God during times of crisis. In contrast to the missionary-founded Presbyterian Church, the moral etiology of evil and suffering within the cosmos is explained more unambiguously by Fang Pentecostals through a rich narrative description of the Devil. By causally explaining witchcraft through biblical demonology, the Devil is bestowed a nearly divine status amongst Pentecostals even amidst hermeneutical reflection upon Christian scripture. For Fang Protestants, the images constructed of God and the Devil conveyed a revealing irony about the substance of popular Christianity in Equatorial Guinea: despite *Nzama* (co-opted as God) being an originally indigenous term and the *deble* (Devil) being a borrowed word, it was the Devil, rather than God, who was portrayed in more robust terms in the interpretation of the book of Job. The apparently alien image of the *deble* reflected a seamless connection with indigenous narrative discourse about the ubiquity of (witchcraft) evil, whereas the image of *Nzama* was theologized using rather remote foreign constructs.

Finally, we concluded this chapter by analyzing two approaches pursued by local Pentecostals in their construction of a theodicy built upon a moral etiology of evil and suffering. The first theodicy of moral etiology depicted amongst Pentecostals was a radical embrace of the causal universe including its most prominent discourse of witchcraft. By carving out a Pentecostal "ritual space" in which *Nzama* (God) could defeat the *deble* (Devil) as embodied by witchcraft, we suggested that the *deble* has become so magnified and enthroned within the cosmos that Pentecostal discourse and praxis tend to revolve around the *deble* as the earth revolves around the sun. In this theological trajectory, *Nzama* (God) essentially becomes meaningless without reference to witchcraft, dependent upon notions of causality, and defined primarily in opposition to the Devil. The second avenue pursued by Pentecostals was an attempt to destabilize the assumptions of the abundant life by rhetorically advocating for the "normalization" of suffering. Yet the existential ambiguities facing Presbyterians vis-à-vis the nature of evil may be instructive here for local Pentecostals: *rhetoric* in the absence of *ritual* is often reflective of those theologies most ambiguous and marginal to the ethos of the church. For many local Pentecostals, the idea that suffering is a legitimate or normal experience in the life of faith is a message which is seriously subverted, if not completely undermined, by the constant ritual concern to combat evil and the Devil.

By analyzing the way in which Fang culture impinges upon Christian reflection upon the nature of evil, we have thus far been content to discuss the conceptualization of suffering and sickness in rather broad categories. In the next chapter, the conversation evolves to become more particular by looking at the book of Job through the experience of those suffering from two stigmatizing diseases: leprosy and HIV/AIDS.

5

The Sting of Retribution and the Promise of Lament

Reading the Book of Job from the Experience of Leprosy and HIV/AIDS

Introduction: *A Letter to Brother Job from Equatorial Guinea*

THIS CHAPTER DISCUSSES THE articulated laments voiced and the retributive blame experienced by leprosy patients and people living with HIV/AIDS (hereafter PLWHA[1]) in Equatorial Guinea. Two Joban texts will feature prominently: Job's lament (in Job 3:1–26) and the series of dialogical texts of Eliphaz, Bildad, and Zophar wherein the theology of retribution is applied to Job's sufferings with unrelenting candor and unsympathetic callousness. For both leprosy patients and PLWHA, the naturalness of lament and the sting of retribution comprise foundational social and theological experiences; both groups were acutely aware of the social exclusion confronted by "Job the *Stigmatized* Sufferer." A central preoccupation of this chapter resides in the concern to listen to these voices "from below" in their appropriation of these texts of Job by offering a descriptive analysis of the primary themes, theologies, and trajectories voiced by the participants themselves.

---

1. Within HIV/AIDS-related research, PLWHA (people living with HIV/AIDS) is a widely used acronym. In this chapter, all names of leprosy patients and PLWHA have been altered to protect anonymity.

Heartfelt lament and retributive blame, however, are hardly confined to stigmatized groups within Fang society. Suffering amongst the Fang is immersed in, if not wholly identifiable with, vehement accusations of moral blame, typically couched in the rhetoric of witchcraft. Retributive blame is an inescapable part of the Fang cultural experience of suffering. This cultural dynamic was poignantly illustrated by Gregorio Nsomboro, a third-year theology student (in 2012) at *Instituto Bíblico "Casa de la Palabra"* (IBCP), a local grassroots seminary. In a classroom assignment under the tutelage of Fang professors, students composed letters to Job based upon their own experiences and understandings of the book of Job. The following is Gregorio's *Letter to Brother Job from Equatorial Guinea*:

> Brother Job,
>
> Each time that I read the Scriptures and meditate on your afflictions and the complaints and accusations that your friends made against you, I ask myself if you have been reincarnated in me. . . . When I look at the situation around me in the land that saw me born, Equatorial Guinea, I can say that it's a photocopy of you.
>
> The truth is that the world is unjust. Just like you, I passed through three horrible years in which I lost two of my children. One died through an illness. After his death, people from the outside, including my own relatives, said that it was through the witchcraft of my wife's family. We almost separated. The other child (six years old) died in a fire in which there was not a chance to remove even one single belonging from the house. . . . The people attributed the fire to my wife being irresponsible, others affirmed that it was a punishment of God against us because we had done something bad—that God had paid us back with his just judgment. Another group said that we had handed over our children as [witchcraft] sacrifices in our churches. My own heart told me: "Where is the God that you serve and how is it that he allowed you to pass through all of this?"
>
> My country is being devastated with all types of epidemics, sicknesses whose origins are still undiscovered, and horrible deaths. But every time that a person suffers from these things, the idea of others is always that the victims have to confess what they have done. . . . I can almost say that the reasoning of your three friends is typical in my culture. All suffering here is linked to witchcraft or to a sin for which God is judging the person or all the family. There is a famous phrase used in my culture: "God

punishes without a stick." I have listened to people lament and cry, saying: "If God exists, why has he permitted this? I don't deserve it, it's not fair!" Others have even taken their lives to prevent further suffering.

In short, this is what we live with every day. With the death of innocent children . . . people who have studied but live poor without jobs, people that suffer sicknesses without knowing where it comes from. Nevertheless many criminals appear increasingly successful in life.

Job, I admire your courage and your mature attitude in responding to your wife and your integrity. Despite everything, you didn't blaspheme against God in all of that (2:9–10). I admire your humble response to God. It's true that the way in which many can demonstrate wisdom is to be silent when the cause is unknown—and not open one's mouth to speak foolishness or falsely accuse the victims.

At least you managed to see restoration in this life. I don't know if Equatorial Guinea and I, if we will have the same grace. Or, perhaps we will have to wait until the redemption of our body when the Lord comes in glory.

Your story truly gives me hope. It gives me the feeling that while man lives on the earth, there is no guarantee that he will not suffer, however innocent or righteous he may be.

I wish that everyone could learn from you.

Sincerely, Your brother Gregorio Nsomboro[2]

Gregorio's *Letter to Brother Job from Equatorial Guinea* may be supplemented by his own testimony during a classroom discussion centering on the retributive theology of Eliphaz, Bildad, and Zophar. Upon arriving at his burned-down house and being confronted with the death of his six-year old son, Gregorio, a young Pentecostal pastor, found himself accused by family, neighbors, and church members of sacrificing his child in witchcraft in order to increase his own religious potency and social prestige:

> *Gregorio*: I could hear the people. "He's already sacrificed his son. He's already sacrificed him. That's why he himself had left [the city of Bata], in order that they might say that he is innocent."

---

2. *Instituto Bíblico "Casa de la Palabra"* (IBCP Seminary), Classroom Assignment on Job. See also Tamez, "A Letter to Job," 50–52; Maluleke, "A Letter to Job—From Africa."

Author: In the church [they said this]?

Gregorio: Yes. They left there and began to blame my wife . . . "Have you now seen that God has taught you that this woman is no longer your wife?" (Because she left the kids in the house.) "Ask her where she was!" . . . I could hear the oppression of the family . . . how they talked. "Now he's sacrificed his child."[3]

Precisely when Job needed consolation, Eliphaz, Bildad, and Zophar mercilessly chided him with truculent accusations and cold-hearted blame. It was the same for Gregorio. This young Pentecostal pastor related to Job as a "brother" not only because of their experiences of tragic suffering but also because their sufferings were exacerbated by cultures of blame which vehemently accuse the sufferer, making tragic situations even worse. For Job and Gregorio, their innocence was forfeited when calamity struck.

Innocent sufferer is virtually an oxymoron both within ancient Israel and amongst the Fang, a category barely perceptible within the community. In an era of HIV/AIDS, this cultural dynamic is toxic. In this chapter, we advance the argument that the paradigm of *Job the Innocent Sufferer* offers churches a dynamic new paradigm for confronting retributive theologies of blame in an era of HIV/AIDS. Yet one of our principal findings from our grassroots research is that ordinary readers are often so captive to "thinking with" retributive blame from the perspectives provided by their culture that many local Christians appear to blunt the force of the paradigm of *Job the Innocent Sufferer* as a potentially sharp instrument for confronting the retributive theologies of blame so prevalent during the HIV/AIDS crisis.

Yet retribution is not the only voice, nor even the most beneficial voice, presented in the book of Job as a response to suffering. In the Bible, the language of suffering arises from the depth of the soul using its own unique language—the lament.[4] Job verbalizes his anguish, leaning into the full weight of his suffering: "I will give free utterance to my complaint; I will speak in the bitterness of my soul" (Job 10:1). After sitting in silence for seven days and seven nights (2:11–13), "Job opened his mouth and cursed the day of his birth" (3:1). As we read Job's *piously irreverent* protest of lament (3:1–26) alongside leprosy patients, PLWHA, and local Christians, various penetrating questions arose. Were they inclined to censure Job's lament or to experience it as cathartic? Was there a difference between the reception of Job's lament amongst stigmatized sufferers and its reception within the churches? As African theologians and biblical scholars Gerald

---

3. *Instituto Bíblico "Casa de la Palabra"* (IBCP Seminary), Class on Job, June 1, 2012.

4. Westermann, *The Structure of the Book of Job*, ix.

West,[5] Emmanuel Katongole,[6] and Denise Ackermann[7] have all recognized, the biblical lament seems to hold a special place of promise for Christians during a time of HIV/AIDS. A pivotal assertion of this chapter is that whilst the biblical lament, and particularly Job's lament, seems ideally suited to provide churches with an authentic theological language capable of embodying compassionate solidarity with PLWHA during the HIV/AIDS pandemic, the reality of how the message of Job was appropriated by Fang Christians in their ecclesial contexts was much more ambiguous.

In the second part of the chapter, therefore, we bring theological reflection into critical dialogue with the stance of local Christian churches regarding their engagement with HIV/AIDS. In terms of numbers, the magnitude of HIV/AIDS in Africa is sobering. Africa comprises only 13 percent of the world's population but more than 70 percent of all people in the world living with HIV reside in Africa.[8] In Equatorial Guinea, the HIV adult (15–49) prevalence rate has been estimated at 6.2 percent[9] with the 30–34 age group (7.9 percent) and men in the 40–44 age group (10 percent) showing higher levels of prevalence.[10] Other segments of the female population are even more vulnerable, including the pregnancies of both agricultural vendors (15.4 percent) and *"comerciantes"* (19.7 percent) who typically sell goods within the informal economy.[11] Needless to say, the HIV/AIDS pandemic is a complex phenomenon. In Africa, HIV/AIDS is embedded in global economic injustice, migratory processes, traditional cultures, local histories, political ideologies, human rights, extreme poverty, sexual ethics, and gender issues. Our focus will necessarily be more cultural and theological by focusing on the complicated relationship between HIV/AIDS and local Fang churches in concert with the symphony of the book of Job whose perspectives seemed, to people living with HIV/AIDS, to provide a particularly relevant text in a time of HIV/AIDS.

---

5. West and Zengele, "Reading Job 'Positively' in the Context of HIV/AIDS in South Africa."

6. Katongole, "Embodied and Embodying Hermeneutics of Life in the Academy," 407–15.

7. Ackermann, "Tamar's Cry," 1–33.

8. "UNAIDS: How AIDS Changed Everything, 2015," *UNAIDS*, 115. "The Global HIV/AIDS Epidemic," *The Henry J. Kaiser Family Foundation*, para. 18.

9. "AIDSinfo: Epidemiological Status, World Overview," *UNAIDS*. The statistic is based upon 2012.

10. *Informe Nacional Sobre los Progresos Realizados en Guinea Ecuatorial*, 7.

11. Ibid., 27.

Reading the Book of Job with Leprosy Patients and People Living with HIV/AIDS

Retribution and Causality

As the curtain descends upon the Joban prologue, the doctrine of retribution comes prominently to the foreground in an increasingly hostile series of dialogues with Job's three friends, Eliphaz, Bildad, and Zophar. Retribution is the notion that "God will punish the wicked and prosper the righteous"[12] and is frequently cited by scholars as embodying "the very heart of Jewish ethics"[13] or as representing the traditional orthodox view of the divine-human relationship in much of the Old Testament.[14] The basis of retribution, to use Pauline language, is that "you reap whatever you sow" (Gal 6:7). From the Deuteronomic covenant which promised blessings for obedience and curses for disobedience (Deut 28–30)[15] to Proverbs and Psalms with their righteous-wicked dichotomy (e.g., Ps 1; Prov 25–29) to Jesus' own disciples who assumed sickness and sin were simplistically related (e.g., "Rabbi, who sinned, this man or his parents, that he was born blind?," John 9:2, cf. Luke 13:1–5), the thematic motif of retribution can be viewed as spanning both Old and New Testaments. Yet no biblical text captures the response of retributive blame more memorably than the book of Job. As the defining theological center comprising the arguments of Eliphaz, Bildad, and Zophar, the theology of retribution "brings together sin and punishment

---

12. Balentine, *Job*, 103. Though Koch prefers to view the concept as a deed-consequence action with no divine juridical action; see Koch, "Is There a Doctrine of Retribution in the Old Testament?" 57–87. For a coherent rebuttal to Koch, see Miller, *Sin and Judgment in the Prophets*, esp. 132–39. For an excellent overview of Koch's argument and the various scholarly reactions to Koch's thesis, see Wong, *The Idea of Retribution in the Book of Ezekiel*, 3–25.

13. Dhorme, *A Commentary on the Book of Job*, cxliii.

14. Pope, *Job*, lxxiii. See also Brueggemann, "A Shape for Old Testament Theology, I: Structure Legitimation," 40; Brueggemann, "A Shape for Old Testament Theology, II: Embrace of Pain," 414. However, it is worth noting the internal heterogeneity of the Jewish ethical tradition, and the existence of alternative models of divine-human encounter alongside that of retribution, as set out, for example, in Martin Buber's "I-Thou" thesis of dialogical existence; Buber, *I and Thou*.

15. See Gammie, "Theology of Retribution in the Book of Deuteronomy," 1–12. For the argument that Deuteronomy may have provided retribution's theological framework against which the writer of Job reacted, see Wolfers, *Deep Things Out of Darkness*, 111–18; Ticciati, *Job and the Disruption of Identity*, 60–64.

in a one-to-one relationship"[16] which "allows no exceptions"[17] for innocent suffering. Of retribution, W. H. Bennett wrote:

> Of all the cruelty inflicted in the name of orthodoxy there is little that can surpass the refined torture due to this Jewish apologetic. Its cynical teaching met the sufferer in the anguish of bereavement, in the pain and depression of disease, when he was crushed by sudden and ruinous losses. . . . Instead of receiving sympathy and help, he found himself looked upon as a moral outcast and pariah on account of his misfortunes; when he most needed divine grace, he was bidden to regard himself as a special object of the wrath of Jehovah.[18]

For the innocent sufferer Job, the retributive theology of the three friends served to isolate Job socially from the community in further burdening him with spiritual and emotional anguish.

Within the causal cosmology of the Fang, the doctrine of retribution made sense as a biblical idea which felt particularly "at home" in Central Africa. As the Congolese priest Ghislain Tshikendwa Matadi writes, "retribution theology is still strong in Africa. In fact, many Africans believe that magic and sorcery are the immediate cause—if not always, at least often—of every type of human suffering."[19] The correspondence between the biblical notion of retribution and the African notion of causality resides in a strong sense of cause and effect wherein earthly happenings are explained as consequences of mystical agency.[20] Most ordinary readers of Job were unaware of retribution as a biblical term, but the theological underpinning which mired Job in blame and accusation was recognized forthrightly and intuitively by Fang interpreters under the cultural rubric of witchcraft:

> *Assembly of the Holy Spirit preacher:* Today, not only in Job—also today! Many times this has occurred in your life. This friend that you so much suffered for him . . . he abandons you when suffering comes to you. You are the worst witch! You are an evildoer!

---

16. Crenshaw, *Defending God*, 117.

17. Ibid., 118.

18. Bennett, *The Books of Chronicles*, 362–63 as cited by Clines, "Job's Fifth Friend," 246.

19. Tshikendwa Matadi, "How Long, O Lord!," 39.

20. Theoretically, retribution and causality differ in that biblical retributive agency is typically linked with God whereas causality, for most African peoples, tends to embrace a diversity of causal agencies. Fang interpreters, however, focused almost exclusively on the commonalities. The correspondence linking retribution and causality is also recognized by academic scholars; see Tsevat, "The Meaning of the Book of Job," 75; Habel, *The Book of Job*, 62.

You are the worst sinner! That's how we Fang are like. *He that is sick is the witch.* Isn't that how it is?

Congregation: Shouts of Amen and Cheers.[21]

Benjamín, Presbyterian Church: This interpretation is not only for the Jews but also for us. Precisely when a person in our culture is sick, we say: "Talk! Talk! Because if you do not 'talk' [i.e. confess your witchcraft] you are not going to get cured. You know what is happening to you!" If the person dies [everybody says]: "Well, he didn't 'talk.'" The interpretation is that since he didn't "talk" [i.e. confess his witchcraft], that's why he's dead. *Therefore, in this book of Job, it seems that the interpretation is the same.* The friends of Job accused him—that if he was passing through suffering, it's because "you have sinned."[22]

For local Christians, the correlation between these accusations urging sufferers to confess their witchcraft and the friends of Job imploring him to repent of his sin was striking. Conceptually, the connections between accusations of Fang witchcraft and the theology of retribution directed at Job by Eliphaz, Bildad, and Zophar are remarkably similar. We can note that in both cases: (1) the accused is experiencing sickness and suffering, (2) the accusers are simply enforcing the traditional wisdom of the community, and (3) the supposed cause of the suffering is hidden from the community's view and known only to the sufferer, whether conceived as nocturnal witchcraft or reckoned as the hidden sin(s) of Job. Thus, the retributive theology of the friends was interpreted by nearly all Fang interpreters—Catholic, Presbyterian, and Pentecostal—as representative of local witchcraft accusations which are often vehemently and oppressively directed against the sick and dying. As has already been discussed at length, suffering and sickness are often the prototypical cultural indication that one's *evus* has been injured in nocturnal flight.[23] Since the confession of witchcraft is considered a vital and indispensable element to begin the healing process, family members often plead with the sick and dying for them to confess their witchcraft:

"*Talk! Talk! You know what you've done. You don't want to die here, do you?*"

---

21. Marcellino Abeso Nse, Assembly of the Holy Spirit, Sermon, Job 19, June 6, 2012.

22. Reformed Presbyterian Church, Bible Study, Job 3, October 18, 2011.

23. See chapter 2, section "The Causal Universe: Sickness and Healing in Fang Cultural Perspective."

> "Talk! You're an old man now. You don't want to go to your grave without having talked!"

It is in this light that the figure of Job was viewed as being accused in an analogous way to a witch in Fang culture. Local Christians identified not only with Job's sufferings *per se* but also with the way in which he suffered in being immersed, like Job, in the midst of blame and accusation.

Leprosy Patients—Retribution as Stigmatization: Witchcraft Accusation, Divine Punishment, and Social Death

For the thirty leprosy patients remaining in the leprosarium of Micomeseng, originally inaugurated on July 11, 1950 under Spanish colonial rule, witchcraft accusations and feelings of divine punishment were central themes in their responses to the book of Job.[24] Remarkably, after the initial reading of Job 1–2 in the leprosarium, *the very first reaction to the Joban text* included a vehement denial of witchcraft from Antonio:

> For my part, I say that I have been sick a long time and nobody can know the truth of one's body when he suffers—many doubt. It is similar to what you just told us of Job. That is similar to what is happening to me. Because I see the truth that I live, but in presenting the truth to the people, they do not believe me. *And I am here, I have not killed anyone, neither have I eaten or sold human flesh.* But I am sick. And increasingly worse since 2004. But praying to God, it's as if I hadn't asked him anything. And each time I pray to God, I am worse off every time. I have a question. How is it that praying to God, you don't have a solution? I have asked this question more than eight times to the many sects[25] that have passed through here and each one has their own response. So again I ask: How is it that praying to God, I am getting worse and have no answer? Sometimes, I forget to pray to God, thinking that he does not listen to me.[26]

Antonio's initial reaction to Job encapsulated many of the themes expressed by leprosy patients during the course of the Bible studies: an intimate identification with Job in his sufferings, denials of witchcraft, disappointment with God that the Fang causal universe would not cooperate with his

---

24. Pujadas, *La Iglesia en la Guinea Ecuatorial: Rio Muni*, 368–69.
25. Antonio's way of referring to all non-Catholic churches.
26. Leprosarium, Bible Study, Job 1–2, October 20, 2011.

prayers, and sober expressions of physical, emotional, and spiritual turmoil stemming from the leprosy itself (see figure 5.1).

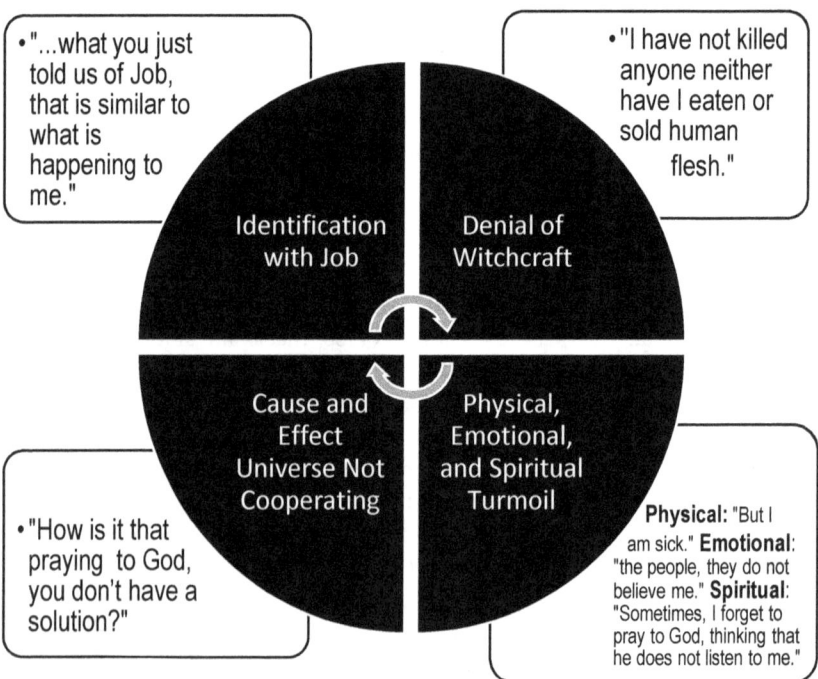

Figure 5.1: Components of Antonio's Initial Reaction to the Book of Job

For the Fang, the most common verbal defense against witchcraft accusation is precisely the language Antonio employs: "I have not killed anyone, neither have I eaten or sold human flesh."[27] This denial, which may be compared to a solemn oath, is a kind of short-hand phrase that the Fang typically employ to deflect charges of witchcraft. At the leprosarium, witchcraft denials became particularly acute as leprosy patients identified movingly and passionately with Job's defense of his innocence against his friends. An elderly woman named Consuela, whose personal history in-

27. Ibid.

cluded a traumatic flight to Cameroon during the Macías years for medical treatment related to her leprosy, was quick to personalize the accusations of Job's friends with her own story of witchcraft denial:

> I saw something similar [to what happened to Job]. I started becoming sick . . . and as I am sick, they began to talk with the mouth. They told me in the mouth that I had something like a crab [note: a common description of the *evus*[28]]; . . . they didn't accept that I told the truth and that I didn't know anything. And they told me that I now had the *evus* and you know that the Fang don't know any other thing other than *mbwo* [witchcraft]. And when they found that a man who was younger than my brother, yes, he died in this village, they said that "Yes, I had eaten him." They treated me more than ten times in the *curanderías* Fang.
>
> I always told them: "I do not know what is happening to me. The sickness that I have seems to me like a crab is in my belly." So they abandoned me saying that now they wouldn't cure me since I had not told them about my witchcraft. And I began to ask God that the sickness [that I have] that I die from it here because I don't know anything. And I asked God to open my eyes that if I know that I did anything that he take my life and if I tell the truth [that God might] give me life. I started to cry. And it turned out that it was an abscess on the belly and it had puss until it exploded. And the puss began to go out and the people began to say that I had spoken the truth. I see that this occurs for the many things that people say without a basis [for saying it].[29]

By linking Consuela's sickness of leprosy with an inexplicable death, the community's accusation that she possessed an anti-social *evus* and had therefore "eaten" a relative served to alienate Consuela from the community as abnormal. *Consuela encountered stigmatization and witchcraft accusation as one interwoven experience.*[30]

Yet the close connection between leprosy and witchcraft does not necessarily eliminate the rhetoric, or the feeling, that leprosy is a result of a divine punishment. Multiple sources of disease causation can comfortably co-exist within the Fang cosmological universe.[31] Both Antonio and

---

28. Mallart Guimera, *Ni Dos Ni Ventre*, 43–54.

29. Leprosarium, Bible Study, Job 4, November 3, 2011.

30. See also Douglas, "Witchcraft and Leprosy," esp. 723–24, 731–35.

31. Many leprosy patients at Micomeseng also believed leprosy was hereditary. Such a view is apparently shared by the Hausa and Fulani peoples and was widespread in the West, being espoused by the Royal College of Physicians in London in 1862, before Hansen's discovery of *mycobacterium leprae* in 1874; Shankar, "Medical Missionaries

Consuela openly expressed the difficulty they had in conceiving of leprosy as anything other than a divine punishment for sin or evil:

> *Antonio*: I have been with a doctor of Japanese nationality. She always told me in our conversations that I "should withdraw the word that many times you repeat 'that it is a punishment' because I don't like that." Therefore I say, what can I call it [leprosy] when I am sick?[32]

> *Consuela*: Yes, I have a question. My question is since the time that I was born from my mother's womb, I was born a leper. Up until now that I am advanced in years, I am still a leper. Now I ask the question. I ask myself if, although doing bad things, is God is going to forgive me of so much evil that I have?[33]

Other leprosy patients explicitly indicated that "God gave me this punishment" or confessed that "on many occasions we believe that God doesn't see us."[34] For the Fang, the word for leprosy (*nzam*) is closely related to the word now used for God (*Nzama*). Native Fang speakers, translating *nzam* into Spanish, frequently refer to leprosy as "*la enfermedad de Dios*" ("the sickness of God"), choosing to call attention to leprosy's relationship with divine punishment. Although reconstructing the precise etymology of the terms remains problematic,[35] *nzam* and *Nzama* may be related to *nzamàn* which signifies "confusion, not fitting in the human mind" which would underscore the vagueness and obscurity which traditionally surrounded both terms for the Fang.[36] While etymological connections are possible,

---

and Modernizing Emirs in Colonial Hausaland," 51; Iliffe, *The African Poor*, 216. Studies in Nigeria and Mali also confirm local theories of the hereditary nature of leprosy; see Varkevisser et al., "Gender and Leprosy," 69; Silla, *People Are Not the Same*, 62–63.

32. Leprosarium, Bible Study, Job 3, October 27, 2011.

33. Leprosarium, Bible Study, Job 1–2, October 20, 2011.

34. Ibid.

35. Tessman, often given to conjuring up etymological connections, posited that leprosy derived from the verb *a săm* meaning "to extend one's hand to punish, to attract punishments"; Tessman, *Los Pamues (Los Fang)*, 493. Yet Allen Pierce, who worked on the translation of the Fang New Testament, in a personal correspondence with the author, writes: "For the word "to reach out the hand/arm," we write /sám/, a single syllable, but with a high tone . . . morphologically Fang would add a nasal at the beginning, and a high tone at the end to produce the past participle of the verb, which would function as a noun, thus- /nsámm/ (noun- "the extension"), which is a different root tone than is "God," or "leprosy"; Allen Pierce, email correspondence with author, February 1, 2012.

36. We owe this point to Samuel Ndong, Director of the Fang New Testament translation project.

the prevailing social stigma of leprosy probably accounts for much of the continuing association of the disease with divine punishment.

In this light, the retribution theology of Job's friends was regarded at the leprosarium as a deeply painful stigmatizing tool, chiefly framed in terms of divine punishment and witchcraft accusation. The visceral identification with Job the Stigmatized Sufferer was profound, sometimes movingly so. Stigmatized leprosy patients stood in solidarity with Job's social exclusion. Yet the divergent reactions to retribution as viewed by Job and the leprosy patients are also illustrative. Whereas Job refuted any acknowledgement of *sin*, leprosy patients deflected charges of *witchcraft*. That is, where Job was concerned to establish his innocence of sin *before God*, leprosy patients were concerned for *communal* absolution from witchcraft, reflecting the antisocial and communal nature of *nsem* ("sin") for the Fang. Such divergences continue poignantly to demonstrate the propensity of local Christians to read the Bible alongside robust fears of witchcraft and their willingness, however unintentional, to conflate biblical and cultural categories.[37] For the leprosy patients, retribution was as much about sociology (and its communal exclusion) as it was about theology (and its "divine mathematics"[38]), as the stories of their lives often made clear:

> *Gabriel*: When a brother-uncle comes here to give you something, he doesn't enter here. He stops on the road and from there calls out to me. He himself does not dare enter here [in the leprosarium]. Never. Never. And he calls me from there: "Gabriel, come, come, come here. I have brought you some things." [And from the car he tosses the bag]. I leave from here, my house in order to find my bag of things. He does not dare enter here. Nobody enters here.[39]

> *Antonio*: All my neighbors from my village are my family. We attended school together, we worked together, we drank together, but nowadays, in the taxi that I get in, not one of them can get in because now I am a leper. Now they are afraid. No longer can they allow their children to enter my house.[40]

In the classic work on stigmatization, *Stigma: Notes on the Management of Spoiled Identity*, sociologist Erving Goffman defined stigma as "an attribute that is deeply discrediting" which diminishes the bearer "from a

---

37. The notion of sin and witchcraft was often equated or conflated.
38. Dhorme, *A Commentary on the Book of Job*, cxxxiv.
39. Leprosarium, Bible Study, Job 42:7–17, November 12, 2011.
40. Ibid.

whole and usual person to a tainted, discounted one."[41] In the memorable words of one leprosy patient, stigmatization feels like "fire in the body," a social death every bit as shameful as leprosy's physical deformities.[42] While stigma scholars have increasingly recognized that stigmatization is a socially constructed phenomenon, no mention is typically made of the close causal relationship that exists between stigmatization and retribution.[43] This is problematic, especially since leprosy-related and HIV/AIDS-related stigma is often littered with the rhetoric of divine punishment and cast within an overarching moral framework. Closer attention to the cultural embeddedness of stigmatization as a phenomenon related to a retributive or causal worldview is critically important if the conversation surrounding stigma in Africa is going to be meaningfully advanced and culturally relevant at the grassroots.

For the Fang, stigmatization and retribution are closely linked. Stigmatization is a *symptom* of the retributive worldview while retributive blame is a *collaborating component* of stigmatization. In the Fang culture which inevitably seeks a personalized causal origin of suffering and sickness, stigmatization is the symptom or logical corollary of a culture of blame and scapegoating. The causal logic is flawless. The quintessential antisocial act of witchcraft is "rewarded" by the quintessential antisocial act of stigmatization and exclusion. An individual who yields to his or her antisocial *evus* will be subjected to stigmatization, a form of antisocial communal punishment. When the communal ontology of "I am because we are" is broken, the community responds by relegating the individual to a kind of social death in exclusion and isolation.[44] Yet retributive blame may also be posited *after* the community decides *whom* and *how* to stigmatize by using those cultural narratives of witchcraft and/or divine punishment which serve to legitimize the community's stigmatizing efforts. In such a case, retributive blame acts as a *collaborating component* of stigmatization, serving to justify the community's social decision to marginalize or exclude the stigmatized person. Therefore, whether stigmatization is the symptom of

41. Goffman, *Stigma*, 3.

42. Leprosarium, Bible Study, Job 4, November 3, 2011.

43. Many, if not most, academic scholars fail to make the connection between stigmatization and retribution. Yet what is most surprising is that even a scholar like Elia Shabani Mligo, who offers an in-depth exploration of stigmatization in the Gospel of John from both academic and popular perspectives, overlooks the connection between retribution and stigmatization in John 9 *even though the doctrine is clearly implicit in the story*; Mligo, *Jesus and the Stigmatized*, 262–81, 327–55. Though see Dube, "Go Tla Siama, O Tla Fola," in *Postcolonial Perspectives*, 486.

44. Mbiti, *African Religions and Philosophy*, 108–9.

the retributive-causal worldview or retributive blame acts as a legitimizing collaborating component within the worldview, the results are the same: social, emotional, and spiritual upheaval often accompany sickness and suffering amongst the Fang. Goffman aptly identified three core types of stigma related to (1) external deformities or physical manifestations, (2) immoral or deviant behavior, and (3) tribal stigma based on membership in a marginalized social group.[45] Leprosy patients in Equatorial Guinea fit into all three category types, indicating the degree to which stigmatization is a life-defining, life-altering, and ultimately a deeply shaming experience.[46]

Leprosy Patients:
Lament and the Internalization of Despair

For Job, tears became prayer in a language known as lament.[47] In suffering, Job reached for a cathartic yet rebellious language that accused God while never relinquishing the grip of faith. "Lament is the language of suffering," writes Claus Westermann, "in it suffering is given the dignity of language."[48] Biblical laments are articulated cries, complaints, or accusations *before* God or *to* God based on circumstances of suffering. Yet not all laments are created equal. While the lament may contain the seeds of personal transformation,[49] re-orientate the sufferer towards God in petitionary prayer,[50] and rejuvenate life's journey with hope[51] and future liberation,[52] the lament can also overwhelm. The lamenter may become stuck in sorrow or devastated by shame. The lamenter may suffer from "the disease of introspection,"[53] a kind of circulatory rumination or oppressive internalization of the suffering which provides neither a window of hope nor an outlet for release:

> In many situations, lament is the only acceptable way of dealing with the tragic break-up and hopelessness that life holds ready

---

45. Goffman, *Stigma*, 4–5.

46. For the same dynamic affecting PLWHA, see Fife and Wright, "The Dimensionality of Stigma," 52.

47. Ackermann, "Tamar's Cry," 25, fn. 87.

48. Westermann, "Role of the Lament in the Theology of the Old Testament," 31.

49. West and Zengele, "Reading Job 'Positively' in the Context of HIV/AIDS in South Africa," 118–22; Wittenberg, "Counselling Aids Patients: Job as a Paradigm," esp. 61–62, 65–66.

50. Brueggemann, "The Costly Loss of Lament," 59.

51. Billman and Migliore, *Rachel's Cry*, 124–27.

52. Kim, "'Outcry': Its Context in Biblical Theology," 230–32.

53. Payne, *The Healing Presence*, 24.

for human beings. *But at the same time engaging in lament can be misleading*—especially when lament leads not to new co-ordinates and structures of orientation, but becomes circular. Circularity is mainly exhibited when the lamenter persists in concentrating on their own suffering, thereby repeating the experience of suffering in their memory. In consequence, lament blocks the sufferer and puts them in the position of not being able to escape from what has happened. The harmful incident and its effects increasingly determine them.[54]

As Job poured his pain into the language of lament by cursing the day of his birth (3:1), leprosy patients recognized that Job meditated profoundly upon the theme of death.[55] Their reactions to Job's lament produced bitter admissions about the possibility of suicide ("one should be born to live well. And when you finish living bad, you are capable of killing yourself"[56]) as well as frustration that death had not yet been granted ("sometimes we yearn for death when God doesn't grant it in that precise moment"[57]). Yet Job viewed death as a welcome, even joyous, release from suffering:

Why is light given to one in misery,

And life to the bitter in soul,

Who long for death, but it does not come,

And dig for it more than for hidden treasures;

Who rejoice exceedingly,

And are glad when they find the grave? (Job 3:20–22)

This Joban perspective was not shared by the leprosy patients at Micomeseng. A theme constantly voiced by leprosy patients centered upon nagging anxieties and disturbing musings that their *present hopelessness would also characterize their eschatological future*. One leprosy patient in his early fifties who epitomized the experience of social death—his wife had not visited him a single time since he had arrived in the leprosarium in 2006—voiced one of the many eschatological concerns articulated at the leprosarium:

---

54. Klein, "The Phenomenology of Lament and the Presence of God in Time," 19, italics added.

55. For example, Job 3:11: "Why did I not die at birth, come forth from the womb and expire?"

56. Leprosarium, Bible Study, Job 3, October 27, 2011.

57. Ibid.

> *Gabriel*: I also have an opinion. I want to ask you a question from so much suffering that I am going through. As I was a soldier, [people said that] "I was very bad." Many say that I killed people, practiced black magic, and that I took forcefully other women. *That if I die, will I go to live bad like I am living now?* I do not admit to having done wrong to anybody.[58]

According to stigma scholars, shame often attacks the stigmatized self as an "inner torment" and a "humiliation in the heart" which internalizes deep within the psyche the feelings of shame that society attaches to the stigma.[59] Psychologists Merle Fossum and Marilyn Mason define shame thus:

> Shame is an inner sense of being completely diminished or insufficient as a person. It is the self judging the self. A moment of shame may be humiliation so painful or an indignity so profound that one feels one has been robbed or her or his dignity or exposed as basically inadequate, bad or worthy of rejection. A pervasive sense of shame is the ongoing premise that one is fundamentally bad, inadequate, unworthy or not fully valid as a human being.[60]

In general, leprosy patients seem to have internalized a deep sense of shame. Acquiescing to society's moral narrative that the disease is a punishment of God, many experienced an almost frightening existential uncertainty before God. The sense of diminishment was palpable. A clear sense of hope before God clearly eluded leprosy patients in their discourses surrounding death, dying, and the afterlife, a kind of generalized anxiety that God's punishment and their present sufferings would extend even to the afterlife. These anxious eschatological laments surfaced repeatedly throughout the Bible studies as the leprosy patients reacted to various Joban passages:

> *Martin, Bible study on Job 1–2*: I say that every person wants to go to God. We all want to see God, although it is difficult to see God if we take into account what you are mentioning about Job's suffering. My heart also tells me this with this punishment [of leprosy] that I have. I pray to God the day that I am not suffering many pains that he might help me. I say to God: "Help me! I am here, [but] I have a family. All my children have remained in the village. I come seeking life." Therefore, I always ask: "Since I

---

58. Leprosarium, Bible Study, Job 1–2, October 20, 2011.
59. Mligo, *Jesus and the Stigmatized*, 72. See also Goffman, *Stigma*, 7.
60. Fossum and Mason, *Facing Shame*, 5, italics removed from the original.

have suffered so much on earth, when I go to God, am I going to suffer as I am suffering here?" Because every person thinks about this part.[61]

Nicolás, Bible Study on Job 3: Let's suppose that when you are suffering, you do not want to be in this world any longer. You prefer to solicit death saying to God, "God, take me out of this world because it might be better up there." Nobody wants their body to suffer which is why we often prefer death instead of suffering. When your body aches, we often say to God: "What am I doing here now? The work that others do, I cannot do it now—really I can't do nothing now." Now that my body is suffering, just as you are seeing me here, I am having pain in my entire body. I can't even stand up. So now that I am suffering, *"Oh God, will I come to suffer up there in your bosom? God?"*[62]

How do we explain these anxious eschatological laments that clearly had become profound spiritual and emotional burdens? The question becomes particularly acute since Fang traditional beliefs and practices do not readily conceive of suffering in the presence of *Nzama*.[63] Four central explanations can be put forward. First, the eschatological apprehension for these Catholic leprosy patients seemed grounded, in part, upon the fear of purgatory. For many leprosy patients, the thought of further *post-mortem* suffering, after the extreme suffering many (if not all) had already experienced in this life, was almost too much to bear. Second, this eschatological hopelessness also seemed rooted in the present anguish and despair of living at the leprosarium itself. Preserving hope at the leprosarium represented an exceedingly difficult task in light of (1) the culture of death and dying which surrounds the leprosarium,[64] (2) the emotional (or absolute) abandonment of families, (3) the loss of (or rejection by) home villages, (4) loneliness and boredom, (5) the loss of careers and abilities, and (6) the numerous physical challenges, most noticeably the daily grind of re-wrapping bandages and attending to large open wound ulcers. Most leprosy patients profoundly resonated with Job's extreme suffering but found it difficult to accept his hope. Third, these eschatological laments may be reflective of how Catholics have inserted *Nzama* into the causal universe wherein *Nzama* is conceived

---

61. Leprosarium, Bible Study, Job 1–2, October 20, 2011.
62. Leprosarium, Bible Study, Job 3, October 27, 2011.
63. Tessman, *Los Pamues (Los Fang)*, 441; Fernandez, *Bwiti*, 236.
64. In recent years, the leprosarium has experienced a reduction of patients from approximately 80 in 2003 to 30 in 2011 mostly due to death from old age and/or from the residual effects of leprosy.

as remote from the experience of suffering despite being credited as responsible for the entire causal universe—including the whole realm of evil—as the Creator God and Supreme Being. For years or even decades, leprosy patients had experienced *Nzama*'s non-cooperation in a causal universe designed to remedy sufferings; hence any basic change in their present sufferings in the eschaton, enacted by *Nzama*, seemed difficult to comprehend.

Finally, we can explain these anxious eschatological laments by noticing the complicated relationship between retribution and lament. On one hand, lament and retributive blame represent two very different, if not wholly incompatible, responses to suffering. Job's lament derives its force and passion from the recognition that his suffering cannot be traced to any conspicuous moral cause. The retributive theology of Job's friends argues in precisely the opposite direction, namely, that conspicuous suffering is the unequivocal sign of Job's sinfulness. Yet on the other hand, the sentiment expressed *ad nauseam* by Job during the dialogues—that God is unjust because Job is innocent—rests securely upon the doctrine of retribution. The notion that "God is unjust" is a statement made not from *without* but from *within* a retributive framework pleading for God to restore order and justice to the universe. In a sense, the leprosy patients shared Job's rather complicated relationship with lament and retribution, even if their experience with both concepts was rather different than Job's. Job's laments were rooted in restoring a *positive* sense of justice to a retributive worldview by accusing God directly and vehemently reacting against the friends' *negative* assessment of his situation. Yet the leprosy patients in general acquiesced to society's *negative* explanation of leprosy as a punishment of God, effectively serving to undermine any *positive* sense of hope and trust in God which continued to characterize the Joban laments.[65] In other words, the patients' fear of divine eschatological *retribution* served to stifle any positive value potentially offered by the Joban *laments*. Moreover, at the leprosarium, laments grew out of a long history of stigmatization and centered *primarily* upon physical ailments, social exclusion, and eschatological retributive anxieties. In contrast, Karl Barth pointed out that Job's sufferings and lamentation arose primarily out of his relationship with Yahweh: "his true sorrow in all his sorrows, and therefore the primary subject of his complaints, consists in the conjunction of his profound knowledge that in what has happened and what has come

---

65. Billman and Migliore's sentiment that the prayer of lament "expresses a trust in the goodness of God so profound that it continues to cry out for God in the agony of God's apparent absence and silence and looks for redemption in the midst of God's terrible hiddenness" surely applies to Job's hope in the midst of lament; Billman and Migliore, *Rachel's Cry*, 114–15. See also Westermann, "Role of the Lament in the Theology of the Old Testament," 32.

on him he has to do with God.... This is the depth and essence of the suffering of the suffering Job. He knows that he has to do with God."[66] The God-centeredness of the lament is indispensable, less the lament collapse destructively into a circularity of despair. Therefore, although Job's laments contained the seeds of trust and hope in Yahweh, the laments of the leprosy patients appeared to provide them with neither an empowering language capable of transcending hopelessness nor a therapeutic perspective of *Nzama*'s redemption in the midst of trouble. By internalizing Job's lament as an acute sense of despair without a corresponding sense of hope, the leprosy patients stifled any cathartic value potentially offered by the Joban laments. For the patients, Job's lament was swallowed up by internalized despair.

People Living with HIV/AIDS: Lament and the Embrace of God through Therapeutic Faith and Renewed Hope

Unlike the Catholic leprosy patients who descended into a circularity of despair, Job's lament offered Pentecostal PLWHA a therapeutically empowering language capable of releasing the emotional avalanche caused by the HIV-positive diagnosis. For the Pentecostal participants in the Good Samaritan HIV/AIDS support group, the Bible study of Job's lament (3:1–26) whereby Job "cursed the day of his birth" (3:1) immediately called to mind "*la noticia*" ("the news")—the initial diagnosis of their HIV-positive status. *La noticia* represented for them the ground zero of a new stigmatized and discreditable identity,[67] a turning point where everything changes and time slows down amidst a blur of incipient feelings:[68]

> *Francisco*: I came to be at home, and I couldn't eat, I couldn't drink, I didn't want to talk to people. Crying on the inside, always when I was alone you found me with tears. Everything was bad, including I thought about committing suicide. Because I was afraid most of the criticism.... What would the people say? And how am I going to be now that I am HIV-positive? Because all of us put in our heads that to be HIV-positive is to die. Now you have an assured death.... I spent one year without being able to tell [the news to] anyone.[69]

---

66. Barth, *Church Dogmatics* 4/3.1: 401.

67. For the distinction between discredited and discreditable, see Goffman, *Stigma*, 57ff.

68. See also West and Zengele, "Reading Job 'Positively' in the Context of HIV/AIDS in South Africa," 117.

69. Interview, Francisco, June 9, 2012.

Yet against this devastating backdrop of *la noticia*, Job's lament was interpreted as a profoundly empowering language capable of transcending the despair of their HIV-positive diagnosis. Job's lament encouraged these Pentecostal PLWHA to confront their anger and face the temptation to deny their *noticia* with a renewed sense of faith and courage.

In reading the Joban lament, PLWHA were equipped with a theologically strong language capable of navigating the pain of anger. Job's lament served to validate biblically and theologically the expression of their own emotional turmoil following *la noticia*. The positive value of Job's lament was often expressed by utilizing the Spanish word *desahogarse* which can be variously translated "share, unburden, vent, get off one's chest" and paints an even better word picture of *not* ("des") *drowning* ("ahogarse," to drown) in the emotional upheaval of HIV/AIDS:

> *Mariana*: It is good that we share (*desahogemos*). Because when we guard everything there inside, we do ourselves damage that we don't realize. . . . Job is also teaching us here that we should get it off our chest (*desahogarnos*). We should not hang on to the bitterness inside.[70]

The participants recognized that without the release of these bitter and angry feelings, the potential for *la noticia* to poison the soul becomes a real possibility. The lament makes the articulation of anger "theologically permissible."[71] For PLWHA, Job's lament served to humanize, even divinely authorize,[72] the feelings which naturally accompany suffering:

> *Ignacio*: Laments are human feelings.
>
> *Mariana*: It is better to express the feelings; . . . if you would have kept [the news] to yourself, you would have made an incorrect decision. "Maybe I'll commit suicide. I'm going to take the medicine like this. Tomorrow when they wake up, the people will see!" This happened to me. If I would have confessed what I feel maybe I would have found someone that could have given

---

70. Good Samaritan HIV/AIDS support group, Bible Study, Job 3, May 25, 2012.

71. West and Zengele, "Reading Job 'Positively' in the Context of HIV/AIDS in South Africa," 119. See also West, "Reading the Bible in the Light of HIV/AIDS in South Africa," 335–44.

72. Nelson, "Justice and Biblical Interpretation beyond Subjectivity and Self-Determination," 447. Similarly, Madipoane Masenya writes that "it is always a good idea for people, particularly those with dreadful diseases, to speak their mind. The talking exercise itself will be found to be therapeutic," Masenya, "Between Unjust Suffering and the 'Silent' God," 196.

> me advice. This is better. What Job did: lament, tell, share (*desahogar*) is the best decision.[73]

For these Pentecostal believers, the praxis of reading the Bible as a therapeutic resource in their journey with HIV/AIDS was profoundly uplifting. One member of the support group, Francisco, spent an entire year refusing to confirm the diagnosis or revisit the hospital, choosing to live on the frontier of fear, disbelief, and denial.[74] With every bout of diarrhea, Francisco thought death to be imminent. After *la noticia*, a confusing therapeutic journey ensued which included urine therapy ("I drank urine in the morning and thought that this could give an effect. And the effect that it gave me was an allergy throughout my whole body . . . because every morning I drank a glass of urine"),[75] an unknown number of injections at Chinese clinics, and treatment at a *curandería* where he was promised a cure by the *ngangan*.[76] Yet it was the Word of God encountered at Joy of My Salvation which was decisive for Francisco: "The Word of God does not cure the disease, the infection, but the Word of God lightens the spirit. Because with this spiritual relief . . . you feel healthy."[77] Francisco testified that he was transformed from an angry and embittered "lion" to a "flower that blossoms everyday."[78] As with many Pentecostals, Francisco employed a *therapeutic hermeneutic* which centered on personal transformation:

> *Francisco*: For me, biblical chapters are used by me as counsel. But in the lament of Job, what I have learned is that whatever happens to me, I have to find a way to share it. And sharing, I unburden myself (*me desahogo*), and I am free. When I learned I was HIV positive, I was not a believer. Because if I was a believer and if you read these chapters, you would know what to do. But really nothing [for me at that time]. That's why, not even the girlfriend that I had for two years [could I share] with her. I couldn't

---

73. Good Samaritan HIV/AIDS support group, Bible Study, Job 3:1–26, May 25, 2012.

74. For an application of Elizabeth Kübler-Ross' stages of dying (denial and isolation, anger, bargaining, depression, acceptance) to PLWHA, see Kgosikwena, "Pastoral Care and the Dying Process," 201–9.

75. Interview, Francisco, June 9, 2012.

76. Ibid. *Francisco*: Both of us [were] in the room [and the *ngangan* asked]: "What's wrong with you?" [*Francisco*:]: "This is the problem that is happening to me." [*ngangan*]: "What problem? I always heal here. I always heal people here of HIV, this isn't anything. But do not tell anyone because if many people find out . . . ." *Author*: Too much fame. *Francisco*: "With this fame people could come to kill me."

77. Ibid.

78. Good Samaritan HIV/AIDS support group, Bible Study, Job 1–2, May 11, 2012.

tell her anything. I couldn't! I had all this inside. But now I know what I can do. Find ways to share and thus be unburdened.[79]

Francisco's therapeutic hermeneutic is unmistakably rooted in local Pentecostal praxis, corresponding closely to the image of God as Healer which is widely prevalent amongst Fang Pentecostals.[80] *For Francisco, the messy cries of lament were interpreted as providing the building blocks of courageous faith and steadfast hope in the midst of the personal crisis of HIV/AIDS.* Pentecostal PLWHA found Job's lament, unlike Catholic leprosy patients, to be profoundly therapeutic in providing an authentic source of emotional and spiritual healing stemming from their HIV-positive diagnosis. Whereas reflecting upon Job's lament, for Catholic leprosy patients, seemed only to reinforce their despair, these Pentecostals living with HIV/AIDS approached scripture therapeutically with the expectation that biblical texts necessarily mediate a divine therapeutic presence in a way that brings healing and wholeness.

Yet Job's lament not only divinely authorized anger for PLWHA but also provided a biblical paradigm for facing denial. Dorothee Soelle writes: "The first step towards overcoming suffering is . . . to find a language that leads out of the uncomprehended suffering that makes one mute."[81] The PLWHA viewed the expression of Job's anguish to God as an important first step in facing their HIV status by moving from denial to acceptance of the disease. In a culture where the topic of HIV/AIDS is taboo, Job's lament provided them with a paradigm for not denying or ignoring HIV-suffering but learning to *"asumir"* or "accept responsibility, come to terms with" the reality of their HIV-positive status:

> *Mariana*: Many of us, one like myself, when this [HIV suffering] happened to me, I blamed my family. And Job did not blame anybody but Job accepted it (*lo asumió*). In other words, he had faith in the Lord. He knew that if the Lord had blessed him, if now the Lord was also giving him [these sufferings], he could accept the responsibility (*asumir*). But many of us, one like myself sincerely it was difficult to accept responsibility (*asumir*), I blamed my family, blamed my father, my mother, my grandmother until the Lord arrived in my life.[82]

---

79. Good Samaritan HIV/AIDS support group, Bible Study, Job 3, May 25, 2012.
80. Davis and Harold, "Theodicy in Job," 9.
81. Soelle, *Suffering*, 70.
82. Good Samaritan HIV/AIDS support group, Bible Study, Job 1–2, May 11, 2011.

However, for many of these Pentecostals living with HIV/AIDS, accepting responsibility and coming to terms with one's HIV-positive status meant acquiescing to the overarching moral narrative attached to HIV/AIDS within the wider society. Amongst the Fang, AIDS is referred to as *okwann binzenzam* (*okwann*—sickness; *binzenzam*—disordered, wild, chaotic) or *okwann endendea* (*okwann*—sickness; *endendea*—excessive, uncontrollable), terms which both refer to someone who engages in a "disordered" or "excessive" sexual life without any control. For the Fang, AIDS is a disease of prostitutes, a disease of death, and *the* dreaded disease in the country which is occasionally referred to as "the big sickness" (*okwann onén*). Moving from denial to acceptance of the disease within this Pentecostal group was often virtually synonymous with accepting the moral blame of sexual promiscuity:

> *Francisco*: We the HIV-positives, we have to put in our head that for every cause, there is a reason. . . . If you don't look for HIV, HIV is not going to find you. You hear? Why? Because the life that I live now, to live it ten years ago, I would not be HIV positive. First, why do I accept responsibility (*asumo*) that I am HIV positive? I take responsibility (*asumo*) because I calculate—how many girls have I slept with? How have I slept with them? To have utilized condoms perhaps I would not be HIV positive. To have only one woman and be with her as the Word of God commands . . . I would not be HIV positive. . . . *Because there are no causes without reasons*. Every HIV positive person that you see today are people that know what they have done.[83]

> *Santiago*: I felt so bad and frustrated—accusing God that perhaps *he* is doing this to me. But after some months, I understood this: we as believers, born-agains, *we should take things as culpable;* . . . after some months, I encouraged myself, I prayed to God and I saw the positive side: that if God has permitted, it's that maybe *I am failing in some things*. I am going to take the responsibility. The pastor talked to me and I told him "I am going to take responsibility—me."[84]

Simply put, the freedom of acceptance came at the price of owning the guilt and shame of sexual bankruptcy, as socially perceived. And while such discourse broadly connects with the movement from repentance to freedom in evangelical piety and potentially encourages personal responsibility

---

83. Interview, Francisco, June 9, 2012.

84. Good Samaritan HIV/AIDS Support Group, Bible Study, Job 1–2, May 11, 2012.

rather than feelings of victimization,[85] these narratives failed to connect with one significant and overarching category of HIV/AIDS in Africa—the category of innocent suffering. In an era of HIV/AIDS, not everyone can, or should, accept moral culpability for having HIV/AIDS. The issues are far more complex. Thus, the HIV-positive Pentecostals, much like the Catholic leprosy patients, continued to interpret their disease in categories associated with retributive blame. Neither stigmatized group fully grasped the paradigm altering implications of Job's *innocent* lament. When Francisco argued that "there are no causes without reasons," he effectively reiterated the retributive theology of Job's friends which—in true Fang fashion—serves to marginalize and dismiss the possibility of *innocent* suffering even amidst the HIV/AIDS pandemic.

HIV/AIDS and the Church: Theological Reflections

The Paradigm of Job the Innocent Sufferer

In response to the HIV/AIDS pandemic, African theologians have often lamented the "massive theological silence"[86] of the church regarding HIV/AIDS or insisted that "the predominant view in most Christian communities is that HIV/AIDS is a punishment from God."[87] The situation in Equatorial Guinea is no different. In over six years of attending various missionary-initiated and Pentecostal churches amongst the Fang, I have *never* heard a pastor address the HIV/AIDS pandemic.[88] Whilst individual theologians portray the HIV/AIDS pandemic as the new *kairos* moment confronting churches in Africa with opportunities for truth-telling and courageous compassion, the silence remains deafening at the grassroots, at least in Equatorial Guinea.[89] And while scholars such as Musa W. Dube argue that the HIV/AIDS pandemic is increasingly being recognized as a

---

85. See also Boyd, "Saving One's Self," esp. 158–215.

86. Maluleke, "The Challenge of HIV/AIDS for Theological Education in Africa," 132.

87. West and Zengele, "Reading Job 'Positively' in the Context of HIV/AIDS in South Africa," 115.

88. I should clarify: I have *often* heard pastors boast about their ability to cure HIV/AIDS in their deliverance ministries, a position very different than addressing the realities of HIV/AIDS. A missionary with twenty years of experience in Equatorial Guinea also testifies that she has *never* heard a pastor address HIV/AIDS from the pulpit.

89. See Maluleke, "The Challenge of HIV/AIDS for Theological Education in Africa," 129–30; Haddad, "Reflections on the Church and HIV/AIDS," 32–33; Ackermann, "Tamar's Cry," 33.

"*social injustice story*,"⁹⁰ the fault line of the conversation at the grassroots—if the conversation is happening at all—continues to be conducted within a moral-religious framework with its connotations of sexual promiscuity and divine punishment.⁹¹ As biblical scholars have occasionally recognized, *the book of Job may provide a pivotal biblical text for empowering churches to move from a retributive theology which blames the sufferer to a paradigm of innocent suffering in the midst of HIV/AIDS.*⁹² At the local level, recalibrating oppressive cultural ideologies of suffering in favor of theologies of compassionate solidarity represents a crucial development for local churches to throw off the yoke of silence and respond with grace and compassion to those infected and affected by the HIV/AIDS pandemic.

For grassroots churches in Africa to respond with compassionate solidarity to the HIV/AIDS pandemic, *a more robust social exegesis of the disease plays a critical role in overturning the culture of blame in an era of HIV/AIDS.* In the midst of HIV/AIDS, the churches' failure to persistently and unwaveringly challenge the dominant cultural paradigm of suffering—that deeds and consequences are causally linked such that people bear the blame for their suffering—is unfortunate. The narrow reductionism of HIV/AIDS to sexual promiscuity and divine punishment not only shackles PLWHA with emotional shame and spiritual angst but also helps buttress stigmatizing attitudes towards PLWHA in the wider society. In Equatorial Guinea, the dearth of secular governmental campaigns to promote awareness of the disease and the virtual non-existence of non-governmental agencies (NGOs) working with HIV/AIDS signifies that the complexities of the HIV/AIDS pandemic are still veiled in obscurity to the majority of people.⁹³ In Africa, the "social embeddedness of vulnerability"⁹⁴ to HIV/AIDS corresponds to complex social realities which include gender, power, and poverty—realities which challenge the basic reductionism of HIV/AIDS to sexual immorality or sexual promiscuity alone. Denise Ackermann indicates that "in many countries in Africa the condition that carries the highest risk of HIV infec-

---

90. Dube, "*Go Tla Siama, O Tla Fola*," *Black Theology*, 219, italics in the original.

91. Good Samaritan HIV/AIDS support group, Bible Study, Job 4:7–9; 8:1–9; 11:13–20, June 1, 2012. *Mariana*: What do the people say [about you having HIV]? *Lucía*: Why have you done bad? *Camila*: We are evil-doers. God punishes us. That's what the people say. *Ana*: They are going to be blaming us: "you serve this God, what for?"

92. See especially Nadar, "Re-reading Job in the Midst of Suffering in the HIV/AIDS Era," 343–357; Masenya, "Between Unjust Suffering and the 'Silent' God." See also the extended footnote in the Introduction, section "Methodology."

93. See Rodríguez et al., "The Pertinence of Applying Qualitative Investigation Strategies," 560–61.

94. Craddock, "Beyond Epidemiology," 4.

tion is that of being a married woman."[95] The relational-power dynamics between the genders embodied in sexual practices in Africa often make women particularly vulnerable to the disease. In *AIDS in the Twenty-First Century: Disease and Globalization*, Tony Barnett and Alan Whiteside write: "It is estimated that 60–80% of African women with HIV have had only one partner but were infected because they were not in a position to negotiate safe sex or prevent their partners from having additional sexual contacts."[96] Moreover, a strictly moral or sexual narrative of HIV/AIDS also fails to recognize the way in which sexual practices are embedded in the prevailing socioeconomic climate of poverty which plagues many African communities. All across Africa, women and young girls are placed in economically vulnerable positions whereby the only "commodity" or "product" which stands between survival and destitution is sex. Variously labeled "survival sex," "transactional sex," or the "sugar-daddy phenomenon," women and young girls often choose to exchange sex for gifts, cash, or favors because of their perilous economic situations. In Tanzania, one study found that 50 percent of sexually experienced young women aged 15–24 reported accepting a "gift" in return for sex.[97] In Uganda, female university students, particularly from poor backgrounds, practice "de-toothing" wherein sex or sexual promises are exchanged for money, cell phones, groceries, or clothes.[98] These are social realities which directly contest the dominant paradigm that exists in many African communities that HIV/AIDS necessarily connotes sexual immorality or sexual promiscuity. For grassroots churches in Equatorial Guinea, however, to become conversant with a more robust social exegesis of the disease which could help instill a more compassionate rhetoric is extremely difficult in a milieu where a deafening silence continues to envelop the epidemic and in a context where the physical disease itself is still much misunderstood. Despite the fact that Equatorial Guinea now boasts the eleventh highest HIV prevalence rate in the world, the issue of HIV/AIDS still has not risen to occupy a prominent level of discourse in the public square.[99]

95. Ackermann, "Tamar's Cry," 12. See also Ackermann, "From Mere Existence to Tenacious Endurance," 233.

96. Barnett and Whiteside, *AIDS in the Twenty-First Century*, 185.

97. Tengia-Kessy et al., "Assessment of Behavioural Risk Factors," 528.

98. Sadgrove, "'Keeping Up Appearances,'" esp. 122–25. Sadgrove explains: "This dynamic, known as 'de-toothing', whereby a woman will analogously extract a man's teeth one by one until he is left with nothing, appears the most salient determinant of sexual behavior amongst university students," 116.

99. See "The World Factbook: Country Comparison, HIV/AIDS—Adult Prevalence Rate," *Central Intelligence Agency*. (Based on 2014 estimates.) See also "AIDSinfo:

For African churches, becoming conversant with the social complexities of the disease is not the only route towards resisting a culture of retributive blame in an era of HIV/AIDS. Scripture also represents a pivotal resource. While theological language can be repressive (i.e., HIV/AIDS is a punishment from God), theological language also holds the promise of new liberatory perspectives.[100] The Old Testament scholar, Johanna Stiebert, in an article entitled "Does the Hebrew Bible Have Anything to Tell Us about HIV/AIDS?" gives the following perspective on illness and disease in the Old Testament:

> [R]eferences to disease and illness are not invariably a matter of simple causality: of constituting a punishment for disobedience or moral shortcoming. There is no logic, or pattern to their distribution: "the good" are afflicted along with "the wicked." Sometimes the reason is to make a theological point, sometimes there appears to be no discernible reason at all. Consequently, it is not possible on the basis of the Hebrew Bible to regard an illness such as HIV/AIDS as a divine punishment for wrongdoing. Instead, it must be acknowledged that the situation is considerably more complex and perplexing. Casting aspersions on the moral character of any person infected with HIV/AIDS is therefore unjust and unacceptable.[101]

In particular, the paradigm of *Job the Innocent Sufferer* seems to represent a unique biblical resource for empowering Christians and churches to stand courageously like Job against cultural ideologies of retributive blame.[102] For the Fang, blame is a veritable cultural *leitmotif* which makes innocent suffering a category barely perceptible, or even non-existent, within the community. At Joy of My Salvation, one woman confessed her struggle to be free from the tendency to accuse the sufferer "because this is how we've been raised—you have to blame."[103] Yet in an era of HIV/AIDS, the marginalization of *innocent* suffering to the periphery of culture is profoundly unfortunate and deeply troubling. Job's fortitude and courage in

---

Epidemiological Status," *UNAIDS*. (Based on 2012 estimates.)

100. Wittenberg, "Counselling Aids Patients," 61–62, 67.

101. Stiebert, "Does the Hebrew Bible Have Anything to Tell Us About HIV/AIDS?" 184.

102. Dube, "Theological Challenges," 545: "It is my contention that the HIV/AIDS era calls the church and its training/theological institutions to re-read scriptures such that they affirm life and counteract death. The church and its scholars need to highlight scriptures, such as Job and John 9, that counteract the notion of associating illness with God's punishment or the sinfulness of the concerned individuals."

103 Joy of My Salvation, Bible Study on Job's Friends, May 16, 2012.

defending himself against the vehement accusations of his friends and the blame of his community makes him a paradigmatic example in an era of HIV/AIDS. As Job recognized, the dominant religious-cultural paradigm of suffering was far too general to account for the specificity of his own suffering. The mystery of Job's innocent suffering explodes traditional categories in their insistence upon simple causality. Suffering is a complex phenomenon which never provides a "one size fits all" paradigm, no matter how much the community wishes for such explanatory simplicity. The Peruvian liberation theologian, Gustavo Gutiérrez, is one scholar who does not miss the paradigmatic implications of Job's innocent suffering:

> The innocence of Job makes it historically possible that there may be *other* innocent human beings. The injustice of his suffering points to the possibility that *other* human beings may also suffer unjustly.... Here we have the potential universality of the figure of Job; it is in fact clear that the poet intends to make a paradigm of him.[104]

With respect to HIV/AIDS, we might say that although sexual promiscuity plays a *role* in the transmission of the disease, no one *deserves* to have HIV/AIDS.[105] Retributive language which declares that HIV/AIDS is a divine punishment for sin or stigmatizes PLWHA as sexually promiscuous overlooks or ignores the complex social exegesis of the disease. From a Christian perspective, when the retributive language of blame and divine punishment rings forth in Christian churches as a prominent discourse in an era of HIV/AIDS, this ecclesial posture also represents an abject failure to integrate biblically the paradigm of Job's innocent suffering into ecclesial discourse and praxis. *Job the Innocent Sufferer* is a paradigm with the potential to shatter the facile assumption that one can divest suffering of its mystery by linking the suffering simplistically to personal sin. Sarojini Nadar has argued that the book of Job instills a valuable pedagogical lesson by instructing churches "how *not to* talk about God in times of suffering" during the HIV/AIDS pandemic by providing an "alternative voice" to the dominant theology of retribution.[106] In other words, whereas the retributive theology of Eliphaz, Bildad, and Zophar provides a blueprint of how *not*

---

104. Gutiérrez, *On Job*, 4, italics added. Similarly, H. H. Rowley writes: "By insisting that there is such a thing as innocent suffering the author of Job is bringing a message of the first importance to the sufferer;" see Rowley, "The Book of Job and Its Meaning," 178.

105. Ryan, "AIDS and Responsibility," 69.

106. Nadar, "Re-Reading Job in the Midst of Suffering in the HIV/AIDS Era," 356, italics in the original.

to talk about suffering in the midst of HIV/AIDS, *Job the Innocent Sufferer* represents a robust biblical paradigm capable of putting a formidable Trojan horse into the citadel of a culture of retributive blame. Job the Innocent Sufferer stands as a paradigmatic counterpoint to a "theology of repression" in providing churches with a new theological language capable of reaching across the chasm of blame and accusation during the HIV/AIDS crisis.[107]

Biblical scholars and professional theologians, therefore, have been unequivocally positive about the value of Job's innocent suffering in providing a crucial biblical resource for empowering churches to move from a retributive theology which blames the sufferer to a paradigm of innocent suffering in the midst of the HIV/AIDS pandemic.[108] As a missionary-professor living and working in Central Africa, I share this hope, namely, that the book of Job might be dropped like dynamite with all its explosive implications into Christian churches, with the ramifications being felt in the surrounding neighborhoods often trapped hopelessly within the causal logic of retribution. However, my research suggests that at the level of popular biblical interpretation, the value of Job's innocent suffering to provide an arresting biblical paradigm to contest and confront the cultural notion of retributive blame is not so straightforward. Occasionally, the negative example of Job's friends served to demonstrate the folly of retributive blame. In his *Letter to Job from Equatorial Guinea*, Gregorio insightfully observed: "It's true that the way in which many can demonstrate wisdom is to be silent when the cause is unknown—and not open one's mouth to speak foolishness or falsely accuse the victim."[109] At Joy of My Salvation, a woman's Bible study recognized that the negative example of Job's friends provided a potentially liberating biblical paradigm not to engage in witchcraft accusation. Yet this group was also outspoken in articulating that witchcraft blame is so entrenched in their communities and culture that escaping entirely from this impulse to blame is extremely difficult even for Christians:

> *Paulina*: All of us blame. Not only the friends of Job here. Also us. We blame others when they go through times like this [of suffering].
>
> *Victoria*: If we have understood Job like this, we should not blame anymore.

---

107. Wittenberg, "Counselling Aids Patients," 64.

108. Masenya, "Between Unjust Suffering and the 'Silent' God."; Nadar, "Re-reading Job in the Midst of Suffering in the HIV/AIDS Era," 343–57.

109. *Instituto Bíblico "Casa de la Palabra"* (IBCP Seminary), Class Assignment, The Book of Job.

> *Sofía*: But this [the tendency to blame] also exists—as the other sisters have said—in the church. When someone comes to church, she leaves from a culture, a way of being in this culture. For example, in our culture, it is considered that nobody dies because the death is natural. You have to attribute the death to a cause, including an accident.... Therefore, when we come to church, although we have accepted Christ, you cannot get rid [of this blame] out of your mind so easily. First, we attribute blame to others. Second, we don't trust [one another].... Always this [blame] is there. Because that's how we've been raised—you have to blame.... "Oh sister, God is sovereign, he is over all things, he is the one who watches over us, he is the one that heals us, and all of that. He will give you the solution." But also, at the bottom of your heart, "Look at her, this sister has *that* kind of sickness?... What has she *done*?" Always blaming. It is difficult to get rid of this from your mind.[110]

Thus, ordinary readers occasionally recognized through the negative example of Job's friends that witchcraft accusations often cause unmerited anguish for the sufferer. Yet contrary to some theologians and biblical scholars, who confidently assert the value of Job's innocent suffering as a liberating biblical resource for overcoming the sting of retributive blame so prevalent during the HIV/AIDS pandemic, local Fang Christians appeared reticent, if the connection was made at all, to apply those same insights to HIV/AIDS. *In fact, the cultural default setting of retributive blame often overwhelmed ordinary readers in their interactions with the text of Job, effectively muzzling or silencing the potential liberating perspectives of the text.* For three straight Sundays, a preacher at Joy of My Salvation portrayed Eliphaz, Bildad, and Zophar as "men of God" and "servants of God" to whom Job "opened his heart" to receive God-ordained counsel.[111] As the preacher put it, "the counsel of the friends brought the first wave of confidence to the heart of Job," by offering God-sanctioned counsel in order for Job to reclaim his blessings.[112] Applying these *positive* exegetical conclusions gleaned from Job's friends, the preacher urged church members to "learn to listen to counsel ... open your heart to receive counsel" so that the advice could "go to work in your life."[113] In other words, rather than portraying Job as vigorously protesting

---

110. Joy of My Salvation, Bible Study, Job 4–5, May 16, 2012.

111. Joy of My Salvation, Sermon, Job 3:1–4, October 16, 2011; Joy of My Salvation, Sermon, Job 4:1–6; 5:1–18; 8:1–7; 11:1–6, 14–20, October 23, 2011; Joy of My Salvation, Sermon, Job 6:3–12; 19:19–25; October 30, 2011.

112. Joy of My Salvation, Sermon, Job 6:3–13, 19:19–25, October 30, 2011.

113. Ibid.

against retributive blame, this Pentecostal preacher depicted Job as being a submissive recipient to the causal logic of his friends. Moreover, even those stigmatized sufferers who had the most to gain by repudiating a theology of retribution—leprosy patients and PLWHA—still interpreted the message of Job through their cultural lenses of retributive blame. In our study, local churches *never* utilized the texts of Job to challenge or contest the retributive blame of stigmatization so prevalent during the HIV/AIDS crisis. Yet even if local preachers or ordinary readers *had* explicitly linked the book of Job to the HIV/AIDS pandemic, there is little certainty that Job would have provided an unequivocal liberating perspective over and against the retributive blame so dominant and prevalent in the culture. Thus, many ordinary Christians severely blunted the paradigm of *Job the Innocent Sufferer* as a sharp object with the potential to counteract the causal logic of retributive blame so prevalent within the culture, a toxic especially damaging during the HIV/AIDS pandemic.

The Ecclesial Censorship of Lament

To lament is to be authentically human. The Catholic leprosy patients lamented, descending into shame and a circularity of despair. The Pentecostal PLWHA lamented, voicing their anger more therapeutically before God. Yet Fang churches of different kinds *censured* Job's lament, often acutely:

> *Reformed Presbyterian Church, Bible Study on Job 3*: I believe that the moral of the story here is that . . . in [any] difficulty that we can have as Christians, the only thing that we should do is give thanks to God and not curse. This is the conclusion. The only thing that we should do in whatever difficult situation that you find yourself in is give thanks to God. Neither curse the day [of your birth] nor wish for death nor curse God. This is the conclusion.[114]

> *Preacher, Assembly of the Holy Spirit, Sermon on Job 3*: Better to be silent than talk. Better that you die with God than without God. . . . When you go through difficult moments, you are going to be quiet. It's better that we are quiet.[115]

Occasionally, Job's lament was censured by reading Job inter-textually through the censuring lens of Job's repentance (Job 42:6) and God's

---

114. Reformed Presbyterian Church, Bible Study, Job 3:1–16, October 18, 2011.
115. Marcellino Abeso Nse, Assembly of the Holy Spirit, Sermon, Job 3–4, May 30, 2012.

chastisement of Job in the Whirlwind Speeches (Job 38:1—41:34). More often, Job was regarded as erupting like a volcano without control, his lament denounced by traditional wisdom which assumed a strict connection between loquaciousness and the inevitability of sin (i.e., "when words are many, transgression is not lacking," Prov 10:19 ESV). Yet the decisive factor serving to censure Job's lament was arguably the way it resonated with traditional Fang mourning practices which are often regarded as excessive by the churches. During the Joban studies, Christians (particularly men) openly mocked the "worldly" way in which Fang traditional culture tends to cope with death and dying, regarding such sullen complaints as incommensurate with Christian hope. For Fang Protestants, traditional mourning and wailing, with its penchant for blaming and accusing God, are ultimately conceived as too blasphemous and irreverent to incorporate into Christian worship.

Yet quite paradoxically, as the churches interacted critically with Job's lament, local stories of lament within the Fang community featured prominently as Christians positioned the Joban lament within the context of their own culture. A Presbyterian elder recalled this story involving a woman and her lost money:

> There was a woman, a woman that went to [the village of] Kogo to sell smoked fish. This woman had already sold 90 percent of her fish. Already she had the money saved. [All of a sudden the purse becomes lost, and she doesn't know where the money is]. It seems that someone took the money. And you know what this woman said? The woman said:
>
> "Oh my God, a poor woman like me! How is it possible that after I have suffered so much, now you allow that they rob me of my money? And I know that you are a God that is always looking, [but] your eyes are in Asia! Now you don't remember what is said in Africa? I can be here praying, praying, praying and you won't listen to me because your attention is on Europe. And I tell you today, God, don't do this to me! Give me the money right now! Give me the money right now because you shouldn't [forget me] like that! Because I know that when you are looking in Europe or Asia, you don't pay attention to Africa. Don't do this to me, God! Give me my money right now!"[116]

During the seminary class on Job, professor Modesto Engonga Ondo set Job's laments against the backdrop of the grieving and mourning practices of the Fang:

116. Reformed Presbyterian Church, Bible Study, Job 3:1–16, October 18, 2011.

> The Fang can bombard [their words] everywhere to find the cause of their situation. I even remember my grandmother, a grandmother-aunt of the family whose only daughter died.... When my aunt was looking at her [deceased] daughter—truthfully I couldn't believe the words that she was saying! (I was a Christian, even a pastor.) She was saying: *"Oh God, Oh God! But God, have you been thinking good? Are you crazy? Now you aren't good like before? To take away my only daughter? God, you haven't thought! Are you now crazy up there in heaven?... Ahhh God, where are you? Where are you? Why haven't you taken me [instead] of taking this poor innocent girl?"* ... I would say that my aunt-grandmother was a typical Fang. A typical Fang would think that if one lifts a bunch of words to God this is going to make God react.[117]

As Mbiti's *Prayers of African Religion* occasionally demonstrates, prayers of lament are not foreign to the traditional religiosity of many African peoples. From Rwanda, Mbiti records this prayer:

> I don't know for what Imana [God] is punishing me: if I could meet with him I would kill him. Imana, why are you punishing me? Why have you not made me like other people? Couldn't you even give me one little child, Yo-o-o! I am dying in anguish! If only I could meet you and pay you out! Come on, let me kill you! Let me run through with a knife! O Imana, you have deserted me! Yo-o-o! [Woe is me!][118]

For the Fang, laments before God seem to have been the product of Christian inculturation. The seismic cosmological changes instigated by Christianity amongst the Fang have led to a robust lament tradition wherein the Fang of today may accuse or blame God directly in the midst of sickness, suffering, and death. Although witchcraft is often believed to be most proximate cause of misfortune, accusatory causal blame may also be directed at God.

Amongst the Fang, laments and cries of anguish are given free expression during periods of mourning, especially by Fang women. Expressive wailing, embodied physicality, and passionate tears amidst communal solidarity often characterize the grieving practices of the Fang. According to Ernst R. Wendland, one of the seven principles typical of Chew and Tonga worldviews is *experientialism* which connotes the unrestrained expression

---

117. *Instituto Bíblico "Casa de la Palabra"* (IBCP Seminary), Class on Job, June 1, 2012.

118. Mbiti, *The Prayers of African Religion*, 86–87.

of feelings and emotions to match the occasion.[119] When Job's friends initially *"raised their voices and wept aloud; they tore their robes and threw dust in the air upon their heads. They sat with him on the ground"* (Job 2:12–13), such responses to suffering are recognized as highly analogous to mourning practices in Central Africa. Nevertheless, in spite of these cultural bereavement practices, or precisely because of them, Fang Protestants appeared reluctant to interpret Job's lament in a favorable light. The censuring of Job's lament, at least amongst non-stigmatized sufferers, was acute and primarily rooted in Christian criticism of traditional practices.

Lament as a Pastoral Response for Churches in a Context of HIV/AIDS

Such censorship of Job's lament by Fang churches poses critical questions during a time of HIV/AIDS. Can the church stand in compassionate solidarity with those infected and affected by HIV/AIDS *without* embracing the lament? How authentic is Spirit-filled (resurrected) praise when it is divorced from God-abandoned (crucified) lament?[120] What role does the community of faith occupy in walking alongside individuals coping with denial, grief, and stigmatization during the HIV/AIDS pandemic? In a seminal essay, "The Costly Loss of Lament," Walter Brueggemann prophetically warns that the church which forfeits lament risks becoming marginalized to the concerns of social justice.[121] Is the hermeneutical censoring of Job's lament intrinsically related to the churches' own silence regarding the HIV/AIDS pandemic? The costly loss of lament during a time of HIV/AIDS tends to place churches on an ecclesial trajectory of embracing a triumphalistic *theologia gloriae* which eclipses a *theologia crucis*.[122] Embracing lament during a time of HIV/AIDS implies recognizing that the whole body of Christ is called to groan together under the weight of the disease as South African Denise Ackermann writes: "If we are truly *one*, we are the church with HIV/AIDS" (1 Cor 12:26; Rom 12:15).[123]

Being the church in an era of HIV/AIDS starts with listening to voices not commonly heard and unlikely to speak for themselves due to

---

119. Wendland, "The Foundation of Religious Belief," 65–122. See also Chilongani, "An African Praying Tradition and Job 7," 65.

120. See Harasta, "Crucified Praise and Resurrected Lament," 204–17.

121. Brueggemann, "The Costly Loss of Lament," 64, 67.

122. See also Louw, "The HIV Pandemic from the Perspective of a *Theologia Resurrectionis*," 100–114.

123. Ackermann, "Tamar's Cry," 18, italics in the original.

the silencing power of HIV-related stigmatization. The more positive reception of Job's lament by the HIV/AIDS group indicates to churches that the lament can occupy an indispensable role in the healing process. Their example suggests that, as PLWHA move from secure *orientation* (before the HIV-positive diagnosis) to painful *disorientation* (the HIV-positive diagnosis) to surprising *reorientation* (acceptance and overcoming denial),[124] the power of lament in articulating the experience of disorientation could be crucial in shattering the silence and overcoming the culture of denial surrounding the disease.[125] As Brueggemann recognizes, "Persons and communities are not fully present in a situation of disorientation until it has been brought to speech."[126] In Africa, healing is not an individual, isolated affair but requires communal empathy and solidarity. Thus, while Job's laments divinely authorized feelings of anger and grief for *individuals* living with HIV/AIDS, the challenge confronting *churches* in an era of HIV/AIDS consists of wearing out a "path between home and sanctuary" by bringing HIV-related suffering into the heart of the church and thereby validating it as a communal affair.[127] Eugene Peterson recognizes that when "others join the sufferer there is 'consensual validation' that the suffering *means* something. The community votes with its tears that there is suffering that is worth weeping over."[128] By lamenting *communally* over HIV/AIDS-related suffering, churches may communicate their compassionate solidarity to those infected and affected by the disease and become instruments in breaking the silence of HIV-related stigma. When a community of faith maintains a polarity of praise and lament[129]—and the experience of the Good Samaritan HIV/AIDS support group provides the example—the church harmonizes its voice with the untold number of sufferers already lamenting internally within its midst:

> *Mariana, Good Samaritan HIV/AIDS Support Group:* There is a moment that I need to pray but in lamentation. Because in that moment you are in communion with God and you don't realize that you are lamenting. You enter into a normal prayer and afterwards you begin to lament and you don't even realize

---

124. Here we are adapting the schema of faith found in Brueggemann, *Praying the Psalms*, 14.

125. For a similar point, see Billman and Migliore, *Rachel's Cry*, 105–7.

126. Brueggemann, *The Psalms and the Life of Faith*, 28 as cited by Byrne, "Give Sorrow Words," 256.

127. Peterson, *Five Smooth Stones for Pastoral Work*, 145.

128. Ibid., 143, italics in the original.

129. Westermann, "Role of the Lament in the Theology of the Old Testament," 27: "Praise can retain its authenticity and naturalness only in polarity with lamentation."

that there are people around you. . . . *There should be a time, like a time of worship, [for] a time of lamentation.*[130]

Practicing *ecclesial* lament, as advised by Mariana, holds the promise of grounding the people of God with a faith in God tied inextricably to the social fabric of the community.

Conclusion

In this chapter, we listened as people living with leprosy and HIV/AIDS interacted with the lament of Job (Job 3:1–26) and the theology of retribution as articulated by Eliphaz, Bildad, and Zophar. From the perspective of stigmatized sufferers, the sting of retribution clearly mirrored their own painful experiences of social exclusion and stigmatization. Both leprosy patients and PLWHA identified profoundly with Job the *Stigmatized* Sufferer. We advanced the argument, based on the fact that leprosy-related and HIV/AIDS-related stigma in Africa is often wedded to a religious-moral narrative of divine punishment, that more careful attention to the cultural embeddedness of stigmatization as a phenomenon centrally related to a retributive-causal worldview is needed for the frank conversations about stigmatization to be meaningfully advanced. Addressing stigmatization *in general* while failing to recognize the *particular* way in which the phenomenon is borne along, and flourishes within, a retributive-causal worldview is to begin a conversation that, at least at the grassroots, will border on being meaningless or irrelevant.

In the reception of Job's lament, the diversity between Catholic leprosy patients and HIV-positive Pentecostals was striking. The dominant discourse of leprosy patients was filled with tropes of internalized despair, unrelenting shame, and anxious eschatological laments while the PLWHA were profoundly empowered to recognize in Job's lament a therapeutic resource sanctioning their own anger which was viewed as a significant step forward in moving from denial to acceptance of the disease. Yet the commonalities were equally profound. Stigmatized sufferers, both leprosy patients and PLWHA, in general acquiesced to the stigmatizing moral framework constructed for them by the Fang community. Whereas leprosy patients fretted about divine (eschatological) punishment, PLWHA continued to accept the prominent discourse of sexual promiscuity, demonstrating the difficulty such sufferers amongst the Fang generally have in conceiving of suffering in terms anything other than retributive blame. In this light,

---

130. Good Samaritan HIV/AIDS support group, Bible Study, Job 3, May 25, 2012.

stigmatized sufferers failed to grasp fully the paradigm-changing potential of Job's innocent suffering to overthrow the negative aspects of a retributive-causal worldview. Even those sufferers who arguably had the most to gain by reorienting their experiences around the paradigm of Job's innocent suffering—leprosy patients and PLWHA—continued to interpret the message of Job through the cultural constructs of retributive blame.

Based on the profound therapeutic experiences of PLWHA to the Joban lament, we put forward the idea that *ecclesial lament* based on HIV/AIDS-related suffering represents one potential way forward for churches to embody compassionate solidarity and break the silence surrounding HIV/AIDS-related stigma. During the HIV/AIDS pandemic, countless people suffer in silence, lamenting internally a disease which often has no voice because of stigmatization. By validating HIV-related suffering through communal lament, the church may join in outspoken solidarity with those PLWHA already lamenting internally within its midst. In an era of stigmatizing silence surrounding HIV/AIDS—to borrow the words of Emmanuel Katongole—"The resurrection of the church begins with lament."[131] By lamenting communally over the HIV/AIDS pandemic, churches may become prophetic voices of hope in showing courageous and compassionate solidarity to those infected and affected by the disease. As the HIV/AIDS support group demonstrated, Fang Christians often tenaciously hope in God in the midst of suffering, sickness, and retributive blame. Our next chapter seeks to analyze precisely these themes of eschatological hope as ordinary readers appropriated Job's hope in the midst of suffering and his final liberation.

---

131. Katongole with Wilson-Hartgrove, *Mirror to the Church*, 163. We owe this reference to Harasta and Brock, "Introduction," 1.

6

Hope in Suffering

*Prayer, Eschatology, and
Job's Final Liberation*

Introduction

IN THIS CHAPTER, WE explore the vision of hope that accompanies local Christians in Equatorial Guinea who often are intimately acquainted with the realities of suffering, poverty, and disease. In portraying the grassroots eschatology of Fang Protestants, we are not primarily interested in a systematic theology of "last things" such as the millennium, the second coming of Christ, or the future of Israel as might be found in creedal statements or formal church documents. Rather, we are concerned to identify the more evasive, but arguably more significant, theologies of hope which sustain local believers in the midst of suffering as they await divine intervention.[1] "I believe that the African reality of suffering is based on the hope that God *knows* and *sees* and *can wake up* at one time or another to lift us up," affirmed Pentecostal pastor Modesto Engonga Ondo, "The African is a man with hope. Though this hope never arrives, yet we hope."[2] In a causal universe where spiritual realities are thought to impinge decisively upon earthly circumstances, *Christian hope is fueled by the stubborn belief that God will intervene in the lives of God's children*. For Christian believers, prayer is the way in which hope is embodied, an ecclesial praxis which

---

1. See also Ross, "The Theology of Hope," 197–211, esp. 199.

2. *Instituto Bíblico "Casa de la Palabra"* (IBCP Seminary), Class of Job, June 7, 2012.

exists in the tension between the expectations of the abundant life and the present sufferings of this world. This divine intervention is based upon the belief that God is not remote or unresponsive to the cries and sufferings of God's people but is willing to be aroused to act in the lives of believers. A primary concern of this chapter, therefore, will be to elucidate this *Deus Victor* paradigm which, arising from sermons and Bible studies, stands in a strict relationship to prayer and serves to comprise the very center of the "theology of hope" espoused by Fang Protestants.

A second major focus of this chapter consists in highlighting the hermeneutical reflections of Joban texts given significant eschatological readings by local Christians. What prominent expressions of eschatology can be identified as grassroots Christians interpreted texts of Job and how do these Christian eschatological themes relate to Fang traditional religiosity? In this chapter, we focus on Job 19 as a significant case study and (to a lesser extent) Job 38–42 to form the basis of this exploration. "I know that my redeemer lives" (Job 19:25) stands as one of the most recognizable phrases in the book of Job, arguably articulating Job's clearest profession of faith and hope in the midst of suffering. Job 38–42 encapsulates Job's final liberation, beginning with the so-called whirlwind speeches of Yahweh and ending with Job's doubly prosperous restoration from suffering. While the former text represents Joban hope in the midst of suffering, the later text portrays hope realized and consummated. By highlighting these texts, we hope to illustrate the way in which Fang Christians formulate eschatology "from below" in lived communities of faith by reading biblical texts in concert with the cultural paradigm of causality and the ecclesial praxis of prayer. This contextually-rooted and ecclesial-driven "theology of hope" is formulated, lived, and enacted by local believers in an effort to provide a vision of hope capable of sustaining the Christian life in the midst of suffering and evil.

Hope and Eschatology in African Christianity

> *For I know that my Redeemer lives, and that at the last he will stand upon the earth; and after my skin has been thus destroyed, then in my flesh I shall see God, whom I shall see on my side, and my eyes shall behold, and not another. My heart faints within me!*
> Job 19:25–27

In the midst of the despair and darkness of suffering, epiphanies of hope and light occasionally lift the countenance of Job's face heavenward. Still suffering terribly on the ash heap, "I know that my redeemer lives" represents arguably the most memorable, if not the most profound, expression of Job's hope in the midst of suffering. As the Old Testament scholar Samuel Balentine writes: "Within Christian tradition, this verse can hardly be read apart from the nexus of faith that associates it with Christ and the promise of resurrection."[3] In the history of Christian interpretation across the centuries and in different contexts—from *the early church fathers* such as Clement of Rome and Origen of Alexandria to *the medieval Catholicism* of St. Thomas Aquinas to *the Reformation period* as viewed through Luther's Bible or Calvin's *Institutes*—Job's hope (19:25–27) has often been cited as the *locus classicus* of the doctrine of the resurrection in the Old Testament.[4] Additionally, Job's hope for a redeemer (*go'el*) has often been identified, however faintly or fleetingly, as referring to the coming Messiah (i.e., the Christ) in a pattern which foreshadows typologically a much fuller and robust expression of Christian eschatology in the New Testament. In other words, in the midst of his sufferings, Job's hope (in Job 19:25–27) has historically been regarded as future-oriented and Christocentric in nature.

In spite of the erosion of this consensus amongst western scholars,[5] the appropriation of Job 19 amongst Fang Christians nevertheless provides a window into the intersection of suffering and eschatology in local faith communities. Yet before delving into Fang interpretations of Job 19, we first turn our attention to the writings of two prominent scholars, John S. Mbiti and Paul Gifford, who have evaluated the eschatological orientation of African Christianity in vastly divergent manners. By briefly delineating their respective arguments, we hope to place this entire conversation of eschatology in an African setting in its proper historical, ecclesial, and theological context.

Escapism or Worldliness? Two Divergent Assessments of the Eschatological Orientation of African Christianity

John Mbiti's major contribution to eschatology is represented by his University of Cambridge doctoral dissertation, completed in 1963 and subsequently published in 1971 as *New Testament Eschatology in an African*

---

3. Balentine, *Job*, 293.

4. Zink, "Impatient Job," 147–48. See also Calvin, *Sermons from Job*, 105–35.

5. This consensus of interpretation linking Job 19 to Christ and the resurrection has largely been eroded amongst western scholars coinciding generally with the rise of the historical-critical method. Though "traditionalist" readings are still advocated by respected scholars such as Janzen, *Job*, 135–50; Balentine, *Job*, 296–301; Andersen, *Job*, 193–94. For a detailing of this phenomenon, see Zink, "Impatient Job."

*Background.*⁶ Although Mbiti's most controversial stance was his argument that most African societies traditionally conceptualized time in terms of a lengthy past, a dynamic present, and virtually no future,⁷ for our purposes *New Testament Eschatology in an African Background* provides an insightful depiction of the eschatology generally characterizing Kenyan, and more generally, African Christianity during the period roughly coinciding with decolonialization. In his work, Mbiti was highly critical of the premillennial, fundamentalist, and future-dominated eschatology of the majority of the missionaries from African Inland Mission (AIM) working in his native Kenya. For Mbiti, the futuristic eschatology of missionary Christianity, focusing predominantly on heaven and hell, not only hindered Christian life and witness in this present world but also combined incoherently with traditional Akamba beliefs and practices which primarily addressed this-worldly concerns. Mbiti argued that when AIM missionaries spoke of the "fire of hell" or "treasures in heaven," these biblical eschatological *symbols* were flatly superimposed as *material* realities upon the Akamba spirit world. Writing with the pastoral sensitivity of a good theologian, Mbiti was clearly concerned that African preoccupations with this present world had been fundamentally co-opted and replaced by eschatological notions of escapism:

> These notions and hopes about a purely materialistic *country* [referring to the "heavenly country" of Heb. 11:14–16] clearly create a false spirituality. They encourage an attitude of indifference to the world in which Christians are called to live; they encourage them to escape from physical reality to a largely fictitious reality; and their Faith is embarrassingly immature.⁸

For Mbiti, this futuristic eschatology of Akamba Christians centering on heaven and hell tended to foster a merit-based or fear-based Christianity while also serving to marginalize Christ to the periphery of eschatology. Mbiti wrote:

> Therefore the *hope of gaining* these heavenly rewards and treasure, and the *fear of losing* them, become the dominant motive in Christian life and service. Thus, the whole concept of heavenly treasure or riches is entirely divorced from Christ except insofar

---

6. Mbiti, *New Testament Eschatology in an African Background*. See also Mbiti, "Eschatology," 159–84.

7. Mbiti, *New Testament Eschatology in an African Background*, 24–32. See also Moreau, "Africa and the Future," 306–20.

8. Mbiti, *New Testament Eschatology in an African Background*, 80, italics added.

as he conveys people from the world of material deprivation to that of rewards and riches.⁹

In the estimation of Mbiti, eschatology was not merely an academic appendix of systematic theology of negligible significance for African Christianity but was profoundly shaping church life and expressions of Christian spirituality: "For many, to be a Christian is to get a passport into Heaven."¹⁰ Mbiti even conjectured that many of the church splits that occurred within African Christianity in the 1960s and early 1970s were due to the profound disappointment some Christians experienced when their escapist spirituality was not forthrightly realized amidst the continuing duress of life.¹¹ In many ways, Mbiti was simply one voice in a chorus of voices protesting this "theology of soul-snatching" of evangelical and fundamental missionaries with respect to African cultures during the 1960s and 1970s.¹² The Dar es Salaam Ecumenical Dialogue of Third World Theologians in August of 1976 heavily criticized western missionaries' other-worldly piety as helping accommodate Africans to suffering, including colonial oppression.¹³

In Pauline terms, Mbiti argued that the already/not yet eschatological tension in the spiritual life had been collapsed in favor of the future dimension for much of African Christianity in the period roughly coinciding with decolonization. But dramatic changes have occurred in the landscape of African Christianity in the last forty-five years since the publication of *New Testament Eschatology in an African Background*. So much has changed, in fact, that Paul Gifford has repeatedly characterized large sections of African Christianity as pitifully shallow *but on precisely the opposite grounds to those once expressed by Mbiti*. In Gifford's estimation, the biblical concept of the afterlife has been "eclipsed" in a capitulation to *this*-worldly concerns and *this*-worldly spiritualities:

> if you asked any African Christian whether he or she believed in an afterlife, the answer would probably be "Yes, of course." If you took a questionnaire into a congregation, all would tick the box indicating a strong belief in the afterlife. Nevertheless, I am convinced from attending African churches over the years that the idea seldom really arises.¹⁴

9. Ibid., 74, italics added.
10. Ibid., 57.
11. Ibid., 60–61.
12. Oduyoye, *Hearing and Knowing*, 37–38.
13. Gifford, *African Christianity*, 31.
14. Gifford, "African Christianity and the Eclipse of the Afterlife," 413.

Gifford's critique of African Christianity's "eclipse of the afterlife" is grounded on two fronts. For the historic mainline or mission denominations, Gifford argues that the churches' involvement in education and health in pre-independent Africa has not decreased but rather expanded exponentially in the 1980s and 1990s. As western donors and NGOs increasingly by-passed the corruption of African states, mainline churches were often co-opted as partners for such diverse interests as micro-finance, agricultural productivity, conflict resolution, water sanitation, or HIV/AIDS education.[15] For Gifford, many such ecclesial projects are not presently being sustained by a robust Christian concern for the transformation of African communities but represent a capitulation to the lure of western opportunities, consistent employment, continuing education, and enhanced modernization. The resulting scenario has resulted in a situation whereby social services "have become increasingly significant for, even constitutive of, parts of mainline Christianity."[16] The crisis confronting the Reformed Presbyterian Church in our own study confirms many of Gifford's concerns insofar as western-funded initiatives for projects such as latrines, the cultivation of rice, and medical clinics played a role in marginalizing traditional Christian emphases of prayer, Bible study, and evangelism to the periphery of church life.[17] In stark contrast to Mbiti's lament of missionary Christianity's other-worldly piety in the 1960s and 1970s, Gifford paints a rather different picture:

> This Christianity brings development as much as redemption. It is associated less with miracle, mystery and magic than with science and technology. It operates with a vocabulary less of grace, sacraments and conversion than of micro-finance, capacity building and women's empowerment. . . . It operates as much from human rights reports and millennium development goals as from biblical texts and creeds.[18]

The second major front where the so-called "eclipse of the afterlife" has occurred resides within African Pentecostalism. Gifford attributes the astounding growth of African Pentecostalism to a multiplicity of factors, but in his estimation Pentecostal churches are *thriving* because their messages of prosperity, health, success, victory, and deliverance profoundly resonate with the socioeconomic plight of millions of Africans who wish to

---

15. Ibid., 418. For the "NGO-ization" of segments of African Christianity, see Hearn, "The 'Invisible' NGO," 32–60.

16. Gifford, "African Christianity and the Eclipse of the Afterlife," 419.

17. See chapter 3, section "Political Ascendancy and Spiritual Decline: The Rise of National Identity and the Decline of the Church."

18. Gifford, "African Christianity and the Eclipse of the Afterlife," 420.

rise above the debilitating effects of poverty.[19] In *Ghana's New Christianity: Pentecostalism in a Globalizing African Economy*, Gifford seeks to capture the recurring emphases of success and financial prosperity by focusing on numerous popular examples of Pentecostal spirituality ubiquitously on display in the city of Accra including *bumper stickers* ("With Jesus I will always win," "Your Success is determined by your Faith"), *names of crusades and conventions* ("Abundance is My Portion," "Experiencing Open Heavens for Divine Blessings," "Taking Your Possessions"), *praise songs and hymns chosen at churches* ("Jesus is a Winner Man," "Abraham's Blessings are Mine"), and *the church slogans and titles of its media productions* ("God's Secrets for Surplus," "Success without Sweat," "Covenant Prosperity is Real") just to name a few.[20] After surveying these popular expressions of Pentecostal spirituality in Accra, Gifford writes:

> In enumerating these examples, the data have not been skewed: examples of other emphases that do not fit our argument have not been left out. Banners or bumper stickers reading "Take up your cross daily (Lk 9.23)," or "I am crucified to the world (Gal. 6.14)," or "Blessed are the Poor (Lk 6.20)" or "My Year of Self-Denial" have not been ignored or overlooked; they simply do not exist and are impossible in this Christianity.[21]

As Philip Jenkins suggests, "Comprehending the prosperity gospel might be the most pressing task for anyone trying to study the changing shape of global Christianity. In West Africa especially, it is hard to avoid churches with a strong prosperity theme."[22] By Gifford's estimation, the prosperity gospel not only is becoming rather ubiquitous within African Pentecostalism but also is threatening to marginalize and displace traditional Christian doctrines such as the cross of Christ and belief in the afterlife—"for it is this-worldly blessings that feature so prominently in African Christianity now."[23]

---

19. Gifford, *Ghana's New Christianity*, ix.

20. Ibid., 44–45.

21. Ibid., 45–46. Gifford also writes: "After 23 years of visiting African churches, I would venture another generalization: the growing Pentecostal churches have one thing in common—a focus on achieving success. Discussing African Pentecostalism without discussing its emphasis on success is like discussing computers without mentioning software;" Gifford, "Expecting Miracles," 20.

22. Jenkins, "The Case for Prosperity," 45.

23. Gifford, "African Christianity and the Eclipse of the Afterlife," 429. See also Gifford, *African Christianity*, 340.

Eschatology and Job 19: A Case Study

While Mbiti and Gifford offer radically divergent portraits of the eschatological orientation of African Christianity, the two scholars are nevertheless united in a common concern. Both scholars have offered a scathing critique of the spirituality of African Christians which is rooted in their unwillingness or inability to live with the inherent tensions of biblical eschatology, but their diagnoses are completely divergent. Do futuristic notions of the Christian afterlife impinge too centrally upon African Christians (Mbiti) or have such concepts become eclipsed (Gifford)? However, neither scholar fully explored a related question: how are contemporary African Christians actually interpreting biblical passages that the church has traditionally associated with the nexus of eschatology, hope, and suffering? By utilizing readings of Job 19 as a case study, the eschatological motifs of Fang Protestants will be analyzed and conclusions will be drawn regarding the nascent theology of hope which undergirds local Christians during times of suffering.

In the Reformed Presbyterian Church of Equatorial Guinea, the hermeneutical appropriation of Job's hope of a redeemer ("I know that my Redeemer lives," 19:25) conveyed a dynamic eschatological tension between a *realized* hope and a much anticipated *future* hope. As Presbyterians interpreted Job 19, their rhetoric reflected the traditional Christian interpretation of the text that began as early as the church fathers:

> *David*: "But I know that my Redeemer lives and that at the end he will arise over the dust." I think that it's a prophecy that Job sees Jesus. He talks of his Redeemer that lives and talks about his death and resurrection. Here it's a prophecy. He sees that his Redeemer lives and will come to be Jesus. That one day He will raise him from the dust. It's a prophecy.[24]

Job's hope provided Fang Presbyterians with an opportunity to meditate robustly on the future afterlife, and their reflections seemed neither to constitute a denial of the realities of this-worldly sufferings nor pacify hopes for a transformed present. An extended conversation about Job 19 amongst ordinary Presbyterians revealed that the eschatological tension between the "already" and "not yet" of God's kingdom was balanced with considerable clarity:

> *Claudia*: What hope did Job have in this case?

---

24. Reformed Presbyterian Church, Bible Study, Job 9:27–35; 13:13–19; 16:18–22; 19:23–27, October 25, 2011.

Tomás: Job knew that apart from this world, there is another life. He hoped to go and see God and be with God apart from this world.... *That's why he endured all the sufferings, hoping that he wanted to reach eternal life.*

Claudia: [Reads Job 19:25-26 again.]

María Carmen: Job understood that there was another life. That's why before, in chapter 13, he says: "Although he slays me, I will hope in him." He knew that this flesh which is decomposing can die.... He had this hope that even though this flesh is corrupted, I know that God himself will raise me up and I will be with him.

Lucas: Before Jesus Christ came to say: "I am the resurrection and the life."... Job was already thinking—you understand me, right?—he is already thinking of the resurrection.

María Carmen: ... I believe that apart from the hope that we have in the life to come, *we also have a hope here*. Because we know that if we go a little bit further than the Old Testament, Christ did not only die to save us—to give us eternal life—but he also carried our infirmities. What this means is that if I have a suffering here in the flesh and I trust in God, I know that this suffering will end [and God] will raise me up not only after death. After death comes, *but also here. He is accompanying us* because he carried our infirmities and sufferings on the cross.

Bartolome: [Job] is in the dust. He is suffering. In addition to the other part [the afterlife] Job had sufficient confidence in God that God can recover all that was lost.... And if not, God will give him a heavenly life never to die.... [This is] the *double trust* that Job had.[25]

For Presbyterians, this vision of hope was a "double trust" that encompassed the future promise of eternal life *and* the comfort in knowing that God "is accompanying us" during an earthly pilgrimage full of sufferings.[26] For the Reformed Presbyterian Church, the afterlife was not eclipsed (as Gifford alleges) but neither was it conceived as a futuristic utopia which encouraged escapism from this world (as Mbiti argued). Rather, heavenly hope was balanced by an earthly realism that clearly recognized that Christians are not immune to the sufferings of this present age: "One has to recognize that with God we do not only receive the good while we are in this

25. Ibid.
26. Ibid.

world but also sufferings. We receive from God the good permanently only in His kingdom."[27]

In stark contrast to Fang Presbyterians who embraced the eschatological tension between the "already" and the "not yet" of God's kingdom while viewing Job's hope Christocentrically through the lens of New Testament eschatology, Fang Pentecostals appropriated Job's hope as centering upon God being the harbinger of solutions, reflecting a certain Old Testament earthiness and materiality of faith rooted almost exclusively in *this-worldly* concerns. In expounding Job 19, the interpretive interest which most captured the hermeneutical imagination of Pentecostals was not first and foremost Job's hope of a Redeemer (Job 19:25–27) but rather the communal and relational problems Job faced which were interpreted in terms of the retributive blame of witchcraft (e.g., Job 19:2–3, 13–19). When Job complains to his friends "how long will you torment me, and break me in pieces with words" (Job 19:2) or laments "my relatives and my close friends have failed me" (Job 19:14), local hermeneutical reflection gravitated to these relational complaints of Job by appropriating them straightaway as representative of their own frustrations with witchcraft. In other words, verses 25–27 of Job 19 (i.e., "My redeemer lives") which historically have been interpreted typologically to refer to Christ and the resurrection were subordinated to verses 2–3 (i.e., "how long will you torment me") and 13–19 (i.e., "my relatives have failed me") in the Pentecostal imagination to refer to witchcraft-related sufferings. Occasionally "witchcraft-centered" readings of biblical texts represented such a dominant concern of Pentecostal interpreters that biblical themes and motifs, often central to the plain meaning of the text itself, were silenced or ignored.

One preacher from the Assembly of the Holy Spirit read and expounded upon every verse in Job 19 except verses 23–28, effectively silencing arguably Job's most famous utterance of "I know that my Redeemer lives" (vs. 25). Nevertheless, skipping from verse 22 ("Why do you, like God, pursue me, never satisfied with my flesh?") to verse 29 ("be afraid of the sword, for wrath brings the punishment of the sword"), served to underscore the main point of Job 19 for this Pentecostal preacher, namely, that the vengeful judgment of God's sword will fall decisively and violently upon witches who dare attack Christians:

> Job says: "Are you not satisfied with my flesh?" [Alluding to Job 19:22.] Who removes the flesh from persons? Is it not witches?

---

27. In this instance, a Presbyterian member is summarizing the main points of the two-week study of Job; Reformed Presbyterian Church, Bible Study, Job 42:7–17, November 2, 2011.

... It is prohibited to touch the body of a Christian. You [witches] can go against all other flesh. But watch out! Don't eat the flesh of a son of God! Because the sword is going to come to chop off [the witches][28] ... Christians are untouchable! Don't touch them![29]

In the hands of this Pentecostal preacher, the text of Job 19 was not devoid of an eschatological perspective. Yet it was rooted neither in a Christocentric hope nor in the eschatological promise of the resurrection but rather in the imprecatory nature of God's judgment against the ubiquitous witches of the Pentecostal hermeneutical imagination. In the Assembly of the Holy Spirit, the eschatological thrust of Job 19 centered upon judgment rather than promise and focused on witches rather than on Christ.

If truth be told, hermeneutical reflection for local Pentecostals often consists of nothing more than an extended exercise of confronting the local narrative of witchcraft with the more powerful Christian narrative known as the Bible. The theme of witchcraft is easily introduced into almost any scriptural passage by local Pentecostals. This interpretative framework for understanding the Bible, with its thick dialogical recourse to witchcraft, itself becomes a type of hermeneutical bondage to witchcraft which local Pentecostals often fail to escape. Rather than meditating on the sustaining love of God in the midst of suffering or the extent of Christ's victory on the cross, hermeneutical reflection tends to echo the dominant discourse of evil so prevalent within the society. With so much hermeneutical energy invested combating witchcraft, one wonders whether Pentecostals have become so exhausted in this all-consuming fight against witchcraft as to fully appreciate biblical doctrines which might point a way "out" of the fight or, better yet, towards a decisive victory in the fight. It often seems like the fight against witchcraft itself has become the means and ends of the Pentecostal Christian existence as well as the main point of its hermeneutical reflection.

Similar to the witchcraft-centered hermeneutic of Assembly of the Holy Spirit's fiery preacher, when young adults at Joy of My Salvation studied Job 19, a myriad of Joban verses provided an alluring invitation to dialogue about witchcraft and suffering in terms of the broken sociocommunal relationships caused by retributive blame. Consider the following verses from Job 19:

> These ten times you have cast reproach upon me; are you not ashamed to wrong me? (vs. 3)

---

28. A homiletical allusion to Job 19:29.
29. Marcellino Abeso Nse, Assembly of the Holy Spirit, Sermon, Job 19, June 6, 2012.

He has put my family far from me, and my acquaintances are wholly estranged from me. (vs. 13)

All my intimate friends abhor me, and those whom I loved have turned against me. (vs. 19)

For these young Pentecostals at Joy of My Salvation, these verses helped build a solid case for witchcraft and retributive blame encompassing the "hermeneutical center" of the passage.

In addition to a witchcraft-centered hermeneutic mined from the quarry of Job 19 at both Pentecostal churches, an eschatologically-oriented reading of Job's hope also characterized the interpretation of Job 19 amongst young adults at Joy of My Salvation. In the midst of suffering, local Pentecostals believe that the eschatological horizon remains unambiguously open for new possibilities, radical breakthroughs, and *Shekinah*-like displays of God's glory. God's power is always "on the way." "Today" always brings the promise of new divine possibilities. God's glory is always visible for those who believe. In short, in Pentecostal rhetoric, God is always in the business of bringing miraculous divine-ordained solutions to disheartening earth-filled problems. At Joy of My Salvation, Job's hope was fundamentally seen as a theocentric hope centering on the arrival of this-worldly solutions framed in terms of divine blessing, healing, and restoration:

> *Justino*: "I know that my redeemer lives. At the end he will arise from the dust." I see this verse as a little summary of the life of Job.... He always knew that one day, God is going to deliver me. God is going to raise me up again.
>
> *Author*: Who is the Redeemer, then?
>
> *Everybody*: God.
>
> *Author*: God. And what was the basis for Job's hope?
>
> *Benedicto*: Job's hope was always based on God. He had a certain confidence that despite everything that could happen to me, I know that God is going to raise me up . . .
>
> *Author*: This was on the earth or on . . . [interrupted]
>
> *Many*: On the earth.
>
> *Benedicto*: When he was on the earth. The hope was not on heaven. Strength, yes, is in heaven, but hope is here on the earth. . . . [Job suffered relationally] with his friends, with his workers, his children, even his own wife threw him out. But Job said: "If

now you don't love me, I will remain here" [on the ashes?]. But he always had a hope saying that "I know my Redeemer lives." ... The hope is in this world.

Noemi: I think that when it comes to Job, Job was on earth, he wasn't in heaven.

Gaspar: Job was on the earth!³⁰

This portrayal of Job's hope as vigorously *this-worldly* is hardly an isolated hermeneutical reflection amongst Fang Pentecostals. Instead, a this-worldly ethos can be viewed as strictly corresponding to the overall shape of local Pentecostalism which has wedded its ecclesial culture to the pragmatic and utilitarian aims of indigenous beliefs and practices.

Kenneth Ross suggests that because divine promises "opening up an eschatological horizon" to a historically distant future "is foreign to the African tradition we might expect that Christianity would have difficulty fully accommodating it."³¹ For Fang Pentecostals, the eschatological horizon remains unambiguously open for new and miraculous possibilities, but these divine solutions almost always center on this-worldly inbreakings of divine intervention.

According to Mbiti, the very concept of time proceeding in a linear fashion towards a distant future represents a quite dissonant concept to African traditional religiosity:

> according to traditional concepts, time is a two-dimensional phenomenon, with a long *past*, a *present* and virtually *no future*. ... *Actual time* is therefore what is present and what is past. It moves "backward" rather than "forward"; and people set their minds not on future things, but chiefly on what has taken place.³²

Mbiti argued that African traditional religion provides no teleology but only deteriology in the sense that time moves *backwards* towards the past.³³ For

---

30. Joy of My Salvation, Bible Study, Job 19, 2012.
31. Ross, "The Theology of Hope," 203.
32. Mbiti, *African Religions and Philosophy*, 17.
33. Mbiti, *New Testament Eschatology in an African Background*, 139. Though Mbiti seems to underestimate the capacity of Africans to view abstract theoretical concepts such as "time" outside the religio-cultural parameters set for them by society, Byang Kato, by arguing that Mbiti's view of time is "illogical," fails to appreciate the way Mbiti has thoroughly embedded his concept of time within indigenous religiosity; Kato, *Theological Pitfalls in Africa*, 63. See also Booth, "Time and Change in African Traditional Thought," 81–91.

the Fang, distant futuristic concepts would have been foreign to the *raison d'être* of traditional rituals which embodied a decidedly this-worldly and anthropocentric orientation. Although ancestors were central to the traditional rituals such as Biéri and Ndong Mba, it was precisely their perceived ability to influence the material world for the living in the here and the now that conferred them such veneration. In this light, even the ancestral realm fails to provide an unequivocal link with the Christian afterlife since, as Mbiti argued, ancestors are essentially forgotten by the community in three or four generations and extinguished as non-entities when no living person is alive to venerate them.[34] Charles Nyamiti, a Tanzanian Roman Catholic priest, has argued that this anthropocentric and utilitarian orientation resides as a distinguishing feature of African traditional beliefs and practices:

> African religious behaviour is centred mainly on man's life in this world, with the consequence that religion is chiefly *functional*, or a means to serve people to acquire earthly goods (life, health, fecundity, wealth, power and the like) and to maintain social cohesion and order.[35]

Mbiti agrees: "The soul of man does not long for spiritual redemption, or for closer contact with God in the next world. . . . Man's acts of worship and turning to God are pragmatic and utilitarian rather than spiritual or mystical."[36] This functional and utilitarian aspect of African religiosities stems most centrally from a critical feature of its internal structure: the belief that humanity lives "in a sacramental universe where there is no sharp dichotomy between the physical and the spiritual."[37] John V. Taylor referred to this dynamic as "the unbroken circle"[38] of African religiosity while Bediako argued that this "unified cosmic system" should be viewed as "the real key to the entire structure."[39] In most African contexts, an underlying unity pervades the cosmos wherein the spiritual and physical realm are so intertwined that it becomes virtually impossible, if not futile, to try to unravel this essential oneness.

When African Pentecostals approach Christianity from these *functional* and *utilitarian* perspectives of indigenous religiosity, hope in God often becomes intertwined with, if not fused to, a hope for divine gifts and

---

34. Mbiti, *New Testament Eschatology in an African Background*, 139.
35. Nyamiti, "The Doctrine of God," 60, italics in the original.
36. Mbiti, *African Religions and Philosophy*, 5.
37. Turner, "The Primal Religions of the World and Their Study," 32.
38. Taylor, *The Primal Vision*, 67–82.
39. Bediako, *Christianity in Africa*, 96.

solutions. No distinction is made between hope *in God* and hope *in God's good gifts*. For Fang Pentecostals, this dynamic was clearly reflected in their hermeneutical appropriation of Job's hope as centering upon an abundant God of solutions who seldom arrives empty-handed or without his promised blessings:

> *Author*: So, the hope [of Job] was on God or that God was going to provide a solution?
>
> *Alejandra*: God will provide a solution. Job had hope that God was going to solve everything that happened to him.
>
> *Benedicto*: That's how it is.
>
> *Justino*: Although I pass through hunger here, I know that one day God is going to open the doors. God can open a door so that I can eat. Because hope—we hope in the Lord—everything is ours for the children of God. Although we suffer, although we pass through difficult moments, always our hope is in Jehovah.
>
> *Paloma*: I have confidence in God. My confidence is addressed to God but this confidence [is that] I expect something to change. *That God is going to do something for me.*
>
> *Bella*: If one has hope, it's *for something*. For example, I want to have a husband. I have hope that God is going to give me one.[40]

The idea of hope being inescapably connected with the notion that "God is going to do something for me"[41] not only resonates with the anthropocentric and functional nature of Fang traditional religiosity but also reflects the characteristic concerns of local Pentecostal ecclesiology. That is, a this-worldly eschatology is reflective of a this-worldly ecclesiology. During the sermon series on Job at Joy of My Salvation, a pragmatic, utilitarian ecclesiology wherein the *church's purpose was clearly tied to earthly solutions* and *spiritual practices were fundamentally oriented towards tangible material results* was plainly articulated:

> If we come here to church . . . it's for this: that we need something. Amen? Because if we were complete—stay at home. When Sunday arrives, [you'd say]: "Well, thanks because I know you, [God]." There is no need [to come to church]. Why should you come? *If an ox has his pasture, why should he leave his house?* He has everything! But if we are here [at church], it's for

---

40. Joy of My Salvation, Bible Study, Job 19, May 19, 2012.
41. Ibid.

something. It's for a need. And this need is that which makes us seek, worship, and cry out. We pass the night worshipping and crying out—not because we have everything! Why can't we go to sleep? Every morning, we arise, "Lord, Hallelujah!" We pray in the afternoon. It's *for something*. There is a problem. There is something that is happening to you. . . . This is what is happening with Job.[42]

At Joy of My Salvation, the pastor can be viewed as clearly articulating what is driving ecclesial praxis: "this *need* is that which makes us seek, worship, and cry out."[43] In other words, prayer and worship are rooted primarily in theodicy's concerns for the removal of evil rather than being explicitly grounded in the relational character of God. By enthusiastically embracing the affirmation of causality and the expectation of the abundant life,[44] Pentecostal praxis often becomes acutely concerned with, if not thoroughly preoccupied by, the presence of evil and suffering within the worldview. In a similar fashion to the way in which the presence of evil galvanized traditional rituals amongst the Fang, the *sine qua non* of Pentecostal praxis is based on pragmatically engaging the causal universe in order to get rid of suffering and evil so people can live an abundant life. Yet within this traditionally inherited framework, the Christian idea that God should be *worshipped* or *pursued* or *enjoyed* for who God is in Godself is largely suppressed. As this Pentecostal preacher approached the matter: "If an ox has his pasture, why should he leave his house?" Or, as we might ask, if a Fang Pentecostal is enjoying the abundant life, why bother seeking God? If one is already enjoying the divine gifts, is there really a need to worship God for who God is?

Yet a striking irony exists in using *the book of Job*, which poses a severe critique to interested forms of piety, to advance a vision of hope centering on God and his gifts. This irony, however, was entirely lost on Fang Pentecostals. Insofar as the entire Joban narrative hinges on the fundamental *dis*-interestedness of religion, Satan's cynical question, "Does Job fear God for nothing?" (Job 1:9) is not only a pivotal, agenda-setting question for the entire book as a whole[45] but also represents an aggressive frontal attack

---

42. Basilio Oyono, Joy of My Salvation, Sermon, Job 6:3–12, 19:19–25, October 30, 2011.

43. Ibid.

44. Issues of causality and the expectation of the abundance life are two foundational elements of the Fang cosmology; see chapter 2, sections "The Causal Universe: Sickness and Healing in Fang Cultural Perspective" and "The Abundant Life and the Presence of Suffering."

45. Ticciati, "Does Job Fear God for Naught?" 353; Lacocque, "Job and Religion at

on self-interested piety.[46] Satan's basic argument is that "Job's godliness is artificial"[47] because material self-interest, or a piety centered upon God *and* his gifts, has a way of inherently adulterating a believer's faith, hope, and love for God. The book's central exploration lies precisely along these lines: can Job (and all who follow in his wake) worship God for nothing and without reward? Or, does piety crumble in the absence of blessings? Moreover, this heavenly wager not only scrutinizes the nature of faith but also the intrinsic worth of God.[48] J. Gerald Janzen rightly identifies this crucial issue at stake in the divine-human relationship when he poignantly asks:

> Is the creator of the world and the divine benefactor of humankind worshipful only by virtue of what deity does for humankind? Or is God intrinsically worshipful? Is deity capable of creating a creature who, somehow, attains to such freedom and independence, such spiritual and moral maturity, as to be in a position to choose to offer God worship and service because of God's intrinsic worthiness to be loved?[49]

The book of Job poses a staunch, direct challenge to advocates of utilitarian versions of religion. Such a vision of hope not only suffers, as Gustavo Gutiérrez argues, from a lack of "depth and authenticity"[50] on the side of faith but also can be characterized as severely malnourished in its diminished vision of God's majestic ontology and intrinsic worth.

The belief that hope in God (piety) and hope in God's good gifts (prosperity) are interconnected, therefore, has more in common with the anthropocentric interests of Fang religiosity than with the biblical book of Job which is making a concerted effort to undermine precisely this causal connection. For Pentecostals, hermeneutical reflection that adamantly asserted that Job hoped in God *and his solutions* tended to mute the pivotal concern for disinterested piety promoted by the Joban prologue. For Fang Pentecostals, the very idea that Job, as a biblical book, might provide a valuable paradigm or an essential biblical model for loosening the physical-spiritual connections within their own indigenous cosmology was completely absent. Considering that the book of Job was arguably penned to provide precisely this oppositional role to the causal cosmology of ancient Judaism by loosening the formulaic connections between sin-and-suffering

---

Its Best," 153.

46. Dhorme, *A Commentary on the Book of Job*, 7.
47. Andersen, *Job*, 84.
48. Balentine, *Job*, 54.
49. Janzen, *Job*, 41.
50. Gutiérrez, *On Job*, 5, cf. 1.

and piety-and-prosperity,[51] this hermeneutical myopia may strike the theologian or biblical scholar as all the more glaring. That appropriation of the book of Job offered virtually no resistance or contestation to the underlying causal cosmology which so informs Pentecostal belief and praxis raises serious questions for the Christian theologian regarding the capacity of local Pentecostals to integrate biblical texts which challenge or contest their basic cultural orientation deriving from indigenous assumptions.

Appropriating the book of Job in contexts of suffering is admittedly complex. The idea that Christians quite naturally or instinctually hope in God *and* health (in contexts of disease) or hope in God *and* prosperity (in contexts of poverty) seems legitimate, even innocent: who does not pray for good health when faced with sickness or for finances to feed one's family when mired in poverty? Yet as Janzen recognizes, the book of Job goes well beyond such anthropocentric interests in setting up a radical, albeit crucial, question based on whether God is "intrinsically worshipful."[52] The book of Job implies that the ontological greatness and majesty of God should alone be capable of sustaining faith and hope not only in the *absence* of blessings but also in the *presence* of sufferings.[53] By insisting wholeheartedly that Christian hope necessarily entails divine gifts, Fang Pentecostals seemed to miss entirely this pivotal perspective on the book of Job without which, it might be argued, the entire book loses its essential meaning. The question may reasonably be asked, in fact, whether local Pentecostals have become so accommodated to a "barter concept of religion"[54] through their cultural paradigms that God essentially becomes reduced to a diminutive "cosmic bellhop"[55] or diminished to a Divine Blessing Dispenser primarily utilized as a *means to an end* insofar as divine blessings, gifts, and solutions are what truly motivate both ecclesial practice and Christian virtue. Such are the radical questions and implications for the divine-human relationship that

---

51. Driver, *An Introduction to the Literature of the Old Testament*, 409; Matthews, *The Religious Pilgrimage of Israel*, 171ff. For background on how the book of Job answers the doctrine of retribution of ancient Israel, see also Dhorme, *A Commentary on the Book of Job*, cxxviii–cli; Pfeiffer, *Introduction to the Old Testament*, 694–707.

52. Janzen, *Job*, 41.

53. As H. H. Rowley argues, the purpose of the book of Job is "to declare to the reader that even such bitter agony as Job endured may be turned to spiritual profit if he finds God in it.... Here is no thought that suffering is itself enriching. Rather is it that the fellowship of God is enriching, and that that fellowship may be found in adversity no less than in prosperity." Rowley, "The Book of Job and Its Meaning," 178–79.

54. Gutiérrez, *On Job*, 1.

55. Jones and Woodbridge, *Health, Wealth & Happiness*, 102 citing Goff, "The Faith That Claims," 21.

the book of Job so insightfully explores. More provocatively, the critique of Gutiérrez of such utilitarian visions of hope and religion is striking:

> The author [of Job] is telling us . . . that a utilitarian religion lacks depth and authenticity; in addition, it has something satanic about it. . . . The expectation of rewards that is at the heart of the doctrine of retribution vitiates the entire relationship and plays the demonic role of obstacle on the way to God. In self-seeking religion there is no true encounter with God but rather the construction of an idol.[56]

The final irony is that Pentecostals, despite their incessant battle against a charismatic Devil, have failed to pay sufficient hermeneutical attention to Satan's pivotal question in the book of Job (i.e., "Does Job fear God for nothing?" Job 1:9). Satan doubts that Job serves God because of God's character and intrinsic worth, but rather for the blessings of riches and prosperity that God has bestowed upon him. The irony only deepens for Pentecostals if the critique of Gutiérrez is on target: in their unrelenting battle against Satan to acquire a material vision of the abundant life, they have not only subverted Job's message that faithfulness to God should be separated from all questions of reward but also have become accomplices, to some degree, of their main archenemy and nemesis.

Deus Victor and the Role of Christ in Hope and Hermeneutics

By using Job 19 as a case study, we have been predominantly concerned in this chapter with sketching the vision of hope undergirding various streams of Protestant Christianity in Equatorial Guinea. Yet eschatology leads naturally into a discussion of Christology, since *Christian* hope divorced from Christ ceases to be distinctively Christian. Perhaps this is one of the reasons why Christian interpreters have historically insisted on making Christological connections principally with Job's redeemer but even with Job himself. On the later connection, Gutierrez observes: "Ever since the time of the church fathers, the book's central character, the Job who suffers but continues to believe, has been regarded as one of the great prefigurations of Christ in the Hebrew scriptures."[57] Considering that grassroots Christians in Africa have generally been immune to western academic readings which suppress Christocentric interpretations of the Old Testament (as ordinary

---

56. Gutiérrez, *On Job*, 5.
57. Ibid., xvii.

readers are generally non-conversant with the historical-critical method), one might conjecture that ordinary readers in Africa would continue to see Christ in the pages of the Old Testament generally and in Job 19 particularly. Exploring this conjecture, the hermeneutics behind it, and the resulting ramifications for Christian hope now occupy our concern.

Charles Haddon Spurgeon, the doyen of nineteenth-century British preachers, once indicated his own hermeneutical method thus:

> I have never yet found a text that had not got a road to Christ in it, and if I ever do find one that has not a road to Christ in it, I will make one; I will go over hedge and ditch but I would get at my Master, for the sermon cannot do any good unless there is a savor of Christ in it.[58]

A prominent evangelical leader in the West explained: "Every single text of Scripture points to Christ.... From Moses to the prophets, He is the focus of every single word of the Bible. Every verse of Scripture finds its fulfillment in Him, and every story in the Bible ends with Him."[59] The argument that a Christocentric orientation should govern biblical hermeneutics, however, is hardly confined to western preachers or exegetes. Asamoah-Gyadu, a Ghanaian Pentecostal scholar, indicates that "Christological hermeneutics" should play a decisive role in the theologies and practices of the church:

> On almost every theological issue, it is important that we apply Christological hermeneutics. This simply means that the Bible must be interpreted and applied with the Christ factor in mind. Jesus Christ, as far as the new covenant goes, is the single most important factor of biblical interpretation. He is the one who came to fulfil the Law of Moses. When the Christ factor is removed from the interpretation of Scripture, Christianity loses its defining model....[60]

The assumption that popular interpreters of the Bible in Africa would be sympathetic to Christ-centered hermeneutical practices is seemingly fueled by scholars of African Christianity who enthusiastically portray grassroots Christians as insatiable sponges who eat, drink, and talk about nothing but Christ from open-aired markets to thatched-roofed churches to everywhere

---

58. As cited by Stetzer, "David and Goliath," para. 4.

59. Mohler, *He Is Not Silent*, 96. See also Moberly, "Preaching Christ from the Old Testament," 233–50; Greidanus, *Preaching Christ from the Old Testament*; Clowney, *The Unfolding Mystery*.

60. Asamoah-Gyadu, *Contemporary Pentecostal Christianity*, 98–99.

in between.[61] For instance, Kwame Bediako points to Afua Kuma's prayers and praises in *Jesus of the Deep Forrest* as indicative of the "deep religious apprehension of Jesus Christ in African terms" which seems to be representative, for Bediako, of much of sub-Saharan Africa.[62] Nevertheless, our own research indicates that such a Christ-centered portrayal of the whole of African Christianity does not correlate with its hermeneutical posture (at least in relationship to the Old Testament). Of the forty-two sermons and Bible studies that we observed amongst Christians in Equatorial Guinea, one solitary Presbyterian Bible study linking Job's hope of a Redeemer to Christ provided the exception, rather than the rule, in its Christocentric interpretation. Local Christians in fact displayed a remarkable propensity and tendency to keep Christ *off* the pages of the Old Testament. Amongst local Pentecostals, Job's hope for a Redeemer was *never* equated with Christ but with a general concept of the Deity.

One might furthermore presuppose, as Gutiérrez assumed in his theological commentary *On Job: God-Talk and the Suffering of the Innocent*, that a Christian meditating upon Job's sufferings would be thrust into the arms of the suffering Christ in being powerfully reminded of Christ's own suffering cry on the cross, "My God, My God, why have you forsaken me?" (Matt 27:46).[63] Yet our research suggests that such a conjecture would also be seriously mistaken for ordinary readers of the Bible in Central Africa. The book of Job sparked meandering conversations about the dynamics of suffering, the problem of evil, and the nature of hope amongst grassroots Christians, but the cross of Christ scarcely registered a blip on the conversational radar. Relatively little concern or pedagogical effort was displayed to place human suffering, or even suffering of the Christian, within a Christocentric framework.

Yet this is not to suggest that Fang Christians feel entirely bereft of Christian resources during times of suffering.[64] For Fang Pentecostals, the

---

61. Matthew Michael's generalization of the Christocentric orientation of African Christianity borders on enthusiastic triumphalism rather than being founded on local realities: "For many Africans, the person of Jesus Christ is such a center and a point of constant fascination. This is easily reflected in the centrality of Christology in their songs, prayers, sermons and various religious observances. Jesus Christ is indeed the centre of African Christianity.... African Christianity is in every aspect Christocentric in profession." Michael, *Christian Theology and African Traditions*, 129–30.

62. Bediako, "The Roots of African Theology," 64; Kuma, *Jesus of the Deep Forest*. For similar enthusiasm about the Christocentric character of African Christianity, see Stinton, *Jesus of Africa*.

63. See Gutiérrez, *On Job*, 101.

64. Though see our previous discussion of the dilemmas facing the Reformed Presbyterian Church, chapter 3, section "Cosmological Maps: Traditional, Presbyterian,

power of witchcraft is tirelessly confronted with the power and promises of God through lively prayer services and times of fasting. The "name of Jesus" to heal is tirelessly proclaimed in deliverance services. However, ordinary Christians *hermeneutically* do not seem particularly concerned with Old Testament texts being fulfilled in Christ nor is Christ perceived as lurking behind every act of God's redemption. From our experience, the biblical narrative, rather than the figure of Christ, is what primarily arouses the interpretive interest of grassroots Christians. *Deus Victor* rather than *Christus Victor* seems to provide the "controlling motif" or "dominant center" that provides the hermeneutical orientation for ordinary African Christians. And this seems particularly so for local Pentecostals. Within Fang Pentecostalism, witches are defeated, curses are blocked, and scriptural promises are claimed but mostly within a framework of the divine-human partnership. The human actor figures prominently but within an overarching perspective that is more theocentric than explicitly Christocentric. Narratives focusing on miraculous healings, changed destinies, and the power to overcome any circumstance are favorite biblical texts. But Elijah, Moses, Daniel, or Joseph often fit as easily into the *Deus Victor* paradigm as Jesus of Nazareth. And even when Christ is preached as healer or deliverer, the emphasis is typically not on creeds—in the sense of communicating classic Christian doctrines such as the incarnation, the deity of Christ, or the substitutionary atonement—but upon the pneumatological encounter with God's victorious power which is claimed in the life of the believer.[65]

Kenneth Ross, after surveying 587 sermons amongst mainstream churches in Malawi, made a striking observation about the marginal role Christ played amongst biblical interpreters in the Malawian churches. Ross writes: "Reading the sermon outlines left me with the impression that, were it not for the Christmas and Easter seasons, there would be relatively little emphasis on Christ himself."[66] Ross indicated that "it was not uncommon to read a sermon outline" which focused upon the themes of "[c]reation, sin and redemption without reference to Christ!"[67] In other words, Malawian preachers seemed to emphasize *Deus Victor* rather than *Christus Victor* in placing redemption in a theocentric, rather than an explicitly Christocentric, framework. Ross surmised that the Christological deficit pervading Malawian sermons—a concern also echoed by Harold Turner who called

---

and Pentecostal Cosmological Maps of the Universe amongst the Fang."

65. Ross, "Preaching in Mainstream Christian Churches in Malawi," 6; Gifford, "The Bible in Africa," 203–18, esp. 217–18.

66. Ross, "Preaching in Mainstream Christian Churches in Malawi," 6.

67. Ibid.

attention to the "muted testimony to Christ" in the preaching of the Aladura churches of Nigeria[68]—seemed to be rooted in the preferential role given to the experiential and subjective aspects of the Christian faith: "It is apparent that it is the subjective rather than the objective pole of the Christian faith which predominates in the preaching.... By comparison, the 'objective' core of Christian faith in the incarnation, the deity and humanity of Christ is given relatively little attention."[69] For Christian theologians, there is a subtle danger in this trajectory: an existential, subjective faith which is not undergirded by robust objective doctrines of the Christian faith—incarnation, atonement, resurrection—easily collapses into a day-to-day reliance on values and patterns of behavior more reflective of African traditional religiosity than on the efficacious life and death of Jesus Christ. An underdeveloped Christological hermeneutic naturally paves the way towards underdeveloped Christocentric doctrines in the preaching and teaching practices of local African churches. The lack of an explicitly Christocentric orientation in the hermeneutics and homilies of African churches from Malawi to Nigeria to Equatorial Guinea raises serious questions as to whether ordinary African believers who fill pews and chairs across the continent are being adequately equipped to apply Christ's efficacious death on the cross to bring definitive victory over evil forces or to fully appreciate the resurrection of Christ in such a way that brings salvific wholeness and healing to all areas of life.

For Mbiti, the lack of a sufficient Christological basis for eschatology was particularly alarming. In *New Testament Eschatology in an African Background*, Mbiti recognized that the object of faith (Christ) should never be confused with, or subverted by, the hope for tangible or materialistic rewards:

> Heaven for its own sake is not heavenly, and has no independent reality as such. *New Testament emphasis is on Jesus* as the One through whom and in whom life is Heaven-ly... The New Testament is explicit that Jesus never promised us a heavenly utopia, *but only His own self and His own companionship* both in Time and beyond, both in space and beyond (cf. Jn: 14:3, Mt. 28:20b; 18:20).[70]

Although the Christian eschatological message of salvation is necessarily holistic (e.g., "The earthiness of African life demands that African salvation

---

68. Turner, *Profile Through Preaching*, 79, cf. 12–13. See also Turner, *Religious Innovation in Africa*, 241.

69. Ross, "Preaching in Mainstream Christian Churches in Malawi," 6.

70. Mbiti, *New Testament Eschatology in an African Background*, 88–89, italics added.

shall be as solidly material as biblical salvation,"[71]) such a holistic accent upon redemption need not eliminate or jeopardize the radical Christological basis of Christian hope. However, any conjecture that Fang Christians would embrace a Christocentric reading of Job's redeemer or of Job himself was dispelled by our research. The contours of Old Testament hermeneutics amongst Fang Protestants appear rather to be shaped by concepts of a divine-human partnership which place human faith and human triumph within a theocentric perspective, rather than within a Christocentric framework.

What does this mean for the eschatology and theology of hope of Fang Protestants? Admittedly, Job's hope for a redeemer, although arguably a hermeneutical cornerstone for developing a Christ-centered eschatology from the Old Testament, is only a dim reflection of the robust Christocentric expression of eschatology as found in the pages of the New Testament. Conceivably, all the Christians participating in the study would have happily affirmed Christ's central role in their own eschatological future. Yet such an affirmation should not be construed as a denial that the causal universe continues to play a fundamental role—and perhaps even the decisive role for some—in the day-to-day vision of hope which undergirds the faith of local Fang Christians. In a causal universe, spiritual realities impinge daily and decisively upon earthly circumstances. Within such a worldview, Christian hope owes a great deal of debt to causality, and prayer becomes the chief embodiment of this hope. In the divine-human relationship, Christians reach out hopefully in prayer to the *Deus Victor* who is conceived as able and willing to respond to their needs. Therefore, the *Deus Victor* paradigm not only represents a dominant center hermeneutically for Fang Christians but also stands in a strict relationship to prayer as comprising the very heart of a theology of hope.

Human Prayer, Divine Sovereignty, and the *Deus Victor*: *Then the Lord answered Job out of the Whirlwind*

> *Then the Lord answered Job out of the whirlwind:"Who is this that darkens counsel by words without knowledge?" Gird up your loins like a man, I will question you, and you shall declare to me. Where were you when I laid the foundation of the earth? . . . And the Lord restored the fortunes of Job. . . . The Lord blessed the latter days of Job more than his beginning. . . . And Job died, old and full of days. Job 38:1–4a, 42:10a, 42:12a, 42:17*

---

71. Walls, *The Missionary Movement in Christian History*, 117.

Our field work has suggested that for Fang Christians, prayer is the embodiment of hope in *Deus Victor*, a practice which clamors for God to liberate, rescue, and redeem in the midst of suffering and evil. Prayerful hope and hopeful praying are essentially an exercise in theodicy. African Christians clamor for the *Deus Victor* to vanquish suffering and evil in order that humanity may be liberated to enjoy the abundant life. In the investigation of Job's final liberation and restoration from suffering by ordinary readers beginning with the so-called Whirlwind speeches (Job 38:1—42:6) and culminating in the Joban epilogue (Job 42:7–17), the emphasis of hermeneutical reflection was placed upon the existential aspects of this contextualized vision of hope which centered upon the *Deus Victor* paradigm expressed and embodied in the Christian practice of prayer.

Of all the intriguing questions potentially explored from the time "the Lord answered Job out of the whirlwind" (38:1) until the restored (and doubly prosperous) Job finally "died, old and full of days" (42:17), *the concern which most intrigued contemporary interpreters was the spirituality which undergirded Job's restoration*. In other words, more than a fascination with the Behemoth (40:15–24) or the Leviathan (Job 41:1–34) or an unsettled feeling that the epilogue (42:7–17) seemingly deconstructs the book as a whole by reinstating the doctrine of retribution,[72] *the nature of Job's spirituality which resulted in divine blessing and liberation from suffering was the theme which most fascinated grassroots interpreters*. The figure of Job and his compelling story—a case of *Deus Victor* wherein Job's dust and ashes are traded for blessings and prosperity—captured the hermeneutical imagination of ordinary readers in a way that might be described as consistent with their overall appropriation of scripture.

Regardless of denominational affiliation, contemporary interpreters sought to discover the connection between Job's spirituality and God's restoration. Or, as Modesto Engonga Ondo succinctly asked during a seminary class on Job: "Did God intervene because Job prayed or because he wanted to show up?"[73] An elderly Presbyterian woman, commenting on Job 42:10 which reads, "And the Lord restored the fortunes of Job when he had prayed for his friends; and the Lord gave Job twice as much as he had before," indicated her belief that a *clear causal connection* seemed to be present between Job's prayer and God's intervention:

> *Claudia*: It seems to be the case that prayer is a strong value. When he had prayed for his friends, everything was increased

---

72. See Clines, "Deconstructing the Book of Job," 106–23.

73. *Instituto Bíblico "Casa de la Palabra"* (IBCP Seminary), Class on Job, June 8, 2012.

twice as much to Job as he had before. When he had prayed. That's when God increased. It comes automatically. The value of prayer.[74]

Yet it was Fang Pentecostals who saw the most unequivocal causal correspondence between the efficacy of Job's prayers and the cessation of his suffering. At Joy of My Salvation, Basilio Oyono expounded upon Job 42:5–6 which reads "I had heard of you by the hearing of the ear, but now my eye sees you; therefore I despise myself, and repent in dust and ashes" by drawing parallels to Israel's own prayers in Egypt as precursors to God's mighty acts of redemption for the people of God:

> Job in this place . . . said, "Lord, Lord, I repent. Lord, help me. Lord, put your hand on me. Lord, restore me. Lord, touch me. Lord, change my situation. Change my life. Change everything that's going on with me." The Bible says that the Lord heard. The Lord heard. *He heard the voice of Job because God listens to the voice of His children. When we pass through difficult times, God hears our voices.* The Bible says that when the people of God were in Egypt, God's people spent 430 years in Egypt. But they cried. They cried. They said, "Lord, we are your people and if we have sinned, forgive us. . . . And the Bible says that God heard from heaven and when God appeared to Moses, he said to Moses: "I have listened. And I heard the voice, the cry of my people, and I've decided to restore their lives. I have decided to [change] the situation of their lives." *In the same way, God made the decision to restore the life of Job.*[75]

The sovereign restorative action of God was never explicitly doubted or disparaged; instead Fang Christians were drawn like a magnet to the role of prayer in the Joban narrative.

For anybody who has spent time amongst African Christians, this hermeneutical attention to prayer hardly comes as a surprise. "What do I know without ambiguity after my years of worshiping with African Christians?" Mark Gornik asks, "They pray. They pray standing up, they pray moving around, they pray kneeling down, they pray in loud voices, they pray all night. . . . Life is about prayer, and prayer is life."[76] The Aladura axiom that "a prayerless Christian is a powerless Christian, while a prayerful Christian is a very powerful Christian" undoubtedly extends as an apt description of Af-

---

74. Reformed Presbyterian Church, Bible Study, Job 42:7–17, November 2, 2011.

75. Basilio Oyono, Joy of My Salvation, Sermon, Job 42:5–17, November 13, 2011. For a similar point, see Kim, "'Outcry': Its Context in Biblical Theology."

76. Gornik, *Word Made Global*, 127.

rican Christianity more broadly.[77] One of the chief distinguishing features of African Christianity lies precisely in its attentiveness to prayer. In Equatorial Guinea, prayer forms a noticeable divide between Protestant churches in a state of decline (the Reformed Presbyterian Church) and those who have embraced pneumatological renewal (Joy of the Holy Spirit, Assembly of the Holy Spirit). Presbyterian leaders cited lack of corporate prayer as one of the precipitating causes of the current spiritual malaise within the church[78] whereas the Pentecostals saw prayer as the catalyst energizing all ecclesial praxis, the life-blood of the church body. In this light, local Presbyterian churches are not viewed in the wider society as the beacon of hope for wounded sufferers as much as Pentecostal churches, though this does not discount the value of private prayer and the hope it instills amongst the Presbyterian faithful.

In a causal cosmology where earthly (visible) realities are often predicated upon spiritual (invisible) entities, prayer represents almost a knee-jerk first-response reaction to situations of suffering and evil. As the Malawian Catholic theologian Patrick Kalilombe writes: "African religion is essentially a way of living in the visible sphere in relation with the invisible world."[79] Or, as Laurenti Magesa recognizes: "When life is threatened or weakened, prayer is most abundant, both private and public prayer: prayer is a means of restoring wholeness and balance in life. In African Religion, prayer is comprehensive, requesting the removal of all that is bad and anti-life in society, and demanding restoration of all that is good. Nothing less satisfies the African religious mind."[80] This posture of African religiosity makes prayer supremely valuable in negotiating the destructive and hostile elements in the cosmology to ensure that the invisible realm yields beneficial, life-affirming results. Prayer thrives in a causal universe. Unlike their western counterparts, African Christians are not stymied by the Enlightenment sacred-secular divide which threatens to marginalize prayer as an outdated relic of Christian spirituality. Particularly for Pentecostals, prayer is an expectant, positive, and hopeful Spirit-led practice seeking to shake the very

---

77. Adogame, "Prayer as Action and Instrument in the Aladura Churches," 118 as cited in Gornik, *Word Made Global*, 152.

78. This was clearly articulated by leaders attending a sparsely attended October 8, 2011 meeting to address the self-diagnosed crisis in the Reformed Presbyterian Church in the city of Bata. Manuel Owono Akara, pastor of Bata's largest Presbyterian Church, also noted the lack of interest in corporate prayer, and blamed this for the spiritual decline of the church in interviews on October 17, 2011 and October 31, 2011.

79. Kalilombe, "Spirituality in the African Perspective," 115.

80. Magesa, *African Religion*, 195.

throne room of God for divine blessings which have been claimed by the believer through the Word of God.

As in the churches, prayer became a focal point of interest at the local seminary in exploring the intersection between Job's hope and God's restoration during the so-called whirlwind speeches (38:1—42:6). The following conversational dialogue between Pentecostal students about the nature of prayer was instructive:

> *Daniel*: In our prayer we always say that I am going to talk to God in order that he knows this: *now I want this. It's mine.* We don't have the thought that God can say "no" or "wait," only [makes a sweeping gesture with his arm].
>
> *Author*: What's this [makes the gesture]?
>
> *David*: Here, take it.
>
> *Daniel*: "Lord, now I want a car." "Lord, look we don't have anything to eat, I want money." "We want children."
>
> *Author*: So you pray in a way that is . . . [interrupted]
>
> *Daniel*: Positive.
>
> *Author*: With expectation.
>
> *Daniel*: "This is what I want *now*." And my Papa says "yes."
>
> *Alejandro*: As if you were manipulating God![81]

Interestingly, two observations about the nature of Fang Pentecostal prayers may be summarized from the above dialogue: (1) prayer is an insistent and bold declaration to God for pragmatic benefits *and* (2) such prayers occasionally encroach upon God's sovereignty in a way that is manipulative or coercive. This tension in Fang Pentecostal theology underscores both the bold and expectant nature of prayer *and* a robust understanding of God's sovereignty. In fact, in the classroom at IBCP seminary, considerable thematic attention was given to upholding precisely this tension between the efficacy of Job's prayers and the priority of God's sovereign action in discussing Job's final restoration. During the dialogical speeches between Job and the friends, Job's speeches were often interpreted as bold petitionary prayers aimed at inciting or provoking God to act or intervene in Job's sufferings.[82]

---

81. *Instituto Bíblico "Casa de la Palabra"* (IBCP Seminary), Book of Job, June 7, 2012.

82. *Instituto Bíblico "Casa de la Palabra"* (IBCP Seminary), Book of Job, June 6, 2012. In discussing Job 9:13–17, Professor Modesto comments: "Job is doubting that

At the same time, God's whirlwind speeches were universally and repeatedly interpreted as "words of intimidation"[83] to Job that not only showcased God's sovereignty but also indicated to Job that his prayers had overstepped their bounds in being presumptuous of God's sovereign nature. As Professor Modesto put it,

> Job began to speak well. And there was no reply because after every prayer he wanted God to react. And he began to say: "You have cheated me, you have lit a fire against me," and such. I believe that this occurs when we incite God to react. We should not oblige God to respond to us.[84]

Modesto often portrayed the nature of Job's petitionary prayers in a positive light. Nevertheless, he viewed God's chastisement of Job (i.e., "Who is this that darkens counsel by words without knowledge," Job 38:2) as entirely appropriate since Job's prayers had overstepped their proper bounds. In this sense, Modesto believed that Job "sometimes was in the right. Sometimes in the dark."[85] For him, Job was *right* in persisting in petitionary prayer but *wrong* in trying to manipulate God. Modesto expressed this "catch twenty-two" situation Job faced by affirming both the necessity of Job's prayer and the sovereign decision of God with respect to Job's liberation:

> The Bible says "call to me and I will respond to you. And you will see great things that you do not know" [alluding to Jer 33:3]. *I believe that God demands that the prophet pray in order that God answers.* . . . I believe that God intervened because Job prayed, but not like Job asked nor in the time that Job wanted.[86]

In other words, God mandated prayer to be an efficacious and essential means of Job's redemption yet God was still sovereign in his liberation of Job. The divine-human partnership stood at the very center of Job's redemption for Professor Modesto but in a way that underscored *both* the efficacious power of human prayer *and* the sovereign restorative power of God.

God would answer his prayer and this is the result that when one has prayed a lot and has not gotten peace, it's a way to incite, to incite God to react. This book is very deep." *Author*: "Incite? In what way?" *Alejandro*: "Provoking God's reaction."

83. *Instituto Bíblico "Casa de la Palabra"* (IBCP Seminary), Book of Job, June 7, 2012.

84. Ibid.

85. Ibid. Modesto also characterizes Job's prayerful dialogues with these words: "It was like here is the road. Job comes to the path and he crosses the path, he leaves the path and crosses the path."

86. *Instituto Bíblico "Casa de la Palabra"* (IBCP Seminary), Class on Job, June 7, 2012.

This mature depiction of the divine-human partnership in Job not only represents an enlightening exegetical insight but also offers a valuable window into a Fang Christian's complex relationship with causality. By contrast, it is interesting to note that western interpreters of Job are often deeply disappointed in the whirlwind speeches, noting their "magnificent irrelevance"[87] to the core question of unjust suffering voiced by Job.[88] Samuel L. Terrien goes to the heart of the concern for western exegetes when he asks provocatively, "Are those interpreters right, therefore, who claim that the Lord scoffs at Job on his pile of manure in a way more reminiscent of a devil than suggestive of a father?"[89] Part of this disconnect from the whirlwind speeches for western exegetes seems grounded in a lack of awareness of, or appreciation for, the potential abuses characterizing a spirituality centered radically upon notions of causality. Whereas the spirituality of western Christianity tends to collapse into secularism, atheism, or deism due to worldviews influenced by the sacred-secular dichotomy stemming from the Enlightenment, the spirituality of African Christians is more susceptible to a functional manipulation of the spirit realm due to notions of causality. This *functional spirituality* tends to manifest itself in two directions, both of which raise difficult questions for Christian theology. First, a *negative* functional spirituality is characterized by retribution theology's mechanistic blame of the sufferer for his or her alleged sin (or alleged witchcraft). In this spirituality, causality is the main actor and God is secondary since God's primary "value" is merely as the mechanistic Judge or Executor of causal logic. This type of spirituality marginalizes the *grace* of God wherein sufferers are labeled "sinners" or "witches" due to the dictates of retribution. (In the previous chapter, we saw how this dynamic adversely affected the lives of leprosy patients and people living with HIV/AIDS.) The second direction taken by a *functional spirituality* applies the same causal logic but in a more *positive* direction towards prosperity. In Christian circles, the biblical metaphor of reaping and sowing becomes particularly important as divine blessings such as prosperity, healing, or success are causally linked with hu-

---

87. Pope, *Job*, lxxxi.

88. Samuel L. Terrien cites a remark made by a clergyman in Charles Williams novel *War in Heaven* as saying: "As a mere argument there's something lacking perhaps in saying to a man who's lost his money and his house and his family and is sitting on the dustbin, all over boils, 'Look at the hippopotamus';" Terrien, "The Yahweh Speeches and Job's Responses," 497. James G. Williams characterizes God as "a Divine Blowhard" mainly interested in overwhelming Job in an arrogant display of divine power: "For what kind of universe must Job now live in? A meaningless universe mismanaged by a chaotic, capricious, jealous Tyrant?"; Williams, "'You Have Not Spoken Truth of Me,'" 247.

89. Terrien, *Job*, 226.

man actions such as prayer, tithing, or fasting. With this type of spirituality, God's ontological greatness suffers a radical diminishment insofar as God is conceived as the mechanistic arbiter of causality, envisioned as a kind of Cosmic Santa Claus or Divine Blessing Dispenser. This type of spirituality marginalizes the *freedom* or *sovereignty* of God, and it was precisely this spiritual danger Professor Modesto recognized in Job because his own Christian context is so susceptible to it. The popular implication, made by many Christian theologians, is that because African Christianity propounds the gospel message within a non-dualistic cosmological framework, forms of African Christianity are afforded a particularly *advantageous* position from which to steer clear of a collapse into secularism (since the sacred pervades all of life) while also avoiding a narrow retreat into pietism (since religion is not confined only to regions of the soul). Andrew Walls claims that "we must conclude that part of the strength of Christianity in Africa today is the fact that it is independent of the Enlightenment."[90] Yet Fang interpreters seemed to understand that a causal cosmology offers its own distinct set of challenges. Gifford's charge of a nascent this-worldly kind of secularism affecting both missionary and charismatic forms of African Christianity and Mbiti's charge of otherworldly escapism or quietism in an earlier period are two scholarly voices which challenge *precisely the benefits supposedly accrued to Christianity from a unified cosmology*. The divergent critiques of Gifford and Mbiti both suggest that the benefits of a unified cosmology may be more imaginary than real, and one suspects that the frequent scholarly lauding of non-dualistic African cosmologies may actually indicate more about the longings for western Christianity to overcome the spiritual-secular dichotomy in its own cosmology than being an unqualified benefit to African forms of Christianity.[91] On the positive side, arguably the central gift bequeathed to Christianity from a causal cosmology is a dynamic sense of prayer. To put it crudely, prayer "works" in a causal universe. Viewed against this backdrop of a causal cosmology, the whirlwind speeches were far from disappointing for Fang interpreters. When Modesto asked, "Did God intervene because Job prayed or because he wanted to show up?" the entire class broke out in laughter.[92] Everyone understood that Modesto

90. Walls, "Christian Scholarship in Africa in the Twenty-First Century," 225. See also Bediako, *Christianity in Africa*, 172–87; Stinton, "Jesus as Healer," 13–35.

91. Philip Jenkins suggests that Northern Churches should "reinterpret their own religion in light of [southern] experiences," Jenkins, *The Next Christendom*, 257. For a rebuttal to the notion that pre-Enlightenment cosmologies are necessarily beneficial to African Christians, see Gifford, "The Southern Shift of Christianity," 202–5.

92. *Instituto Bíblico "Casa de la Palabra"* (IBCP Seminary), Class on Job, June 8, 2012.

had framed the whirlwind speeches with a perfectly impossible question. In a causal universe, where the functionality of prayer occasionally serves to diminish God to a "cosmic bellhop,"[93] the divine "words of intimidation"[94] from the whirlwind were not regarded as cruel or disappointing but as a confrontational *but necessary* reminder to Job that God could not be manipulated or obliged to answer Job's prayers.

Modesto's mature portrayal of Job's final liberation and restoration helpfully illustrates the *Deus Victor* paradigm which stands at the heart of a theology of hope for African Christians. The *Deus Victor* paradigm underlying Fang Pentecostal readings of Job entailed an eminently strong and mighty God capable and willing to intervene in human suffering in order to heal, redeem, and deliver. Yet God's power was not conceived as a cause for humble passivity before the throne of grace. Instead of eliminating or diminishing prayer, the *Deus Victor* paradigm established prayer as a vital, indeed imperative, ingredient in the divine-human partnership. *Deus Victor* left ample space for the suffering cries of humanity. Listen to Modesto again:

> When we suffer, how should we pray? In the first place, the book of Job enlightens us as to the direction of our prayers. That we should address ourselves to a *Sovereign God* who is omnipotent, omnipresent, and omniscient to whom we owe all human solutions. We must also know that we should not provoke God for anything that we want from him. That is, when we address God, we should know these attributes of God. That he has *all the strength to answer, he is present when I pray,* and *he knows everything*. But he is sovereign. God does things in his time, as he wants to do them. I cannot incite him. I cannot oblige him.[95]

It was noticeable that Professor Modesto construes God's sovereignty in a way that is good news for prayer: God's omnipotence is his "strength to answer," God's omnipresence means "he is present when I pray," and God's omniscience signifies that "he knows everything," all divine attributes which are envisioned, if not constituted, as being deeply compatible with human prayer.[96] By embodying hope in prayer directed to the *Deus Victor*,

---

93. Jones and Woodbridge, *Health, Wealth & Happiness*, 102 citing Goff, "The Faith That Claims," 21.

94. Instituto Bíblico "Casa de la Palabra" (IBCP Seminary), Book of Job, June 7, 2012.

95. Instituto Bíblico "Casa de la Palabra" (IBCP Seminary), Class on Job, June 8, 2012.

96. Ibid.

grassroots Christians are sustained in the midst of suffering, evil, poverty, and disease.

Conclusion

By listening to hermeneutical reflections of Joban texts that were given prominent eschatological readings by local Christians, we have argued that a contextualized vision of Christian hope is embodied in prayer and centered upon the *Deus Victor* paradigm. Whereas Mbiti and Gifford predominantly sought to illustrate how the inability of African Christians to navigate the "already" and "not yet" tension of biblical eschatology had led some segments of African Christianity to become either escapist (Mbiti) or worldly (Gifford), our own attention to actual hermeneutical reflection amongst Fang Protestants, utilizing Job 19 as a case study, demonstrated a considerable variety of eschatological motifs across the denominational spectrum. Consistent with their missionary origins, reflections in the Reformed Presbyterian Church stood closest to traditional and historical interpretations of Job 19 in reading Job's hope for a redeemer through the Christocentric lens of New Testament eschatology. Amongst Fang Pentecostals, Job 19 primarily provided a launching pad into a discussion of the nature of retributive witchcraft blame which was viewed as conceptually analogous to Job's own relational complaints. At Joy of My Salvation, Job's hope for a redeemer was given a decidedly theocentric and this-worldly eschatological reading, imbibing the contour and shape of Fang traditional religiosity as well as being reflective of its ecclesial foundations. Yet Pentecostal hermeneutical reflection upon Joban hope tended to mute the pivotal message of the book of Job about the fundamental disinterestedness of religion. By insisting that Job hoped in God *and his gifts*, local Pentecostals showed little inclination to allow the biblical text to challenge or contest those elements of indigenous religiosity which undergird Pentecostal ethos and praxis. The central message of Job that faithfulness to God may occur in the midst of suffering without the hope of material reward remained conspicuously absent in Pentecostal hermeneutical reflection.

This chapter has also featured Job 19 as a case study for exploring the conjecture of whether Fang Christians would interpret an Old Testament text through the Christocentric lens of the New Testament. What we found is that local Christians showed themselves to be profoundly unconcerned to read the Old Testament story of Job through any Christocentric framework which placed the sufferings of Christians in the redemptive shadow of Christ or his cross. Despite a solitary Bible study amongst Presbyterians linking Job's hope for a *goèl* (redeemer) to Christ, grassroots interpreters did not seem particularly predisposed to read Old Testament texts through the Christocentric lens of the New Testament. For most Fang interpreters, the divine-human partnership figured prominently in the interpretation of biblical narratives but in a way that *highlighted the centrality of human triumph* in a theocentric, rather than explicitly Christocentric, framework. This hermeneutical orientation also characterized the vision of hope undergirding Fang Protestants: hope is embodied by local Christians as they reach out in prayer to the *Deus Victor*. Indeed, in the appropriation of Job's final liberation from suffering in the final chapters of Job (38–42), the spirituality of prayer which undergirded Job's restoration was given prominent attention by local Christians. In a causal cosmology, prayer is frequently robust, representing a key resource for confronting the destructive spiritual forces that populate the universe. However, within such a milieu, as mature reflection by local Christians recognized, prayer can occasionally devolve into a functional spirituality mainly interested in coercing or manipulating God. It is in this light that Professor Modesto at the local seminary appropriated the whirlwind speeches of God as a confrontational but necessary reminder to Job that the sovereign God could not be manipulated or coerced by his prayers. Yet even in this recognition, the efficacious nature of human prayer *and* the sovereign decision of God in securing Job's final restoration and liberation was underscored. Thus, a contextualized theology of hope in Central Africa is embodied in the practice of prayer, as Christians cry out to the *Deus Victor* who is conceived as able and willing to respond to human suffering.

7

Conclusion

African Christianity between Indigenization and Diabolization

IT HAS BEEN NO part of the intention of this book to offer a commentary-style treatment of the book of Job from an African context. Rather this study has sought to utilize Job as a catalyst and entry-point into crucial conversations relating to the wider contours of contemporary African Christianity. Its central argument has been that the experiences of the Christian faith and the dominant themes, theologies, and trajectories adopted by local believers in Africa are uniquely informed by the dialogical intersection of biblical interpretation, local culture, and ecclesial practice, a dynamic we have named the *hermeneutics-culture-praxis triad*. In this book, the hermeneutical circle of (biblical) text and (cultural) context that most biblical scholars argue characterize the ethos and orientation of African Christianity was joined by a third participant: ecclesial praxis. Analyzing African Christianity from a bi-polar approach (text-in-context) not only isolates biblical texts from their main interpretative community (the church) but also fails to understand how ecclesial communities dynamically engage, re-engage, or dis-engage their cultural backgrounds through lively dialogue and debate. In this respect, we have argued that the *hermeneutics-culture-praxis triad* is pivotal to understanding both the biblical hermeneutics of grassroots African Christians and the critical beliefs, dominant values, and indispensable theologies which undergird expressions the Christian faith across the African continent.

As ordinary readers engaged with the quintessential biblical book on suffering, the most pervasive, recurring, and foundational question which reverberated against the backdrop of their own lives—whether young or old, layperson or pastor, Presbyterian or Pentecostal—was some harmonic reiteration of the following sentiment:

> *"Put yourself in the story. You are there in Job's place. How would you react? How would you respond?"*

Rather than reading "behind" the text (the historical-critical approach) or positioning themselves "upon" the text (the literary approach), ordinary readers dynamically entered the interpretative process personally and existentially to explore the book of Job from "within" the story, bringing with them their distinct cultural paradigms as well as the dominant ecclesial practices of their local church traditions. After listening to these ordinary readers perform contextual theology in dialogical conversation with the three sources of the *hermeneutics-culture-praxis triad*, it may be helpful to take a step back and look at the road these ordinary readers traversed in their appropriation of the book of Job. In other words, what dialogical interactions were observed between text, culture, and praxis? And how was Christian scripture utilized by the ordinary readers in our study? Three lines of inquiry may be broadly identified.

Three Trajectories on the Use of Christian Scriptures in African Christianity

As Andrew Walls has observed, "The conditions of Africa . . . are taking Christian theology into new areas of life, where Western theology has no answers, because it has no questions."[1] Ordinary readers in Equatorial Guinea turned to the text of Job to provide answers to pressing existential questions arising out of their indigenous culture meditated through the lens of ecclesial practices. For Fang Christians, this principally meant a hearty and robust dialogue between the biblical text and witchcraft. The theme of witchcraft was so central for ordinary readers that one can scarcely talk intelligently of popular African hermeneutics without acknowledging its controlling influence. As ordinary readers bring their concerns, questions, and pre-understandings of the cosmos to bear upon Christian scriptures, the theme of witchcraft is continuously refracted through the prism of their biblical interpretation. By appropriating the Bible from a positionality extremely close to the text itself—we have argued that the epistemological distance between *meaning* and *application*

---

1. Walls, "Structural Problems in Mission Studies," 146–47.

is fundamentally foreshortened in African hermeneutics—the fear, blame, and anxiety of witchcraft which impinge upon the lives of ordinary readers come quickly to the surface in the interpretive process. In short, witchcraft is ubiquitously present in the interpretation of Christian scriptures as ordinary readers approach biblical texts.

The landscape of African Christianity has changed dramatically since missionary Robert Moffat's Bible was confused with witchcraft *bola* by certain Batswana observers in the mid-nineteenth century.[2] Yet a central preoccupation African Christians bring to the biblical text, consisting of the longing for spiritual protection against witchcraft, remains essentially unchanged nearly two centuries later. By some accounts, witchcraft anxieties have intensified by the conditions created by modernity as traditional rituals which sought to curb the malevolent effects of witchcraft (such as the anti-witchcraft cult of *Nguí* for the Fang) were driven underground by colonial governments or aggressively stamped out by missionary Christianity.[3] In this sense, Gerald West's discerning plea for scholars of African Christianity to follow "traces of the Bible as *bola* into the present" represents a penetrating insight.[4] West relies heuristically on Vincent Wimbush's assertion that the earliest formative encounters of African-Americans with the Bible—as slaves seeking to wrestle away the Bible from their white masters and construct their own interpretive agenda against oppression—have become a foundational hermeneutical experience for African-Americans "in the sense that all other African American readings are in some sense built upon and judged by" this earliest experience of oppression vis-à-vis slavery.[5] In a similar vein, West argues that since the earliest African ancestors often regarded the white man's Bible as another potential sacred object in their quest for spiritual protection—the Bible as *bola*—that all subsequent uses of the Bible trace their origins to this formative experience.[6] If West's provocative assertion is right, that the Bible as *bola* has a long history both *within* and on the *periphery* of African Christianity, then scholars of African Christianity would be wise to pay closer attention biblically and theologically to witchcraft as the single biggest cultural prism through which ordinary readers interpret their Bibles and live out the Christian faith.

A second common use of the Bible in African Christianity resides in the therapeutic appropriation of the *Deus Victor* paradigm where God

2. Moffat, *Missionary Labours and Scenes in Southern Africa*, 384
3. See Fernandez, "Christian Acculturation and Fang Witchcraft," 244–70.
4. West, "The Bible as Bola," 35.
5. Ibid., 34.
6. Ibid., 24–31, 34–36.

is conceived as a powerful interventionist willing and able to liberate his children from evil and suffering. For Fang Christians, the spiritual correspondence between human prayers and divine restoration in the life and sufferings of Job deeply resonated with local believers. The motif seemed to confirm their own instinctual sense of the efficacious nature of prayer, especially in the midst of suffering. In a causal universe, Christian prayers benefit from many of the same cosmological presuppositions as traditional rituals, with both practices being profoundly rooted in theodicy. In African traditional rituals, ancestors or divinities are beseeched and ritually leveraged in order to overthrow mystical evil forces and restore the abundant life when the well-being of the community is perceived to be threatened. In Christian prayers, believers call upon the *Deus Victor* to rescue and redeem from suffering (i.e., sickness, poverty, witchcraft) in order to restore the abundant life which normally is thought to characterize the Christian life. In this sense, the text of Job provided promising perspectives for grassroots believers mired in suffering since the text of Job's restoration offered ordinary readers a high degree of correspondence with their own cultural notions of causality and their ecclesial practices of prayer.

For African Christians, a lively sense of causality serves to strengthen prayer and sustain hope in the midst of suffering and evil. As the Latin axiom expressed it, *lex orandi, lex credendi*: the law of prayer determines the law of belief.[7] The way people pray is expressed by what they believe; what people believe is demonstrated by the way people pray.[8] As our own study revealed, from a Christian perspective, the *Deus Victor* paradigm frequently begged for a more robust Christological grounding in hermeneutical praxis and homiletical reflection to anchor the paradigm more solidly within the biblical framework. Notwithstanding this critique of the Christological deficit pervading the image, the *Deus Victor* paradigm nevertheless stands entrenched as a positive overarching catalyst for prayer within large segments of the African church.

However, this rather optimistic assessment of the reading practices of ordinary African Christians, who appropriate the *Deus Victor* paradigm *hermeneutically* in their reading practices and *existentially* in their personal lives, needs to be balanced by a reflection of a more sobering kind. The third trend vis-à-vis the use of scripture witnessed by this study is that the text of Job was frequently silenced or muzzled in its ability to challenge or contest dominant cultural paradigms and prevailing ecclesial practices. For a Christian optimist, biblical texts are often thought to be the basis driving

---

7. Stanley, "Inculturation," 23.
8. Bevans, *Models of Contextual Theology*, 23.

ecclesial praxis while possessing the latent capacity to radically shape cultural contexts; yet in reality, cultural contexts and ecclesial practices in both northern and southern hemispheres frequently minimize, or even entirely mute, the impact of biblical texts.

One critical juncture where cultural motifs and ecclesial practices served to severely overshadow a key perspective from the text of Job was in the silencing of Satan's pivotal question in the prologue: "Does Job fear God for nothing?" (Job 1:9). In Africa, traditional religiosity is chiefly anthropocentric, pragmatic, and functional, with rituals performed as a means to acquire earthly goods. In other words, African traditional religiosity is never "for nothing" but always "for something," whether long life, fertility, abundant crops, good health, or protection from evil forces. As the Christian faith becomes irrevocably intertwined with African traditional religiosity (a process which has occurred organically throughout the continent), faith in God often becomes fused to, if not confused with, a hope for divine gifts and solutions. As Christianity encounters the rich tapestry of African cultures, the Christian faith often changes the content, substance, and beliefs of African traditional religiosity: worship and prayers are now directed to God in the name of Jesus, and the Christian experience is lived in the power of the Holy Spirit. Yet the Christian faith in African contexts often absorbs uncritically the basic structure of African traditional religiosity (anthropocentric rather than God-centric) as well as its overarching goals and objectives which are principally functional and pragmatic (i.e., "what practical benefits do I receive if I adopt this new faith"?). Thus, Satan's question revolves around his doubts of whether Job can serve God "for nothing," that is, without receiving any pragmatic divine blessings. Satan suspects that Job serves God, not because of God's character and intrinsic worth, but rather for the functional rewards and riches which God has bestowed upon him. In the book of Job, Satan's question represents a frontal attack on forms of self-interested piety. The entire narrative framework of Job is deeply committed to unraveling this thorny issue of whether Job can remain faithful to God not only in the *absence* of blessings but also in the *presence* of suffering. In principle, this Joban perspective represents a very counter-intuitive insight for African traditional religiosity, just as it did for its original hearers in the ancient Near East, cutting acutely against the grain of the *raison d'être* of indigenous beliefs and rituals which assumes a symbiotic relationship, if not a reciprocal correspondence, between religious adherence and material well-being. Yet amongst the more than 200 ordinary readers observed in this study, this critical perspective of the book of Job was silenced or muzzled by the basic orientation of Fang traditional religiosity. In effect, the material anthropocentric quest for the abundant life, one of the foundational features of Fang culture, severely overshadowed this key perspective from the text of Job. Yet the idea that hope in God (piety) and hope in God's good gifts (prosperity) are interconnected has more in common with the anthropocentric interests of Fang religiosity than with the book of Job which is making a concerted effort to undermine precisely this connection. For Christian exegetes, the silencing of this crucial and prominent theme in Job is akin to missing the theme of the "righteousness of God" in Romans or the "suffering servant" motif in Isaiah, leading to an impoverishment of the thematic core of the book as the inescapable result. In particular, Fang Pentecostals continued, on the basis of the book of Job, to advocate material and pragmatic visions of faith and hope in God *and his gifts* to an extent that questions how far they may be able to integrate biblical texts which challenge or contest indigenous religiosity into their ecclesial worldview.

African biblical scholars and theologians often make much of the cultural parallels between ancient Israel and modern-day Africa. For example, West has observed nearly thirty cultural motifs from the text of 2 Samuel which correspond to contexts of Southern Africa.[9] The implication is often made that these cultural parallels facilitate a deep contextualization of the biblical message within indigenous African cultures. Yet our own study has shown that it is precisely these cultural parallels that often subverted a plain sense reading of the text of Job, which derives its power precisely from its counter-cultural character. Philip Jenkins' judgment that "while some resemblances might be superficial, their accumulated weight adds greatly to the credibility of the text" is too simplistic, even bordering on naiveté.[10] Cultural congruencies with the text of scripture may garner a credible hearing within local cultures but these cultural parallels also represent potential *cultural blinders* capable of reducing the dialogical interaction between text and context to a one-way conversation where the voice of the scripture becomes muted or drowned out by the culture.

A second critical Joban theme silenced by the prevailing cultural instincts of ordinary readers was the paradigm of *Job the Innocent Sufferer*. In theory, Job's innocent suffering represents a uniquely suited biblical antidote to challenge the repressive cultural ideology of retributive blame so prevalent amongst the Fang. The Joban idea that suffering cannot be simplistically or formulaically reduced to personal offence or wrongdoing is a radically liberating message—potentially—for those ensnared by the dictates of Fang causal logic which typically conceives of suffering as a tell-tale sign of a deeper causal evil. The book of Job appears to present a strategic biblical

---

9. West, "1 & 2 Samuel," 94.
10. Jenkins, *The New Faces of Christianity*, 69.

message during a time of HIV/AIDS and witchcraft to counteract the cultural proclivity to blame the sufferer by exposing the friends as incompetent and fraudulent counselors. Nevertheless, the cultural mechanism of retributive blame is so entrenched within the cultural psyche of the Fang that the biblical text of Job provided little or no contestation of dominant cultural paradigms and ecclesial practices despite the fact that many ordinary Christians recognize the toxicity of retribution. Even leprosy patients and people living with HIV/AIDS who had the most to gain by repudiating a theology of retribution, with its accompanying social exclusion of stigmatization, still interpreted the message of Job through their cultural lenses of retributive blame. This deeply ingrained cultural dynamic of retribution, with its tendency to produce vehement accusations, harsh discord amongst families, and explosive divisions within neighborhood churches, is genuinely troubling to ordinary Fang Christians. Nevertheless, many ordinary readers of Job blunted the paradigm of Job's innocent suffering as a potentially liberating message, falling back on the trusted cultural trope of retributive blame to help explain incidences of sickness and suffering.

Cultural blind spots, which are in no way unique to African churches, being present in a myriad of forms within western Christianity, nevertheless often do irreparable damage to the character and authentic witness of the church. In reality, the figure of Job stands like a giant oak tree against the prevailing winds of retribution in the Hebrew Bible. Especially in a time of HIV/AIDS, the paradigm of Job the Innocent Sufferer *does* seem uniquely suited to provide a pivotal biblical resource for empowering grassroots Christians and churches to confront the cultural captivity to retributive blame by offering a more compassionate response than the frequent stigmatization of the surrounding culture. In a causal universe which excludes or dismisses the category of innocent suffering, the possibilities for churches to re-orientate their language around the paradigm of *Job the Innocent Sufferer* seems to represent a critical step, at least from a biblical perspective, in challenging the repressive and marginalizing language of sexual promiscuity and divine punishment so often attached to the HIV/AIDS pandemic. Job's innocent suffering provides churches with a language capable of articulating theologically the social complexities of the disease, communicate to all that no one deserves HIV/AIDS, and help mend broken fences with those people living with HIV/AIDS already stigmatized by the dominant cultural discourse of retributive blame. However, when these potentially liberating perspectives are not recognized or realized in Christian churches, especially in an era of HIV/AIDS, the church's ability to walk compassionately in solidarity with people living with HIV/AIDS is severely diminished. In this respect, to borrow the words of Esther Acolatse, "African Christianity has yet to truly transcend its cultural moment."[11] And perhaps this cultural captivity to traditional religiosity is no *more* true that when biblical texts are silenced or muzzled from damaging cultural *leitmotifs* such as the causal logic of retribution.

The Nature of the Indigenization of the Christian Faith in Africa

Part of this dynamic of biblical texts being silenced by the power of inherited cultural concepts is rooted not simply in the adherence to deeply rooted cultural paradigms but also in the implicit and at times facile endorsement by theologians, biblical scholars, and missiologists of the theological method of inculturation. Referring specifically to African Pentecostals, David Ngong argues that "the theology of inculturation has been marked by a tendency to be critical of wholesale appropriation of theology couched in Western concepts and background but less so with its appropriation of central elements of African culture."[12] In part, this is understandable as western colonialism, with western missionaries riding on its coattails, often denigrated and demonized African indigenous cultures. The pleas of the late Kwame Bediako, who argued that African theology must pursue inculturation with a view towards the establishment of a Christian identity which was thoroughly Christian and thoroughly African, can be understood, in part, as a reaction to a kind of theologizing within missionary forms of Christianity which was reticent to integrate fully non-Enlightenment paradigms of indigenous religiosity into the theology and praxis of local churches.[13] Yet is this narrative, that grassroots Christians are fundamentally estranged from their indigenous cultures, still an adequate description of African Christianity in the twenty-first century? In the light of the Pentecostalization of much of African Christianity, the theology of inculturation touted by Bediako, which was rooted chiefly in a concern to remedy the fundamental existential estrangement of grassroots Christians from African cultures, was arguably based upon a description of local realities that is now becoming increasingly outdated. Today, a more pertinent question might be to ask whether the inculturation of African Christianity is being limited or restricted to those aspects of indigenous culture which conceptually overlap with Christianity.[14]

11. Acolatse, *For Freedom or Bondage?* 5.

12. Ngong, "Theology as the Construction of Piety," 356.

13. See Bediako, *Theology and Identity*. See also Ferdinando, "Christian Identity in the African Context," 121–43.

14. Ngong, "Salvation and Materialism in African Theology," 4.

Are the proliferating Pentecostalized forms of Christianity fundamentally transforming those aspects of culture which display little continuity or even sharp discontinuity with the message of Christianity? Is Christianity making inroads into substantially altering not only the content and beliefs of African traditional religiosity (i.e., prayers are now offered in the name of Jesus), but also deeply converting its basic structure, goals, and objectives? For example, take the issue of prayer: are these African Christian prayers simply baptizing the anthropocentric aspirations of African traditional religion with the name of Jesus or are these prayers giving evidence of a new-found biblical worldview which centers on the intrinsically worshipful God of the scriptures? In other words, is God being leveraged and used as a *means to an end* or being worshipped for his ontological greatness and majesty? As Andrew Walls has recognized, the *indigenizing principle* which seeks to make Christianity "at home" in any culture only represents a viable expression of Christian inculturation insofar as the *pilgrim principle* which puts the Christian "out of step" with the culture equally holds true.[15]

Scholars of African Pentecostalism such as Allan Anderson, Ogbu Kalu, and J. Kwabena Asamoah-Gyadu frequently portray the movement as the embodiment of an enduring Christian inculturation in Africa, arguing that the felt existential and religious needs of Africans, including their most pressing concerns of witchcraft and evil, have been adequately and profoundly addressed by Pentecostal theologies and practices.[16] In our study, Fang Pentecostals were shown to place theodicy and the nature of witchcraft evil at the center of hermeneutical reflection and ecclesial praxis, thus aligning their Christian faith and ecclesiology more centrally than missionary forms of Christianity to the preoccupations which traditionally galvanized Fang traditional rituals. For Fang Pentecostals, it was argued, the image of the Devil connects powerfully and viscerally to narrative discourses about the ubiquity of evil and witchcraft which so fascinate the Fang. Yet the issue confronting Fang Pentecostals resides precisely in this dilemma: many adherents of the movement are so concerned with the Devil and his machinations of witchcraft that reflection upon *Nzama* (God) often takes a backseat to the Devil. We have suggested that local Pentecostals have constructed their image of *Nzama* through the lens of a moral etiology of evil and suffering, meaning that the Christian God often becomes dangerously dependent upon causality, a figure who is meaningless without reference to witchcraft, and who is defined primarily in relationship to the Devil. Through radi-

---

15. Walls, *The Missionary Movement in Christian History*, 7–9.

16. Anderson, *Zion and Pentecost*, 258, cf. 29; Kalu, "Preserving a Worldview," 137; Asamoah-Gyadu, "Signs, Wonders, and Ministry," 32–46.

cally embracing the causal universe with its basic affirmation of witchcraft, local Pentecostals arguably enthrone God's dark counterpart so centrally within the cosmos that the Devil becomes absolutely indispensable as their primary "sparring partner" supporting the very life-blood of their ecclesial orientation even as God is relegated to second-tier status in hermeneutical reflection.

For scholars such as Paul Gifford, Abraham Akrong, and David Ngong, this dynamic represents a troubling, even disturbing, trend for Christianity in Africa and problematizes the opinion of those scholars who frequently laud the Pentecostal and charismatic movements as representing a profound inculturation of the Christian message in Africa.[17] Scholars have touted *ad nauseam* that African Pentecostalism appeals quite widely to the African masses, but equally there is a need for scholars to evaluate theologically the rampant demonology which is presently characterizing Pentecostalized forms of African Christianity, a point Ngong makes with considerable clarity:

> many African Christians are functional Manicheans because the satanic principle looms large in their psyche. It may not be wrong to say that the evil principle looms so large in the psyche of many African Christians that they spend more time thinking about the devil and evil spirits that may be lurking around them than they do thinking about God. This way of thinking is one that needs to be challenged rather than simply endorsed for the reason that it contributes to the spread of Christianity.[18]

African Christianity between Indigenization and Diabolization

As we have seen, many of the issues facing Protestant Christianity amongst the Fang is grounded upon the way indigenization and diabolization has actually occurred at the popular level. With respect to indigenization, our study has shed light on the marked difference between the God-centered

17. See Gifford, "The Southern Shift of Christianity," esp. 197–205; Gifford, "African Christianity and the Eclipse of the Afterlife," esp. 422–29; Akrong, "Neo-Witchcraft Mentality in Popular Christianity," 1–12; Akrong, "Towards a Theology of Evil Spirits and Witches," 18–26; Ngong, "Theology as the Construction of Piety," esp. 354–62; Ngong, "Salvation and Materialism in African Theology," 1–21; Ngong, *The Holy Spirit and Salvation in African Christian Theology*, esp. 8–11; Ngong, "Reading the Bible in Africa," 174–91.

18. Ngong, "Salvation and Materialism in African Theology," 14–15.

religious tradition of Christianity and the anthropocentric this-worldly concerns of Fang religiosity, a point underscored by Keith Ferdinando referring to Africa more broadly:

> The fundamental difference between African and biblical conceptions of the spirit and occult world stems from essentially different notions of the Supreme Being. One of the pre-eminent dimensions of the biblical doctrine of God is his *universal sovereign government*: for the biblical writers the whole cosmos, visible and invisible, is dominated by him, and religious attitudes and practices are shaped accordingly. It is this which is absent from African traditional religion, whose Supreme Beings are not generally understood to exercise such a sovereignty.... Rather, in the living experience of its adherents, it is the world of lesser spirits and of witches and sorcerers which is of dominant spiritual and existential concern.[19]

The anthropocentric this-worldly cosmology of the Fang, despite the elevation of the indigenous figure *Nzama* to occupy the role of God within the Judeo-Christian tradition, has not been as pliable in absorbing the God-centered religious tradition of Christianity as one might have expected. In general, local Fang Christians would have no fundamental problem ascribing to *Nzama* all the attributes of the Creator God and Supreme Being of the Judeo-Christian scriptures. In practice, however, their hermeneutical reflection tended to marginalize *Nzama* to the periphery of the Joban text in much the same manner *Nzama* was traditionally marginal to indigenous Fang religiosity, suggesting that the indigenous cosmology has reserved a rather rigid place-holder for *Nzama* even amidst Christian reflection. In other words, the indigenization of *Nzama* has not resulted in a process whereby *Nzama* has been extracted wholesale out of his indigenous cosmology and dropped seamlessly into the God-centered religious tradition of Christianity. This was evident amongst Fang Presbyterians *and* Fang Pentecostals. Within the Presbyterian Church, the existential frustration with the causal universe was shown to reside precisely in *Nzama*'s supposed inability to affect the causal universe. Whilst this dynamic is partly reflective of Enlightenment models of ministry that continue to inform church praxis, it also implies that many local Presbyterians continue to perceive *Nzama*'s role in the cosmos as fundamentally incapable of dealing with evil and suffering, thus aligning their perception of *Nzama* quite closely to his marginal role within the indigenous cosmology. For Fang Pentecostals, it has been argued that deliverance ministries have given *Nzama* a "ritual

---

19. Ferdinando, *The Triumph of Christ in African Perspective*, 379, italics added.

space" in which to operate within the cosmos. Yet this dynamic begged the question of whether *Nzama* has effectively been restricted to the sole task of running the gauntlet of indigenous religiosity in dealing with evil and suffering, thus defining *Nzama* rather exclusively in terms of his cosmological functionality. In light of these dynamics amongst the Fang, what are we to make of Bediako's unequivocal enthusiasm for indigenous concepts of God being a key element in the profound indigenization of the faith in Africa? Bediako implies that, unlike forms of European Christianity which did not incorporate Zeus, Jupiter, and Odin into the Judeo-Christian tradition,[20] the indigenization of African Christianity, by finding deities "not too distinguishable from the God of the Bible"[21] in the primal worldviews of Africans' pre-Christian past, has been afforded a dynamic idiom to express Christian theological concepts. Yet once the connection has been made between "the God of the Bible" and the African "deity," as dubious as these connections might be, as our own discussion of *Nzama* has shown, African theologians such as Bediako, like his predecessor and theological hero John Mbiti,[22] typically proceed in a unidirectional manner by investing this African deity of the pre-Christian past with all the attributes of God as found in the Christian scriptures. In our experience, this dynamic also mirrors the theologizing that occurs at the level of popular African Christianity. Although African proverbs or refrains are often referred to tangentially, the personality of this pre-Christian "God" is often forsaken and this "deity's" traditional place within the cosmological universe is forgotten as Christians engage in theology by re-writing the deity's pre-Christian religious past. Thus, when critics such as Okot p'Bitek and James L. Cox[23] object to the works of John S. Mbiti[24] or E. Bolaji Idowu[25] or Geoffrey Parrinder[26] on the grounds that these authors are "intellectual smugglers" who have imposed

---

20. Bediako, "The Significance of Modern African Christianity—A Manifesto," 54.

21. Bediako, "Biblical Christologies in the Context of African Traditional Religions," 88–89 as cited by Wagenaar, "Theology, Identity and the Pre-Christian Past," 368.

22. See Katongole, "A Different World Right Here,'" 211.

23. Whereas p'Bitek is highly critical of Idowu and Mbiti, Cox's primary dialogical partner in this regard has been Parrinder. See p' Bitek, *African Religions in Western Scholarship*, 80–120; Cox, *From Primitive to Indigenous*, 16–22; Cox, "The Invention of the Christian God in Africa." See also Cox, "The Globalization of Localized African Religions," 56–65.

24. Mbiti, *Concepts of God in Africa*.

25. Idowu, *Olódùmarè*. See also Idowu, *African Traditional Religion*.

26. Parrinder, *West African Religion*; Parrinder, *African Traditional Religion*.

Greek metaphysical categories[27] or "a non-empirical Christian theological construct"[28] upon African religious thought or, in seeking to de-hellenize this trend, state categorically that "the idea of a high God among the Central Luo was a creation of the missionaries,"[29] one could argue that the critics of Mbiti and Idowu object to this kind of theologizing on the basis of a social scientific study of religions but leave largely unanswered the question of how this type of theologizing of the pre-Christian past may affect academic or popular forms of African theology. What our own study suggests is that for Fang Christians, the pre-Christian religious past of *Nzama*—particularly his marginality to the causal universe—continues to affect their theologies implicitly and virtually unconsciously. This raises critical issues for the process of indigenization, such as the way in which cosmological structures and theology are necessarily intertwined and points to evidence that the pre-Christian religious past of African deities are not so easily whitewashed by Christian theological concepts. At least for *Nzama*, his pre-Christian past continues to affect his conceptual appropriation by present-day Fang Christians—yet often in a way which displays a tendency towards muting and marginalizing, to paraphrase Ferdinando's words, the biblical doctrine of God's universal sovereign government over creation.[30]

Our study has also raised several issues with respect to the diabolization that has occurred amongst the Fang, including the point already raised implicitly by Ngong in his allusion above to Manicheaism, namely, that Pentecostalized forms of African Christianity have "accentuated the move towards dualism."[31] As was the case for the Fang, a Machichean duality between good and evil was absent in many indigenous African cultures[32] which possessed no intrinsically evil entity, spirit, or deity before the arrival of Christianity.[33] Although the evil *actions* of individuals known as witches were dealt with ritualistically by the community through recourse to the traditional rites, a larger-than-life Devil-figure held to be *ontologically* responsible for evil in the entire causal universe represents, by and large, an importation bequeathed to Africa cultures via the frequent demoniza-

27. p' Bitek, *African Religions in Western Scholarship*, 88.

28. Cox, "The Classification 'Primal Religions' as a Non-Empirical Christian Theological Construct," 55–76.

29. p' Bitek, *Religion of the Central Luo*, 50.

30. Ferdinando, *The Triumph of Christ in African Perspective*, 379.

31. Akrong, "Towards a Theology of Evil Spirits and Witches," 18.

32. As the Fang proverb says, "good and bad walk together" (*abe ye mbeng ba wulu nsama*); Fernandez, *Bwiti*, 215, 227. See also Meyer, *Translating the Devil: Religion and Modernity*, 86, 94–96; Parkin, "Entitling Evil," 224–43.

33. Bosch, "The Problem of Evil in Africa," 40.

tion of African religiosity by the early missionaries. One of the unintended consequences of the missionary enterprise in Africa was that the existence of witchcraft was reinforced, perhaps even strengthened, by a diabolization which linked indigenous witchcraft with the activity of a powerful causal being known as the Devil.[34] This radical intensification of diabolization, however, has today become a central feature of many, if not most, of the Pentecostal churches in Equatorial Guinea. By relating to Fang traditional beliefs and practices predominantly through the figure of the Devil, these indigenous practices, particularly *mbwo* (witchcraft), have not only been thoroughly demonized in the Pentecostal imagination but also have become indispensable foundational structures for the Pentecostal faith, albeit negatively defined.[35] Practically, this diabolization of indigenous practices magnifies the Devil so extensively within the causal universe that engaging with the demonic activity of witchcraft becomes such an integral and vital part of hermeneutical reflection and ecclesial practice that the whole edifice of African Pentecostalism might well collapse without the integrative function provided by the Devil. This rampant demonology amongst Fang Pentecostals, a characteristic shared with many African Pentecostals more broadly, raises several wider questions for Christian theologians. Three perspectives which have emerged from our own study can be addressed here.

The Rampant Diabolization within African Christianity: Some Concerns

First, our study has argued that Christian theodicy decisively impinges upon the theological vision of grassroots Christians, leaving an indelible imprint upon the fabric of African Christianity. This contextualized vision of theodicy—what we termed a moral etiology of evil and suffering—provides a critical lens through which local Christians interpret scripture, reconceptualize the cosmology, and construct images of God and the Devil which critically impacts the nature and expression of the Christian faith. Inquiring about the "cause behind the cause," a practice so prevalent in Fang religiosity, equally represents a pervasive practice within Pentecostal deliverance ministries which require people to confess their *nsem* (sin) in order to be healed from demonic spirits. Yet this confession of *nsem* is often not connected in a meaningful way to living a moral life (other than in the perceived immorality of visiting a traditional healer or participating

---

34. See also Meyer, *Translating the Devil: Religion and Modernity*, 103–8.
35. Ibid., 100; Meyer, "'If You Are a Devil, You Are a Witch,'" 106, 108.

in traditional rituals which are viewed as doorways to the demonic). The preoccupation with finding the "cause *behind* the cause" often reinforces the notion that *nsem* is fundamentally external, rather than profoundly internal, to the Christian. Sexual purity, refraining from alcoholic drink, and basic holiness principles are often touted as indispensable for living the "blessed life," but these moral practices frequently have nothing to do with battling sin or resisting evil *since the decisive causative factors of evil and suffering are often imagined to be external to the individual*. As Gifford recognizes, this creates an unfortunate "disconnect between leading a moral life and fighting evil forces."[36]

Yet when spiritual causality becomes fundamentally external, rather than internal, to the person, not only does deliverance from demonic activity become a *de facto* substitution for personal repentance from sin but also the person often develops an unhealthy kind of spiritual dependency on religious specialists.[37] In the Pentecostal tradition, pastors or prophets anointed with the gift to discern witchcraft, spiritual curses, ancestral blockages, territorial spirits, and demonic gateways often become intrinsically necessary for fighting external evils which are unknown to the sufferer. A rampant demonology thus displays a tendency towards externalizing evil, making sufferers profoundly and thoroughly dependent upon "Big Men" Pentecostal leaders for their ability to mediate God's "solutions" which typically last only until the next onslaught of witchcraft fears, incurable sickness, or prolonged suffering. This rampant conceptualization of evil as fundamentally external to the believer not only frequently enmeshes believers in a never-ending cycle of religious dependency on African Pentecostal pastors but also "betrays a failure to understand the nature of true evangelical freedom" as personal responsibility for battling sin is forfeited and outsourced to deliverance ministry practitioners.[38]

Second, our study has presented Fang Pentecostals as touting an instrumentalist view of God and the church. Pentecostal praxis, backed by hermeneutical reflection, has been shown to be tied almost exclusively to this-worldly problems rooted in the causal universe and thereby *ipso facto* to the activity of the Devil. Anderson argues that the Pentecostal "message of receiving the power of the Holy Spirit—a power greater than any of the powers which threaten this existence—is good news" for many Africans caught in the throes of a cosmos with a multiplicity of unseen malevolent forces.[39] Yet

---

36. Gifford, "The Southern Shift of Christianity," 194.
37. Akrong, "Neo-Witchcraft Mentality in Popular Christianity," 4–5.
38. Acolatse, *For Freedom or Bondage?* 22.
39. Anderson, "Pentecostal Pneumatology and African Power Concepts," 73.

in many Pentecostal circles amongst the Fang, the appropriation of the Holy Spirit's operational gifts of deliverance from demonic spirits, healing from sicknesses, and combating witchcraft often borders upon a "barter concept of religion" implying that God is utilized and leveraged more as a means to an end—and set in a strict oppositional role to the Devil—than worshipped for his intrinsic worth.[40] In this trajectory of the Christian faith, attention to God's ontological greatness is severely diminished. Therefore, despite Anderson's insistence that African Pentecostals dynamically contextualize the Holy Spirit as a life-giving power which meets the existential needs of deliverance from evil[41] far better than the "sterile pneumatology imported from the West,"[42] one cannot rule out *a priori* the judgment of Akrong that the Holy Spirit is often reduced to "a spiritual principle"[43] or Birgit Meyer's estimation that for many Pentecostal churches in Ghana "Christology thus boils down to an image of Jesus driving away demons"[44] or Acolatse's view that the name of Jesus essentially "becomes the charm *par excellence* against all magical charms."[45] Akrong holds that African Pentecostals often adopt uncritically the functional or utilitarian aspects of African indigenous religiosity, resulting in a diminished view of Christ's person and work:

> The Christology of the Charismatic movement can be described as an instrumental Christology in which Christ is also sublimated into the mode of the Holy Spirit within the theology of dispensation. The main value of Christ is the blood of Christ, which is used as a weapon that one could use to fight evil spirits. . . . In the final analysis we have a docetic Christ who is reduced to a power or spiritual principle for exorcism.[46]

Implicit in this critique of the rampant demonology of African Pentecostals is that by adopting an instrumentalist view of God and church practices, many within the movement can be viewed as departing rather significantly from the relational ontology that is widely regarded as typically characteristic of African thought. Rather than conceiving of the Christian life as a dynamic participation in God, which portrays human personhood as radically defined in relationship to others (e.g., Mbiti's axiom "I am because we

---

40. Gutiérrez, *On Job*, 1.
41. Anderson, *Zion and Pentecost*, 253.
42. Anderson, "Pentecostal Pneumatology and African Power Concepts," 72.
43. Akrong, "Neo-Witchcraft Mentality in Popular Christianity," 8.
44. Meyer, *Translating the Devil: An African Appropriation*, 235.
45. Acolatse, *For Freedom or Bondage?* 44.
46. Akrong, "Neo-Witchcraft Mentality in Popular Christianity," 8.

are"[47]), many African Pentecostals appear content to conceive of God as a means to an end, or as a figure fundamentally external, rather than internal, to the basic personhood of the Christian, thus fundamentally jettisoning this relational ontology with respect to God.

Third, our study has portrayed Fang Pentecostals as occasionally cognizant of the need to normalize the concept of suffering in the lives of Christians since their churches are so aggressively committed to the elimination of witchcraft in the pursuit of the abundant life. Yet because the Fang Pentecostalized worldview can generally be described as bursting at the seams with demonic powers responsible for every imaginable type of suffering in strict opposition to the will of God, *the framework of their demonology often leaves little room for conceiving of suffering as a normal part of the Christian life*. The cosmic battle against the Devil so consumes hermeneutical reflection and is so entrenched in ecclesial praxis that many Fang Pentecostals could scarcely appreciate the sentiment expressed by the Old Testament scholar H. H. Rowley who, when writing about the central meaning of the book of Job, compared Job's suffering to those of the apostle Paul: "Paul ceases to cry out for deliverance from his suffering, but finds enrichment in his suffering, so that he comes to rejoice in the suffering itself because it has brought him a new experience of the grace of God. This is fundamentally the same as have found in the book of Job."[48] The rampant demonology characterizing the Pentecostal movement amongst the Fang and many other African peoples virtually excludes such a view.

In conclusion, these processes of indigenization and diabolization raise important questions for scholars, theologians, and biblical scholars of African Christianity. If, on the one hand, (1) the Devil has been incarnated *at a more profound level* than God due to the cosmological structure of African traditional religiosity which, in typical fashion, tends to marginalize God to the periphery of religious consciousness, and, on the other hand, (2) the Devil has ascended to become a *disturbingly central* and *indispensable element* within Pentecostalized forms of African Christianity without whose presence the whole edifice of Pentecostalized Christianity in Africa would come crumbling down, then this theological trajectory not only raises serious questions and concerns as to the actual process of Christian inculturation taking place in Africa but also warrants considerable biblical attention and theological response from scholars of African Christianity as well as from its pastors, its churches, and its millions of ordinary believers.

---

47. Mbiti, *African Religions and Philosophy*, 127.
48. Rowley, "The Book of Job and Its Meaning," 183.

Appendix 1

The "Pentecostal Deliverance Liturgy" of Apostle Agustín Edu Esono

"Power against Incurable Sicknesses"

APOSTLE AGUSTÍN EDU ESONO of Assembly of the Holy Spirit was liberally utilizing *Poder contra las Enfermedades Inmedicables* ("Power against Incurable Sicknesses") during his morning deliverance and healing sessions during April and May of 2012. We have referred to this document as a "Pentecostal Deliverance Liturgy," which illustrates the way in which Fang Pentecostals display creative innovation in their deliverance and healing ministries. In the liturgy, Esono augments the more customary deliverance practices of prayer and the oil of anointing by leading the participants in the repetition of mantras accompanied by physical-symbolic enactments designed to bring about God's healing and the destruction of demonic forces believed to be causing physical illnesses.

In addition to the corporate liturgy, Esono indicated that he frequently prescribed *Oración de Siete Días* ("Prayer of Seven Days") to church members and people in the surrounding neighborhood in order that suffering and sick people might individually continue their healing and deliverance at home. "Prayer of Seven Days" may be viewed as a kind of "Individual Healing Liturgy" wherein certain biblical chapters and verses are read daily with certain prayers being "prescribed" during particular hours of the day in order to procure healing and deliverance from various sicknesses. The use of the Christian Scriptures to enact healing by Apostle Esono is highly analogous of the use of the Psalms by the Aladura Churches of West Africa as portrayed by David T. Adamo.[1] The original Spanish documents have

---

1. See Adamo, *Reading and Interpreting the Bible in African Indigenous Churches.*

been translated from Spanish into English by the author, and the original capitalization has been preserved from the original documents.

Poder contra las Enfermedades Inmedicables
("Power against Incurable Sicknesses")

CONFESSIONS

Jeremiah 32:27: "See, I am the Lord, the God of all flesh, is anything too hard for me?"

Mark 10:27: "Jesus looked at them and said, 'For mortals it is impossible, but not for God; for God all things are possible.'"

Luke 1:37: "For nothing will be impossible with God."

Isaiah 53:5–6: "But he was wounded for our transgressions, crushed for our iniquities; upon him was the punishment that made us whole, and by his bruises we are healed. All we like sheep have gone astray; we have all turned to our own way, and the Lord has laid on him the iniquity of us all."

Colossians 2:15: "He disarmed the rulers and authorities and made a public example of them, triumphing over them in it."

Acts 10:38: "How God anointed Jesus of Nazareth with the Holy Spirit and with power; how he went about doing good and healing all who were oppressed by the devil, for God was with him."

PRAISE AND WORSHIP

1. Confess your sins and ask God for forgiveness that the blood of Jesus will purify you.
2. I command every evil plantation in my life JUMP WITH ALL YOUR ROOTS IN THE NAME OF JESUS (put your hands on your belly and keep repeating this prayer many times).
3. I cough and vomit any food that I ate at the table of the devil, in the name of Jesus.

APPENDIX 1: THE "PENTECOSTAL DELIVERANCE LITURGY"

4. May all negative materials circulating in my blood be evacuated, in the name of Jesus.
5. I drink the blood of Jesus. (Swallow it physically by faith. Repeat this prayer for a long time.)
6. (Place a hand on your head and the other hand on your belly and begin to pray like this): FIRE OF THE HOLY SPIRIT BURN FROM MY HEAD TO THE BOTTOM OF MY FEET. (Mention all the organs of the body: kidneys, liver, intestines, stomach, blood, etc. At this point in prayer, you should not be in a hurry because the fire will surely descend. You should pray until you start to feel warm.)
7. Let the blood of Jesus be transfused in my blood vessels, in the name of Jesus.
8. I command every agent of disease in my blood and in my bodily organs die, in the name of Jesus.
9. Let my blood reject every evil and strange entity, in the name of Jesus.
10. Holy Spirit speak your freedom and healing over my life, in the name of Jesus.
11. Let the blood of Jesus proclaim the disappearance of all disease in my life.
12. I have the blood of Jesus against the spirit of . . . (Mention the name of the sickness), you need to flee, in the name of Jesus.
13. Oh Lord, may your healing hand be extended right now over my life.
14. Oh Lord, may your hand of miracles be extended right now over my life.
15. Oh Lord, may your hand of deliverance be extended right now over my life.
16. I reduce to nothing all compromise with the spirit of death, in the name of Jesus.
17. I rebuke any headquarters of disease in my life, in the name of Jesus.
18. I destroy every place of refuge for sickness in my life, in the name of Jesus.
19. I destroy the dominion and the operation of sickness in my life, in the name of Jesus.
20. Every sickness in my life, kneel down, in the name of Jesus.

21. Oh Lord, may my negativity be transformed into positivity, in the name of Jesus.
22. I command the death of every agent of sickness in any dominion of my life, in the name of Jesus.
23. I shall not see more of this sickness (name it) in my life, in the name of Jesus.
24. Father Lord, may the whirlwind of God disperse any force of sickness manufactured or invented against my life, in the name of Jesus.
25. May any spirit hindering my perfect cure fall and die right now, in the name of Jesus.
26. Father and Lord may every employer of death in my life begin to kill themselves, in the name of Jesus.
27. Father and Lord, may every cell of sickness in my life die, in the name of Jesus.
28. Father and Lord, may every agent of sickness operating against my health disappear, in the name of Jesus.
29. Fountain of bodily discomfort in my life, dry up now, in the name of Jesus.
30. Every dead organ in my body, receive life now, in the name of Jesus.
31. Father and Lord, may the blood of Jesus be transfused in my blood to carry out my perfect cure, in the name of Jesus.
32. Every disorder in my body, receive the order of God, in the name of Jesus.
33. Any disease in my body, jump with all your roots, in the name of Jesus.
34. I take back any conscious or unconscious cooperation with sickness, in the name of Jesus.
35. Oh Lord, may the whirlwind of God expel any wind of sickness in my life.
36. I take back my body from every curse of sickness, in the name of Jesus.
37. Oh Lord, may the blood of Jesus cleanse every evil plantation in my blood.
38. I take back every organ of my body from every evil altar, in the name of Jesus.
39. I take back my body from the manipulation of any chain of the darkness, in the name of Jesus.

APPENDIX 1: THE "PENTECOSTAL DELIVERANCE LITURGY"

40. Fire of the Holy Spirit, destroy every stubborn agent of sickness in my body, in the name of Jesus.
41. I stop every demon of incurable sickness, in the name of Jesus.
42. I annul every clinical prophecy concerning my life, in the name of Jesus.
43. Fire of the Holy Spirit, boil every sickness that is in my body, in the name of Jesus.
44. I annul every verdict of witchcraft against my life, in the name of Jesus.
45. Oh earth, vomit everything that has been buried in you against my health, in the name of Jesus.
46. Every tree that sickness planted in my blood, be pulled out with its roots for the fire of God, in the name of Jesus.
47. I command every arrow of witchcraft out of my: spinal cord, spleen, umbilicus, heart, throat, my eyes, my head, in the name of Jesus.
48. I tie up and may the fire of God burn all evil presence in my bodily system:

    —Reproductive   —Skeletal
    —Digestive   —Endocrine
    —Nervous   —Musculatory
    —Circulatory   —Excretory
    —Respiratory

49. I break the backbone and destroy the root of every spirit that is speaking against me, in the name of Jesus.
50. Begin to give thanks to God for your healing.

Oración de Siete Días ("Prayer of Seven Days")

1) REPENTANCE

Psalm 32:1–5	James 5:1–6
Psalm 139:23–24	Romans 2:1–11
Acts 19:18–19	Daniel 9:18
Daniel 9:5	Matthew 6:14–15
Amos 3:3	Psalm 103:3
Ezekiel 20:43	Psalm 130:4

Proverbs 28:13	Ezekiel 18:21–23
Matthew 18:21–35	Matthew 3:7–8
James 4:6–7	Isaiah 1, Isaiah 59

2) INVOCATION OF THE BLOOD OF JESUS FOR TOTAL PURIFICATION

Romans 3:25	Ephesians 1:7
Romans 5:9	Ephesians 2:13–16
Hebrews 9	1 John 1:5–10
Hebrews 10:29	Revelation 5:9
Hebrews 13:12	Revelation 1:5
John 6:56	Acts 20:28
John 19:34	Acts 20:28
Revelation 7:14	1 Peter 1:18–19

3) PRAYER OF COMBAT AGAINST THE NEGATIVE AND ABOMINIDABLE WORKS OF MY ENEMIES

2 Samuel 22 (All) at 24:00 and upon waking up in the morning

Psalm 27 at 12:00

Psalm 35 at 18:00

4) PRAYER OF COMBAT AGAINST WITCHCRAFT, OCCULT, WIZARDRY, SEXISM, MARABOUTS, MYSTICISM, AND SATANISM

Psalm 59 (All) at 24:00 and at 5:00 in the morning

Psalm 69 (All) at 12:00h

Psalm 91 (All) at 18:00h

5) PRAYER OF REVERSAL OF CURSES PLACED UPON SATANIC ALTARS

Isaiah 41	Galatians 3:314
Isaiah 43	Psalm 109 (All)
Nehemiah 13:2	Judges 6 (All)
Proverbs 26:2	

6) PRAYER OF FAITH (THE DESIRES OF YOUR HEART)

Matthew 19:26	Matthew 21:21–22
Luke 1:37	Hebrews 4:16
Isaiah 38:1–6	Jeremiah 5:14
Hebrews 11 (All)	John 7:15
Psalms 50:14–15	Lucas 21:15
Psalms 34:8–10; 18–23	

7) PRAYER OF THANKSGIVING

Deuteronomy 8:12–20	Psalm 100
Luke 17:11–19	Psalm 126
Psalm 150	

Appendix 2

Reading the Book of Job at Six Distinct Locations in Equatorial Guinea

The following six venues (#1–#6) participated in the study by interpreting and appropriating the book of Job through sermons, Bible studies, and seminary classroom instruction and dialogue. In addition, semi-structured interviews were conducted with leprosy patients and people living with HIV/AIDS. Over 200 ordinary readers of the Bible in Equatorial Guinea participated in the study (not counting church members who listened to the Joban sermons). The primary textual blocks of Job and the specific dates each group participated in the study are listed below.

#1: Reformed Presbyterian Church of Equatorial Guinea

Sermons (recorded and transcribed):

1. Preacher: Manuel Owono Akara Oke; Text: Job 1; October 9, 2011
2. Preacher: Adam Miguel Etame Mayoko; Text: Job 3:1–16; October 16, 2011
3. Preacher: Alberto Mañe Ebo Asong; Text: Job 4:1–11; October 23, 2011
4. Preacher: Manuel Owono Akara Oke; Text: Job 9:27–35; November 6, 2011
5. Preacher: Pamela Idjabe; Text: Job 29:1–11; November 13, 2011
6. Preacher: Juan Ebang Ela; Text: Job 42:1–6; November 20, 2011

APPENDIX 2: READING THE BOOK OF JOB AT SIX DISTINCT LOCATIONS 263

Bible Studies (recorded and transcribed):

1. Text: Job 1–2; October 17, 2011
2. Text: Job 3; October 18, 2011
3. Text: Job 11:1–20; October 24, 2011
4. Text: Job 9:27–35; 13:13–19; 16:18–22; 19:23–27; October 25, 2011
5. Text: Job 29–30; October 26, 2011
6. Text: Job 32–37; October 31, 2011
7. Text: Job 38:1—42:6; November 1, 2011
8. Text: Job 42:7–17; November 2, 2011

#2: Joy of My Salvation

Sermons (recorded and transcribed):

1. Preacher: Basilio Oyono; Text: Job 1–2; October 9, 2011
2. Preacher: Basilio Oyono; Text: Job 3:1–4; October 16, 2011
3. Preacher: Basilio Oyono; Text: Job 4:1–6; 5:1–18; 8:1–7; 11:1–6, 14–20; October 23, 2011
4. Preacher: Basilio Oyono; Text: Job 6:3–12; 19:19–25; October 30, 2011
5. Preacher: Rafael Nze; Text: Job 17; November 2, 2011
6. Preacher: Basilio Oyono; Text: Job 38:1–12, 16–21, 28–29, 39–42; 39:1; 40:1–5; 42:1–6; November 6, 2011
7. Preacher: Basilio Oyono; Text: Job 42:5–17; November 13, 2011

Bible Studies (recorded and transcribed):

1. Text: Job 1–2; November 16, 2011
2. Text: Job 3; November 19, 2011
3. Text: Job 4–5; May 16, 2012
4. Text: Job 19; May 19, 2012
5. Text: Job 38:1—42:6; June 2, 2012
6. Text: Job 42; June 6, 2012

#3: Assembly of the Holy Spirit

Sermons (recorded and transcribed):

1. Preacher: Liborio Nvo Ndong; Text: Job 1; May 9, 2012
2. Preacher: Liborio Nvo Ndong; Text: Job 2; May 11, 2012
3. Preacher: Marcellino Abeso Nse; Text: Job 3–4; May 30, 2012
4. Preacher: Marcellino Abeso Nse; Text: Job 19; June 6, 2012
5. Preacher: Frederic Fouahouly; Text: Job 1:1–5 and various; June 15, 2012
6. Preacher: Lupercio Mbembo Ivenda; Text: Job 42; June 17, 2012

#4: Leprosarium of Micomeseng

Bible Studies (recorded and transcribed):

1. Text: Job 1–2; October 20, 2011
2. Text: Job 3; October 27, 2011
3. Text: Job 4; November 3, 2011
4. Text: Job 9; November 11, 2011
5. Text: Job 38, 42:1–9; November 12, 2011
6. Text: Job 42:7–17; November 12, 2011

Semi-Structured Interviews (recorded and transcribed):

1. "Gabriel"; October 20, 2011
2. "Alvaro"; November 3, 2011
3. "Claudia"; November 12, 2012
4. "Consuela"; November 12, 2012

#5: Good Samaritan HIV/AIDS Support Group

Bible Studies (recorded and transcribed):

1. Text: Job 1-2; May 11, 2012
2. Text: Job 3; May 25, 2012
3. Text: Job 4:7–9; 8:1–9; 11:13–20; June 1, 2012

> *Unfortunately, due to rain and scheduling conflicts, the last three planned Bible studies on Job with people living with HIV/AIDS (PLWHA) were not realized. Nevertheless, Job's lament (Job 3) and Eliphaz, Bildad, and Zophar's dialogical speeches were appropriated by PLWHA which ultimately proved sufficient for analyzing the promise of lament and the sting of retribution amongst PLWHA.*

Semi-Structured Interviews (recorded and transcribed):

1. "Francisco"; June 9, 2012
2. "Elena"; June 9, 2012
3. "Anunciación"; June 14, 2012
4. "Linda"; December 2, 2012

#6: *Instituto Bíblico "Casa de la Palabra"* (IBCP Seminary)

Classes (recorded and transcribed):

1. May 31, 2012
2. June 1, 2012
3. June 2, 2012
4. June 6, 2012
5. June 7, 2012
6. June 8, 2012

> *The participants involved in the class "The Book of Job" included Professor Modesto Engonga Ondo, Professor Esteban Ndong, and eight third-year theology students in the midst of their ministerial practicum in the local churches.*

Semi-Structured Interviews Cited in the Book
(not transcribed, ordered by date)

Interview, Basilio Oyono, October 12, 2011.

Interview, Alberto Mañe Ebo Asong, October 14, 2011.

Interview, Manuel Owono Akara, October 17, 2011, October 31, November 9, 2011.

Interview, Manuel Nzôh Asumu, October 24, 2011.

Interview, Damián Ángel Asumu, October 27, 2011.

Interview, Modesto Endo Ongonga, November 20, 2011.

Interview, Martin Mbeng Nze, April 24, 2012.

Interview, Vicente Ndong Esono with Deogracias Bee, May 1, 2012.

Group Interview, Modesto Engonga Ondo, Antonio Hill, Leoncio Ndong, May 9, 2012.

Interview, Maria Dolores Nchama, May 18, 2012.

Interview, Agustín Edu Esono, May 18, 2012.

Bibliography

A'Bodjedi, Enènge. "Las Iglesias Presbiterianas Ndòwě." Translated by Josef Maria Perlasia. *Oráfrica: Revista de Oralidad Africana* 2 (2006) 49–74.

———. "Los Pastores Presbiterianos Ndòwě." Translated by Josef Maria Perlasia. *Oráfrica: Revista de Oralidad Africana* 4 (2008) 73–100.

Ackermann, Denise M. "From Mere Existence to Tenacious Endurance." In *African Women, Religion, and Health: Essays in Honor of Mercy Amba Ewudziwa Oduyoye*, edited by Isabel Apawo Phiri and Sarojini Nadar, 221–42. Maryknoll, NY: Orbis, 2006.

———. "Tamar's Cry: Re-Reading an Ancient Text in the Midst of an HIV/AIDS Pandemic." In *Reformed Theology: Identity and Ecumenicity II: Biblical Interpretation in the Reformed Tradition*, edited by Wallace M. Alston Jr. and Michael Welker, 1–33. Grand Rapids: Eerdmans, 2007.

Acolatse, Esther E. *For Freedom or Bondage?: A Critique of African Pastoral Practices*. Grand Rapids: Eerdmans, 2014.

Adamo, David Tuesday. *Reading and Interpreting the Bible in African Indigenous Churches*. Eugene, OR: Wipf and Stock, 2001.

———. "The Use of the Psalms in African Indigenous Churches in Nigeria." In *The Bible in Africa: Transactions, Trajectories, and Trends*, edited by Gerald O. West and Musa W. Dube, 336–49. Leiden: Brill, 2001.

Ademiluka, Sola. "The Use of Therapeutic Psalms in Inculturating Christianity in Africa." *African Ecclesiastical Review* 37, no. 4 (1995) 221–27.

Adeyemo, Tokunboh, ed. *Africa Bible Commentary*. Grand Rapids: Zondervan, 2006.

Adogame, Afe. "Prayer as Action and Instrument in the Aladura Churches." In *Opfer Und Gebet in Den Religionen*, edited by Ulrich Berner et al., 115–31. Gütersloh: Bertelsmann, 2005.

Adogame, Afe, and Lazio Jafta. "Zionists, Aladura, and Roho: African Instituted Churches." In *African Christianity: An African Story*, edited by Ogbu Kalu, 271–87. 1st Africa World Edition. Trenton, NJ: Africa World, 2007.

"AIDSinfo: Epidemiological Status, World Overview." *UNAIDS*. http://www.unaids.org/en/dataanalysis/datatools/aidsinfo/.

Akper, Godwin I. "The Role of the 'Ordinary Reader' in Gerald O. West's Hermeneutics." *Scriptura* no. 88 (2005) 1–13.

Akrong, Abraham. "Neo-Witchcraft Mentality in Popular Christianity." *Research Review* 16, no. 1 (2000) 1–12.

———. "Towards a Theology of Evil Spirits and Witches." *Journal of African Christian Thought* 4, no. 1 (June 2001) 18–26.

Alexandre, Pierre, and Jacques Binet. *Le Groupe Dit Pahouin: (Fang, Boulou, Beti)*. Paris: Presses Universitaires de France, 1958.

Andersen, Francis I. *Job: An Introduction and Commentary*. Third American Printing. London: IVP, 1976.

Anderson, Allan. "African Independent Churches and Pentecostalism: Historical Connections and Common Identities." *Ogbomoso Journal of Theology* 13, no. 1 (January 2008) 22–42.

———. *African Reformation: African Initiated Christianity in the 20th Century*. Trenton, NJ: Africa World, 2001.

———. "Deliverance and Exorcism in Majority World Pentecostalism." In *Exorcism and Deliverance: Multi-Disciplinary Studies*, edited by William K. Kay and Robin Parry, 101–19. Milton Keynes, UK: Paternoster, 2011.

———. "Exorcism and Conversion to African Pentecostalism." *Exchange* 35, no. 1 (2006) 116–33.

———. "Pentecostal Pneumatology and African Power Concepts: Continuity or Change?" *Missionalia* 19, no. 1 (April 1991) 65–74.

———. *Zion and Pentecost: The Spirituality and Experience of Pentecostal and Zionist/Apostolic Churches in South Africa*. Pretoria: University of South Africa, 2000.

Anim, Emmanuel Kwesi. "Who Wants to Be a Millionaire? An Analysis of Prosperity Teaching in the Charismatic Ministries (Churches) in Ghana and Its Wider Impact." PhD diss., Open University, 2003.

Anum, Eric. "Comparative Readings of the Bible in Africa: Some Concerns." In *The Bible in Africa: Transactions, Trajectories, and Trends*, edited by Gerald O. West and Musa W. Dube, 457–73. Leiden: Brill, 2001.

———. "The Reconstruction of Forms of African Theology: Towards Effective Biblical Interpretation." PhD diss., University of Glasgow, 1999.

Arden, Donald S. "Out of Africa Something New." *Anglican Theological Review* 6 (January 1976) 17–36.

Asamoah-Gyadu, J. Kwabena. *African Charismatics: Current Developments within Independent Indigenous Pentecostalism in Ghana*. Leiden: Brill, 2005.

———. "Conquering Satan, Demons, Principalities, and Powers: Ghanaian Traditional and Christian Perspectives on Religion, Evil, and Deliverance." In *Coping with Evil in Religion and Culture: Case Studies*, edited by Nelly van Doorn-Harder and Lourens Minnema, 85–104. Amsterdam: Editions Rodopi B.V., 2008.

———. *Contemporary Pentecostal Christianity: Interpretations from an African Context*. Eugene, OR: Wipf & Stock, 2013.

———. "'The Evil You Have Done Can Ruin the Whole Clan': African Cosmology, Community, and Christianity in Achebe's Things Fall Apart." *Studies in World Christianity* 16, no. 1 (2010) 46–62.

———. "Signs, Wonders, and Ministry: The Gospel in the Power of the Spirit." *Evangelical Review of Theology* 33, no. 1 (2009) 32–46.

Asongu, J. J. "A Curse or Blessing: Oil and Human Security in Equatorial Guinea." In *2009 Business, Society and Government Proceedings*, 7–38. Chicago, IL, 2009.

Awolalu, J. Omosade. "Sin and Its Removal in African Traditional Religion." *Journal of the American Academy of Religion* 44, no. 2 (1976) 275–87.

Balandier, Georges. *Afrique Ambiguë*. Paris: Plon, 1957.

———. *Ambiguous Africa: Cultures in Collision*. Translated by Helen Weaver. London: Chatto & Windus, 1966.

———. *The Sociology of Black Africa: Social Dynamics in Central Africa*. London: Deutsch, 1970.

Balentine, Samuel E. *Job*. Macon, GA: Smyth & Helwys, 2006.

Barnett, Tony, and Alan W. Whiteside. *AIDS in the Twenty-First Century: Disease and Globalization*. New York: Palgrave Macmillan, 2002.

Barth, Karl. *Church Dogmatics*. 4/3.1: *The Doctrine of Reconciliation*. Translated by Geoffrey William Bromiley. London: T. & T. Clark, 1961.

Barton, John. *The Nature of Biblical Criticism*. Louisville: Westminster John Knox, 2007.

Baudin, Noël. *Fetichism and Fetich Worshipers*. Translated by Mary McMahon. New York: Benziger Brothers, 1885.

Bayart, Jean-François. "Africa in the World: A History of Extraversion." *African Affairs* 99, no. 395 (2000) 217–67.

———. *The State in Africa: The Politics of the Belly*. London: Longman, 1993.

Bediako, Kwame. "Biblical Christologies in the Context of African Traditional Religions." In *Sharing Jesus in the Two Thirds World: Evangelical Christologies from the Contexts of Poverty, Powerlessness and Religious Pluralism*, edited by Vinay Kumar Samuel and Chris Sugden, 81–122. Grand Rapids: Eerdmans, 1984.

———. *Christianity in Africa: The Renewal of a Non-Western Religion*. Edinburgh: Edinburgh University Press, 1995.

———. "The Roots of African Theology." *International Bulletin of Missionary Research* 13, no. 2 (1989) 58–62.

———. "The Significance of Modern African Christianity—A Manifesto." *Studies in World Christianity* 1, no. 1 (1995) 51–67.

———. *Theology and Identity: The Impact of Culture Upon Christian Thought in the Second Century and in Modern Africa*. Oxford: Regnum, 1992.

———. "Toward a New Theodicy: Africa's Suffering in Redemptive Perspective." *Journal of African Christian Thought* 5, no. 2 (2002) 47–52.

———. "Understanding African Theology in the 20th Century." *Themelios* 20, no. 1 (1994) 14–20.

Behrend, Heike. "The Rise of Occult Powers, AIDS and the Roman Catholic Church in Western Uganda." *Journal of Religion in Africa* 37, no. 1 (2007) 41–58.

Bennett, W. H. *The Books of Chronicles*. London: Hodder and Stoughton, 1894.

Bevans, Stephen B. *Models of Contextual Theology*. Rev. and expanded ed. Maryknoll, NY: Orbis, 2002.

Bibang Oyee, Julián. *La Migración Fang: (según Dulu Bon Be Afri Kara)*. Avila: Malamba, 2002.

Billman, Kathleen D., and Daniel L. Migliore. *Rachel's Cry: Prayer of Lament and Rebirth of Hope*. Eugene, OR: Wipf & Stock, 2006.

Boocock, Nathaniel. *Our Fernandian Missions*. London: Hammond, 1912.

Booth, Newell S. "Time and Change in African Traditional Thought." *Journal of Religion in Africa* 7, no. 2 (1975) 81–91.

Bosch, David J. "The Problem of Evil in Africa: A Survey of African Views on Witchcraft and of the Response of the Christian Church." In *Like a Roaring Lion*, edited by Pieter G. R. de Villiers, 38–62. Pretoria: University of South Africa Press, 1987.

Boyd, Lydia C. "Saving One's Self: Ugandan Youth, Sexual Abstinence, and Born-Again Christianity in the Time of AIDS." PhD diss., New York University, 2010.

Brown, Arthur Judson. *One Hundred Years: A History of the Foreign Missionary Work of the Presbyterian Church in the U. S. A., with Some Account of Countries, Peoples and the Policies and Problems of Modern Missions*. Vol. 1. New York: Fleming H. Revell Company, 1936.

Brueggemann, Walter. "The Costly Loss of Lament." *Journal for the Study of the Old Testament* 36 (1986) 57–71.

———. *Old Testament Theology: An Introduction.* Nashville: Abingdon, 2008.

———. *Praying the Psalms.* Winona, MN: Saint Mary's, 1993.

———. *The Psalms and the Life of Faith.* Edited by Patrick D. Miller. Minneapolis: Fortress, 1995.

———. "A Shape for Old Testament Theology, I: Structure Legitimation." *Catholic Biblical Quarterly* 47, no. 1 (1985) 28–46.

———. "A Shape for Old Testament Theology, II: Embrace of Pain." *The Catholic Biblical Quarterly* 47, no. 3 (1985) 395–415.

———. *Theology of the Old Testament: Testimony, Dispute, Advocacy.* Minneapolis: Fortress, 1997.

Buber, Martin. *I and Thou.* 2nd ed. London: Continuum, 2004.

Bucher, Hubert. *Spirits and Power: An Analysis of Shona Cosmology.* Oxford: Oxford University Press, 1980.

Burnett, David. *Unearthly Powers: A Christian Perspective on Primal and Folk Religions.* Eastbourne, England: MARC, 1988.

Byrne, Patricia Huff. "'Give Sorrow Words': Lament—Contemporary Need for Job's Old Time Religion." *Journal of Pastoral Care & Counseling* 56, no. 3 (2002) 255–64.

Calvin, John. *Institutes of the Christian Religion.* Edited by John T. McNeill. Translated by Ford Lewis Battles. London: SCM, 1961.

———. *Sermons from Job.* Translated by Leroy Nixon. Grand Rapids: Eerdmans, 1952.

Chamberlin, Christopher. "The Migration of the Fang into Central Gabon during the Nineteenth Century: A New Interpretation." *The International Journal of African Historical Studies* 11, no. 3 (1978) 429–56.

Chilongani, Dickson Daud. "An African Praying Tradition and Job 7." *The ANITEPAM Journal* (November 2006) 64–74.

Chima, Alex. "Story and African Theology." *African Ecclesiastical Review* 26, no. 1–2 (1984) 52–65.

Claretian Missionaries. *Cien Años de Evangelización En Guinea Ecuatorial (1883–1983).* Barcelona: Editorial Claret, 1983.

Clines, David J. A. "Deconstructing the Book of Job." In *What Does Eve Do to Help?: And Other Readerly Questions to the Old Testament*, 106–23. Sheffield, UK: JSOT, 1990.

———. *Job 1–20.* Word Biblical Commentary. Dallas: Word, 1989.

———. "Job's Fifth Friend: An Ethical Critique of the Book of Job." *Biblical Interpretation* 12, no. 3 (2004) 233–50.

Clowney, Edmund P. *The Unfolding Mystery: Discovering Christ in the Old Testament.* Colorado Springs: NavPress, 1988.

Cobb, John B., and David Ray Griffin. *Process Theology: An Introductory Exposition.* Belfast: Christian Journals, 1977.

Coll, Armengol. *Segunda Memoria de Las Misiones de Fernando Póo y Sus Dependencias.* 2nd ed. Madrid: Imprenta Ibérica de Estanislao Maestre, 1911.

Coordinating Council Conference: Report and Recommendations. Bulstrode, Gerrards Cross, England: WEC International, June 1982.

"Country Profile: Equatorial Guinea 2008." *The Economist Intelligence Unit*, 2008.

"Country Profile: Equatorial Guinea 2009." *The Economist Intelligence Unit*, 2009.

Cox, Harvey Gallagher. *Fire from Heaven: The Rise of Pentecostal Spirituality and the Reshaping of Religion in the Twenty-First Century*. London: Cassell, 1996.

Cox, James L. "The Classification 'Primal Religions' as a Non-Empirical Christian Theological Construct." *Studies in World Christianity* 2, no. 1 (1996) 55–76.

———. *From Primitive to Indigenous: The Academic Study of Indigenous Religions*. Aldershot, UK: Ashgate, 2007.

———. "The Globalization of Localized African Religions: The Case of Kwame Bediako." In *World Christianity in Local Context: Essays in Memory of David A. Kerr*, edited by Stephen R. Goodwin, 56–65. London: Continuum, 2009.

———. *The Invention of God in Indigenous Societies*. Durham: Acumen, 2014.

———. "The Invention of the Christian God in Africa: Geoffrey Parrinder and the Study of God in African Indigenous Religions." In *Le Monothéisme: Diversité, Exclusivisme Ou Dialogue?*, edited by André Caquot and Charles Guittard, 315–28. Paris: Sociéte Ernest Renan, 2010.

Craddock, Susan. "Beyond Epidemiology: Locating AIDS in Africa." In *HIV and AIDS in Africa: Beyond Epidemiology*, edited by Ezekiel Kalipeni et al., 1–10. Oxford: Blackwell, 2004.

Craig, William Lane. *Reasonable Faith: Christian Truth and Apologetics*. 3rd ed. Wheaton, IL: Crossway, 2003.

Crenshaw, James L. *Defending God: Biblical Responses to the Problem of Evil*. Oxford: Oxford University Press, 2005.

Creus, Jacint. *Curso de Literatura Oral Africana: Lecturas Comentadas de Literatura Oral de Guinea y del África Negra*. Barcelona: CEIBA Ediciones, 2005.

Cronjé, Suzanne. *Equatorial Guinea—The Forgotten Dictatorship: Forced Labour and Political Murder in Central Africa*. London: Anti-Slavery Society, 1976.

Daneel, Marthinus L. "Coping with Wizardry in Zimbabwe in African Initiated Churches (AICs)." In *Coping with Evil in Religion and Culture: Case Studies*, edited by Nelly van Doorn-Harder and Lourens Minnema, 51–70. Amsterdam: Editions Rodopi B.V., 2008.

———. "Exorcism as Combating Wizardry: Liberation or Enslavement?" In *All Things Hold Together: Holistic Theologies at the African Grassroots: Selected Essays*, 311–40. Pretoria: Unisa, 2007.

Daughrity, Dyron B. *The Changing World of Christianity: The Global History of a Borderless Religion*. New York: Lang, 2010.

Davies, Evan. *Whatever Happened to C. T. Studd's Mission? Lessons from the History of WEC International*. Gerrards Cross, UK: WEC, 2012.

Davis, R. E. (Ronnie), and Godfrey Harold. "Theodicy in Job: Ancient Word, Modern Reflections." *South African Baptist Journal of Theology* 20 (2011) 1–18.

Decalo, Samuel. *Psychoses of Power: African Personal Dictatorships*. Boulder, CO: Westview, 1989.

Dhorme, E. *A Commentary on the Book of Job*. Translated by Harold Knight. London: Nelson, 1967.

Dickson, Kwesi A. "Continuity and Discontinuity Between the Old Testament and African Life and Thought." In *African Theology En Route: Papers from the Pan-African Conference of Third World Theologians, December 17–23, 1977, Accra, Ghana*, edited by Kofi Appiah-Kubi and Sergio Torres, 95–108. Maryknoll, NY: Orbis, 1979.

———. "'Hebrewisms of West Africa': The Old Testament and African Life and Thought." *Legon Journal of Humanities* 1 (1974) 23–34.

———. "The Old Testament and African Theology." *Ghana Bulletin of Theology* 4, no. 4 (1973) 31–41.

———. *Theology in Africa*. London: Darton Longman & Todd, 1984.

Douglas, Mary. "Witchcraft and Leprosy: Two Strategies of Exclusion." *Man* 26, no. 4 (December 1991) 723–36.

Draper, Jonathan A. "The Bible as Poison Onion, Icon and Oracle: Reception of the Printed Sacred Text in Oral and Residual-Oral South Africa." *Journal of Theology for Southern Africa* no. 112 (March 2002) 39–56.

———. "Old Scores and New Notes: Where and What Is Contextual Exegesis in the New South Africa?" In *Towards an Agenda for Contextual Theology: Essays in Honour of Albert Nolan*, edited by M. T. Speckman and L. T. Kaufmann, 148–68. Pietermaritzburg: Cluster, 2001.

Driver, S. R. *An Introduction to the Literature of the Old Testament*. 9th ed. Edinburgh: Clark, 1913.

Dube, Musa W. "*Go Tla Siama, O Tla Fola*: Doing Biblical Studies in an HIV and AIDS Context." *Black Theology* 8, no. 2 (2010) 212–41.

———. "*Go Tla Siama, O Tla Fola*: Doing Biblical Studies in an HIV and AIDS Context." In *Postcolonial Perspectives in African Biblical Interpretations*, edited by Musa W. Dube et al., 483–508. Atlanta: Society of Biblical Literature, 2012.

———. "Theological Challenges: Proclaiming the Fullness of Life in the HIV/AIDS & Global Economic Era." *International Review of Mission* 91, no. 363 (October 2002) 535–49.

Duffy, Eamon. *The Stripping of the Altars: Traditional Religion in England, c.1400–c.1580*. New Haven: Yale University Press, 1992.

Dy'Ikengue, Ibia. *Costumbres Bengas y de los Pueblos Vecinos: Mbangwe-Corisco, 1872*. Translated by Práxedes Rabat Makambo. Madrid: SIAL, 1872.

Ekomo, Mariano et al., eds. *Palabras Que No Tienen Boca: Relatos Urbanos de Guinea Ecuatorial*. Barcelona: CEIBA, 2009.

Engelke, Matthew, "Text and Performance in an African Church: The Book, 'Live and Direct.'" *American Ethnologist* 31, no. 1 (February 2004) 76–91.

Englund, Harri. "Christian Independency and Global Membership: Pentecostal Extraversions in Malawi." *Journal of Religion in Africa* 33, no. 1 (2003) 83–111.

"Equatorial Guinea." *World Atlas*. http://www.worldatlas.com/webimage/countrys/africa/gq.htm.

"Equatorial Guinea." *The World Bank*. http://data.worldbank.org/country/equatorial-guinea.

"Evangelical Presbyterian Church of Ghana." *ARC: Alliance of Religions and Conservation*. http://www.arcworld.org/downloads/Christian-Ghana-Presbyterian-7YP.pdf.

Evans-Pritchard, E. E. *Witchcraft, Oracles and Magic Among the Azande*. New ed. Oxford: Clarendon, 1976.

"Fang." *Encyclopedia Britannica*. http://www.britannica.com/EBchecked/topic/201505/Fang.

"Fang Homeland." *Joshua Project*. https://joshuaproject.net/assets/media/profiles/maps/m11187_cf.pdf.

Fegley, Randall. *Equatorial Guinea*. Vol. 136. World Bibliographical Series. Oxford: Clio, 1991.

———. *Equatorial Guinea: An African Tragedy*. New York: Lang, 1989.
Ferdinando, Keith. "Christian Identity in the African Context: Reflections on Kwame Bediako's Theology and Identity." *Journal of the Evangelical Theological Society* 50, no. 1 (March 2007) 121–43.
———. *The Triumph of Christ in African Perspective: A Study of Demonology and Redemption in the African Context*. Carlisle, UK: Paternoster, 1999.
Fernandez, James. "The Affirmation of Things Past: Alar Ayong and Bwiti as Movements of Protest in Central and Northern Gabon." In *Protest and Power in Black Africa*, edited by Robert I. Rotberg and Ali A. Mazrui, 427–57. New York: Oxford University Press, 1970.
———. *Bwiti: An Ethnography of the Religious Imagination in Africa*. Princeton: Princeton University Press, 1982.
———. "Christian Acculturation and Fang Witchcraft." *Cahiers d'Études Africaines* 2, no. 6 (1961) 244–70.
Fife, Betsy L., and Eric R. Wright. "The Dimensionality of Stigma: A Comparison of Its Impact on the Self of Persons with HIV/AIDS and Cancer." *Journal of Health and Social Behavior* no. 41 (2000) 50–67.
Finnegan, Ruth H. *The Oral and Beyond: Doing Things with Words in Africa*. Oxford: Currey, 2007.
Fossum, Merle A., and Marilyn J. Mason. *Facing Shame: Families in Recovery*. New York: Norton, 1989.
Foucault, Michel. *The Archaeology of Knowledge*. London: Routledge, 1989.
Fowl, Stephen E., and L. Gregory Jones. *Reading in Communion: Scripture and Ethics in Christian Life*. Grand Rapids: Eerdmans, 1991.
Frank, Barbara. "Permitted and Prohibited Wealth: Commodity-Possessing Spirits, Economic Morals, and the Goddess Mami Wata in West Africa." *Ethnology* 34, no. 4 (1995) 331–46.
Fuller, J.J. *Cameroons and Fernando Po*. Unpublished manuscript. London: Baptist Missionary Society, 1887.
Frynas, Jędrzej George. "The Oil Boom in Equatorial Guinea." *African Affairs* 103, no. 413 (2004) 527–46.
Gammie, John G. "Theology of Retribution in the Book of Deuteronomy." *Catholic Biblical Quarterly* 32, no. 1 (January 1970) 1–12.
Gbádégesin, Enoch Olújídé. "Changing Roles of Èsù: Yorùbá Traditional and Christian Religious Concepts in a Globalized Era." *Dialogue & Alliance* 21, no. 2 (Fall/Winter 2007) 33–53.
Geschiere, Peter. "Witchcraft and New Forms of Wealth: Regional Variations in South and West Cameroon." In *Powers of Good and Evil: Social Transformations and Popular Belief*, edited by Paul Glough and John P. Mitchell, 43–76. New York: Berghahn, 2001.
Gifford, Paul. "African Christianity and the Eclipse of the Afterlife." In *The Church, the Afterlife and the Fate of the Soul: Papers Read at the 2007 Summer Meeting and the 2008 Winter Meeting of the Ecclesiastical History Society*, edited by Peter D. Clarke and Tony Claydon, 413–29. Woodbridge, UK: Boydell, 2009.
———. *African Christianity: Its Public Role*. London: Hurst, 1998.
———. "The Bible in Africa: A Novel Usage in Africa's New Churches." *Bulletin of the School of Oriental and African Studies* 71, no. 2 (2008) 203–18.

———. "Expecting Miracles: The Prosperity Gospel in Africa." *Christian Century* 124, no. 14 (2007) 20–24.

———. *Ghana's New Christianity: Pentecostalism in a Globalizing African Economy.* Bloomington: Indiana University Press, 2004.

———. Review of *The Bible in Africa: Transactions, Trajectories, and Trends,* edited by Gerald O. West and Musa W. Dube. *Journal of Religion in Africa* 34, no. 3 (2004) 397–401.

———. "The Southern Shift of Christianity." In *Veränderte Landkarten Auf Dem Weg Zu Einer Polyzentrischen Geschichte Des Weltchristentums: Festschrift Für Klaus Koschorke Zum 65. Geburtstag,* edited by Ciprian Burlaciouiu and Adrian Hermann, 189–205. Wiesbaden: Harrassowitz Verlag, 2013.

Global Christianity: A Report on the Size and Distribution of the World's Christian Population. Pew-Templeton: Global Religious Futures Project. Pew Research Center, December 2011.

"Global Health Observatory (GHO) Data." *World Health Organization.* http://www.who.int/gho/hiv/epidemic_status/deaths_text/en/.

———. http://www.who.int/gho/mortality_burden_disease/life_tables/en/

"The Global HIV/AIDS Epidemic." *The Henry J. Kaiser Family Foundation.* http://kff.org/global-health-policy/fact-sheet/the-global-hivaids-epidemic/.

Goff, James R., Jr. "The Faith That Claims." *Christianity Today* 34, February 1990, 18–21.

Goffman, Erving. *Stigma: Notes on the Management of Spoiled Identity.* London: Penguin, 1968.

Goldingay, John. *Models for Interpretation of Scripture.* Grand Rapids: Eerdmans 1995.

Gornik, Mark R. *Word Made Global: Stories of African Christianity in New York City.* Grand Rapids: Eerdmans, 2011.

Gray, Richard. *Black Christians and White Missionaries.* New Haven: Yale University Press, 1990.

Gregor, Schmidt. "Evil and Salvation in African Religion and Christianity." Maryknoll Institute of African Studies of Saint Mary's University of Minnesota and Tangaza College, Nairobi, 2006. http://www.comboni-missionare.de/literatur/schmidt_gregor_evil_and_salvation.pdf.

Greidanus, Sidney. *Preaching Christ from the Old Testament: A Contemporary Hermeneutical Method.* Grand Rapids: Eerdmans, 1999.

Grubb, Norman P. *C. T. Studd, Cricketer and Pioneer.* Fort Washington, PA: Christian Literature Crusade, 1985.

———. *Penetrating Faith in Spanish Guinea.* London: Worldwide Evangelization Crusade, 1941.

Gunner, Liz. "Africa and Orality." In *African Literature: An Anthology of Criticism and Theory,* edited by Tejumola Olaniyan and Ato Quayson, 68–73. Malden, MA: Blackwell, 2007.

Gutiérrez, Gustavo. *On Job: God-Talk and the Suffering of the Innocent.* Translated by Matthew J. O'Connell. Maryknoll, NY: Orbis, 1987.

Habel, Norman C. *The Book of Job: A Commentary.* London: SCM, 1985.

Habtu, Tewoldemedhin. "Job." In *Africa Bible Commentary,* edited by Tokunboh Adeyemo, 571–604. Grand Rapids: Zondervan, 2006.

Haddad, Beverley. "Reflections on the Church and HIV/AIDS: South Africa." *Theology Today* 62, no. 1 (2005) 29–37.

Harasta, Eva. "Crucified Praise and Resurrected Lament." In *Evoking Lament: A Theological Discussion*, edited by Brian Brock and Eva Harasta, 204-17. London: T. & T. Clark, 2009.

Harasta, Eva and Brian Brock. "Introduction." In *Evoking Lament: A Theological Discussion*, edited by Brian Brock and Eva Harasta, 1-11. London: T. & T. Clark, 2009.

Harries, Jim. "Good-by-Default and Evil in Africa." *Missiology* 34, no. 2 (2006) 151-64.

Hastings, Adrian. *A History of African Christianity, 1950-1975*. Cambridge: Cambridge University Press, 1979.

"Health Profile: Equatorial Guinea." *World Health Rankings*. http://www.worldlife expectancy.com/country-health-profile/equatorial-guinea

Healy, Nicholas M. *Church, World, and the Christian Life: Practical-Prophetic Ecclesiology*. Cambridge: Cambridge University Press, 2000.

Hearn, Julie. "The 'Invisible' NGO: US Evangelical Missions in Kenya." *Journal of Religion in Africa* 32, no. 1 (2002) 32-60.

Hick, John. *Evil and the God of Love*. London: Collins, 1968.

"HIV/AIDS Fact Sheet No. 360, Updated November 2015." *World Health Organization*. http://www.who.int/mediacentre/factsheets/fs360/en/.

Holmes, Rebecca. *Social Protection to Tackle Child Poverty in Equatorial Guinea*. Project Briefing. Overseas Development Institute, September 2009.

Holter, Knut. *Old Testament Research for Africa: A Critical Analysis and Annotated Bibliography of African Old Testament Dissertations, 1967-2000*. New York: Lang, 2002.

"Hopeless Africa." *The Economist*, May 13, 2000.

Horton, Michael S. *The Christian Faith: A Systematic Theology for Pilgrims on the Way*. Grand Rapids: Zondervan, 2011.

Hume, David. *Dialogues Concerning Natural Religion*. Reproduced with introduction by Bruce M'Ewen. Edinburgh: Blackwood, 1907.

Idowu, E. Bọlaji. *African Traditional Religion: A Definition*. London: SCM, 1973.

———. *Job: A Meditation on the Problem of Suffering*. Ibadan: Daystar, 1977.

———. *Olódùmarè: God in Yoruba Belief*. London: Longmans, 1962.

Iliffe, John. *The African Poor: A History*. Cambridge: Cambridge University Press, 1987.

"Infant Mortality Rate (Total Deaths per 1,000 Live Births) 2012." *U.S. Global Health Policy*. http://www.globalhealthfacts.org/data/topic/map.aspx?ind=91.

Informe Nacional Sobre los Progresos Realizados en Guinea Ecuatorial: Indicadores Básicos Para el Seguimiento de la Declaración Política Sobre el VIH/Sida. Republica de Guinea Ecuatorial Programa Nacional de Lucha Contra el SIDA, April 12, 2012. http://www.unaids.org/en/dataanalysis/knowyourresponse/countryprogre ssreports/2012countries/ce_GQ_Narrative_Report.pdf.

Janzen, J. Gerald. *Job*. Atlanta: John Knox, 1985.

Jenkins, Philip. "The Case for Prosperity." *Christian Century* 127, no. 24 (2010) 45.

———. *The New Faces of Christianity: Believing the Bible in the Global South*. Oxford: Oxford University Press, 2008.

———. *The Next Christendom: The Coming of Global Christianity*. Rev. and expanded ed. Oxford: Oxford University Press, 2007.

Johnson, Todd M., and Kenneth R. Ross, eds. *Atlas of Global Christianity, 1910-2010*. Edinburgh: Edinburgh University Press, 2009.

Jones, David W., and Russell S. Woodbridge. *Health, Wealth & Happiness: Has the Prosperity Gospel Overshadowed the Gospel of Christ?* Grand Rapids: Kregel, 2010.

Kalilombe, Patrick A. "Spirituality in the African Perspective." In *Paths of African Theology*, edited by Rosino Gibellini, 115-35. London: SCM, 1994.

Kalu, Ogbu, ed. *African Christianity: An African Story*. 1st Africa World Press ed. Trenton, NJ: Africa World Press, 2007.

———. *African Pentecostalism: An Introduction*. Oxford: Oxford University Press, 2008.

———. "Estranged Bedfellows? The Demonisation of the Aladura in African Pentecostal Rhetoric." *Missionalia* 28, no. 2/3 (2000) 121-42.

———. "Preserving a Worldview: Pentecostalism in the African Maps of the Universe." *Pneuma: The Journal of the Society for Pentecostal Studies* 24, no. 2 (2002) 110-37.

Kanyoro, Musimbi. "Reading the Bible from an African Perspective." *Ecumenical Review* 51, no. 1 (1999) 18-24.

Kaplan, Robert D. "The Coming Anarchy." *The Atlantic*, February 1994. http://www.theatlantic.com/magazine/archive/1994/02/the-coming-anarchy/304670/.

Kato, Byang H. *Theological Pitfalls in Africa*. Kisumu, Kenya: Evangel, 1975.

Katongole, Emmanuel M. "'A Different World Right Here, A World Being Gestated in the Deeds of the Everyday': The Church within African Theological Imagination." *Missionalia* 30, no. 2 (2002) 206-34.

———. "Embodied and Embodying Hermeneutics of Life in the Academy: Musa W. Dube's HIV/AIDS Work." In *Postcolonial Perspectives in African Biblical Interpretations*, edited by Musa W. Dube et al., 407-15. Atlanta: Society of Biblical Literature, 2012.

Katongole, Emmanuel M., and Jonathan Wilson-Hartgrove. *Mirror to the Church: Resurrecting Faith After Genocide in Rwanda*. Grand Rapids: Zondervan, 2009.

Kgosikwena, Kagiso Billy. "Pastoral Care and the Dying Process of People Living with HIV/AIDS: Speaking of God in a Crisis." *Missionalia* 29, no. 2 (2001) 200-19.

Kifleyesus, Abebe. "Cosmologies in Collision: Pentecostal Conversion and Christian Cults in Asmara." *African Studies Review* 49, no. 1 (2006) 75-92.

Kim, Ee Kon. "'Outcry': Its Context in Biblical Theology." *Interpretation* 42, no. 3 (1988) 229-39.

Kiriaku Kinyua, Johnson. *Introducing Ordinary African Readers' Hermeneutics: A Case Study of the Agĩkũyũ Encounter with the Bible*. New York: Lang, 2011.

Klein, Rebekka A. "The Phenomenology of Lament and the Presence of God in Time." In *Evoking Lament: A Theological Discussion*, edited by Eva Harasta and Brian Brock, 14-24. London: T. & T. Clark, 2009.

Klinteberg, Robert af. *Equatorial Guinea—Macías Country: The Forgotten Refugees; An International University Exchange Fund (IUEF) Field Study on the Equatorial Guinea Refugee Situation*. Geneva: International University Exchange Fund, 1978.

Koch, Klaus. "Is There a Doctrine of Retribution in the Old Testament?" In *Theodicy in the Old Testament*, edited by James L. Crenshaw, 57-87. Philadelphia: Fortress, 1983.

Konings, Piet. "Religious Revival in the Roman Catholic Church and the Autochthony-Allochthony Conflict in Cameroon." *Africa: Journal of the International Institute of African Languages and Cultures* 73, no. 1 (2003) 31-56.

Kuma, Afua. *Jesus of the Deep Forest*. Accra: Asempa, 1981.

Kyriakakis, Ioannis. "Traditional African Religion, Cosmology and Christianity." *Journal for the Study of Religions & Ideologies* 11, no. 32 (2012) 132–54.
Laburthe-Tolra, Philippe. *Initiations et Sociétés Secrètes au Cameroun: Les Mystères de la Nuit.* Paris: Karthala, 1985.
Lacocque, André. "Job and Religion at Its Best." *Biblical Interpretation* 4, no. 2 (1996) 131–53.
Lado, Ludovic. "African Catholicism in the Face of Pentecostalism." *African Christianities* (2006) 22–30.
Largeau, Victor. *Encyclopédie Pahouine, Congo Français: Éléments de Grammaire et Dictionnaire Français-Pahouin.* Paris: Leroux, 1901.
Lash, Nicholas. *Theology on the Way to Emmaus.* London: SCM, 1986.
Leibniz, Gottfried Wilhelm. *Theodicy: Essays on the Goodness of God, the Freedom of Man, and the Origin of Evil.* Edited by Austin Farrer. Translated by E. M. Huggard. London: Routledge & K. Paul, 1951.
LeMarquand, Grant. "The Bible as Specimen, Talisman, and Dragoman in Africa: A Look at Some African Uses of the Psalms and 1 Corinthians 12–14." *Bulletin for Biblical Research* 22, no. 2 (2012) 189–99.
Lessing, Gotthold Ephraim. "On the Proof of the Spirit and of Power." In *Lessing's Theological Writings: Selections in Translation*, translated by Henry Chadwick, 51–56. London: A. & C. Black, 1956.
Liniger-Goumaz, Max. *Historical Dictionary of Equatorial Guinea.* Metuchen, NJ: Scarecrow, 1979.
———. *Small Is Not Always Beautiful: The Story of Equatorial Guinea.* London: Hurst, 1988.
"List of Least Developed Countries (as of 16 February 2016)". *United Nations.* http://www.un.org/en/development/desa/policy/cdp/ldc/ldc_list.pdf.
"Literacy Rate, Adult Total (% of People Ages 15 and Above)—Country Ranking." *Index Mundi.* http://www.indexmundi.com/facts/indicators/SE.ADT.LITR.ZS/rankings.
Louw, D. J. "The HIV Pandemic from the Perspective of a *Theologia Resurrectionis*: Resurrection Hope as a Pastoral Critique on the Punishment and Stigma Paradigm." *Journal of Theology for Southern Africa* no. 126 (2006) 100–14.
Lowrie, John Cameron. *A Manual of Missions: Or, Sketches of the Foreign Missions of the Presbyterian Church; with Maps, Showing the Stations and Statistics of Protestant Missions among Unevangelized Nations.* New York: Randolph, 1854.
———. *A Manual of the Foreign Missions of the Presbyterian Church in the United States of America.* 3rd ed. New York: Rankin, 1868.
Lwendo, Habakuki Y. "The Significance of the Doctrine of Retribution in Old Testament Job for Pastoral Counselling in Aids." Master's thesis, School of Theology, University of Natal, Pietermaritzburg, 2000.
Magesa, Laurenti. *African Religion: The Moral Traditions of Abundant Life.* Maryknoll, NY: Orbis, 1997.
———. "The Present and Future of Inculturation in Eastern Africa." In *Inculturation: Abide by the Otherness of Africa and the Africans: Papers from a Congress (October 21–22, 1993, Heerlen, the Netherlands) at the Occasion of 100 Years SMA-Presence in the Netherlands*, 57–71. Kampen: Uitgeversmaatschappij J. H. Kok, 1994.
Mallart Guimera, Louis. *Ni Dos Ni Ventre: Religion, Magie et Sorcellerie Evuzok.* Paris: Société d'ethnographie, 1981.

Maluleke, Tinyiko Sam. "Black and African Theologies in the New World Order: A Time to Drink from Our Own Wells." *Journal of Theology for Southern Africa* no. 96 (November 1996) 3–19
———. "The Challenge of HIV/AIDS for Theological Education in Africa: Towards an HIV/AIDS Sensitive Curriculum." *Missionalia* 29, no. 2 (2001) 125–43.
———. "A Letter to Job—From Africa." *Tam Tam* 5 (October 1997) 5.
Mandryk, Jason. *Operation World*. 7th. ed. Colorado Springs: Biblica, 2010.
Mañe Ebo Asong, Alberto. "Misioneros Protestantes Presbiterianos Norteamericanos." Unpublished manuscript. Bata: Equatorial Guinea, n.d.
———. "Resumen Histórico de La Misión Protestante Presbiteriana en Guinea Ecuatorial." Unpublished manuscript. Bata: Equatorial Guinea, n.d.
Marshall-Fratani, Ruth. "Mediating the Global and Local in Nigerian Pentecostalism," in *Between Babel and Pentecost: Transnational Pentecostalism in Africa and Latin America*, ed. André Corten and Ruth Marshall-Fratani, 80–105. London: Hurst, 2001.
Martrou, L. "Les 'Eki' Des Mfang." *Anthropos* 1 (1906) 745–61.
Masenya, Madipoane J. "All from the Same Source? Deconstructing a (Male) Anthropocentric Reading of Job (3) through an Eco-Bosadi Lens." *Journal of Theology for Southern Africa* no. 137 (July 2010) 46–60.
———. "Between Unjust Suffering and the 'Silent' God: Job and HIV/AIDS Sufferers in South Africa." *Missionalia* 29, no. 2 (2001) 186–99.
———. "Her Appropriation of Job's Lament? Her-Lament of Job 3, From an African Story-Telling Perspective." In *Postcolonial Perspectives in African Biblical Interpretation*, edited by Musa W. Dube et al., 283–97. Atlanta: Society of Biblical Literature, 2012.
Masenya, Madipoane J., and Rodney Steven Sadler. "Job." In *The Africana Bible: Reading Israel's Scriptures from Africa and the African Diaspora*, edited by Hugh R. Page, 237–43. Minneapolis: Fortress, 2010.
Matthews, I. G. *The Religious Pilgrimage of Israel*. New York: Harper, 1947.
Maxwell, David. "'Delivered from the Spirit of Poverty?' Pentecostalism, Prosperity and Modernity in Zimbabwe." *Journal of Religion in Africa* 28, no. 3 (1998) 350–73.
———. "In Defence of African Creativity." Review of *African Christianity: Its Public Role*, by Paul Gifford. *Journal of Religion in Africa* 30, no. 4 (2000) 468–81.
———. "The Spirit and the Scapular: Pentecostal and Catholic Interactions in Northern Nyanga District, Zimbabwe in the 1950s and Early 1960s." *Journal of Southern African Studies* 23, no. 2 (1997) 283–300.
Mbana, Joaquin. *Brujeria Fang en Guinea Ecuatorial (El Mbwo)*. Madrid: SIAL Ediciones, 2004.
Mbiti, John S. *African Religions and Philosophy*. London: Heinemann, 1969.
———. "The Bible in African Culture." In *Paths of African Theology*, edited by Rosino Gibellini, 27–39. London: SCM, 1994.
———. "The Biblical Basis for Present Trends in African Theology." In *African Theology En Route: Papers from the Pan-African Conference of Third World Theologians, December 17–23, 1977, Accra, Ghana*, edited by Kofi Appiah-Kubi and Sergio Torres, 83–94. Maryknoll, NY: Orbis, 1979.
———. *Concepts of God in Africa*. London: SPCK, 1970.
———. "Eschatology." In *Biblical Revelation and African Beliefs*, edited by Kwesi A. Dickson and Paul Ellingworth, 159–84. London: Lutterworth, 1969.

———. "God, Sin, and Salvation in African Religion." *Journal of the Interdenominational Theological Center* 16, no. 1–2 (1989) 59–68.

———. *New Testament Eschatology in an African Background: A Study of the Encounter between New Testament Theology and African Traditional Concepts.* London: Oxford University Press, 1971.

———. *The Prayers of African Religion.* London: SPCK, 1975.

"McNeill Family Papers, 1918–1970." Presbyterian Historical Society. http://www.history.pcusa.org/collections/findingaids/fa.cfm?record_id=284.

McNeill, Lois Johnson. *Compilation of the First Half-Century of Mission Work in Rio Muni 1850–1900: The West African Mission of the Presbyterian Church in the U.S.A.* Swarthmore, PA: Unedited, 1972.

McSherry, Brendan. "The Political Economy of Oil in Equatorial Guinea." *African Studies Quarterly* 8, no. 3 (Spring 2006) 23–45.

Meadowcroft, Tim. "Relevance as a Mediating Category in the Reading of Biblical Texts: Venturing beyond the Hermeneutical Circle." *Journal of the Evangelical Theological Society* 45, no. 4 (2002) 611–27.

Merz, Johannes. "'I am a Witch in the Holy Spirit': Rupture and Continuity of Witchcraft Beliefs in African Christianity." *Missiology: An International Review* 36, no. 2 (2008) 201–18.

Mesters, Carlos. "The Use of the Bible in Christian Communities of the Common People." In *The Bible and Liberation: Political and Social Hermeneutics*, edited by Norman K. Gottwald and Richard A. Horsley, 3–16. Rev. ed. Maryknoll, NY: Orbis, 1993.

Meyer, Birgit. "Christianity in Africa: From African Independent to Pentecostal-Charismatic Churches." *Annual Review of Anthropology* 33 (2004) 447–74.

———. "'Delivered from the Powers of Darkness': Confessions of Satanic Riches in Christian Ghana." *Africa* 65, no. 2 (1995) 236–55.

———. "'If You Are a Devil, You Are a Witch And, If You Are a Witch, You Are a Devil.' The Integration of 'Pagan' Ideas into the Conceptual Universe of Ewe Christians in Southeastern Ghana." *Journal of Religion in Africa* 22, no. 2 (1992) 98–132.

———. "Pentecostalism and Neo-Liberal Capitalism: Faith, Prosperity and Vision in African Pentecostal-Charismatic Churches." *Journal for the Study of Religion* 20, no. 2 (2007) 5–28.

———. *Translating the Devil: An African Appropriation of Pietist Protestantism; the Case of the Peki Ewe in Southeastern Ghana, 1847–1992.* Amsterdam: Universiteit van Amsterdam, 1995.

———. *Translating the Devil: Religion and Modernity Among the Ewe in Ghana.* Trenton, NJ: Africa World, 1999.

Michael, Matthew. *Christian Theology and African Traditions.* Eugene, OR: Resource, 2013.

Mijoga, Hilary B. P. "Hermeneutics in African Instituted Churches in Malawi." *Missionalia* 24, no. 3 (1996) 358–71.

"The Millennium Development Goal Report 2010." *Millennium Development Goals Indicators.* http://mdgs.un.org/unsd/mdg/Resources/Static/Products/Progress2011/11-31339%20%28E%29%20MDG%20Report%202011_HR_4%20Addendum%20NEW.pdf.

Miller, Patrick D. *Sin and Judgment in the Prophets: A Stylistic and Theological Analysis.* Atlanta: Scholars, 1982.

"Ministerio de Sanidad y Bienestar Social de Guinea Ecuatorial. La Extensión de Diagnóstico Precoz de VIH, Barreras Y Facilitadores, Informe de Situación. Estudio ESEVIGUE. 1st Ed. Malabo: MINSABS." 2011.

Mligo, Elia Shabani. *Jesus and the Stigmatized: Reading the Gospel of John in a Context of HIV/AIDS-Related Stigmatization in Tanzania*. Eugene, OR: Pickwick Publications, 2011.

Moberly, R. W. L. "Preaching Christ from the Old Testament." In *"He Began with Moses . . .": Preaching the Old Testament Today*, edited by Grenville J. R. Kent et al., 233–50. Nottingham, UK: IVP, 2010.

Moffat, Robert. *Missionary Labours and Scenes in Southern Africa*. London: Snow, 1842.

Mohler, Al. *He Is Not Silent: Preaching in a Postmodern World*. Chicago: Moody, 2008.

Moreau, A. Scott. "Africa and the Future: An Analysis of John Mbiti's Concept of Time." In *Issues in African Christian Theology*, edited by Samuel Ngewa, et al., 306–20. Nairobi: East African Educational, 1998.

Morrow, Lance, et al. "Africa: The Scramble for Survival." *Time*, September 7, 1992.

Mosala, Itumeleng J. "Race, Class, and Gender as Hermeneutical Factors in the African Independent Churches' Appropriation of the Bible." *Semeia* 73 (1996) 43–57.

Mosupole, Augustine C. "Stigma and Discrimination: Job 3:1–26." In *AfricaPraying: A Handbook on HIV and AIDS, Sensitive Sermon Guidelines and Liturgy*, edited by Dube W. Musa, 125–27. Geneva: World Council of Churches, 2003.

Mudimbe, V. Y. *The Invention of Africa: Gnosis, Philosophy, and The Order of Knowledge*. Bloomington, IN: Indiana University Press, 1988.

Mukenge, André Kabasele. "Une Lecture Populaire de La Figure de Job Au Congo." *Bulletin for Old Testament Studies in Africa* no. 16 (May 1, 2004) 2–6.

Mvone-Ndong, Simon-Pierre Ezéchiel. *Imaginaire de la Maladie au Gabon: Approche Épistémologique*. Paris: L'Harmattan, 2007.

Mwombeki, Fidon. "Reading the Bible in Contemporary Africa." *Word & World* 21, no. 2 (2001) 121–28.

Nadar, Sarojini. "'Barak God and Die!' Women, HIV and a Theology of Suffering." In *Grant Me Justice!: HIV/AIDS & Gender Readings of the Bible*, edited by Musa W. Dube and Musimbi R. A. Kanyoro, 60–79. Maryknoll, NY: Orbis, 2004.

———. "Re-Reading Job in the Midst of Suffering in the HIV/AIDS Era: How Not to Talk of God." *Old Testament Essays* 16, no. 2 (2003) 343–57.

———. "Studying the Book of Job Part 1: Women and the Poor in HIV and AIDS Contexts." In *Studying the Hebrew Bible in HIV and AIDS Contexts*, 103–18. Theology in the HIV and AIDS Era Series: The HIV and AIDS Curriculum for TEE Programmes and Institutions in Africa Module 3. Geneva: World Council of Churches, 2007.

———. "Studying the Book of Job Part 2: Suffering, Stigma, and Discrimination in HIV and AIDS Contexts." In *Studying the Hebrew Bible in HIV and AIDS Contexts*, 119–36. Theology in the HIV and AIDS Era Series: The HIV and AIDS Curriculum for TEE Programmes and Institutions in Africa Module 3. Geneva: World Council of Churches, 2007.

Nassau, Robert Hamill. *Corisco Days: The First Thirty Years of the West African Mission*. Philadelphia: Allen, Lane and Scott, 1910.

———. *The Gabon and Corisco Missions*. New York: Presbyterian Board of Foreign Missions, 1873.

———. *My Ogowe: Being a Narrative of Daily Incidents During Sixteen Years in Equatorial West Africa*. New York: Neale, 1914.
Ndong Mbá Nnegue, Jesús. *Origen e Implantacion de La Iglesia Católica en Guinea Ecuatorial (1469–1883)*. Malabo: Guinea Ecuatorial, 2006.
Ndongo Mba-Nnegue, Jesús. *Los Fan: Cultura, Sociedad y Religión*. Madrid: J. Ndongo, 1985.
Ndung'u, Nahashon W. "The Role of the Bible in the Rise of African Instituted Churches: The Case of the Akurinu Churches in Kenya." In *The Bible in Africa: Transactions, Trajectories, and Trends*, edited by Gerald O. West and Musa W. Dube, 236–47. Leiden: Brill, 2001.
Neiman, Susan. *Evil in Modern Thought: An Alternative History of Philosophy*. Princeton: Princeton University Press, 2002.
Nelson, Alissa Jones. "Justice and Biblical Interpretation Beyond Subjectivity and Self-Determination: A Contrapuntal Reading on the Theme of Suffering in the Book of Job." *Political Theology* 11, no. 3 (2010) 431–52.
———. *Power and Responsibility in Biblical Interpretation: Reading the Book of Job with Edward Said*. Sheffield, UK: Equinox, 2012.
Nerín, Gustau. "El Barco de las Chinas en Guinea Ecuatorial: Entre la Leyenda Urbana y el Culto Cargo." *ORÁFRICA: Revista de Oralidad Africana* 4 (April 2008) 129–36.
Ngong, David Tonghou. *The Holy Spirit and Salvation in African Christian Theology: Imagining a More Hopeful Future for Africa*. New York: Lang, 2010.
———. "Reading the Bible in Africa: A Critique of Enchanted Bible Reading." *Exchange* 43 (2014) 174–91.
———. "Salvation and Materialism in African Theology." *Studies in World Christianity* 15, no. 1 (2009) 1–21.
———. "Theology as the Construction of Piety: A Critique of the Theology of Inculturation and the Pentecostalization of African Christianity." *Journal of Pentecostal Theology* 21, no. 2 (2012) 344–62.
Ntreh, Benjamin Abotchie. "Job." In *Global Bible Commentary*, edited by Daniel Patte, 141–50. Nashville: Abingdon, 2004.
Nyamiti, Charles. "The Doctrine of God." In *A Reader in African Christian Theology*, edited by John Parratt, 58–68. London: SPCK, 1987.
Obeta, Julius Sunday. "Eschatological Concepts in Job." PhD diss., University of Nigeria, 2000.
Ocha'a Mve Bengobesama, Constantino. *Tradiciones del Pueblo Fang*. Madrid: RIALP, S.A., 1981.
Oduyoye, Mercy Amba. *Hearing and Knowing: Theological Reflections on Christianity in Africa*. Maryknoll, NY: Orbis, 1986.
Okpewho, Isidore. *African Oral Literature: Backgrounds, Character, and Continuity*. Bloomington, IN: Indiana University Press, 1992.
Omenyo, Cephas. "From the Fringes to the Centre: Pentecostalization of the Mainline Churches in Ghana." *Exchange* 34, no. 1 (2005) 39–60.
———. "William Seymour and African Pentecostal Historiography: The Case of Ghana." *Asian Journal of Pentecostal Studies* 9, no. 2 (2006) 244–58.
Ondo Mangue, Florencio. "El Culto a los Ancestros de los Fang." *Atanga*, October 2010, 32–35.
Onyinah, Opoku. "Akan Witchcraft and the Concept of Exorcism in the Church of Pentecost." PhD diss., University of Birmingham, 2002.

———. "Deliverance as a Way of Confronting Witchcraft in Modern Africa: Ghana as a Case History." *Asian Journal of Pentecostal Studies* 5, no. 1 (2002) 107–34.

p'Bitek, Okot. *African Religions in Western Scholarship*. Kampala: East African Literature Bureau, 1970.

———. *Religion of the Central Luo*. Nairobi: East African Literature Bureau, 1971.

Parkin, David J. "Entitling Evil: Muslims and Non-Muslims in Coastal Kenya." In *The Anthropology of Evil*, edited by David J. Parkin, 224–43. Oxford: Blackwell, 1985.

———, ed. *The Anthropology of Evil*. Oxford: Blackwell, 1985.

Parrinder, Geoffrey. *African Traditional Religion*. 3rd ed. Westport, CT: Greenwood, 1976.

———. *West African Religion: Illustrated from the Beliefs and Practices of the Yoruba, Ewe, Akan and Kindred Peoples*. London: Epworth, 1949.

Pawlikowski, John T. "The Judaic Spirit of the Ethiopian Orthodox Church: A Case Study in Religious Acculturation." *Journal of Religion in Africa* 4, no. 3 (1971) 178–99.

Payne, Leanne. *The Healing Presence: How God's Grace Can Work in You to Bring Healing in Your Broken Places and the Joy of Living in His Love*. Westchester, IL: Crossway, 1989.

Peel, J. D. Y. *Religious Encounter and the Making of the Yoruba*. Bloomington, IN: Indiana University Press, 2000.

Pélissier, René. "Autopsy of a Miracle." *Africa Report* 25, no. 3 (June 1980) 10–14.

———. "Spain Changes Course in Africa." *Africa Report* 8, no. 11 (December 1963) 8–11.

Peterson, Eugene H. *Five Smooth Stones for Pastoral Work*. New ed. Grand Rapids: Eerdmans, 1992.

Pfeiffer, Robert H. *Introduction to the Old Testament*. Rev. ed. New York: Harper, 1948.

Phillips, Clifton Jackson. *Protestant America and the Pagan World: The First Half Century of the American Board of Commissioners for Foreign Missions, 1810–1860*. Cambridge: East Asian Research Center, Harvard University Press, 1969.

Pierce, Allen, et al. "Findings of Church Language Use, Based on Socio-Linguistic Survey for the Languages of Equatorial Guinea." Bata, Equatorial Guinea: Unpublished report, November 1996.

Pobee, John S. *Toward an African Theology*. Nashville: Abingdon, 1979.

Pope, Marvin H. *Job: Introduction, Translation, and Notes*. 3rd ed. Garden City, NY: Doubleday, 1973.

Pujadas, Tomas L. *La Iglesia En La Guinea Ecuatorial: Fernando Poo*. Vol. 1. Madrid: Iris de Paz, 1968.

———. *La Iglesia En La Guinea Ecuatorial: Rio Muni*. Vol. 2. Barcelona: Editorial Claret, 1983.

"Quarterly Economic Review of Congo, Gabon, Equatorial Guinea." *The Economist Intelligence Unit* (1985).

Quinn, Frederick. "The Desert People, 250 to 500, Coptic Church, Egypt." *Dictionary of African Christian Biography*. http://www.dacb.org/stories/egypt/desert_people.html.

Rabat Makambo, Práxedes. "Estudio Preliminar." In *Costumbres Bengas y de los Pueblos Vecinos: Mbangwe-Corisco, 1872*, 3–33. s.l.: s.n., n.d.

"Reformed Presbyterian Church of Equatorial Guinea." *World Council of Churches*. http://www.oikoumene.org/member-churches/regions/africa/equatorial-guinea/reformed-presbyterian-church-of-equatorial-guinea.html.

Riches, John. "Interpreting the Bible in African Contexts: Glasgow Consultation." *Semeia* 73 (1996) 181–88.

Robinson, Haddon W. *Biblical Preaching: The Development and Delivery of Expository Messages*. 2nd ed. Grand Rapids: Baker Academic, 2001.

Rodríguez, Carmen, et al. "The Pertinence of Applying Qualitative Investigation Strategies in the Design and Evaluation of HIV Prevention Policies." In *Recent Translational Research in HIV/AIDS*, edited by Yi-Wei Tang. Vol. 2. Open Access Book: InTech, 2011.

Roe, Henry. *Fernando Po Mission: A Consecutive History of the Opening of Our First Mission to the Heathen, with Notes on Christian African Settlers, African Scenery, Missionary Trials and Joys*. London: Woburn Sands, 1882.

Ross, Kenneth R. "Preaching in Mainstream Christian Churches in Malawi: A Survey and Analysis." *Journal of Religion in Africa* 25, no. 1 (1995) 3–24.

———. "The Theology of Hope: A Missing Link in Africa Christianity?" *Africa Theological Journal* 19, no. 3 (1990) 197–211.

Roth, John K. "A Theodicy of Protest." In *Encountering Evil: Live Options in Theodicy*, edited by Stephen T. Davis, 1–20. Louisville, KY: Westminster John Knox, 2001.

Rowlands, Michael, and Jean-Pierre Warnier. "Sorcery, Power and the Modern State in Cameroon." *Man* 23, no. 1 (1988) 118–32.

Rowley, H. H. "The Book of Job and Its Meaning." In *From Moses to Qumran: Studies in the Old Testament*, 141–86. London: Lutterworth, 1963.

Ryan, Charles. "AIDS and Responsibility." In *Reflecting Theologically on AIDS: A Global Challenge*, edited by Robin Gill, 60–76. London: SCM, 2007.

Sadgrove, Jo. "'Keeping Up Appearances': Sex and Religion amongst University Students in Uganda." *Journal of Religion in Africa* 37, no. 1 (2007) 116–44.

Sanneh, Lamin. *Summoned from the Margin: Homecoming of an African*. Grand Rapids: Eerdmans, 2012.

Shankar, Shobana. "Medical Missionaries and Modernizing Emirs in Colonial Hausaland: Leprosy Control and Native Authority in the 1930s." *The Journal of African History* 48, no. 1 (2007) 45–68.

Shaw, Rosalind. "The Invention of 'African Traditional Religion.'" *Religion* 20, no. 4 (1990) 339–53.

Shenk, Calvin E. "The Ethiopian Orthodox Church: A Study in Indigenization." *Missiology* 16, no. 3 (1988) 259–78.

Shorter, Aylward. *Jesus and the Witchdoctor: An Approach to Healing and Wholeness*. Maryknoll, NY: Orbis, 1985.

Silla, Eric. *People Are Not the Same: Leprosy and Identity in Twentieth-Century Mali*. Oxford: Currey, 1998.

"Sixty Killed in Equatorial Guinea Plane Crash." *The Sydney Morning Herald*, July 18, 2005. http://www.smh.com.au/news/world/sixty-killed-in-equatorial-guinea-plane-crash/2005/07/18/1121538897104.html.

Soelle, Dorothee. *Suffering*. Translated by Everett R. Kalin. London: Darton, Longman and Todd, 1975.

Stanley, Brian. *The History of the Baptist Missionary Society, 1792–1992*. Edinburgh: T. & T. Clark, 1992.

———. "Inculturation: Historical Background, Theological Foundations and Contemporary Questions." *Transformation* 24, no. 1 (2007) 21–27.
"The State of the World's Children 2009: Maternal and Newborn Health." UNICEF. http://www.unicef.org/sowc09/docs/SOWC09-FullReport-EN.pdf.
Stetzer, Ed. "David and Goliath: Christ-Centered Preaching." *Christianity Today*, July 1, 2013. http://www.christianitytoday.com/edstetzer/2013/july/david-and-goliath-christ-centered-preaching.html.
Stiebert, Johanna. "Does the Hebrew Bible Have Anything to Tell Us About HIV/AIDS?" *Missionalia* 29, no. 2 (2001) 174–85.
Stinton, Diane B. "Jesus as Healer: Reflections on Religion and Health in East Africa Today." In *Religion and Health in Africa: Reflections for Theology in the 21st Century*, edited by Adam K. A. Chepkwony, 13–35. Nairobi: Paulines Publications Africa, 2006.
———. *Jesus of Africa: Voices of Contemporary African Christology*. Maryknoll, NY: Orbis, 2004.
Sugirtharajah, R. S. *The Bible and the Third World: Precolonial, Colonial, and Postcolonial Encounters*. Cambridge: Cambridge University Press, 2001.
Sundiata, Ibrahim K. *From Slaving to Neoslavery: The Bight of Biafra and Fernando Po in the Era of Abolition, 1827–1930*. Madison: University of Wisconsin Press, 1996.
———. "The Roots of African Despotism: The Question of Political Culture." *African Studies Review* 31, no. 1 (1988) 9–32.
Sundkler, Bengt. *Bantu Prophets in South Africa*. London: Lutterworth, 1948.
Surin, Kenneth. "Theodicy?" *The Harvard Theological Review* 76, no. 2 (1983) 225–47.
———. *Theology and the Problem of Evil*. Oxford: Blackwell, 1986.
Tamez, Elsa. "A Letter to Job." In *New Eyes for Reading: Biblical and Theological Reflections by Women from the Third World*, edited by John S. Pobee and Barbel von Wartenberg-Potter, 50–52. Geneva: World Council of Churches, 1986.
Taylor, John V. *The Growth of the Church in Buganda: An Attempt at Understanding*. London: SCM, 1958.
———. *The Primal Vision: Christian Presence amid African Religion*. London: SCM, 1963.
———. *Processes of Growth in an African Church*. I.M.C. Research Pamphlets no.6. London: SCM, 1958.
Tengia-Kessy, A., et al. "Assessment of Behavioural Risk Factors Associated with HIV Infection among Youth in Moshi Rural District, Tanzania." *East African Medical Journal* 75, no. 9 (1998) 528–32.
Tennent, Timothy C. *Theology in the Context of World Christianity: How the Global Church Is Influencing the Way We Think About and Discuss Theology*. Grand Rapids: Zondervan, 2007.
Terrien, Samuel L. *Job: Poet of Existence*. Indianapolis: Bobbs-Merrill, 1957.
———. "The Yahweh Speeches and Job's Responses." *Review & Expositor* 68, no. 4 (1971) 497–509.
Tessman, Günter. *Los Pamues (Los Fang): Monografía Etnológica de Una Rama de Las Tribus Negras Del África Occidental*. Edited by José Manuel Pedrosa. Translated by Erika Reuss Galindo. 2 vols. Spanish Translation of *Die Pangwe. Völkerkundliche Monographie Eines Westafrikanischen Negerstammes* (Berlin: Ernst Wasmut, 1913). Alcalá, Spain: Universidad de Alcalá, 2003.

Thorne, Alec. *God at Work in Spanish Guinea.* London: Evangelical Publishing House, 1943.
Ticciati, Susannah. "Does Job Fear God for Naught?" *Modern Theology* 21, no. 3 (2005) 353–66.
———. *Job and the Disruption of Identity: Reading beyond Barth.* London: T. & T. Clark International, 2005.
"Treatment of Children Living with HIV." *World Health Organization.* http://www.who.int/hiv/topics/paediatric/hiv-paediatric-infopage/en/.
Tsevat, Matitiahu. "The Meaning of the Book of Job." *Hebrew Union College Annual* 37 (1966) 73–106.
Tshikendwa Matadi, Ghislain. "How Long, O Lord!" In *AIDS in Africa: Theological Reflections,* edited by Bénézet Bujo and Michael Czerny, 31–42. Nairobi: Paulines Publications Africa, 2007.
———. *Suffering, Belief, Hope: The Wisdom of Job for an AIDS-Stricken Africa.* Translated by Joseph P. Newman and Robert S. Czerny. Nairobi: Paulines Publications Africa, 2007.
Turner, Harold W. "The Primal Religions of the World and Their Study." In *Australian Essays in World Religions,* edited by Victor C. Hayes, 27–37. Bedford Park, South Africa: Australian Association for the Study of Religions, 1977.
———. *Profile Through Preaching.* London: Edinburgh House, 1965.
———. *Religious Innovation in Africa: Collected Essays on New Religious Movements.* Boston: Hall, 1979.
Tyrrell, George. *Christianity at the Cross-Roads.* London: Longman Green, 1910.
Ukpong, Justin S. "Developments in Biblical Interpretation in Africa: Historical and Hermeneutical Directions." In *The Bible in Africa: Transactions, Trajectories, and Trends,* edited by Gerald O. West and Musa W. Dube, 11–28. Leiden: Brill, 2001.
———. "Popular Readings of the Bible in Africa and Implications for Academic Readings: Report on the Field Research Carried out on Oral Interpretation of the Bible in Port Harcourt Metropolis, Nigeria under the Auspices of the Bible in Africa Project, 1991–1994." In *The Bible in Africa: Transactions, Trajectories, and Trends,* edited by Gerald O. West and Musa W. Dube, 582–94. Leiden: Brill, 2001.
———. "Rereading the Bible with African Eyes: Inculturation and Hermeneutics." *Journal of Theology for Southern Africa* no. 91 (1995) 3–14.
"UNAIDS: How AIDS Changed Everything, 2015." *UNAIDS.* http://www.unaids.org/sites/default/files/media_asset/MDG6Report_en.pdf.
Van Dijk, Rijk. "Witchcraft and Scepticism by Proxy: Pentecostalism and Laughter in Urban Malawi." In *Magical Interpretations, Material Realities: Modernity, Witchcraft and the Occult in Postcolonial Africa,* edited by Henrietta L. Moore and Todd Sanders, 97–117. London: Routledge, 2001.
Van Dyk, P. J. "The Tale of Two Tragedies: The Book of Job and HIV/AIDS in Africa." *Bulletin for Old Testament Studies in Africa* 16 (2004) 7–13.
Varkevisser, Corlien M., et al. "Gender and Leprosy: Case Studies in Indonesia, Nigeria, Nepal and Brazil." *Leprosy Review* 80, no. 1 (2009) 65–76.
Wagenaar, Hinne. "Theology, Identity and the Pre-Christian Past: A Critical Analysis of Dr. K. Bediako's Theology from a Frisian Perspective." *International Review of Mission* 88, no. 351 (1999) 364–380.
Walls, Andrew F. "African Christianity in the History of Religions." *Studies in World Christianity* 2, no. 2 (1996) 183–203.

———. "Christian Scholarship in Africa in the Twenty-First Century." *Transformation* 19, no. 4 (October 2002) 217–28.

———. "Eusebius Tries Again: Reconceiving the Study of Christian History." *International Bulletin of Missionary Research* 24, no. 3 (2000) 105–11.

———. *The Missionary Movement in Christian History: Studies in the Transmission of Faith*. Maryknoll, NY: Orbis, 1996.

———. "Structural Problems in Mission Studies." *International Bulletin of Missionary Research* 15, no. 4 (1991) 146–55.

———. "Worldviews and Christian Conversion." In *Mission in Context: Explorations Inspired by J. Andrew Kirk*, edited by John Corrie and Cathy Ross, 155–65. Farnham, UK: Ashgate, 2012.

Wendland, Ernst R. "The Foundation of Religious Belief: Key Aspects of the Chewa and Tonga World-View." In *Bridging the Gap: African Traditional Religion and Bible Translation*, edited by Philip C. Stine, 65–129. Reading, UK: United Bible Societies, 1990.

"The Wesleyan Church." http://www.wesleyan.org/about.

West, Gerald O. "1 & 2 Samuel." In *Global Bible Commentary*, edited by Daniel Patte, 92–104. Nashville: Abingdon, 2004.

———. *The Academy of the Poor: Towards a Dialogical Reading of the Bible*. Pietermaritzburg: Cluster, 2003.

———. "(Ac)claiming the (Extra)ordinary African 'Reader' of the Bible." In *Reading Other-Wise: Socially Engaged Biblical Scholars Reading with Their Local Communities*, edited by Gerald O. West, 29–47. Atlanta: Society of Biblical Literature, 2007.

———. "The Bible as Bola: Among the Foundations of African Biblical Apprehensions." *Journal of Theology for Southern Africa* no. 112 (2002) 23–37.

———. "Biblical Hermeneutics in Africa." In *African Theology on the Way: Current Conversations*, edited by Diane B. Stinton, 21–31. London: SPCK, 2010.

———. "Hearing Job's Wife: Towards a Feminist Reading of Job." *Old Testament Essays* 4, no. 1 (1991) 107–31.

———. "Mapping African Biblical Interpretation: A Tentative Sketch." In *The Bible in Africa: Transactions, Trajectories, and Trends*, edited by Musa W. Dube and Gerald O. West, 29–53. Leiden: Brill, 2001.

———. "The Poetry of Job as a Resource for the Articulation of Embodied Lament in the Context of HIV and AIDS in South Africa." In *Lamentations in Ancient and Contemporary Contexts*, edited by Nancy C. Lee and Carleen Mandolfo, 195–214. Atlanta: Society of Biblical Literature, 2008.

———. "Reading the Bible in the Light of HIV/AIDS in South Africa." *Ecumenical Review* 55, no. 4 (2003) 335–44.

West, Gerald O., and Bongi Zengele. "Reading Job 'Positively' in the Context of HIV/AIDS in South Africa." *Concilium* 4 (2004) 112–24.

West, Gerald O., and Musa W. Dube, eds. *The Bible in Africa: Transactions, Trajectories, and Trends*. Leiden: Brill, 2001.

Westerlund, David. "Pluralism and Change. A Comparative and Historical Approach to African Disease Etiologies." In *Culture, Experience and Pluralism: Essays on African Ideas of Illness and Healing*, edited by Anita Jacobson-Widding and David Westerlund, 177–218. Uppsala: Uppsala University, 1989.

Westermann, Claus. "Role of the Lament in the Theology of the Old Testament." *Interpretation* 28, no. 1 (1974) 20–38.

———. *The Structure of the Book of Job: A Form-Critical Analysis*. Philadelphia: Fortress, 1981.

Wijsen, Frans. "Popular Christianity in East Africa: Inculturation or Syncretism?" *Exchange* 29, no. 1 (2000) 37–60.

Williams, James G. "'You Have Not Spoken Truth of Me': Mystery and Irony in Job." *Zeitschrift Für Die Alttestamentliche Wissenschaft* 83, no. 2 (1971) 231–55.

Wittenberg, Gunther H. "Counselling Aids Patients: Job as a Paradigm." *Journal of Theology for Southern Africa* no. 88 (1994) 61–68.

Wolfers, David. *Deep Things Out of Darkness: The Book of Job, Essays and a New English Translation*. Kampen: Kok Pharos, 1995.

Wong, Ka Leung. *The Idea of Retribution in the Book of Ezekiel*. Leiden: Brill, 2001.

"The World Factbook: Equatorial Guinea." *Central Intelligence Agency*. https://www.cia.gov/library/publications/the-world-factbook/fields/2075.html.

"The World Factbook: Country Comparison, HIV/AIDS—Adult Prevalence Rate." *Central Intelligence Agency*. https://www.cia.gov/library/publications/the-world-factbook/rankorder/2155rank.html.

Wood, Geoffrey. "Business and Politics in a Criminal State: The Case of Equatorial Guinea." *African Affairs* 103, no. 413 (2004) 547–67.

"World Population Prospects, The 2010 Revision: Volume 1: Comprehensive Tables." United Nations. New York 2011. http://esa.un.org/unpd/wpp/Documentation/pdf/WPP2010_Volume-I_Comprehensive-Tables.pdf.

Wright, Christopher J. H., et al. "Lausanne Theology Working Group Statement on the Prosperity Gospel." *Evangelical Review of Theology* 34, no. 2 (2010) 99–102.

Young, Frances M. *Art of Performance: Towards a Theology of Holy Scripture*. 1st ed. London: Darton, Longman & Todd, 1990.

Zink, James K. "Impatient Job: An Interpretation of Job 19:25–27." *Journal of Biblical Literature* 84, no. 2 (1965) 147–52.

Index

A'Bodjedi, Enènge, 81–82
abók misémm (Fang dance of/against sins), 51
abundant life theology
　African theodicy and, 123–27
　centrality in Fang culture of, 71–74
　Fang Pentecostal theodicy and, 158–59
　normalization of suffering and destabilization of, 160–62
Ackermann, Denise, 169, 190–91, 199–201
Acolatse, Esther, 252
Adamo, David t., 22
ádzémé awú (celebration of death), 54–55
Africa, morbidity and mortality statistics for, 31
African Bible Commentary, 14
African Christianity
　Christian Scripture use in, 238–44
　Christological hermeneutics and, 222–26
　critique of spirituality in, 210–21
　culture and, 19–22
　Deus Victor paradigm and, 227–35
　eschatological orientation in, 205–9
　Fang cosmological mapping of universe and, 127–38
　Hebrew narratives and, 26–30
　hermeneutics-culture-praxis triad in, 15–25, 237–38
　independence movement and role of, 85–88
　indigenization and diabolization in, 237–53
　interpretations of Job in, 1–2
　readings of Book of Job by, 13–35
　rise pentecostalism in, 90–91
　scope of study of, 6–7
　suffering and sickness in, 22, 30–32
　theodicy in, 117–19, 121–27
　theology of hope in, 204–5
　traditional cultural synthesis with, 96–99
African Christianity: Its Public Role (Gifford), 102
African cosmology
　Bible study and role of, 21–22
　causality in, 32–34
　in Fang culture, 57
　sickness and health in, 70–71
African Cup of Nations (football), 102
African extraversion, 104–5
African Indigenous Churches (AICs), 8–10. *See also* indigenous religiosity
　affinity for Judaism in, 26–30
　founding story of, 92
　Malawian exegesis in, 24
　Pentecostalization and theodicy in, 154–59
　Pentecostal movement and, 110–12
African Inland Mission (AIM), 206
Africanization process, 144
　indigenous cosmology and, 133–34
African religiosity, cultural roots of, 20–21
African Union Summit, 102
Afri Kara (mythical patriarch of Africa), 48–49
afterlife, in Fang Christianity, 210–21
agency in African Christianity
　Fang evangelization and, 82–83
　indigenous autonomy and, 7, 101–5

289

agency in African Christianity
    (continued)
    Pentecostalism in Equatorial Guinea
        and, 100–112
    social-human agency of witchcraft
        and, 68–69
*AIDS in the Twenty-First Century:
    Disease and Globalization*
    (Barnett and Whiteside), 191
Akamba culture, 206–7
akomnge (prepared/initiated people),
    63–66
Akrong, Abraham, 156, 246, 252
Akurinu African Indigenous Church,
    27n.67
akwann misémm (sicknesses of sin), 49,
    68–71k
Alar Ayong movement, 49
Alexandre, Pierre, 58
Alliance of Religions and Conservation
    (ARC), 88
All Nations for Christ Bible Institute, 92
Amin, Idi, 37
ancestor rituals in Fang culture
    Biéri ancestral ritual, 54–58
    disease etiology and, 67–71
    Pentecostal eschatology and, 216–21
Andekĕ ya Injĭnji, 80–81
Anderson, Allan, 245, 251–52
Anglican Church, mission in Buganda
    of, 85–88
Annabón, 38–40
anti-witchcraft cults. *See* Nguí (Fang
    anti-witchcraft cult)
Anum, Eric, 21n.38
application, in African Bible study,
    18–19, 238–44
Aquinas, St. Thomas, 205
Arden, Donald S., 71
Asamoah-Gyadu, J. Kwabena, 222,
    245–46
Assemblies of God, 91n.74
Assembly of the Holy Spirit (Asamblea
    del Espíritu Santo), 9, 100–112
    deliverance ministry of, 154
    Devil narrative in, 148–50
    eschatology in preaching at, 212–21
    external agency and indigenous
        autonomy and, 101–5
    hermeneutic interpretations of, in
        Equatorial Guinea, 139–41
    prayer in, 229–35
    prophetic seminars held by, 105–9
    readings of Book of Job in, 264
Association of Evangelical and
    Pentecostal Churches of
    Equatorial Guinea, 9
asumir (acceptance of responsibility),
    for HIV/AIDS patients, 187–89
Asumu, Damián Ángel, 91–99, 103–4,
    112–13
Asumu, Manuel Nzôh, 134n.42
Awono Akara, Manuel, 89, 133–34

Balentine, Samuel, 205
Baptist Missionary Society, 77–82
Barnett, Tony, 191
Barton, John, 24n.54
Bata Prison, 43
Baudin, Noël, 32–33, 66–67
Bayart, Jean-François, 103
BEAC (Banque des etats de l'Afrique
    central) French monetary zone,
    44–45
Bediako, Kwame, 13, 15n.10, 223, 244,
    248
Bennett, W. H., 171
Berlin Conference (1884-85), 38
Bevans, Stephen B., 2
biang (eye medicine), 59
Bible study
    in African Christianity, 6–7, 13–15,
        238–44
    African culture and, 19–22
    African hermeneutics and, 15–19
    HIV/AIDS discourse and, 192–96
    indigenous equivalents for Satan
        and, 137–38
The Bible in Africa (West and Dube), 14
biblical interpretation in African
    Christianity, role of narrative in,
    27–30
Biéri ancestral ritual, 49–50, 54–58
    Fang cosmological mapping of
        universe and, 129–31

Pentecostal eschatology and, 216–21
Bildad (friend of Job), 56–57
    dialog with Job, 165, 167–69
    retribution doctrine and, 170–73
Binet, Jacques, 58
Bioko. *See* Fernando Po
biyem (witches), 63–66
blame and accusation
    disease etiology and, 67–71
    in Fang witchcraft culture, 61–66
"bola" (Botswana witchcraft), Bible
    mistaken for, 21–22, 22n.45, 239
Bosch, David, 137, 153–54
Brazilian Catholicism, 23
Brueggemann, Walter, 199–201
Buber, Martin, 170n.14
Burnett, David, 33

cacao plantations, 39–44
Calvin, John, 126–27
Cameroon
    Fang culture in, 132n.37
    indigenous Christian migrants
        from, 83, 100
causality
    in African cosmologies, 32–34
    African theodicy and, 123–27
    diabolization of indigenous
        religiosity and, 251–53
    Fang cosmological mapping of
        universe and, 129–38
    normalization of suffering and,
        160–62
    Pentecostalization and theodicy and,
        153–59
    Pentecostalization and theodicy in
        relation to, 154–59
    prayer and, 229–35, 240–44
    Presbyterian Image of God and,
        142–50
    retribution and, 33–34, 170–73
    sickness and health in Fang culture
        and, 52–53, 66–71
    suffering in Fang culture and, 71–74
centralization, of missions in Africa,
    85–88
Charismatic church
    prosperity gospel in, 22n.45
    role of Devil in, 30n.75
chequeos (check-ups), in deliverance
    ministries, 154–59
Chinese pharmacies, 68, 96
Christianity, global demographics of,
    15–19
Christological hermeneutics, hope
    theology and, 222
Claretian order, 82–83
Clement of Rome, 205
clericalism, missions in Africa and,
    85–88
Clines, David, 33
colonialism
    African Christianity and, 75–76
    in Equatorial Guinea, 37–44
    Fang cosmological mapping of
        universe and, 129–38
    Fang culture and, 48–49
    Fang Nguí anti-witchcraft cult and,
        59–60
    inculturation theology and, 244–46
    post-colonial rise of independent
        churches and, 90
    Reform Presbyterian Church
        struggle against, 84–88
communication of ideas, oral narration
    and, 29–30
communities of disciples, African
    Christians as, 23–25
community
    Biéri cult and acquisition of, 54–58
    Fang social classifications in, 63–66
    sickness and, in Fang culture, 52–53
contextuality
    African Christianity and, 2
    Bible study and, 17–19
    Job figure in reader-centered
        hermeneutics and, 138–41
    of live objects, theodicy and, 153–62
conversion, deliverance ministry and,
    94–99
Corisco
    map of, 78
    Reformed Presbyterian Church on,
        77–82

cosmology
    Devil in Fang witchcraft narrative and, 147–50
    Job figure in, 141–42
    mapping of universe in Fang cosmology, 127–38
    parameters of African theodicy in context of, 123–27, 162–64
    retribution doctrine and, 171–73
"The Costly Loss of Lament" (Brueggemann), 199–201
Costumbres Bengas y de los Pueblos Vecinos, 81
Council of Evangelical Churches of Equatorial Guinea, 8–10
Cox, Harvey, 91
Cox, James L., 125n.16, 248–49
Craig, William Lane, 139
cross-cultural partnerships, African Christianity and, 103–5
Cruzada churches, 77–82, 87–88
culture
    in African Christianity, 19–22
    comparisons of African and ancient Israel cultures, 242–44
    deliverance ministries and boundaries of, 97–99
    Fang Biéri ancestral ritual and procurement of, 54–58
    Fang indigenous beliefs and practices, 46–73
    of Fang people, 36
    hermeneutics-culture-praxis triad and, 16
    official *vs.* popular inculturation debate and, 131–32
    orality and story-telling in, 29–30
    theodicy in Africa and, 117–19
curanderías (traditional healing places), 89, 96, 98–99
    deaths of priests at, 133
    for HIV/AIDS patients, 186–89
    indigenous suspicion of, 133–34, 158–59
    Pentecostalism and, 155–59

Dar es Salaam Ecumenical Dialogue of Third World Theologians, 207

deble (Fang Satan figure), 137
deity, African theodicy and focus on, 123–27
deliverance ministry
    Esono's "Pentecostal Deliverance Liturgy" of, 255–61
    Fang cosmology and, 137–38, 247–50
    HIV/AIDS in, 189n.88
    of Joy of My Salvation Church and, 93–99
    liturgy of, 110–12
demonic expulsion, deliverance ministry and, 94–99
despair, internalization in leprosy patients of, 179–84
Deus Victor paradigm
    African Christian appropriation of, 239–44
    hope theology and, 204, 221–26
    prayer and, 4, 226–35
Deuteronomy, retribution doctrine and, 170n.15
Devil
    diabolization of indigenous practices and, 250
    embodiment of, in Pentecostal churches, 73, 98–99, 135–38, 156–59
    Fang witchcraft and narrative of, 147–50
    Job's struggle between God and, 117–19, 138–53
    in Presbyterian causality, 142–50
    theologized God and narrative of, 150–53, 241–44
diabolization
    in African Christianity, 237–53
    consequences of, 250–53
    indigenous religiosity and, 246–50
Dickson, Kwesi A., 27
disease etiology
    in Fang culture, 49–53, 66–71
    typology in Africa of, 67–68
disengagement of missionary churches, independence movement and, 85–88

divine-human partnership, *Deus Victor* paradigm and, 226–35
divine punishment
　HIV/AIDS as, 190–96
　leprosy as, 173–79
divine sovereignty of God, 232–35
"Does the Hebrew Bible Have Anything to Tell Us about HIV/AIDS?" (Stiebert), 192
double exogamy, Fang practice of, 51
Dube, Musa W., 14, 189–90, 192n.102
Dulu Bon be Afri Kara (The Journey of the Children of Afri Kara), 49–50

ecclesial ethnography, 8–10
ecclesial praxis, hermeneutics-culture-praxis triad and, 16, 22–25
economic conditions
　in Equatorial Guinea, 37–45
　Pentecostal church and influence of, 208–9
　prevalence of HIV/AIDS and, 191–96
　prosperity gospel focus on, 107–9
ecumenical partnerships i, in Equatorial Africa, 87–88
education
　Catholic baptism as access to, 39–40, 131–32
　Macías dictatorship and decline of, 42–44
ekí (prohibitions or taboos), disease typology in Fang culture and, 68–71
Ekong form of witchcraft, 107n.131, 152n.91
Eliphaz (friend of Job), 56–57
　dialogged with Job, 165, 167–69
　retribution doctrine and, 170–73
elite in African society, independence movement and, 85
Emvelo, Gustavo, 84
Engelke, Matthew, 138n.53
Engutu, Ondoua, 49n.63
epistemology, orality in Africa of, 28–30
Equatorial Guinea
　contextual theology in, 2
　HIV/AIDS in, 169, 191–96
　Macías dictatorship in, 37, 40–43
　map of, 38, 78
　oil industry in, 44
　Pentecostalism in, 90–100
　prayer in churches of, 229–35
　Protestant denominations in, 3–4, 8–10
　reading locations for Book of Job in, 262–66
　rise of national identity in, 84–88
　silence about HIV/AIDS in, 189–96
　socio-political history of, 37–45
　stereotypes of Christianity in, 76n.5
eschatology
　in African Christianity, 205–9
　hope theology and, 204–5
　Job Chapter 19 as case study in, 210–21
Esono, Agustín Edu, 9, 101, 105, 111, 154
　"Pentecostal Deliverance Liturgy" of, 255–61
Èsù (Yoruban Satan figure), 137
Ethiopian orthodox church, 26n.66
Evangelical Presbyterian Church (Ghana), 133–34
Evans-Pritchard, Hugh, 70, 151
evil
　African Christianity and focus on, 125–27
　Fang Christianity and concepts of, 4
　leprosy as punishment for, 175–79
　Pentecostalization and theodicy concerning, 153–59
　theodicy and nature of, 117–64
　theologized God and narrated Devil and, 151–53
　in Western theodicy, 120–21
evus (witchcraft entity)
　as apotheosis of evil, 126–27
　appearance of, 59–60
　deliverance ministry and, 93–99
　disease etiology and, 69–71
　healing ministry of Pentecostalism and, 95–99
　leprosy linked to, 175–79

INDEX

evus (witchcraft entity) *(continued)*
  Mbwo (witchcraft) dynamics and, 60–66
  sickness and healing in Fang culture and, 146
Ewe culture
  Devil in, 150–51
  Evangelical Presbyterian Church and, 133–34
  Legba in, 137
external networks, African Christianity and role of, 101–5
eyima Biéri (Biéri figure), 54

Fang culture
  abundant life and presence of suffering in, 71–74
  biblical text interpretation in, 238–44
  contextualization of theodicy in, 123–27
  cosmological mapping by, 127–38, 141–42, 247–50
  Cruzada churches of Okak, 77–82
  defense against witchcraft in, 174–79
  deliverance ministry in, 94–99
  Deus Victor paradigm and, 228–35
  Devil in witchcraft narrative of, 147–53
  dialectical subgroupings of, 47n.55
  eschatology in churches of, 210–21
  evus figure in, 61
  hope theology in Pentecostalism of, 212–21
  inculturation theology and, 245–46
  indigenous beliefs and practices of, 46–73
  Macías dictatorship and, 41–43
  map of territory of, 47
  migration history of, 48–49
  moral etiology in, 121–22, 166–69
  normalization of suffering and destabilization of abundant life in, 160–62
  Pentecostalism and, 134–38, 152–53, 247–50

  population and geographical distribution of, 46–48
  Presbyterian evangelization and, 82–83
  principal rituals of, 49–50
  resistance to colonialism by, 39–44
  retribution doctrine in cosmology of, 171–73
  sickness and health in, 66–71
  social classifications in culture of, 62–63, 146–47
  stigmatization and retribution in, 177–79
  suffering in, 166–69
fasting
  in Biéri ancestral cult, 54
  in healing ministries, 22, 24, 98–99
  in prosperity gospels, 107–9
Federation of Evangelical and Pentecostal Churches of Equatorial Guinea, 8, 99–100
Fegley, Randall, 80–81, 83
Ferdinando, Keith, 247
Fernandez, James, 51–53, 55–56, 58–60, 71–72, 132n.37
Fernando Po, 38–40
"fetish," Bible as, 21–22
fetishism, causality and, 32
Fossum, Merle, 181
Fouahouly, Frederic (Prophetic Frederic), 106–9, 139–41
Foucault, Michel, 120–21
Fowl, Stephen, 23
Francophone "Men of God"
  Assembly of the Holy Spirit and, 101–5
  prosperity gospel dissemination by, 105–9
functional spirituality, in African Christianity, 232–35

Gabon
  Fang culture in, 132n.37
  migration to Equatorial Guinea from, 100–101
gender, HIV/AIDS pandemic and role of, 190–96

Ghana, Evangelical Presbyterian Church in, 133–34
Ghana's New Christianity: Pentecostalism in a Globalizing African Economy (Gifford), 209
Gifford, Paul
  on African Christianity, 5, 14, 102–3, 233, 235
  on deliverance ministries, 93–94
  on eschatology, 207–210
  on inculturation theology, 246
  on independence movement, 88
globalization, African Christianity and, 102–5
God
  Fang Pentecostal doctrine of, 156–59
  hope theology in Fang Pentecostalism and, 212–21
  sovereignty of, 232–35
Goffman, Erving, 177–79
Good Samaritan (NGO), 9–10
  HIV/AIDS support group, 184–89, 264–65
Gornik, Mark, 228
grassroots Christian communities
  Bible study in, 14–15, 34
  biblical text and witchcraft in, 238–44
  consequences of diabolization and, 250–53
  eschatology of, 203–4
  hope theology and, 221–26
  interpretations of Job in, 165–69
  silence about HIV/AIDS in, 189–96
Gutiérrez, Gustavo, 193, 223

Hastings, Adrian, 90
healing ministries
  of African Indigenous Churches (AICs), 110–12
  cosmological mapping of, 133–34
  God as Healer in Fang Pentecostalism, 187–89
  of Joy of My Salvation church, 95–99
Hebrew narratives, African Christianity and, 26–30
Hellenistic theology
  African Christianity and, 248–50
  God image in, 152–53
hermeneutics
  in African Christianity, 5–6
  African hermeneutics, 15–19
  Job figure in reader-centered hermeneutics, 138–41
  role of Christ in, 221–26
  study of Job Chapter 19 and, 211–21
  therapeutic faith and, 186–89
hermeneutics-culture-praxis triad, 2–4
  in African Christianity, 15–25, 34–35
  African Christianity and, 15–25, 237–38
  culture and, 19–22
  current and future challenges for, 112–13
  Fang indigenous beliefs and practices, 46–73
  hermeneutics and, 15–19
  praxis, 22–25
Hick, John, 119
historical criticism, Bible study and, 17–19, 237–38
HIV/AIDS in Africa
  African Christianity's engagement with, 169
  Fang Christianity and, 4
  lament of, and embrace of God by patients of, 184–89
  paradigm of Job the Innocent Sufferer and, 189–96
  retributive blame doctrine and, 168–69
  role of Pentecostal church in managing of, 199–201
  statistics on, 31–32
Holiness ethos, in Joy of My Salvation Church, 90–93
holistic ministry, in Joy of My Salvation Church, 93–99
homooúsios (of the "same substance"), Fang cultural concept of, 137–38

hope, theology of
  Deus Victor paradigm and, 221–26
  eschatology in African Christianity and, 204–5
  in Reformed Presbyterian Church, 210–21
  suffering and, 203–4
Hume, David, 119–20

Idahosa, Benson, 92
Idowu, E. Bolaji, 4–5, 248–49
Iglesia Betania, 100–101
Iglesia del Cristianismo Celeste, 110
Iglesia Paloma, 92
Imùnga ja Nyèmbanyango, 79–82
incest, Fang taboos concerning, 51
inculturation
  African theological endorsement of, 244–46
  official *vs.* popular debate over, 131
independence
  post-colonial rise of independent churches and, 90
  Reform Presbyterian Church advocacy for, 84–88
indigenous religiosity. *See also* African Indigenous Churches (AICs)
  African Christianity and, 237–53
  Assembly of the Holy Spirit and, 100–112
  birth of, in Equatorial Guinea, 100–101
  Catholic Church incorporation of, 80–81, 131n.35
  diabolization and, 246–50
  external African agency and, 101–5
  Fang culture and, 46–73
  functionalism of, 241–44
  hope theology and, 216–21
  Joy of My Salvation Church and, 90–100
  Pentecostalism and, 91n.74, 155–59
  prayer and, 228–35
  Presbyterian evangelization and, 82–83
  Reform Presbyterian Church and, 83

  theologized God *vs.* narrated Devil, 150–53
innocent suffering, retributive blame doctrine and, 166–69
institutionalization of missionary churches, 85–88
Instituto Bíblico "Casa de la Palabra" (IBCP), 166–69, 230–31, 265
Israel (ancient), modern Africa compared with, 20, 27, 71, 89, 168, 203, 228, 242–44

Jenkins, Philip, 13–14, 209, 233n.91, 242
Jesus, hermeneutic interpretations of, in Equatorial Guinea, 139–41
Jesus of the Deep Forest (Kuma), 223
J'Ikěngě, Ibiya, 80–82
Job, Book of
  academic research on, 1–2
  African Christian study of, 8–10, 13–35, 238–44
  appropriations of, 3–4
  Biéri cult religiosity compared with, 55–58
  causality in, 33–34
  Chapter 19 in, 210–21
  in context of African sickness and suffering, 32
  Deus Victor and, 227–35
  dialogical texts in, 165
  discourse on African continent and, 25–26
  eschatology and hope in African Christianity and, 204–5
  in Fang cosmology, 141–42
  grassroots interpretations of, 1–2
  hope theology and, 217–21
  lament (Job 3:1-26) in, 165, 179–84, 184–89
  leprosy and HIV/AIDS in Africa and reading of, 165–202
  Pentecostal HIV/AIDS patients and, 184–89
  Reformed Presbyterian Church interpretations of, 210–21
  stigmatization of leprosy in context of, 173–79

struggle between God and Devil in, 117–19, 138–53
textual and thematic blocks in, 6
venues in Equatorial Africa for reading of, 262–66
whirlwind speeches in, 230–35
Job the Innocent Sufferer paradigm
HIV/AIDS and, 189–96, 242–44
retributive doctrine and, 166–69
Jones, Gregory, 23
Joy of My Salvation Church (*Gozo de la Salvación*), 8, 90–100. *See also* Pentecostal church
anti-witchcraft rituals in, 107
Deus Victor paradigm and, 228–35
growth and conflict in, 90–93, 112–13
Guinean Protestant Christianity and, 99–100
HIV/AIDS in congregation of, 192–96
holistic ministry of, 93–99
Job narrative in sermons at, 195–96
normalization of suffering in, 161–62
prayer in, 229–35
readings of Book of Job in, 263
study of Job Chapter 19 by, 213–21
Judaism
African Christian affinity for, 26–30
ethical tradition in, 170–73
Fang ties to, 48
Judeo-Christian tradition, western theodicy and, 124–27
Juventud en Marcha con Macías (Youth on March with Macías), 41

kairos movement, 85
HIV/AIDS pandemic and, 189–96
Kalilombe, Patrick, 229
Kalu, Ogbu, 97–99, 245
Kanyoro, Musimbi, 19
Katongole, Emmanuel, 169
Kirundi Bible, 137
Klinteberg, Robert, 43
Koch, Klaus, 170n.12
ko-mbot (non-person), 61

Kuma, Afua, 223

lament
ecclesial censorship of, 196–99
in Job 3:1-26, 165, 179–84
of leprosy patients, 179–84
as pastoral response to HIV/AIDS, 199–201
of people living with HIV/AIDS, 184–89
la noticia ("the news") of HIV-positive status, 184–89
Latino evangelism, African Christianity and, 103–5
Legba (Ewe Satan figure), 137
Leibniz, Gottfried, 119
Leprosarium of Micomeseng, 9, 173, 175n.31, 180–81, 264
leprosy
Book of Job in context of, 170–84
in Fang culture, 52n.77 (*See* leprosy)
as hereditary, belief in, 175n.31
internalization of despair in patients with, 179–84
retribution as stigmatization for patients with, 173–79
Letter to Brother Job from Equatorial Guinea, 166–69, 194–96
Liborio Nvo Ndong, 150, 154, 161
literacy
African Christianity and, 16n.17
in Equatorial Africa, 39–40
Macías dictatorship and decline of, 42–43
literary approach to Bible study, 17–19
liturgy
in deliverance ministry, 110–12
Esono's "Pentecostal Deliverance Liturgy," 255–61
live object, contextualized theodicy of, 153–62
Luther, Martin, 13–14

Macías Nguema, Francisco
dictatorship of, 37, 40–44
elite clergy and, 84–85
harassment of missionaries by, 87

Mackay, James L., 79
Magesa, Laurenti, 20–21, 72–73, 131, 229
malan (hallucinogen), 54
Malawian churches
   exegesis, 24
   marginalization of Christ in, 224–25
Mallart Guimera, Louis, 61n.126, 63, 69–71
Malukeke, Sam Tinyiko, 5
Mami Wata (water spirit), 152n.92
Mañe, Acacio, 84
Mañe Ebo Asong, Alberto, 117, 134n.42
Manicheanism, African Christianity and, 249–50
Martrou, L., 53
Masenya, Madipoane, 5
Mason, Marilyn, 181
Masowe weChishanu church, 138n.53
matrimonial rituals, in Fang culture, 51–53
Maxwell, David, 103, 131n.35
Mbana, Joaquín, 60
Mbàyi a Moliko Indigenous Presbyterian Church, 80
Mbiti, John S.
   on African Christianity, 14, 23, 215–16, 233, 235, 252–53
   on eschatology in African Christianity, 205–10, 225–26
   on Fang culture, 53, 72–73, 146, 248–50
mbwo (Fang witchcraft), 55
   deliverance ministry and, 93–99
   Devil in, 147–50
   diabolization of in Pentecostalism, 250
   evus and dynamics of, 60–66
   Fang cosmological mapping of universe and, 132–38, 163
   Pentecostalization and theodicy in relation to, 154–59
   sickness and health and, 67–71
McNeill, Joseph, 84
Meadowcroft, Tim, 20n.31
meaning, in African Bible study, 18–19, 238–44
mebara (yaws), Fang cultural view of, 52

Mebege (Fang supreme god), 57–58
   Fang cosmological mapping of universe and, 129
medicine in Equatorial Africa
   healing ministry of Pentecostalism and, 96–99
   Macías dictatorship and decline of, 42–44
   medicinal use of Bible and, 22
Mesters, Carlos, 23
Meyer, Birgit, 93, 133–34, 144, 150–51, 155–56, 252
Michael, Matthew, 223n.61
miemie (innocent person), 55, 63–66, 70–71
missionaries in Africa
   futuristic eschatology of, 206–9
   history of, 77–82
   independence movement and role of, 85–88
   indigenous agency and, 82–83
Modesto Engonga Ondo, 9–10, 203, 227–28, 231–32, 232–35
Moffat, Robert, 21–22, 239
moral etiology
   African theodicy as, 121–22
   Fang Devil narrative and, 149–50
   for HIV/AIDS patients, 188–89
   Job figure in reader-centered hermeneutics and, 138–41
Mosala, Itumeleng, 24
mvwaa, centrality in Fang culture of, 71–74
mwan biang (child of medicine) figure, 54–56

narrative
   role of, in African Christianity, 27–28
   theologized God and narrated Devil in, 150–53
   in Western preaching, 28–30
national identity
   in Equatorial Guinea, 84–88
   inculturation theology and, 244–46
natural/physical disease etiology, in Fang culture, 67–71
Nchama, Maria Dolores, 100–101

INDEX

Nchama, Mba, 84
Ndong, Esteban, 9–10
Ndong Mba purification ritual, 49–53
    Fang cosmological mapping of universe and, 129–31
    Pentecostal eschatology and, 216–21
Ndowe peoples, 77n.12, 82–83
Neiman, Susan, 120
Nerín, Gustau, 66
New Testament
    eschatology in, 205–9
    Satan in, 137
New Testament Eschatology in an African Background (Mbiti), 205–9, 225–26
The New Faces of Christianity: Believing the Bible in the Global South (Jenkins), 14
ngangan (Fang healers), 63–64, 68–71, 146
    Fang cosmological mapping and, 133
    for HIV/AIDS patients, 186–89
    Pentecostalism and, 155–59
ngbel (Fang nocturnal realm), 61–66
Ngong, David, 246, 249–50
Ngubi, Mbula, 84
Nguí (Fang anti-witchcraft cult), 49–50, 58–60. *See also* anti-witchcraft cults; witchcraft
    colonial suppression of, 132n.37, 239–40
    Fang cosmological mapping of universe and, 129–31
    initiation process in, 61–66
Nigeria, relations with Equatorial Africa, 39–43
Nigerian Aladura (Praying) Churches, 22, 228–29
nnénnáng (hemorrhoids), Fang cultural perspective on, 51
nonconfessional hermeneutics, Bible study and, 24n.54
nsem (sin)
    deliverance theology and, 250–53
    Fang cultural perspective on, 52–53
    leprosy as retribution for, 176–79

Nsomboro, Gregorio, 166–69
Nvo, Enrique, 84
Nyamiti, Charles, 216
Nzama (Supreme Being)
    in African theodicy, 122, 125–27, 152–53
    Devil narrative and, 151–53
    Fang cosmological mapping and, 129–38, 247–50
    in Fang culture, 56–60, 72–73
    Fang Pentecostal theodicy and, 156–59, 245–46
    leprosy as sickness from, 175–79, 182–84
    Presbyterian causality and role of, 142–50, 162–64

Obiang, Samuel Zoe, 84
Obiang Nguema Mbasogo, Teodoro, 44, 85
oil industry, in Equatorial Africa, 44–45
okwann binzenzam (Fang terminology for AIDS), 188–89
Old Testament
    resurrection doctrine in, 205
    retribution doctrine in, 170–73
oñang (glaucoma), Fang cultural view of, 52
Ondo Edu, Bonifacio, 84
On Job: God-Talk and the Suffering of the Innocent (Gutiérrez), 223
Onyinah, Opoku, 96–99
oral theology
    African Christian Bible study and, 14, 24–25
    communication of ideas and, 29–30
Origen of Alexandra, 205
Owono Akara, Manuel, 86, 229n.78
Oyono, Basilio, 97–99, 117, 228

Parrinder, Geoffrey, 248–49
Partido Unico Nacional de Trabajadores (PUNT) (Sole National Workers' Party), 41–42
paternalism, missions in Africa and, 85–88
patriarchy, witchcraft and, 143n.67

Pauline theology
  eschatological perspective in, 207–9
  retribution paradigm, 170
p'Bitek, Okot, 248–49
Pélissier, René, 43
Pentecostal Bible School, 101
Pentecostal church. *See also* Joy of My Salvation Church (*Gozo de la Salvación*)
  African Indigenous Churches (AICs) and, 110–12
  censorship of Job's lament by, 196–99
  consequences of diabolization in, 251–53
  cosmological mapping and, 127–38
  current status and future challenges for, 112–13
  defined, 91n.74
  deliverance ministry in, 93–99
  demographic shifts in, 76n.5
  Devil as scapegoat in, 73, 147–50
  in Equatorial Guinea, 9–10
  Fang culture and, 134–38
  growth in Africa of, 208–9
  HIV/AIDS in Africa and, 189–96
  inculturation theology and, 244–46
  indigenous Guinean Pentecostalism in, 90–91, 100–112
  normalization of suffering in, 160–62
  people living with HIV/AIDS in, 184–89
  prosperity gospel in, 22n.45, 66
  theodicy and, 153–59, 163–64
  theologized God and narrated Devil in, 151–53
performative ritual speech, 138n.53
physicality, in deliverance ministry, 96–99
Pierce, Allan, 176n.35
pilgrim principle, in African Christianity, 245–46
Pioneer Bible Translators, 91n.75
Playa Negra prison, 43
pneumatological soteriology
  in Fang Pentecostalism, 94–99
  prayer in, 229–35

Pobee, John S., 23
politics, Reform Presbyterian Church involvement in, 84–88
post-mortem suffering, leprosy patient's fear of, 181–84
praxis
  of deliverance ministries, 98–99
  of Job's lament, for HIV/AIDS patients, 186–89
prayer
  in African Christianity, 24, 27n.67, 30
  Biéri ancestral cult and, 55–56
  deliverance ministry at Joy of My Salvation Church and, 93–99
  Deus Victor paradigm and, 4, 226–35
  holiness ethic at Joy of My Salvation Church and, 92
  indigenous Pentecostalism and, 100–105
  Job as model for power of, 26, 240–44
  oral theology and, 14
  prosperity gospel and role of, 105–9
  in Reformed Presbyterian Church, 84–90
Presbyterian Church
  causality and Image of God in, 142–50
  Fang cosmological mapping and, 132–38
  history in Equatorial Guinea of, 77–82
  indigenous agency and, 82–83
  Job figure in reader-centered hermeneutics of, 139–41
Primitive Methodist Missionary Society, 77–82
prophetic seminars, prosperity gospel and, 105–9
prosperity gospel, 22n.45, 66
  deliverance ministry and, 93–94
  economic conditions in Africa and, 208–9
  Francophone "Men of God" dissemination of, 105–9
  Job narrative in context of, 139–41

prophetic seminars and, 105–9
Protestant churches in Africa
　Fang cosmology and, 132–33
　Joy of My Salvation Church in Guinean Protestant Christianity, 99–100
　Pentecostalization and theodicy in relation to, 154–59
　study of Job and, 8–10
Psalms, appropriation of, in traditional healing practices, 22, 95–99
purification, Fang Ndong Mba purification ritual, 49–53

Reading in Communion (Fowl and Jones), 23
Reformed Presbyterian Church of Equatorial Guinea (Iglesia Reformada Presbiteriana de Guinea Ecuatorial), 8, 76n.3
　early Presbyterian history and, 77–82
　ecumenical partnerships formed by, 87–88
　eschatology and, 210–21
　Fang cosmological mapping and, 132–38, 162–64, 247–50
　indigenous religiosity and, 82–83, 89–90
　political ascendancy and spiritual decline of, 84–88
　prayer in, 229–35
　present crisis and future challenges for, 89–90, 112–13, 229n.78
　readings of Book of Job in, 262–63
　western-funded initiatives and marginalization of, 208–9
religious/supra-human disease etiology, in Fang culture, 67–71
Renan, Ernest, 140
retribution, doctrine of
　causality and, 33–34, 170–73
　in Fang culture, 166–69
　HIV/AIDS and, 191–96
　negative functional spirituality and, 232–33
　stigmatization of leprosy patients and, 173–79

study of Job Chapter 19 and, 214–21
Rio Muni, 38–40, 80–82
Roman Catholic Church
　deliverance ministry demonization of, 95–99
　education in Equatorial Guinea linked to baptism in, 39–40, 131–32
　in Equatorial Africa, 42–44, 75–76, 82–83
　Fang beliefs concerning, 64–66
　Fang Nguí suppressed by, 59–60
　festive events of, 76n.5
　incorporation of indigenous religiosity in, 80–81, 131n.35
　Pentecostalization and theodicy in relation to, 154–59
Ross, Kenneth, 215, 224
Roth, John, 120n.9
Rowley, H. H., 220n.53, 253
Rwuba (Kirundi Satan figure), 137

Samuel 2, Book of, 242
self-identity of African Christians, 15n.10
sexual promiscuity, HIV/AIDS as retribution for, 190–96
Shabani Mligo, Elia, 178n.43
shame, stigmatization and, 181–84
Sialo, Joaquin Maria, 80–81
sickness and health
　in African Christianity, 22, 30–32
　causality and retribution and, 170–73
　in Fang culture, 49–53, 66, 71
　holistic ministry of Joy of My Salvation Church and, 93–99
　Pentecostal deliverance liturgy and, 111–12
Simpson, George L., 79
sin, Fang *akwann nisémm* (sicknesses of sin) purification ritual and, 49–53
slavery, in Equatorial Africa, 43, 79–80
social death, leprosy as, 173–79
social/human disease etiology
　in Fang culture, 67–71, 146–47
　HIV/AIDS and, 190–96

Soo Ndong Mba (Fang initiatory ritual), 52–53
South Africa, Biblical motifs in, 242
Spain, colonization in Africa by, 37–40
specialization, of missions in Africa, 85–88
Spurgeon, Charles Haddon, 222
Stiebert, Johanna, 192
Stigma: Notes on the Management of Spoiled Identity (Goffman), 177–79
Studd, C. T., 77–82
suffering
  in African Christianity, 30–32
  Book of Job in context of, 217–21
  in Fang culture, 71–74, 179–84
  hope in, 203–36
  moral etiology in African theodicy and, 121–22
  normalization of, in Fang theodicy, 160–62
  retributive blame and experience of, 166–69, 171–73
Surin, Kenneth, 120
symbolic theology
  African Christian Bible study and, 14
  deliverance ministry and, 96–99

Tanzania, transactional sex in, 191
Taylor, John V., 85–88
Terrien, Samuel, 57–58, 232
Tessman, Günter, 57–58, 68, 71, 132n.37, 176n.35
theodicy
  in African Christianity, 121–27
  consequences of diabolization and, 250–53
  contextualization in African Christianity of, 123–27
  in Fang Christianity, 4, 123–27, 162–64
  Fang cosmological mapping of universe and, 127–38
  live objects contextualization in, 153–62
  as moral etiology, 121–22
  nature of evil and, 117–64
  normalization of suffering in, 160–62
  Pentecostalization and, 153–59, 163–64
  in Western theology, 119–21, 123
Theology and Identity (Bediako), 15n.10
theology of hope, Fang Christianity and, 4
therapeutic faith, Pentecostal people living with HIV/AIDS and, 184–89
time, in African eschatology, 215–16
Tiv Nongo u Kristu church, 86
traditional healing, appropriation of Psalms in, 22, 95–99
transactional sex, prevalence of HIV/AIDS and, 191–96
Treaty of Paris (1900), 38, 82
Tshikendwa Matadi, Ghislain, 171–73
Turner, Harold, 224o225
Tyrell, George, 139

Uganda, transactional sex in, 191
Ukpong, Justin, 17–19, 20n.32
Unearthly Powers (Burnett), 33
Único Milagro, 43
United States, African Christianity links to, 102–5
universe, Fang cosmological mapping of, 127–38
urine therapy, 186
utilitarian ecclesiology, hope theology and, 216–21

van Dijk, Rijk, 110
Vatican II, impact in Equatorial Guinea of, 131n.35

Walls, Andrew, 26–27, 124–25, 132, 135–36, 233, 245
WEC International, 77n.8
Wesleyan Church, Joy of My Salvation Church partnership with, 92–93, 103–4
West, Gerald O., 4–5, 14, 168–69, 239, 242
Westerlund, David, 67
Westermann, Claus, 179–80

Western theology
    inculturation in Africa and, 244–46
    preaching and narrative in, 28–30
    theodicy in tradition of, 119–21, 123
    whirlwind speeches in Job and, 232–35
Whiteside, Alan, 191
witchcraft. *See also* anti-witchcraft cults; Nguí (Fang anti-witchcraft cult)
    biblical text and, 238–44
    Biéri cult and, 55
    cosmological mapping of universe and, 132–38
    deliverance ministry of Joy of My Salvation Church and, 93–99
    Ekong form of, 107n.131
    evil linked to discourse on, 126–27
    in Ewe culture, 133–34
    in Fang Pentecostalism, 213–21
    initiation process in Fang culture and, 61–66
    leprosy and, 52n.77, 173–79

"witchdemonology" concept, Pentecostal healing ministry and, 96–99
women in Africa, prevalence of HIV/AIDS in, 191–96
World Council of Churches (WCC), 8, 87–88
Worldwide Evangelization Crusade, 77–82
written theology, African Christian Bible study and, 14

Yoruba Bible, 137
Yoruba culture
    Èsù in, 137
    incest in, 51n.72

Zande culture, witchcraft in, 70
Zophar (friend of Job), 56–57
    dialog with, 165, 167–69
    retribution doctrine, 170–73

About the Author

Jason Carter (PhD, World Christianity, The University of Edinburgh) is a professor at *Instituto Bíblico "Casa de la Palabra"* (IBCP) of Equatorial Guinea. At IBCP, he serves on the Executive Leadership Team and as the Director of International Relations. Dr. Carter is also Central American Theological Seminary's Coordinator for the Master of Arts (MA) in Ministry program extension site in Equatorial Guinea, the first Master's degree program for Christian pastors and leaders ever offered in the country. Dr. Carter has been training and equipping pastors and leaders for 10+ years in Central Africa.